Suspect Relations

Suspect Relations

Sex, Race, and Resistance
in Colonial North Carolina

KIRSTEN FISCHER

Cornell University Press
Ithaca & London

First published 2002 by Cornell University Press
First printing, Cornell Paperbacks, 2002

Printed in the United States of America

Library of Congress Cataloging-in-Publication Data

Fischer, Kirsten, 1963–
    Suspect relations : sex, race, and resistance in colonial North
Carolina / Kirsten Fischer.
        p. cm.
    Includes bibliographical references and index.
    ISBN 978-0-8014-3822-6 (cloth : alk. paper)
    ISBN 978-0-8014-8679-1 (pbk.alk.paper)

    1. North Carolina—History—Colonial period, ca. 1600–1775.   2. North Carolina—
Race relations.   3. North Carolina—Social conditions—18th century.   4. Indians of
North America—North Carolina—Social conditions—18th century.   5. African
Americans—North Carolina—Social conditions—18th century.   6. Man-woman
relationships—North Carolina—History—18th century.   7. Sex role—North Carolina—
History—18th century.   8. Social classes—North Carolina—History—18th century.
9. Government, Resistance to—North Carolina—History—18th century.   I. Title.
    F257 .F53 2002
    306.7'09756'09033—dc21   2001003357

Cornell University Press strives to use environmentally responsible suppliers and materials to the fullest extent possible in the publishing of its books. Such materials include vegetable-based, low-VOC inks and acid-free papers that are recycled, totally chlorine-free, or partly composed of nonwood fibers. For further information, visit our website at www.cornellpress.cornell.edu.

Cloth printing   10 9 8 7 6 5 4 3 2 1
Paperback printing   10 9 8 7 6 5 4 3

For Nancy and Jürgen Fischer, ever my "proud parentals"

Contents

Illustrations

Acknowledgments

It is a great pleasure to thank those who helped me write this book. This project received generous institutional and financial support, beginning with a Chairman's Fellowship from Duke University and a small but helpful grant from Smith College, my alma mater. A Michael Kraus Research Grant from the American Historical Association, an F. K. Weyerhaeuser Fellowship from the Forest History Society in Durham, North Carolina, and a grant from the National Endowment for the Humanities allowed me to research and write the early drafts. A Research and Creative Scholarship Grant from the University of South Florida and an Archie K. Davis Fellowship from the North Caroliniana Society supported further summer research. Thanks to the wonderful staff members at libraries and archives in North Carolina where I spent much time: the North Carolina State Archives in Raleigh, the Special Collections Library at Duke University in Durham, the Southern Historical Collection at the University of North Carolina in Chapel Hill, and the Friends Historical Collection at Guilford College in Greensboro. A postdoctoral fellowship at the Tanner Humanities Center at the University of Utah and an NEH / Lloyd Lewis postdoctoral fellowship at the Newberry Library in Chicago came at a crucial time and enabled me to complete the manuscript. Dan McCool at the American West Center at the University of Utah generously provided me with an office during my last summer of revisions. I am very grateful for all of this assistance.

At Duke University I benefited immensely from the intellectual and moral support of professors William Chafe, Peter Wood, Nancy Hewitt,

Julius Scott, and Cynthia Herrup—outstanding historians all, who care-fully read and commented on my work. Peter Wood's ability to impart a sense of immediacy, urgency even, about early America is the reason I be-came a colonial historian in the first place, and the brilliance and subtlety of his historical analysis continue to inspire my writing and teaching. Nancy Hewitt (now at Rutgers University) generously improved every chapter with her keen insights and editorial pen and helped me think about the complexities of gender, race, and class. Bill Chafe is in many ways responsible for the completion of this book. He whole-heartedly sup-ported this project from its nebulous beginnings and gave me encourage-ment and excellent advice at critical moments throughout the writing process. Bill, Peter, and Nancy tirelessly supported my professional en-deavors long after I left Duke University, and they have been writing letters of recommendation all this time. I thank them for their faith and enthu-siasm and for being role models of professional mentoring.

I am greatly indebted to friends who willingly consented to the invalu-able but difficult task of commenting on unpolished chapters. Arun Agrawal, Nick Biddle, Sharon Block, Caitlin Crowell, Mary Ellen Curtin, Laura Edwards, Sabine Engel, Ann Farnsworth-Alvear, Andrew Frank, Elliott Gorn, Robin Grey, Christina Greene, Eric Hinderaker, Kathy Howe, Steve Johnston, Jane Kamensky, Marjoleine Kars, Ann Little, Patrick Miller, Jennifer Morgan, Lucy Murphy, Jean O'Brien, Ann Plane, Greg Smoak, Neva Specht, Tim Tyson, Barbara Welke, and Alfred Young: you are my he-roes—thank you. Laura Edwards, Sabine Engel, Ann Little, and Greg Smoak deserve special mention for the insightful engagement with which they read many chapters, many times over, and helped me clarify my ar-guments. My readers for Cornell University Press, Carol Karlsen and Wal-ter Johnson, made wonderfully creative suggestions that improved the book significantly and inspired me more than they can ever know.

Stimulating conversations with colleagues in many different settings shaped the book as well. For their thoughtful comments on my confer-ence papers I thank Peter Bardaglio, Herman Bennett, Virginia Bernhard, Victoria Bynum, Patricia Cline Cohen, Cornelia Hughes Dayton, Wilma King, Mindie Lazarus-Black, Jan Lewis, Theda Perdue, Robert Reid-Pharr, Hortense Spillers, and the participants at the October 1997 session of the Newberry Seminar in Early American History and Culture. Two anthology essays provided a testing ground for my ideas: "'False, Feigned, and Scan-dalous Words': Sexual Slander and Racial Ideology Among Whites in Colo-nial North Carolina," in *The Devil's Lane: Sex and Race in the Early South*, ed. Catherine Clinton and Michele Gillespie (New York: Oxford University Press, 1997) and "'Common Disturbers of the Peace': The Politics of White

Women's Sexual Misconduct in Colonial North Carolina," in *Beyond Image and Convention: Explorations in Southern Women's History* (Southern Women Series) ed. Janet Lee Coryell et al. (Columbia: University of Missouri Press, 1998). Portions of those essays are reprinted here with the publishers' permission. My colleagues at the University of South Florida gave friendly support, and Giovanna Benadusi and Bob Ingalls were especially good about reminding me to "get it done." The USF History Department's Faculty and Graduate Student Seminar provided very helpful comments on chapter 5. In the short time I have been at the University of Minnesota, my new colleagues already have been splendid, and the Comparative Women's History Workshop gave me excellent suggestions for chapter 4. Special thanks to the staff and fellows at the Tanner Humanities Center at the University of Utah and the Newberry Library in Chicago (1998–99), whose inspirational company and careful attention to my seminar papers helped me finish the manuscript and put it in the mail. At Cornell University Press, Peter Agree (now at the University of Pennsylvania) waited patiently for the manuscript and then ushered it quickly through the review process. Sheri Englund graciously and ably took up where Peter left off, and the Cornell team transformed a pile of papers into a book. My sincere thanks to all.

I am blessed with friends, of historical bent and otherwise, who in one way or another helped me write this book. For being themselves and for enjoying at least some of my idiosyncrasies, I thank Golfo Alexopoulos, Nick Biddle, Mara Brown, Heidi Clark, Jim Conway, Mary Ellen Curtin, Laura Edwards, Carolyn Eichner, Carolin Emcke, Sabine Engel, Elliott Gorn, Christina Greene, Gurleen Grewal, Eric Hinderaker, Shreeram Krishnaswami, Ann Little, Jennifer Morgan, Perri Morgan, Lee Rech, Erica Scatchard, Catharina Schuchmann, Ann Settle, Katie Tenpas, Tim Tyson, and Mary Wingerd. Special thanks to Greg Smoak for sharing with me his passion for the past and for present-day adventures.

My family is a source of great joy. Thanks to Mom and Dad, Eric, Simone, Nikolas, Monique, and Gramma for giving me so many reasons to celebrate.

A Note on Editorial Method

I have retained original spelling and punctuation when quoting from the records with the exception of expanding archaic contractions and replacing "ye" with "the." I have also added small editorial changes in brackets when it seemed necessary to clarify the text's meaning. Dates have been modernized throughout, beginning the year on January 1 rather than on March 25 as England and its colonies did according to the Old Style, or Julian, calendar until 1752. I have also converted the numerical days and months used by Quakers into the current-day standard.

Suspect Relations

Introduction: Changing Conceptions of Race

S exual relationships and their social repercussions in colonial North
Carolina can tell us much about eighteenth-century constructions of
race. In the intimate interactions of ordinary people, we can see ideas
about race and a social hierarchy based on racial distinctions taking shape.
Scholars have analyzed how well-educated men in the eighteenth century
conceptualized race, gender, and class in their letters, essays, and scientific
tracts. We know much less, however, about the way non-elite people—Africans,
Native Americans, and Europeans—contributed to the construction of these
social categories. How did they reinscribe or contest developing meanings
of race? By what means did racial prejudice become attached to ideas of permanent bodily difference, and what role did sexual relations play in this development? How did specific relations of gender and class aid or disrupt the
imposition of a racial hierarchy? Building on scholarship about the racial aspects of colonial legislation, prescriptive literature, and the writings of an
educated elite, this book draws on court records and travel literature to show
how a wide range of people shaped race relations and racial thinking in their
personal (and yet often very public) sexual lives. In their illicit sexual behavior
and in their responses to the unlawful conduct of others, ordinary people
participated in the development of a new racial order. As they did so, they
reenacted and reshaped relations of gender and class as well.[1]

The eighteenth century marks a watershed in racial thinking. By the
close of that century, European Americans generally believed that race was

1

inherent to the body and visible in physical traits that in turn revealed the moral and intellectual capacities of an individual. This conception of race as biological would eventually become so entrenched as to seem timeless, but in fact the idea represents a significant shift from previous notions of difference. Formerly, racial difference appeared external and mutable, a matter of culture and geography as much as anything else, and susceptible to changes in either. Climate, for example, served to explain European perceptions of Africans' appearance and temperament: proximity to the sun in tropical zones scorched Africans' skin, while the region's heat led to their dissolute behavior. Enough time spent in northern climes, however, would turn lazy, passionate, dark-skinned people into industrious, self-controlled, and light-skinned ones. Similarly, many Europeans believed that Native Americans were born white, and that outdoor living and the application of oil and paint gradually stained their bodies. In this view, racial affiliation resulted from geographical circumstances and culturally determined choices. The same was true for Europeans: just as Africans and American Indians could blanch over time and assimilate European culture, so too could northern Europeans become dark-skinned and uncivilized if left among African or American "savages."[2]

The shift toward a biological view of race began in the late seventeenth century.[3] Elaborating on Sir William Petty's *The Scale of Creatures* (1676) and François Bernier's division of humankind into at least four categories in 1684, philosophers in England and northwestern Europe divided the world's people into groups and debated the possibility that distinct human species, each with their own physical, moral, and mental abilities, had evolved from separate origins. In the 1730s, the Swedish botanist Linnaeus devised *A General System of Nature* that classified all living beings, whereupon Enlightenment thinkers wondered whether the human category itself encompassed a hierarchy of types. In 1754 the Scottish philosopher David Hume supposed "the negroes and in general all other species of men (for there are four or five different kinds) to be naturally inferior to the whites." Most eighteenth-century writers who speculated about distinct human species eventually rejected the idea of multiple human origins in favor of the biblical recounting of a single pair of ancestors for all people. Still, what stands out in the array of competing explanations for human differences is the growing emphasis on anatomy rather than on culture or environment as the underlying cause. The term *biology* would not be used among scientists until 1802, but during the eighteenth century the idea of physically distinct groups of people—what the next century's scientists would call "races"—gained wider currency than ever before. By the nineteenth century, the origins of this idea had disappeared behind the presumption of naturalness, and it was commonly understood in Europe and the United States that race was (and always had been) a biological given, incontestably real and physically obvious.[4]

Scholars disagree over how to describe and evaluate eighteenth-century ideas about race.[5] Some argue that the widespread belief in one shared origin for all of humanity and the touting of universal laws that applied (at least in theory) to all members of the human family represent a form of racial thinking that was not as racist as the next century's "scientific racism" with its theories of measurably distinct and unequal human species. While the specific underpinnings of racial theories are important, racism does not, to my mind, hinge on any one particular explanation of human origins. Enlightenment thinkers, positing a single human origin only to claim that groups of people had either evolved or degenerated to different and unequal rungs on the evolutionary ladder, created a racial hierarchy that proved just as expedient in justifying "race"-based enslavement as did accounts of polygenism. The conception of human characteristics as physical, inheritable, and permanent enough (how long does it take to move from one evolutionary stage to the next?), together with the idea that physical traits reliably portend intellectual and moral qualities, helped justify the enslavement and exploitation of Africans for the benefit of Europeans. Despite a rhetoric of "one human family," then, Enlightenment accounts of racial difference proved no less harmful than later versions, and eighteenth-century formulations often appear as racist as the next century's more thoroughly biological definitions of race. Theories of race defined and explained difference in various ways, but all could justify oppression. The following discussion of "race" and "race relations" excavates the eighteenth-century manifestations of these concepts without losing sight of either their historical specificity or their uses in the justification of slavery. Informed by the extensive scholarship on race as a social construct, "races" appear here as socially defined categories that can have severe social and economic effects. Although the terms *black* and *white* are problematic because they reinscribe the very categories whose construction I examine in this book, I nonetheless use these as convenient synonyms for *African American* and *European American*. The term *interracial sex* is similarly misleading, because it presupposes two fixed and distinct races that then mix, but I have used the term when its paraphrasing would be too unwieldy, hoping the reader will add imaginary quotation marks.

Like ideas about race, assumptions about sexual difference also changed dramatically in the eighteenth century. Early modern Europeans believed that physical differences between men and women resided less in their reproductive organs than in humoral physiology. Based on the teachings of

Galen of Pergamum (ca. A.D. 130–200), the early modern idea of physiology explained the health and personality of an individual in terms of the balance of four "humors" in the body: blood, phlegm, black bile, and yellow bile. The predominance of hot and dry humors in men made them more rational than women, who were characterized by cold and moist qualities. The mixture of humors in the body created a gradient of sexual difference to which anatomy was relatively unimportant, as women and men were essentially the same. Women, for instance, represented inverted versions of men with similar if not identical sexual organs placed inside their bodies rather than on the outside. Under certain circumstances, in fact, abrupt and unexpected sex changes were thought to happen to women (although not to men). In sum, the sex of an individual existed on a continuum of unstable possibilities rather than in one of two fixed poles.[6]

Furthermore, there was little doubt that both men and women were sexual beings. Female orgasm was long considered a prerequisite for conception, and sensuality and sexuality were thought to constitute a woman's very being. Biblical accounts of womankind as the "weaker vessel" buttressed the notion that women lacked the moral compass and the capacity for rationality and self-control that defined honorable manhood. The assumption of female immorality provided the imperative for men to rule over women, but it also led husbands to fear being cuckolded by an adulterous wife. Dire images of sexually aggressive women fill the pages of scriptural warnings, and advice books on proper behavior continually enjoined women to chastity. Nowhere, however, did the prescriptive literature assume that women's sexuality was inherently different from men's.[7]

In the two centuries after 1600, ideas about the physical and behavioral differences between men and women changed. Among scientists, the "one sex" model gave way to the idea that men and women were so anatomically different as to constitute two distinct entities rather than two versions of the same thing. The new "two-sex" model depicted women not as inverted men, but as the complementary, inherently different, and even "opposite" sex. Concurrently, this model ascribed to women a nature distinctly different from that of men, depicting women as naturally (and hence ideally and appropriately) modest and reserved. Virtuous women were submissive and chaste, and those who did not fit this image now appeared deviant. These new notions of womanhood (embedded especially in prescriptions for genteel behavior), produced some favorable images of women as more moral and sensitive than men, but they still employed a reductionist definition of femininity that grounded women's nature in their bodies.[8]

Ideas about race, sex, and gender changed significantly in the eighteenth century, but how did these ideological shifts inform each other, if at all? In particular, how did they interact and shape the developing racial hierarchy in American colonies increasingly dependent on slave labor? Scholars have produced an impressive body of work on race and sex, respectively, and I rely heavily on both in my efforts to see the connections in North Carolina.[9] A third investigative thread involves gender more generally. From the first extensive family and community studies written by social historians in the 1970s, to more recent work on the profound (but often less visible) impact of gender on political ideologies and socioeconomic structures, the scholarship on gender covers a vast terrain and continues to reshape our understanding of the colonial era.[10] Most recently, historians have begun to explore the links between gender systems and the racial order. Kathleen Brown's work on the role of gender in structuring the social relations of racial slavery in colonial Virginia through 1750 is especially path-breaking in this regard. It is now clear, for example, that colonial marriage laws defined racial boundaries with increasing specificity, and that legislation regulating the interactions of servants and slaves proved crucial to the way racial hierarchies were made and upheld. But we still know much less about how individuals, in their everyday interactions, shaped racial ideology and race relations in eighteenth-century slave societies. This book examines illicit sexual practices to gain insight into the way ordinary people participated in the making of a racial hierarchy.[11]

Historians interested in the causal relations of social change are tempted to prioritize one form of oppression over another, often with insightful results.[12] Nonetheless, rather than argue for a shift in the priority of one category over another, this book examines the continual contestation, reassertion, and reconfiguration of racial categories within the context of sexual relations. It seeks especially to show how assumptions of gender, race, and class difference propped each other up in the developing social hierarchy. That does not mean that these constructs of difference were all equally powerful or equally up for grabs; they were not. Ideas about hierarchical relations of gender and class preceded chronologically those about race and may have seemed more obvious and natural to eighteenth-century colonists. But as racial prejudice was reformulated into biological racism (that is, into the idea that one's "race" consisted of an inherited and immutable set of moral, intellectual, and physical qualities), ideas about class and gender were also always in play. Sometimes certain aspects of social organization appeared more fluid and contestable than others, but in fact ideas about proper relations of gender, class, and race were always informing each other in ways that remained remarkably flexible. When I describe how race became more "fixed" or a racial hierarchy "hardened," I mean to say that racial and social boundaries came to *seem* permanent and natural, but not that racial ideas (or relations, for that matter) became rigid. Like perceptions of gender and class, racial concepts continued to adapt to circumstance, engaging in all kinds of acrobatics so that race as a construct would seem natural, permanent, and timeless.[13]

Sexual relations provide a useful analytical window onto the past because bodies in the eighteenth century were public and private at the same time. On the one hand, of course, bodily experience remained intensely personal. As the most immediate means by which people experienced themselves as individuals, one person's physical sensations could, in the last instance, never be felt by another. Yet, at the same time, bodies had a strikingly public dimension. For example, slaves disfigured with branding and whiplashes embodied the power of their owners. Bodies could also signal resistance to coercion; they were, after all, the very vehicles by which people ran away or engaged in prohibited sexual behavior. One's physical self became both a site and a means for the expression of power relations, and sex was an important part of such experiences. Sexual relations, in turn, had social meanings and economic repercussions that shaped the developing racial order. Sexual relations were racialized, for example, when courts punished some forms of interracial sex and not others, thereby linking a person's sexual prerogatives or sexual vulnerability to their race (in addition to their gender and status). At the same time, race relations were sexualized when, for example, masters sexually exploited their slaves, castrated them, or broke up slave families. When sexual coercion was linked to a racial hierarchy, each made the other seem more "natural," that is, the result of innate, biological facts. This book shows how people defined, conducted, punished, resisted, and understood sexual relations in ways that made race seem physically real, even as some also struggled against racialized forms of oppression.[14]

Foucault used the term *bio-power* to describe the regulation and discipline that the state began to impose on individual bodies and on entire populations in the eighteenth century. A new "technology of sex" drew on medicine, education, and demography to promote norms by which the state would subjugate individuals and control populations. These techniques of power, Foucault said, served to reproduce a large labor force for the growing capitalist economy, and they "also acted as factors of segregation and social hierarchization." This book focuses on the latter effects of bio-power and explains how efforts to regulate women's sexual behavior also underscored racial boundaries. But in its investigation of the regulatory power of legal and social rules about sex, this study keeps its sight on the experience and agency of the women targeted by such measures. Far from being passive recipients of a new social order, their resistance and accommodations to the exigencies of bio-power fundamentally influenced race relations in the colonial setting. Lower-class women, in particular, found themselves the focus of legislative efforts to outlaw certain kinds of unions, with the result that when they struggled to determine their own intimate relationships, they necessarily shaped relations of race and class as well.[15]

The assertion of difference, then, met with contestation, and there was no simple linear development in the eighteenth century from a racialist or protoracist mentality to a racist one. Women and men made personal choices based on many contingencies, of which racial or ethnic identity was only one. Some sexual relations were based on inclination, mutual attraction, shared interest, and love. Ideas about racial difference may have played only a small role in shaping these liaisons, and some of them, by demonstrating more egalitarian forms of intimacy, could inadvertently or self-consciously challenge the supposed naturalness of the racial order. Other sexual encounters, however, were purposefully abusive. In other words, there was no single or overdetermined relationship between illicit sex and other relations of power. Unlawful sex occurred in circumstances that were oppressive, liberating, violent, collaborative, loving, and compromising. As race became an important, even defining, element in eighteenth-century sexual relations, illegal liaisons—some voluntary, others coerced—variously disrupted and reinforced the idea of race as an inherited and immutable fact, and not always in predictable ways.

Colonial North Carolina is ideal for this study for the very reasons historians have largely overlooked it. The colonial population grew only slowly in the first half century of settlement because the shallow and shifting Outer Banks hindered the establishment of permanent harbors, and the rivers that fed into the Albemarle Sound hampered travel by land. Scholars have generally preferred to study the wealthier and more populous colonies to the north and south, and those historians who do study North Carolina have often described the settlement as woefully primitive and even of criminal bent. The weak control exerted by the elite, the argument goes, allowed the rest of the population to behave in unruly fashion, making North Carolina an embarrassingly unsophisticated link in the chain of otherwise thriving and orderly British colonies along the Atlantic coast. Certainly the Anglican Church and a moneyed elite established themselves only gradually in the colony, but what at first glance may seem an unfortunate circumstance in fact conceals a treasure trove. The prolonged political instability in North Carolina resulted in extensive eighteenth-century court records that chart the transition from a relatively fluid social structure to a firmly stratified slave system. North Carolina differed from neighboring colonies in its relatively slow settlement before about 1730, but many of the processes that shaped the colony were not unique. As in other colonies, laws that regulated the interactions of servants and slaves concurrently drew boundaries of race. The social hierarchy emerged not only from racial legislation, however, but also from the everyday behavior of ordinary women and men who often, but not always, complied with the law. Such unlawful conduct, so visible in North Carolina's extensive court records, also shaped ideas about racial difference.[16]

My focus remains largely on northeastern North Carolina because records for the oldest counties along the Albemarle Sound allow a reconstruction of the hardening racial hierarchy from as early as the 1680s through the eve of the American Revolution. This study draws heavily on unpublished lower court records to understand how people negotiated sexual relations. It has been worth the effort to sift through hundreds, if not thousands, of original, unindexed lower court records looking for cases involving women, because many such cases were heard and dismissed at this level and never appeared in the higher court records. The lower court records are challenging sources. Many names appear only once, making it hard to pinpoint a person's social and economic standing in the community or to excavate their kinship ties. Court records are also skewed toward illegal behavior and say less about those who complied with the laws. Furthermore, people on trial spoke defensively, not freely, about their transgressive behavior. Nonetheless, the records discussed here are invaluable for the way they show how ordinary people engaged with each other in private and in public spaces, in households, taverns, and Quaker meetings, on the street and on the run, in the birthing chair and on the courtroom bench. Depositions often include ordinary language (the repetition of slander, for example), and they provide unique glimpses of otherwise undocumented social relationships. Despite their lacunae, colonial court records provide evocative source material for the reconstruction of the racial politics of illicit sex.

The chapters in this book are thematic and loosely chronological. Chapter 1 explores female behavior that thwarted Anglican gender norms and explains why it mattered to authorities in early North Carolina. The focus here is not on illicit sex so much as on an Anglican gender order and its discontents in the decades of settlement to 1710. The private and public realms were inseparable in the colonial era, and clergymen, government officials, court magistrates, and male heads of households all represented a larger patriarchal authority. In the context of North Carolina's political instability, the presence of alternative gender norms—those of Native Americans and of Quakers—accentuated the already precarious position of North Carolina's Anglican elite. Frustrated government officials found that to establish a "proper" social order, they had to enforce as normative their notions of female propriety and patriarchal gender relations.

Colonial observers displayed an avid interest in Native American sexual behavior, and chapter 2 explores the rhetoric and the reality of Euro-Indian relations. Some colonial writers employed a gendered accounting of racial difference, one that discerned between Indian men and women and focused on their sexual behavior, to promote the colonial appropriation of Indian land. Sexual representations of Indian women thus became part of an ideology of conquest. In real life, Native Americans experienced colonialism in distinctly gendered ways. Over time, native women who had liaisons with English traders went from being cultural brokers, whose sexual relations with outsiders served a traditional role in diplomacy and trade, to being more liminal figures whose alliances with English husbands accommodated some degree of private property and patriarchal gender relations. This chapter shows how intimate Anglo-Indian relations became a forum, both representational and real, in which people on both sides negotiated shifting power relations and ideas of racial difference.

The third chapter argues that the establishment of a racial hierarchy relied on the sexual regulation of single women, especially lower-class white and free black servants. Increasingly detailed colonial legislation regarding sex and marriage defined racial boundaries and adjudicated the status of illegitimate children. By 1715, the North Carolina legislature had prohibited servants from marrying, outlawed interracial sex, and burdened the mixed-race children of white mothers and the offspring of free black women with long terms of service. But the hardening of racial categories in colonial statutes did not necessarily translate into a fixed ideology of race. Women resisted the restraints on their personal lives: some ran away to get married, and others struggled to hold together families that did not receive legal sanction. Sexual misconduct often occurred together with theft, illegal trade, irreverent speech, and aid to runaway servants and slaves. The combination of social and sexual transgressions could undermine conventional relations of gender, race, and class and marked the limits of elite control. Placing ordinary women at the center of historical analysis enables us to understand, as the colonial elite also did, that the sexual behavior of women was not peripheral to the project of colonization but rather a crucial part of the struggle for control in an expanding slave society.[17]

Despite continuing challenges to the emerging hierarchy, racism among whites deepened as slavery became more widespread in the colony after about 1730. Ideas about race found expression in the sexual slander European Americans spread about one another, and chapter 4 uses defamation cases as a measure of whites' growing concern about racial distinctions.

Slanderous allegations of interracial sex depicted the act as a transgression against a natural boundary as well as a legal one, making the liaison seem more unnatural and more abhorrent than fornication between white partners. The graphic nature of the insults strengthened the idea that interracial sex represented a degradation of the most serious kind, especially for white women. These charges prompted vehement courtroom denials in which plaintiffs defended their reputations by underscoring racial boundaries. Sexual slander cases mark the limits placed on acceptable sex within the context of rising racial divisions, highlighting how the white community understood and regulated its own behavior while reinforcing hierarchies of gender, race, and class.

By the end of the eighteenth century, the concept of race as physical and hereditary had become much more firmly entrenched. The final chapter argues that this was partly the result of the diverging treatment of black and white bodies. As eighteenth-century statutes first regulated and then prohibited branding, whipping, and amputations for white servants but not for slaves, the divergence in legally condoned acts of violence reinforced the idea that the bodies of African Americans were inherently different. The brutality that could be legally inflicted on slaves signaled to white viewers the innate difference of the victims. In particular, punishments that targeted the sexual agency of the victim (such as the castration of male slaves) served as sexualized markers of race. In the context of slavery, sexualized violence became an especially vivid means of marking a body as "black" or "white."

Illicit sexual relations in the eighteenth century constituted dangerous liaisons on a number of counts. They were dangerous for people without much social power, because harsh punishments could be the result. Fines, public whippings, and even banishment from the colony were court-ordered penalties for unlawful sex. But illicit liaisons also seemed dangerous to government officials who saw in them a challenge to their own authority. Interracial liaisons among the lower classes were particularly threatening because they portended other kinds of illegal cooperation and because children from such unions blurred racial boundaries. The adjudication of illicit sex did more than attempt to control certain groups of people: it also bolstered the notion that race was a physical fact, one that justified enslavement and exploitation. Over the course of the eighteenth century, indeterminate ideas about racial distinctions melded with notions of gender and class differences to form a new amalgam, a fully biological notion of race, one that seemed as natural as sexual difference already did and as divinely ordained as the social order. How these concepts of difference related to one another, how racial ideas gained substance in the social relations of individuals, and how some people resisted its implications is explored in the chapters that follow. In illicit affairs and unlawful transactions, people tested and contested ideas about gender, class, and race. Whether these suspect relations were discussed in travel literature, Quaker meetings, tavern slander, or courtroom testimony, their public explication, denial, confession, and punishment further enhanced the status of race as a biological given. In a broad array of personal interactions and courtroom exchanges, unlawful sex was symbolically linked to ideas of racial difference in ways that made race seem as corporeal as sex. In the context of colonization and slavery, contests over illicit sex went a long way toward making race seem real.

Disorderly Women
and the Struggle for Authority

To men in positions of authority in early North Carolina, the adultery of one wife or the escape of one servant woman meant more than an individual flouting the law; to colonial leaders, defiant women personified the social disorder they deplored in a colony they were still trying to control. In August 1697, for example, magistrates heard the case against Dorothy Steel, a white woman who in early June had run away from her husband William in Albemarle County in northeastern North Carolina. Seeking refuge further south, Steel hired William Lee and John Spellman "to goe with her to Ashley River." Three other men—James Seserson, John Hardy, and Henry Hayes—also joined the expedition, and together the renegades stole what they could from William Steel, including one bed, one rug, a pot, a trunk in which to carry their loot, three firelock guns, and their mode of transport: "a Canoe and Sailes." Forty miles from Cape Fear, Dorothy and her companions encountered "sum Indians" and gladly "bought sum venson of them." The next day, however, Indians "Came Creeping up in the bushes" and shot at them, wounding Henry Hayes in the shoulder. The travelers returned fire and reversed their tracks, planning now to go north to Virginia. Halting in their old neighborhood, Dorothy persuaded thirty-year-old Elizabeth Vina to join them. A neighbor spied the fugitives and asked "whi thay stayed and lurked about thare," advising them to "begon spedyly or he would go and fetch the Constable and sese [seize] them." Vowing "thay would dey before they would be taken," the runaways set off again. For two days they rowed along the shore until they saw three head of cattle. John Spellman shot the smallest one, which the hungry crew gutted, quartered, and roasted. Disembarking at Thomas Pollock's plantation on Salmon Creek, the runaways enjoyed "sum tobaco and Rosting yeares of Corn of Colonel Pollickes negro Manuell," a slave who, with his wife, managed the plantation without supervision. The fugitives then traded one of William Steel's guns to Tom Andover, a free black man who agreed to "pilaite [pilot] them to south Key." Relying on theft and trade, the runaways survived on the loose for two months. In August, however, their luck ran out. They were apprehended, brought to court, and deposed by Thomas Harvey, deputy governor of North Carolina and chief justice of the General Court. Lee, Spellman, and Steel kept their accounts brief, but Elizabeth Vina and James Seserson added that Lee and Steel "did Ly together upon one bed all the voige." William Lee eventually admitted as much in court, and the grand jury indicted him and John Spellman (who did not make a confession) for "ravishing" Dorothy Steel. When the court reconvened in October, Lee and Spellman were convicted and sentenced to thirty-nine lashes for the "Ravishment of the wife and goods of Wm. Steel." Dorothy herself suffered thirty stripes for "Unlawfull Departing from her husband and going away with an adulteror." In addition, John Spellman was banished from the colony for four years for "feloniously killing a Beast."[1]

Dorothy Steel's transgressions had a political dimension because patriarchal household government, political rule, and property rights were tightly intertwined in early modern Europe and its American colonies. The patriarchal household was crucial to the social order; it served as metaphor and microcosmic example of the divinely ordained social hierarchy. As the monarch expected obedient subjects, so did the patriarch demand submissive household dependents (namely his wife, children, and servants). Households also controlled property and regulated its transfer from one male owner to his heirs. As a married woman, Dorothy Steel had no legal identity apart from that of her husband and could claim no property of her own. She violated William's property rights by stealing valuable objects, but also by running away and depriving him of his right to sole access to her body and her labor. Steel's adventure disrupted prescribed relations between husband and wife at the same time that it showed disregard for property rights and for the deference required of subordinates in general. Given the links between individual households and the social order, women's misconduct took on a political cast that the perpetrators themselves did not always intend.[2]

Illicit behavior like Steel's (which was certainly not unique to North Carolina) acquired special meaning in the context of the Albemarle Sound, a fledgling colony marked in its early decades by considerable social flu-idity, political instability, and religious dissent. Government officials, them-selves often recent arrivals without the impressive plantations and houses of wealthy men elsewhere, struggled to establish their authority in the new settlement. Generally modest living conditions in the young colony blurred distinctions of status, and members of the budding elite—the governor's council, court magistrates, and prominent assemblymen—were hard pressed to distinguish themselves socially from most other colonists. They could do little to quell complaints from wealthy colonists elsewhere that North Carolina settlers routinely refused to curtail smuggling, pay quitrents, or show respect to appointed officials. Dorothy Steel's trial substantiated the suspicion that stolen goods circulated among white, free black, and enslaved traders: Tom Andover, the free black ferrier, accepted William Steel's purloined gun in exchange for transportation, and Manuel and his wife shared Colonel Pollock's corn and tobacco with the fugitives. To court magistrates and other critics, Steel's flight and adultery, combined with the apparent ease with which she and others engaged in theft and unlaw-ful trade, exemplified the general unruliness that marked the settlement on the Albemarle Sound. Disorderly women confirmed the perception of well-to-do onlookers that North Carolina harbored dissenters and delin-quents alike.

The misconduct of colonial women in North Carolina gained further resonance from the fact that alternative gender roles existed among Native Americans and Quakers, respectively. These culturally distinct gender norms contrasted with mainstream English ideas about the place of women in pa-triarchal households, and they contributed to the perception of social dis-order in the colony. This was especially true in the case of Native Americans in the region, whose customs of matrilineage, land use, property holding, and gender relations represented a visible and viable alternative to colonial norms. Although Indian men held official positions of power in their so-ciety, native women controlled significant aspects of community life and influenced political decisions. Native American gender roles and arrange-ments of property holding in North Carolina presented a strong challenge to the interlaced English norms of patriarchy and private property. Another alternative to English gender roles appeared in the Society of Friends (called Quakers), a politically influential minority in the early colony. Quakers lived in patrilineal households, and they held private property and owned slaves as did members of the Church of England. Yet Quakers allowed women to travel in pairs and preach to meetings throughout the colonies. Women Friends also met monthly to discuss, vote on, and record community mat-ters. Among both Indians and Quakers, then, albeit in very distinctive ways, women gathered together, talked, and acted in consultation and often in concert with one another *as women*. They had socially sanctioned channels of influence that appeared aberrant to people accustomed to English familial norms of subordinate wives and daughters without access to an institutionalized and influential forum for the public expression of their opinions.[3]

To colonial critics (who often exaggerated the degree of self-determination and political power that Indian and Quaker women enjoyed), such alternative gender relations appeared threatening because they seemed to give women inordinate power and implicitly challenged the presumed naturalness of the patriarchal order. Dorothy Steel may not have been thinking about Indians or Quakers when she fled her husband, but to colonial magistrates her behavior illustrated more than the homegrown disorder that characterized England and colonial settlements alike: her actions reminded such men of the alternative relations of gender, property, and authority in and near colonial settlements that might spread and more radically undermine their own versions of law and order. Part of the quest for authority among colonial lawmakers and magistrates thus involved the establishment of their own gender ideals as normative. Seeking legitimacy as an elite when they did not yet have the accoutrements of that class, these men in positions of authority tried to assert their place at the top of the social hierarchy in part by enforcing one set of gender relations over other available options. Dorothy Steel's public whipping, which included nine lashes more than usual for adultery, served to demonstrate the enormity of her crimes against her husband as well as the power of local authorities to punish transgressions of prescribed relations of property and respect. But such punishments could not halt the misconduct of colonial women, nor could they erase the presence of gender relations among Indians and Quakers that contrasted starkly with English ideals.

English Gender Relations—Real and Ideal

Dorothy Steel's adventure rankled the General Court precisely because patriarchal gender relations, like divisions of class, were the bedrock of English society. The family served explicitly as a training ground for lessons in hierarchy. As one seventeenth-century English tract explained, "A family is . . . a little Commonwealth . . . a school wherein the first principles and grounds of government and subjection are learned." In the model English household, virtuous women were quiet, obedient, and chaste; along with the children and servants, they deferred to the family patriarch. Legally,

English wives' identities were subsumed by their husbands'. A woman who married became a *feme covert,* which meant "under the protection and influence of her husband, her *baron* or lord." A married woman could not legally own property or claim her own earnings (all of which belonged to her husband), nor could she sue or be sued, have legal say over her children, or object to her husband's right to the "moderate correction" of his wife, children, and servants (which included the use of a whipping switch no bigger than the size of his thumb). Patrilineal families conveyed property from one generation of male owners to the next, and the legal apparatus of the state protected marital boundaries and punished sexual transgressions that could result in illegitimate offspring and tangled lines of inheritance. Estranged spouses could sometimes gain a legal separation without the ability to remarry, but marriages were usually unseverable, with divorce granted only in extraordinary circumstances such as bigamy, consanguinity, or a husband's impotence. Since legal divorce was difficult for husbands to obtain and nearly impossible for wives, unhappy men could and did desert their spouses, leaving women unable to remarry, claim or sell property, or gain custody of their children.[4]

As authority was divided in the English household, so were responsibilities. Husbands and sons engaged in agricultural work and the public business of the household. Although wives and daughters helped in the fields at harvest time and sometimes worked at weeding and hoeing, their primary responsibilities remained within the sphere of the house, garden, dairy, and poultry yard. They churned butter, brewed ale, spun thread, sewed, washed and mended clothes, and tended the garden. Wives also cooked, cared for the children, and—as an extension of their husband's authority—oversaw any servants. Although women made crucial contributions to the domestic economy, they were mostly excluded from those tasks that, when hired out, received more pay (plowing, for example) or that garnered more public respect (such as artisanry of the kind dominated by men). Women's work was presumed secondary and supplemental in relation to men's labors.[5]

Chastity (virginity for unmarried women, monogamy for wives, and abstinence for widows) comprised the crucial female virtue, especially for middle- and upper-class women. Where property was at stake, husbands wanted to ensure that only their biological offspring became heirs. But even where lack of property made the issue of inheritance less pressing, a "cuckolded" husband unable to control his wife's sexual behavior forfeited respect as the head of his household. Since both women's virtue and men's honor were at stake in cases of female misconduct, sermons and advice manuals insisted on the vigilant surveillance of women and control of their sexual behavior. In carefully supervised courtships, couples were to become

acquainted but abstain from sexual relations. Only after the public an-
nouncements of plans to wed (called marriage banns) did prospective partners receive sanction to proceed with the ceremony and conjugal intimacy.[6]

In real life, however, people's behavior did not conform to the prescriptive literature. Women and men in early modern England who engaged in
premarital sex encountered wide tolerance, especially among the lower and
middling classes. An exchange of gifts could signal "betrothal" and with it
the informal license to have sex based on the prospect of future marriage.
Once married, women's work took them outside the household. They carried their wares to market, for example, where they made deals, joked, flirted,
and fought. In the give-and-take of everyday life, conjugal couples worked
out their own particular relationships. While companionate marriages
marked some households, shouting matches and marital violence testified
to a "struggle for the breeches" in others. Given the symbolic importance of
patriarchal domesticity (and the general lack of privacy), gender role transgressions often became a matter of public concern. When wives "hen-pecked"
their husbands or husbands did not discipline wayward members of their
household, the community might sanction one or both spouses. Women accused of promiscuity were carted through town on an open wagon and as-
sailed with insults, while parades (called the skimmington or charivari) served
to humiliate the husband with taunting songs about his wife's profligacy. Female subservience remained an elusive ideal and people knew it, but in the
pageantry of public humiliation and the dramatic reassertion of prescriptive roles, men and women alike reaffirmed the salience of gender norms.
Although women might thwart prescribed behavior, hierarchical gender relations remained an organizing principle of both real and symbolic power.[7]

As in England, families in the colonies provided a critical means of social organization. In an upstart society without entrenched institutions, family order was all the more important. Where colonies were sparsely settled
and less effectively supervised by the authorities, some feared that "masterless" people might more likely engage in aberrant behavior. In response
to the "grave Inconvenience" that followed from single people "being for
themselves" and not living in "well Governed families," New England legislators, for example, required in 1636 and 1669 that no single person shall
"be suffered to live of himself." Such injunctions in the colonies were limited to the seventeenth century and did not appear in North Carolina, but
the importance of the family as a means of ordering social relations persisted there as well. Colonial women received admonishments to defer to
their husbands, and settlers in North Carolina would have been familiar
with the kind of advice provided by the *Virginia Gazette* in 1737: a wife should
"Never dispute with him [her husband] whatever be the Occasion . . . And

if any Altercations or Jars happen, don't separate the bed, whereby the Animosity will cease . . . by no Means disclose his imperfections, or let the most intimate Friend know your Grievances . . . Read often the Matrimonial Service, and overlook not the important word OBEY." Perhaps especially in outlying settlements marked by political instability, orderly households became the symbol of, and prerequisite for, a functioning government.[8]

Even so, this ideal was neither universally held nor an everyday reality. Some colonial couples created their own (officially unrecognized) wedding ceremonies or dispensed with wedding vows altogether, which in turn led to large numbers of illegitimate children. Migration between colonies and the delay in communication by mail made it difficult to hinder bigamy or to know if an absented husband had died and his wife was free to remarry. Even lawfully married couples did not necessarily contribute to social stability, since households remained a contested space in which men and women continually renegotiated their relations of power. In frontier conditions, furthermore, gender roles blurred, as women engaged in work traditionally thought to be men's. One colonial woman in the North Carolina backcountry, for example, had to "carry a gunn in the woods and kill deer, turkeys, &c., shoot doun wild cattle, catch and tye hoggs, knock down beeves with an ax and perform the most manfull Exercises as well as most men in those parts." Rigid gender distinctions were a luxury that few could afford, and shared responsibilities led, if not to more equal relations of authority, then at least to the perception among some observers that the patriarchal mainstays of frontier families were in danger of unraveling.[9]

Because the symbolic importance of patriarchal families persisted even in (perhaps especially in) the face of divergent practice, a wife's disobedience to her husband could represent a larger gesture of dissent. When Dorothy Steel fled her husband and took on other lovers, she not only wounded William's status as the head of his household, she also broke the domestic rules that lay at the heart of the social order. Her defiant declaration that she would rather "dey" than return to her husband demonstrated a deliberate rejection of the social and sexual behavior expected of her by the colonial government and the Anglican Church. To disapproving members of North Carolina's General Court, Dorothy Steel's attitude epitomized the irreverence that plagued colonial authorities.[10]

"The Refuge of our Renegadoes"

North Carolina had not always been so troublesome. The colony appeared promising in 1629 when Charles I named it "Carolana" after himself and granted all the land between thirty-six and thirty-one degrees latitude to his attorney general Sir Robert Heath. This vast tract of land between Virginia and the Spanish colony of Florida stretched theoretically from the Atlantic to the western sea. Heath did not actively promote colonization, however, and when Charles II was restored to the throne after the English Revolution, he revoked his father's grant to Heath and transferred the land to eight loyal supporters, making them in 1663 the "Lords Proprietors" of "Carolina." This generous grant of unknown proportions—the distance to the Pacific Ocean was still a matter of conjecture—had as its aim the enrichment of the royal favorites. In contrast to the religious settlements in New England, colonies in the South were mercantilist ventures, and the Proprietors looked forward to the annual quitrents that planters would pay for their plots of land, together with the taxes levied on corn, wheat, tobacco, and lumber exports. To entice planters, the Proprietors established a "headright" system in which they granted a certain amount of acreage per person or "head" brought into the colony: "eighty acres English measure to every freeman and as much to his wife if he have one," and eighty acres to a master or mistress "for every able man Sarvant he or shee hath brought or sent" and forty acres for every "weaker Sarvant [such] as woeman children and slaves above the age of fowerteene yeares." Indentured servants would receive forty acres after the expiration of their terms of service.[11]

Investors had good reason for optimism. Surveyors returned from expeditions with enthusiastic reports of fertile soil and dense pine forests that reached from the Outer Banks on the Atlantic Ocean through the hilly Piedmont to the Appalachian Mountains in the west. As early as 1622 the secretary for Virginia, John Pory, visited the Albemarle region and found "great forests of Pynes 15 or 16 myle broad and above 60 mile long, which will serve well for Masts and for Shipping, and for pitch and tarre . . . On the other side of the River there is fruitfull Countrie blessed with aboundance of Corne, reaped twise a yeere." For men on the make who could not travel to the "southern plantation," promotional literature tempted with such titles as *Virginia: More Especially the South Part thereof, Richly and Truly Valued: Viz. The Fertile Carolana, And No Lesse Excellent Isle of Roanoke, of Latitude from 31. to 37. Degr. Relating the Meanes of Raysing Infinite Profits to the Adventures and Planters*. The prospective settlement in Albemarle appeared to have all the makings of a windfall.[12]

Despite the promise of natural bounty, the region's geography impeded travel and trade, isolating the new colony. The shifting sands of the Outer Banks defeated attempts to establish permanent harbors, and the swamps and rivers around the Albemarle Sound made travel by land arduous. The Albemarle settlement was so far away from its political hub in Charlestown (later Charleston), that after 1664 the "Countie of Albemarle" received its own county governor and assembly. Governor William Drummond, his chosen Council, and twelve elected assemblymen made laws, levied taxes, and established courts in Albemarle. Around 1668 Albemarle County was divided into precincts—Currituck, Pasquotank, Perquimans, and Chowan—each with its own court. Beginning in 1689 the governor of Albemarle County was replaced by a deputy governor for "that part of our province of Carolina that lyes north and east of Cape feare." This deputy governor reported to the governor of Carolina in Charlestown until 1712, when the Proprietors began to address their instructions directly to the "Governor of North Carolina." What once had been Albemarle County had become a separate colony (see figures 1 and 2 for maps of the region).[13]

Along with its government institutions, the colonial population of Albemarle grew only slowly. To entice wealthier investors, surveyor Thomas Woodward pressed the Proprietors in 1665 to allow larger land grants for those who could afford them, "It being only land that they come for." Woodward explained that "Rich men (which Albemarle stands much in need of) may perhaps take up great Tracts; but then they will endeavor to procure Tenants to helpe towards the payment of their Rent, and will at their own charge build howseing (which poor men cannot compasse) to invite them." To have "some men of greater possessions in Land then others" better served "the well being and good Government of the Place than any Levelling Paritie." But not all immigrants shared Woodward's dislike for a flattened social hierarchy. From the start, the Albemarle settlement encompassed a sizable presence of non-elite whites, many of whom had been shut out of the Virginia real estate market by large-scale land speculators. (In 1658, thirty people alone held title to over 100,000 acres of land in Virginia, and by 1666 all desirable land between the York and James Rivers had been patented.) Virginians who could not afford to buy land at high prices, and who were reluctant to test the Piedmont Indians to the west, turned their attentions southward. Beginning in the 1650s, small farmers and fur traders sought their livelihood south of the Virginia border, and in the next decades, a steady stream of migrants followed. Most early settlers in the Albemarle Sound region were English men and women from the Chesapeake, especially from the southern counties of Virginia. Decades later, in the mid eighteenth century, large numbers of African, German, Scots-Irish, Welsh, and French immigrants changed the ethnic makeup of the colony. They either traveled south from Pennsylvania and Virginia down the Great Wagon Road and spread throughout the Piedmont, or they arrived in Cape Fear by boat or by land from South Carolina (as was especially the case with enslaved Africans after about 1730). But in the first decades of colonial settlement, Europeans

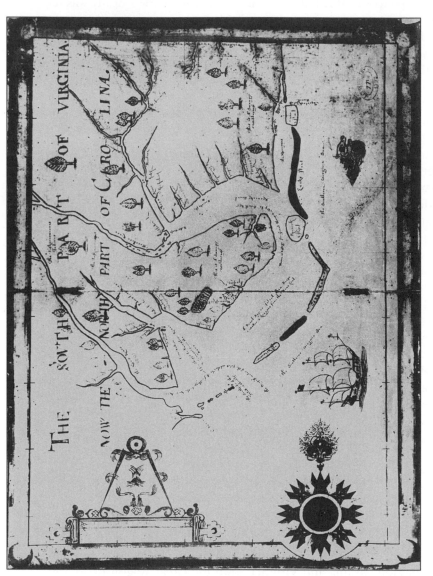

Figure 1. The map of "The South Part of Virginia Now the North Part of Carolina," made in 1657 by London chartmaker Nicholas Comberford, shows the Chowan, Roanoke, Pamlico, and Neuse rivers as well as the outer banks that made maritime travel hazardous. The second line of writing was added to the original title in a different hand in the seventeenth century. Courtesy of the North Carolina Division of Archives and History.

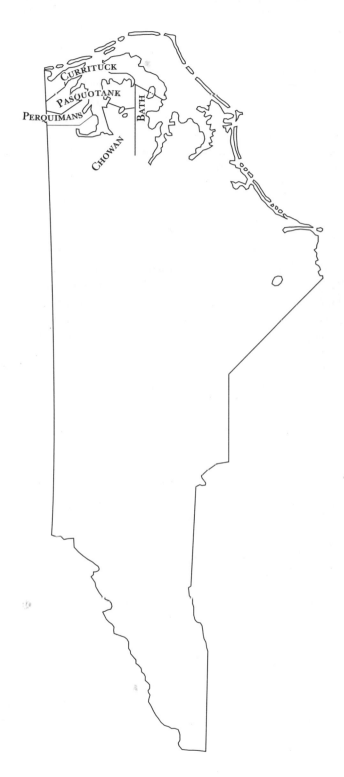

CURRITUCK

PASQUOTANK

PERQUIMANS

CHOWAN

BATH

Figure 2. North Carolina colony in 1700.

in North Carolina hailed mostly from England (often via Virginia), and they frequently traveled in small groups, sometimes as families.[14]

Many of the newcomers were former servants who sought independence and a plot of their own when their indentures expired. The president of the Virginia Council reported in 1708 that "many of our poorer sort of Inhabitants daily remove into our neighboring Colonies, especially to North Carolina." The Virginia Council noted the departure of a "great number of young people & servants just free to seek for settlements in the province of North Carolina where land is to be had on much easier Termes than here." Land was available at low prices, and young men could realistically hope to own small tracts within a few years. Others traveled south to escape debt collectors. As Colonel Joseph Seymour of Maryland complained in 1707, North Carolina's five-year postponement of debt repayment "has occasioned great numbers to flye from this Province thither to the great detriment of Merchants in England and cheating the honest well meaning people of this Country." The Virginia Council agreed. The exemption in North Carolina "for being sued for debts contracted in other places" only "encourages a great many people of uneasy circumstances or dishonest inclinations to run thither to avoid their creditors & secure themselves a safe retreat . . . [in] that Country which has no settled Government." Elites in Virginia and Maryland worried that disaffected servants, runaway slaves, debtors, and thieves congregated south of the Virginia border to pursue their criminal ways outside the purview of the law. For decades, wealthy observers echoed the 1681 warning of Virginia's governor Thomas Culpeper that "Carolina (I meane the North part of it) always was and is the Sinke of America, the Refuge of our Renegadoes, and Till in better order, Dangerous To us." As late as 1732, Governor Burrington still lamented that "there are not a sufficient number of Gentlemen in it [North Carolina] fitt to be Councellors, . . . Justices of the Peace, . . . [or] officers in the Militia." He deplored that "there is no difference to be perceived in Dress and Carriage" between the common people on the one hand and court justices and government officials on the other, "which Parity," Burrington complained, "is in no other Country but this."[15]

From the start, political upheavals underscored the bad reputation of Albemarle settlers. In 1677, an antiproprietary faction protested the enforcement of the Plantation Duty Act of 1673, a duty of one penny per pound of exported tobacco. The protesters, themselves among the most prominent settlers, imprisoned the substitute governor and customs collector, Thomas Miller. The conflict, known as Culpeper's Rebellion, began as a quarrel among North Carolinians engaged in intercolonial and transatlantic trade, but it spread to those with other grievances. Miller later testified that "by beat of Drum and a shout of one and all of [the] rabble" he had been "accused of blasphemy, treason and other crimes, and so upon a shout of one and all of [the] rabble" he was "clapt in Irons" and then the "stocks and pillory [were] overturned and throwne into the river by this rabble." Some observers feared the uprising would spread among laboring people and entice them to flee or rebel. "If they not be suddenly subdued," one report warned, "hundreds of idle debters, theeves, Negros, Indians and English servants will fly into . . . the vast coast and wild woods of the backside of Virginia." The rebellion subsided, but political strife did not. Between 1670 and 1712 the Albemarle settlers sent six of their first fourteen governors back to England, some of them in chains. Governor Seth Sothell, for example, himself a Proprietor, was ousted in 1689 for multiple acts of corruption. In 1729, seven of the eight exasperated Proprietors gave up the enterprise (the earl of Granville retained his portion), and North Carolina became a royal colony. Looking back on the proprietary period in 1732, George Burrington, the first crown-appointed governor, described the inhabitants of North Carolina as "not Industrious but subtle and crafty." They "allways behaved insolently to their Governours," Burrington reported, and "some they have Imprisoned, drove others out of the Country, at times sett up two or three supported by Men under Arms," so that "all the Governors that ever were in this Province lived in fear of the People (except myself) and Dreaded their Assemblys."[16]

Such obstreperous behavior may have been encouraged by the rough and relatively equal living conditions of white settlers in early North Carolina. Landholding was more evenly distributed in North Carolina than in Virginia or South Carolina: quitrent lists compiled in 1735 for the northeastern counties of Currituck, Pasquotank, Perquimans, Chowan, Bertie, Tyrrell, and Edgecombe show that while nearly three quarters of the heads of households owned land, the majority of planters owned less than 250 acres, and few owned more than 1,000. The houses on these tracts were built to serve in the short term, not to last or to create an imposing specter of wealth (see figure 3, Boyette House). Most initially had one or two rooms, often with dirt floors, and they were made of hewn logs, the cracks filled in with clay, moss, sticks, and straw, although some houses had clapboard siding and a few were made of brick and had more than one story. North Carolina had no towns at all in the seventeenth century. Bath, the oldest, was incorporated on the Pamlico Sound in 1706, but three years later it still consisted of only twelve houses. In Chowan County, Edenton (called Queen Anne's Creek until 1722) became the colony's largest town (and remained so until mid-century), but as late as 1728, William Byrd of Virginia found that it boasted only "forty or fifty houses, most of them small, and built without expense. A Citizen here is counted extravagant, if he has Ambition enough to aspire to a Brick-chimney. Justice herself is but indifferently Lodged, the

Figure 3. The Boyette House in Johnston County from the early nineteenth century consists of horizontal sawn planks dovetailed together at the corners and a wooden chimney daubed with clay. This kind of one-room dwelling was typical in eastern colonial North Carolina. Courtesy of the North Carolina Division of Archives and History.

Court-House having much the Air of a Common Tobacco-House." The men who made up the governor's council and the justice system did not yet have the available income or the access to imported goods that would have allowed the ostentatious display of wealth with which Virginians were familiar. In Williamsburg, organized horse races, carriage rides through town, the seating of well-dressed families in the front pews of the Anglican Church, and courtroom rituals in impressive brick buildings routinely reinscribed class difference and commanded gestures of respect from the lower orders. North Carolina's leading men could not yet engage in such public exhibitions of privilege (the first Anglican church was a wooden structure built in 1701), nor could they claim to be from a long line of prominent families in the colony. From the point of view of wealthy men elsewhere, and probably also from that of resident settlers, the elite in North Carolina was still trying very hard to become an "upper" class.[17]

As a result of the slower accumulation of wealth in North Carolina, large-scale slaveholding grew only slowly. Nonetheless, African Americans came with at least four of the ten English settlers who obtained land prior to 1663, and many more migrated in the following decades. In 1705, about 1,000 slaves lived in the colony. The most populous county (Pasquotank) had 1,121 white and 211 black inhabitants by 1709. Thirty years later, when 103 of Pasquotank County's 283 households paid taxes for slaves, thirteen slave-holders owned between six and ten slaves; the remaining owned five slaves or fewer. North Carolinians began to catch up with slaveholders elsewhere when Albemarle planters such as Edward Moseley, Alexander Lillington, and the Swann family moved to the Cape Fear region where they and investors from South Carolina began to amass huge tracts of land and import slaves in large numbers. In the early 1730s, Governor George Burrington estimated North Carolina's population at about 6,000 blacks and 30,000 whites. (At that time nearly 50,000 blacks and over 100,000 whites lived in Virginia, and more than 21,000 slaves constituted a two-to-one black majority in South Carolina.) By 1748, slaves outnumbered servants in North Carolina, and by 1763 slaves outnumbered indentured servants in the Albemarle region by three to one.[18]

Although the slave labor system did not boom until well after the colony was established, laboring people of different backgrounds lived and worked together from the earliest days of settlement. English, African, and Indian servants worked together planting tobacco, corn, and other vegetables, raising many pigs and some cattle, and processing pines for the naval stores industry: they boiled sap for pitch, tar, and turpentine, and cut logs into boards, shingles, and barrel staves. The inventory for Captain Valentine Bird in 1680, for example, listed eleven Negro slaves, one Indian woman slave, and one indentured white woman. In 1693, two whites, four Indians, and eleven blacks worked for Quaker Esau Albertson in Albemarle County. In January 1694 Quaker Francis Tomes claimed headrights for ten people, including "Two Indians, three Negrose," and two white servant women. When John Bentley filed for headrights the following month, he listed "a negroe Boy a Negroe Woman an Indian Boy." Similarly, Isaac Wilson claimed land in January 1706 for "Negroe Phebe Indian Mall Negroe Patt Negro Maria." These close living and working conditions lent themselves to interracial cooperation. In July 1698, for example, "two negroes & one Indian" belonging to James Cole ran away together, but only after they "rob[b]ed the house and Caryed away Severall Goods and a trunk with wearing Cloaths." A white woman named Rebekah Baily was arrested in 1706 for "unlegally receiving Six pair of Buttons" belonging to Mr. Thomas Peterson and delivered to her by a "Negroe Woman belonging to William Glover Esquire." Whites and blacks on the Glover and Peterson estates had moved the buttons (and perhaps other goods) smoothly from one place to the other. Close working arrangements enabled a swift trade in stolen articles, and networks of communication aided runaways seeking temporary shelter. As Dorothy Steel's case illustrates, such illicit activity was hard to repress, and it added to the frustration of government officials who yearned for tighter social controls.[19]

Servants and slaves sometimes cooperated with each other, but they likely held prejudices as well. Although an ideology of racial difference as something innate and hereditary was still under construction, cultural chauvinism had a long history. English people, for example, no matter how lowly, could readily avail themselves of the widespread belief that protestant English culture was far superior to that of Catholic Spain, France, and Gaelic Ireland. English commoners heard much about a "barbaric" Ireland, where the importance of clans (rather than individual households), the nomadic and wide-ranging grazing of animals, the common arrangement for partible inheritance rather than primogeniture, a syncretic religion of Catholicism and non-Christian beliefs, the possibility of divorce and remarriage, and apparent tolerance of loose sexual morals all seemed evidence of a primitive, uncivil people. Irish beliefs and relations of property and gender served, in the minds of ambitious Englishmen, as evidence of an uncivilized country that was available for the taking, even at the cost of violent expropriation and brutal repression. When the Irish fought back, stereotypes of Irish savagery gained further credence. Even lower-class English servants, who were themselves often accused of the same kind of vagrancy and degeneracy that caricatured Irish people, may have felt pride and relief at being English at least, heirs to presumed cultural superiority despite their poverty.[20]

English chauvinism extended beyond the bounds of Europe to include Africans as well, whose rendition in early modern English art and literature was marked by a fascination for the "exotic," mingled with a fearful disdain of "blacknesse." Writers of travel accounts (many of whom never left England) represented black women and men as strangely different in manners and appearance. African women, for example, materialized in these narratives as both mothers and monsters. Descriptions of breasts so long that women could nurse over their shoulders evoked images of animal teats, while the portrayal of painless childbirth (a common theme in accounts of Irish and American Indian women as well) made African women's reproduction, like their nursing, seem mechanical and effortless. Depicted as both sexual and savage, African women appeared perfectly suited for the productive and reproductive labor of slavery. Such images had permeated English culture by the late seventeenth century, and they informed English responses to people of different cultures they encountered in the New World.[21]

In the North American colonies, however, everyday interaction soon dispelled fantasies of monstrous humans. To the Indians, Africans, and Europeans working in North Carolina's corn and tobacco fields, cultural ways that were initially strange soon became less fearsome. In the first few decades of settlement, shared housing, joint labor in the fields and forests, and community efforts to establish a settlement under frontier conditions hindered rigid distinctions of living conditions or work responsibilities along racial lines. Servants of different backgrounds who shared houses, food, and tools discovered mutual interests that could lead to joint enterprises such as theft, running away, and sexual liaisons. Many servants, white and black, had come from Virginia, where the condition of African Americans was not necessarily that of enslavement: until the late seventeenth century, some free black families in Virginia managed to own property, win lawsuits against whites, and acquire slaves themselves. Interracial marriage was not explicitly prohibited in Virginia until 1691. The humanity of people from different backgrounds and of distinctive appearance was not in doubt, and living conditions in the less developed North Carolina colony fostered acts of cooperation. Not that perfect understanding or full acceptance of others' ways prevailed. Prejudice against people who dressed, ate, looked, celebrated, and mourned differently combined with the belief in one's own cultural superiority most certainly persevered. But adaptation to new living and working conditions sparked curiosity about cultural differences and customs that might prove useful in new surroundings. One such set of customs involved gender roles. Recent arrivals to North Carolina looked with great interest—some with fear, others with admiration—at the way Native American arrangements of gender seemed to make a world of difference.[22]

"Plantinge Corne without Fence": Native American Land Use and Gender Roles

By the time Dorothy Steel and her companions exchanged goods and gunfire with "sum Indians," the latter had been greatly affected by well over a century of European contact. The Spanish explorer Hernando de Soto traveled through the region in 1540, Giovanni da Verrazano sailed up the coast for the French in 1542, and Juan Pardo explored in 1566–68. The English founded their first colony on the island of Roanoke in 1585 (although it soon disintegrated). Diseases imported during these sixteenth-century European expeditions spread rapidly among Indians who had no immunity to Old World microbes, and recurring epidemics continued to devastate native populations. The Cherokee in the mountains, for instance, numbered approximately 30,000 in 1660, but an outbreak of smallpox in 1697 cut the population in half. The Tuscarora and Algonquian tribes in the coastal region also numbered about 30,000 in 1660, but by 1685 the coastal plains Indians were reduced to about 10,000, and at the turn of the century their number was half that. In 1700 only about 4,000 Tuscarora Indians and fewer than 1,000 members of smaller tribes—some of whom had been reduced to a single village—occupied the region between Virginia and the Neuse River. Although Native Americans had vastly outnumbered the newcomers throughout the early decades of colonial settlement, by 1700 the newcomers were in the majority: roughly 9,400 Europeans, 7,200 Indians, and 400 African Americans lived east of the mountains.[23]

The Indians in the region that became North Carolina belonged to three linguistic groups (see figure 4). The largest of these was Iroquoian and included the Cherokee in the mountains and the Tuscarora in the coastal plain. In between, in the Piedmont, lived Siouan-speaking people, while smaller groups of Algonquian Indians, the Machapunga, Chowan, Pamlico, Meherrin, and Bear River Indians, for example, populated the coast and the regions around the Albemarle and Pamlico Sound. Even within a single linguistic family, people spoke mutually unintelligible languages. Surveyor John Lawson, who in 1701 traveled five hundred miles through South and North Carolina, found that "Altho' their Tribes or Nations border one upon another, yet you may discern as great an Alteration in their Features and Dispositions, as you can in their Speech, which generally proves quite different from each other, though their Nations be not above 10 or 20 Miles in Distance." While distinctive traits marked the region's native cultures, there were also widely shared customs of lineage, land use, property, and relations of authority that contrasted notably with English customs.[24]

Europeans understood Indian customs from within their own cultural framework, and their observations often reveal their own assumptions about appropriate gender relations. John Lawson, for example, described the reasons for Native American matrilineage in terms that would make sense to (and possibly amuse) his English readers, saying that "the Female Issue [carried] the Heritage, for fear of Imposters; the Savages well knowing, how much Frailty possesses the *Indian* Women, betwixt the Garters and the Girdle." Concerns about female infidelity and assumptions of women's weak moral fiber pervaded English culture; it is hard to know whether this was a concern as well among Indian groups or simply Lawson's gloss on the situation. Historians must treat these narratives with care, reading for the author's audience and motives as well as for content. Nonetheless, these

Native Americans in North Carolina

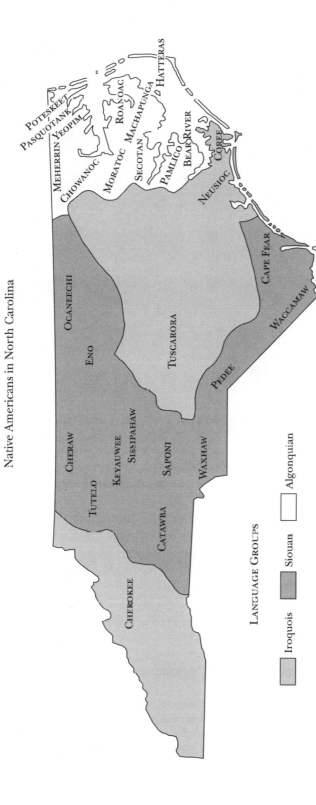

LANGUAGE GROUPS

Iroquois

Siouan

Algonquian

Figure 4. Indians in early North Carolina belonged to three linguistic groups: the Iroquois-speaking Cherokee and Tuscarora, the Siouan speakers in the Piedmont, and Algonquian speakers in the coastal plain.

Figure 5. John White's drawing of Secota village in 1585 depicts distinct activities including dancing, feasting, hunting, tending sacred fires, and watching the fields for birds and other scavengers. Viewed from above, the human figures are small, and Indian life appears orderly and bountiful. Courtesy of the North Carolina Division of Archives and History.

writings provide rich ethnographic detail that can be checked against the findings of ethnohistorians, historical anthropologists, and archeologists. Eighteenth-century ethnography and travel literature (genres that often blurred) remarked most often on the inhabitants of Indian villages and seldom on Indians who lived in colonial settlements. Similarly, North Carolina's court records give only sporadic glimpses of the many Indians who undoubtedly lived among the settlers as artisans, servants, and slaves. (I have found no court cases involving sexual relations between Indians and settlers—white or black.) The following discussion, therefore, focuses mostly on Piedmont Indians and the Cherokee within the changing context of their Indian villages.[25]

Europeans found especially remarkable the matrilineal kinship system they encountered in much of the Southeast. Families were traced through the mother's line, and blood relatives included one's mother, her mother, the mother's siblings and one's own siblings. The biological father and the mother's father were not considered kin, nor were the children of the mother's brother, as they were members of their own mothers' families. Families were members of clans (the Cherokee counted seven clans, for example), each of them stemming from their own fictive ancestor, so that all members of a clan, whether or not they had ever met and no matter which village they were from, recognized each other as kin. Adopted family members were considered as much a part of the clan as those born into it. Members of different clans lived in each village and married exogamously as it was incestuous to marry within one's clan. When a man married, he moved from the household of his mother to that of his wife, but he remained a member of his mother's clan. A man who married more than one wife often married sisters, enabling him to stay in one household rather than divide his time among two. If a couple separated, the woman and children remained in their matrilocal multigenerational households, and the man returned to his family. While biological fathers might take an interest in their children, a child's most important male relative was the mother's brother who played a more active role in the child's upbringing. Women were most responsible for raising children. Alexander Longe, a trader who lived with the Cherokee for ten years, noted that when a child was born, "all the feemale Relations lokes one the Child to be thire proper doughter." If the mother of the newborn dies, "aney of the womens Relations that gives milke will teake the Child and give itt sucke and they will make noe distinchon betwixt That Child and thire own proper Chilldrin." Indeed, "they will Rather be more kinder to itt then to thire own proper Chilldrian" and the husband "must shoe more kindness to that Child than to his own or Els he must Expect but letell quite [little quiet] of his wife." Longe's depiction reveals his own understanding of kinship based on "blood" (and not adoption), as well as his sympathy for husbands he describes as hen-pecked, but he also shows a community of "female Relations" responsible for raising children.[26]

Matrilineality was not the same as matriarchy (women were generally not chiefs, for example), yet the custom of tracing families through the female line gave women important responsibilities. The clan, and the women at its core, decided how to respond to the death of a relative. The tradition of blood vengeance required that the murder of kin be avenged—and a kind of cosmic balance reestablished—by killing the perpetrator or a close relative of the perpetrator. That is why "*Indians* ground their Wars on Enmity, not on Interest, as the *Europeans* generally do." Lawson explained that "for the loss of the meanest Person in the Nation, they will go to War and lay all at Stake, . . . till the Nation they were injur'd by, be wholly destroy'd, or make them that Satisfaction which they demand." Indian women decided, too, whether war captives should be adopted to replace lost family members or tortured and killed in retribution for the loss. When women chose torture they enacted it themselves, beating the victim with canes and burning torches, occasionally reviving the victim with a douse of cold water, all the while singing and laughing, especially if the captive showed fear of death. Women were central figures in war-related rituals, and as a group they made important decisions over life, death, and membership in the clan.[27]

Indian women also acquired status from indigenous customs of property holding and land use. Many Indian groups such as the Cherokee, for example, discerned between different kinds of property that could be claimed by the entire tribe, a family, or an individual, respectively. While whole tribes laid claim to certain hunting grounds, women in matrilineal families controlled the fields they tended, the corn and other crops they produced, and the houses in which family members lived. Individuals owned personal possessions such as tools, jewelry, and weapons, but such goods were generally not passed on to heirs. Native Americans in North Carolina recognized claims to territory based on usufruct rights—the specific uses people made of the land—rather than exclusive ownership of land within permanently fixed boundaries. The allocation of hunting, fishing, and planting to different villages within the same territory allowed different groups to benefit from the same area without infringing on one another's activities. Claims to land remained contingent upon active use, and people who did not return annually to their fields lost their right to them, making the land available to anyone else who planted it. North Carolina Indians usually divided work responsibilities by gender, although entire Indian villages prepared and planted the fields. Men removed trees by setting fires to the trunks or stripping the bark so the trees would die, then men and women planted the fields together. James Adair, an Irishman who spent over thirty years among the Cherokee and Chickasaw Indians, remembered that "Indian law obliged every town to work together in one body, in sowing or planting their crops; though their fields are divided by proper marks, and their harvest is gathered separately." The work did not seem disagreeable as they "fall to work with great cheerfulness" while an orator "cheers them with jests and humorous old tales, and sings several of their most agreeable wild tunes" while beating on a drum as "they proceed from field to field, till their seed is sown."[28]

Though men and women shared some tasks, most responsibilities divided along gender lines. Men fished with spears and elaborate fishing weirs and hunted game in the winter, leaving the women, children, and older men in the villages. In warmer months, groups of women tended the fields of corn, beans, squash, and peas, while older women, perched on scaffolds, kept vigilant watch for crows and other scavengers. Women also planted smaller vegetable gardens near their houses, gathered nuts, berries, honey, and edible roots, baked bread, cooked soups, and pressed oil from nuts. Adair admired the "great variety of dishes they make out of wild flesh, corn, beans, peas, potatoes, pompions [pumpkins], dried fruits, herbs and roots," and claimed that "They can diversify their courses, as much as the English, or perhaps the French cooks." Women also made their own household utensils: baskets from woven cane, an array of glazed pottery, bottles from hollowed gourds, and deerskin flasks. They used bone needles and sinew to fashion clothing from dressed animal hides and from fabric made with fibrous hemp stalks.[29]

The segregation of responsibilities dove-tailed with the belief that men and women had distinct powers that existed in a delicate balance with each other. This balance required careful tending lest a transgression of gender roles cause terrible disruptions. Blood, for example, was thought to have great powers that accrued differently to men than to women, requiring gender-specific cleansing rituals. Women, for example, were thought to have special powers related to menstruation and their ability to give birth. Their menstrual blood was considered a powerful substance that required abstinence, isolation in separate huts, and ritual purification. In turn, male warriors returning from battle were thought to ruin the cornfields if they entered them before completing rituals of seclusion and purification, and wounded men lived in isolation for four months to avoid spreading pollution. Both men and women had powers related to blood, but the effects of that power were markedly distinct. Native American men and women operated from within separate realms of responsibility, and Indian women generally had less public authority than men, but their well-defined gender roles neither demanded nor justified a gender hierarchy of the kind Europeans believed God had imposed on the descendents of Adam and Eve.[30]

Nonetheless, some Europeans viewed the multiple responsibilities of Indian women as oppressive. Commentators described the "squaw drudge" as a primitive and pathetic woman who worked in the fields while her lazy husband enjoyed hunting and fishing. The image of Indian women as quasi-slaves appeared early in colonial accounts and had a tenacious history. In 1607, the English aristocrat George Percy said that Powhatan women in Jamestown, Virginia, "doe all their drugerie. The men takes their pleasure in hunting and their warres." In 1728, William Byrd of Virginia employed a well-worn trope when he wrote that "The little Work that is done among the Indians is done by the poor Women, while the men are quite idle, or at most employ'd only in the Gentlemanly Diversions of Hunting and Fishing." In England, hunting was a leisure activity reserved for the wealthy, so English observers often misunderstood both the social value of hunting game and the respected role of women's agricultural work. Honest misunderstanding or not, the image of the "squaw drudge" served other purposes as well. Depictions of lazy Indian men exploiting female relatives emphasized Englishmen's roles as providers for European women (whose daily "drugerie" went unremarked). Englishmen could also fancy themselves welcome civilizers: European gender roles would relieve grateful Indian women of their agricultural servitude and draw them into the appropriately domestic work done by English women.[31]

In fact, however, native women gained power from their agricultural work. Aside from the common crib into which women annually put as much corn as they saw fit, individual households stored their own harvest. The supervision of food stores gave women influence in decisions of diplomacy—when to go to war, for example. The fact that women controlled the fruits of their labor and shared in the resources and responsibilities of the village may explain why they did not seem to feel unduly burdened by their work. One long-time visitor among the Cherokee noted that "Though custom attached the heaviest part of the labour to the women, yet they were cheerful and voluntary in performing it." In his nineteen years among the Cherokee, missionary Butrick continued, "I have seen nothing of that slavish, servile fear, on the part of women, so often spoke of."[32]

Even though women gained status through the production of food, the accumulation of personal wealth did not figure prominently in the indigenous social order. Indians owned personal possessions, but these were not amassed to show economic or social power, nor were they passed on to heirs. Pottery, jewelry, and weapons were buried with the owners when they died (to be used in the afterlife). At harvest time, individuals made a contribution to the public granary "according to his ability or inclination, or none at all if he so chooses," to which "every citizen has the right of free and equal access, when his own private stores are consumed." When the next harvest began to ripen, the stores of corn were destroyed at the annual Green Corn Ceremony. Adair believed this ceremony contributed to the "spirit of hospitality" he saw among the Indians, and he admired their "community of goods": "An open generous temper is a standing virtue among them; to be narrow-hearted, especially to those in want, or to any of their own family, is accounted a great crime." Lawson believed that because Indians garnered respect based on their "natural Vertues and Gifts, and not Riches," they did not "contemplate on the Affairs of Loss and Gain; the things which daily perplex us." They "never work as the *English* do, taking care for no farther than what is absolutely necessary to support Life." Though Lawson, Bartram, and Adair may have used idealized images of community-oriented goodwill as an oblique attack on social conditions in Britain, they had aptly recognized that honor and rank among the Indians they visited did not stem from the accumulation of property. Positions of leadership were inherited, but respect had to be earned and maintained through demonstrations of skill, not a show of wealth.[33]

Property arrangements and sexual customs were linked in native cultures, albeit differently than in European ones. Indians in North Carolina did not transfer personal property from one generation to the next, making superfluous any effort to control a wife's sexuality for the purpose of passing wealth onto her husband's biological sons. Nor did unhappily married spouses feel compelled to remain together. One Indian explained to Adair that "marriage should beget joy and happiness, instead of pain and misery," and for a couple that "could not love each other afterwards, it was a crime to continue together, and a virtue to part, and make a happier choice." Lawson found that in Carolina, Indian women could dissolve unhappy marriages easily, since their unions "are no farther binding, than the Man and Woman agree together. Either of them has Liberty to leave the other," Lawson explained, in which case the woman remained in her house and kept the fields she cultivated, and "all the Children go along with the Mother, and none with the Father." If the wife had an extramarital affair, she "was not punish'd for Adultery, but 'tis the Man that makes the injur'd Person Satisfaction." The "Rival becomes Debtor" to the husband, paying certain goods agreed upon between the two men, after which "all Animosity is laid aside betwixt the Husband, and his Wife's Gallant." Amazed at what seemed an unnatural breach of patriarchal authority, Englishmen marveled that Indian husbands submitted to a "petticoat-government" and let themselves be cuckolded by promiscuous wives.[34]

But these outsiders may also have exaggerated the extramarital activity of Indian spouses, either for their sensationalist value, or because they did not recognize Indians' marriages as such. Long-term conjugal relations were celebrated with a bridewealth (a dowry) and a ritualized feast. John Lawson said he knew "several Couples" who remained "faithful to each other, admitting none to their Beds but such as they own'd for their Wife or Husband: So continuing to their Life's end." Other unions incurred fewer reciprocal obligations between partners and may have begun and ended with less formality. Because many English observers did not discern between different kinds of conjugal relations, they often described Indian nuptial rites as spurious and "marriages" as fickle. Despite such misunderstandings, intrigued Europeans rightly noted that Indian wives generally enjoyed more social and sexual leverage than did European women. To a greater extent, native women retained control over their agricultural produce, their children, and their sexuality. Men held most positions of power, but women's responsibilities gave them publicly acknowledged influence over community decisions.[35]

Though colonists' ideas about property differed from those of the Indians they encountered, the English themselves had no consensus regarding appropriate land use. Precisely because property rights were contested in England, Native American arrangements appealed to some migrants and seemed foolish to others. Since the sixteenth century, the landed elite had been reasserting their rights to property for which they held titles but which generations of tenant families had farmed or used as commons for grazing animals. Eager to evict tenants and enclose the land with fences to graze wool-bearing sheep for the expanding textile industry, titleholders insisted that property ownership was a private, permanent affair, that ownership of land was absolute and remained unaffected by its uses, and that property could be legally transferred to another owner only through inheritance or sale. The enclosure movement fueled bitter contention. A steep rise in the population exacerbated problems of homelessness and unemployment, and beggars roamed the countryside in search of subsistence. Harvest failures compounded the crisis, leading to a rise in food prices while high unemployment held wages low. During the English Revolution, radical thinkers like the Diggers argued that private property was unethical and based on violence, and they promoted a communal tilling of the land. This tradition of radicalism persisted into the eighteenth century, and even less radical villagers tenaciously defended the custom of commonly held grazing lands and communal rights to forest timber. Upon arriving in America, some settlers may well have appreciated Native American customs of shared land use. Others, however, believing it immoral to hold land and not till it, would have found spurious the Indians' claims to hunting territory. They may have seen "lazy" Indian men as comparable to aristocratic English landowners who retained uncultivated fields and forests for their own pleasure.[36]

Whether sympathetic to Indian uses of land or not, most English immigrants craved an independence they understood to be literally grounded in freeholdings. Land-hungry and enticed by reports that acreage could be had on "easy terms" from the Indians, English migrants to North Carolina acquired land and began the process of fencing and planting. As early as 1648, aspiring landowners from Virginia bought land from North Carolina Indians, and by the 1660s such transactions had become general practice. The Lords Proprietors deplored that settlers in the Albemarle region independently "bought great tracts of land from the Indians, which if they shall injoye will weaken the plantation." Accordingly, the "Fundamental Constitutions of Carolina," penned in 1669 by John Locke, stipulated that "no person whatever, shall hold or claim any land in Carolina, by purchase or gift, or otherwise, from the natives or any other whatsoever; but merely from and under the Lords Proprietors, upon pain of forfeiture of all his estate, moveable or immoveable, and perpetual banishment." Despite these proprietary efforts to control land deals in the colony, settlers continued to make their own arrangements with Indian neighbors.[37]

Culturally distinct notions of property soon clashed. Native Americans willing to share territory or barter with Europeans for certain uses of the land could not readily comprehend the idea of selling land outright. The idea of "trespassing" on the newcomers' now "privately" owned property remained alien. Tensions rose as English settlement patterns impinged on ancient hunting grounds and when settlers' livestock trampled unfenced Indian gardens and cornfields. In the colony's first decades, conflict mingled with gestures of reconciliation. Skirmishes broke out repeatedly (Indians attacked the Albemarle settlement in late September 1666, for example), while at other times Anglo-Indian relations took a friendly turn, as in 1670, when the English found that "all our provisions was gone soe wee were fiorst to live upon the indeans who are very kinde to us." Overall, however, Indians found themselves increasingly hemmed in by settlers whose land claims were defended by the courts.[38]

The fate of one Algonquian town shows the radical changes that occurred in a short amount of time. Chowanoc, located on the west side of the Chowan River, had been inhabited for more than a thousand years, and in the 1580s was home to seven hundred warriors and their kin, some 2,500 in all. In November 1694, the Chowan Indians complained to the General Court that "they are much Injured by the English seating soe near them."

The magistrates initially ordered that "noe more [land] Entrys or settle-ment of land be made higher than the plantations which are alreddy seated above the Old towne Creeke," but they could hardly prevent settlers' con-tinuing encroachments on Indian territory. A year later, an Indian named John King reported in court that Englishmen John Parish and William God-frey "offered some abuse to him and other Indians" and "denied their lib-erty of Hunting." This time the court's response was stingy: the Indians had "liberty to hunt on all wasteland that is not taken up and liberty to pass through the lands that are seated in their goeing to and from the said Wast land," but only under the stipulation that they conduct themselves "sivilly and doeing noe Injury." Native Americans soon found that when they continued to hunt or plant in familiar terrain they stood accused of breaking treaties and ignoring land sales. By 1709, Chowanoc had been reduced to fifteen fighting men and their families. After the Tuscarora War ended in 1713, the Chowan were confined to a reservation of six square miles in Bertie County called Indian Woods. Many Chowan Indians may have entered the colonial settlements as laborers, joined larger tribes, or fled their homes altogether, but by 1752, the ancient town consisted of only a few families with hardly any land at all.[39]

The very seasonal mobility of Indians added to the colonial perception that Indian communities were unstable and without legitimate claim to the land. There were Indian villages, of course, but during winter hunts men left them for months at a time, adding to the perception of Indians as roaming and unsettled people. When the Meherrin Indians complained to the Virginia Council in 1707 about the "encroachments" made on them by North Carolina colonists, North Carolina assemblymen Edward Mose-ley, William Glover, Francis Foster, and Samuel Swann composed their own counter-charge: "the stragling and vagrant Indians of that Nation" had been "plantinge Corne without fence so that no English can seate near them without danger of trespassing [with] their Cattle and Horses," which the Meherrin Indians "Revenge without measure." The real question at hand, the writers continued, was "whether near a hundred familys of her Majesty's subjects of Carolina should be disseased [deceased] of their freehold to lett a few vagrant and Insolent Indians rove where they please." The depiction of Indians as vagrants ignored the obvious presence of Indian fields and gardens and overlooked the agricultural labor done by women (perhaps precisely because as "women's work" it seemed less legitimate to colonial observers). From this perspective, Indians had no claim to the land because they did not properly use it, whereas Englishmen who provided for their families had a right to farm the land. Having rhetorically erased Native American agriculture from the landscape (with language that recalled the unemployed gangs of England), these assemblymen proposed a solution in the form of surveillance: "we have always thought it necessary that the Indians should live together in towns where all their young men may be under the immediate inspection of their own Governors to prevent their private mischiefs that may be more easily done and concealed in single and separate familys."[40]

English objections to indigenous patterns of land use thus merged with their reservations about Native American family structures. Colonial leaders found Indian families insufficient as a means of controlling the behavior of young men because families played a very different role in Native American society than they did among the English. In English society, male heads of household were charged with maintaining order, preferably leading by their own example, but failing that, by inflicting corporal punishment on wayward family members and servants. In Native American society, by contrast, the entire village policed social boundaries by ridiculing or shunning those who behaved in unacceptable ways. Indians shamed transgressors with a "keen irony and satyr, that kills whom it praises," and they deployed "an ironic way of jesting. . . . with severe sarcasms which wound deeply." Relatives and neighbors, not household patriarchs, used verbal pressure to enforce good behavior within the villages. Because the larger community exerted social control, individual marriages could form and dissolve without disrupting the social order.[41]

In both colonial and native societies in North Carolina, albeit in very different ways, property arrangements and familial relations provided interconnected structures of social organization. Native women's social authority resided substantially in their responsibility for agricultural work and in their control over its produce. Matrilineal social organization and the absence of property inheritance allowed Indian women considerable sexual self-determination. Among the English, by contrast, married women could not own property themselves, and rules about female chastity sought to ensure the transference of real property to their husband's male heirs. English men tilled the land and controlled its resources, and although women's work was crucial to the domestic economy, a wife's productivity did not lead to an expansion of her authority vis-à-vis her spouse. Cultural differences regarding gender roles mattered to colonial authorities precisely because of the links between property-holding, inheritance, lineage, marriage, sexual behavior, and relations of authority. Some feared an alternative culture might attract too many disaffected colonists. A few traders in the backcountry did no harm, even when they remained there for decades and lived in Indian villages with native spouses and children. Too many such cultural converts, however, undermined claims about the cultural superiority of the English. Uncertain about their own status, furthermore, would-be leaders had an exaggerated sense of the impact of alternative systems of property, gender, and power on colonial society. After all, some, but certainly not the majority of colonists, viewed social relations in Tuscarora, Waxhaw, or Cherokee villages as admirable and worthy of emulation. Still, the paranoia was real enough, and it put misconduct like Dorothy Steel's in a new light. Her willingness to take property from her husband, engage in sex with other men, and trade freely with Indians and Africans gained new meaning in the light of Indian ways. To government officials and court magistrates, her behavior seemed more than simply the acts of a delinquent English housewife; it portended just the kind of cultural conversion they feared. Whose relations of gender and property would ultimately prevail seemed an open question in the late seventeenth century. In the meantime, colonial presumptions about the natural order of patriarchal households faced another challenge. This one came from the radical Protestantism of the Society of Friends.[42]

Inner Light and Sexless Souls: The Society of Friends

Women in the Society of Friends had roles and responsibilities greatly at odds with English gender norms. Quakers' belief that women and men could in equal measure be infused with divine "Inner Light" meant that women who experienced godly inspiration spoke with as much religious authority as their male peers. Women Quakers, like men, could become "Public Friends," respected public speakers on religious matters who received certificates to travel and preach to mixed groups of men and women. In a radical departure from the teachings of Apostle Paul that women must remain silent in church and submissive to their husbands, women preachers left their husbands and domestic duties behind to serve the larger cause of bringing unconverted women and men "into the Light." In an effort to encourage Friends and convert non-Quakers, women preachers bore public testimony to the workings of God, gave sermons explicating the Scriptures, and published their writings. Furthermore, Quaker women, like men, met in gender-segregated meetings where they discussed community affairs and sent groups to investigate Friends accused of misconduct and couples planning to marry. Quaker women thus had a formalized and regular means of making decisions that shaped their community. They also had an identity apart from their familial responsibilities. In the first decades of settlement on the Albemarle Sound, the gender norms of the growing minority of Quakers in the colony represented to Anglican men a world turned upside down and a hindrance to the establishment of proper social relations and respect for their authority.[43]

The Society of Friends, founded by George Fox in England in 1648, proclaimed a theology of universal love that was available to all human beings, regardless of skin color, sex, or status. Anyone willing to strip away the superficial layers of egotism could be flooded by the "inner light" that was the godliness in every human being. Imbued with a feeling of divine love, Friends called out their inspirations, speaking as vessels of the Lord; for the way they shook with the power of their visions, critics derisively labeled them "Quakers." The Society of Friends dismissed the notion of a covenant of works—the idea that one could influence one's salvation with good behavior. They also discarded outward signs of deference and social conventions of authority. In the 1650s Fox rejected all formal structures of organized religion, including baptism and marriage ceremonies performed by a minister, as well as the paying of tithes. He replaced the pagan language of the calendar with numerical indications for days and months. Quakers refused to swear oaths of any kind, including oaths of allegiance to the crown. They ceased doffing their hats or bowing to social superiors and began addressing everyone with the informal "thee" and "thou" rather than the more formal "you." In their desire to shed vanity and pride, Quakers dressed in simple, modest clothing. As an antiformalist sect that believed that "once in the light, men and women were out of the law," Quakers soon became subject to severe persecution in England.[44]

This persecution followed Quakers to America. It gained a legislative toehold in the southern colonies when the Governor's Council in Maryland, briefly under Puritan control, arrested itinerant preachers and in 1658 ordered that all Quakers cease their religious practices or "depart the Province on paine due to rebels and traitors." In 1660, lawmakers in Virginia passed "An Act for Supressing the Quakers," those "unreasonable and Turbulent sort of people" who teach "lies, miracles, false visions, prophecies and doctrines" in an effort to "destroy religion, lawes, communities and all bonds of civil societie." The act ordered the arrest and deportation of any Quaker to arrive in the colony and imposed a fine of a hundred pounds of tobacco on anyone who owned Quaker literature or allowed meetings in or near their home. Two laws passed in 1662 ordered a fine of two hundred pounds of tobacco for anyone caught attending a Quaker meeting, a penalty of twenty pounds in cash for every month of missed attendance at an Anglican church service, and a fine of two hundred pounds of tobacco for every child not baptized (with no limit placed on the number of times a parent could be fined). The next year the Virginia government stipulated that when five or more non-Anglican adults—Quakers or "any other separatists whatsoever"— gathered together for a religious meeting, each had to pay two hundred pounds of tobacco for the first offense, five hundred pounds for the second, and suffer deportation for the third. Shipmasters who transported Quakers to the colony had to pay five thousand pounds of tobacco and ship them out again on the same vessel; anyone who offered shelter to Quakers would be fined the same amount, and local officials who failed to enforce the law could forfeit two thousand pounds in the loose-leaf currency. Although these laws were enforced only intermittently, the threat of such penalties hung over the heads of all dissenters, and occasional punishments served as dire warnings. When Quakers Mary Tomkins and Alice Ambrose entered Virginia a second time in 1663, they each suffered thirty-two lashes at the pillory and were expelled without their personal belongings. Virginia lawmakers did their utmost to prevent the spread of "this Pestilent sect."[45]

North Carolina differed from Virginia and Maryland in that it offered liberal provisions for religious dissenters. Seeking to encourage settlement, the Proprietors expressly granted "freedom and liberty of conscience in all religious or spiritual things." Certain restrictions remained, however. The "Fundamental Constitutions" of the colony, written by John Locke, pronounced atheists officially unacceptable. No one was allowed to live in or own land in Carolina "who doth not acknowledge a God, and that God is publicly and solemnly to be worshipped." Religious diversity was permitted only as long as it did not lead to political dissent: no one was to "speak any thing in their religious assembly irreverently or seditiously of the government or governors, or of state matters." Moreover, the Church of England, "which being the only true and orthodox, and the national religion of all the king's dominions, and so also of Carolina," was the only church that received public maintenance. Nonetheless, the constitutions were generous in their allowance that "any seven or more persons agreeing in any religion, shall constitute a church or profession, to which they shall give some name, to distinguish it from others." Despite its restrictions, therefore, North Carolina (like Rhode Island, New Jersey, and Pennsylvania) was much more tolerant than other colonies in which Quakers suffered imprisonment, fines, banishment, or even hanging for their beliefs.[46]

Hannah Phelps appreciated the relative religious freedom available in Albemarle County. She had migrated first from England to the Massachusetts Bay Colony where she and her husband hosted the first recorded Quaker meeting in Salem in June 1658. That year, Quakers were banned from the colony on pain of death. Despite the danger, Hannah continued to hold meetings at her house and was fined every year from 1658 to 1663 for not attending the Salem church. When she traveled to Boston in autumn 1659 to visit two Quakers from England who had been sentenced to death, she and five other Friends were summarily arrested and imprisoned. Two weeks after the execution of the condemned Friends, Hannah and her cohorts were admonished, whipped, and sent home, and the Salem Court seized her house and lands in payment of the fines levied against her and her husband. In July 1664, Hannah and Henry Phelps sought refuge along the Albemarle Sound. As early as May 1672, the Quaker minister William Edmundson visited these Carolina Friends. The renowned Irish missionary found the watery landscape south of the Virginia border "all wilderness" with "no English inhabitants or pathways, but some marked trees to guide people." When he finally arrived at the Phelps's house on Perquimans River, Edmundson dried his sopping clothes and held the first meeting of the Society of Friends (and the first recorded religious service) in the Albemarle settlement, gratified that despite his weariness several people "were tendered and received the testimony." Spurred by a visit from George Fox later that year, the fledgling Society continued to grow. When Edmundson returned to the colony in 1676, he found the people generally "tender and loving" with "no room" for "priests" (paid ministers) since "Friends were finely settled."[47]

By 1700 there were three thriving monthly meetings in the Albemarle area, two in Perquimans (held at the houses of Francis Tomes and Jonathan Phelps) and one in Pasquotank. Monthly meetings also convened at the Nicholson, Bundy, Scott, and White households until, by the first decade of the eighteenth century, Friends had built separate meetinghouses (see figure 6). Prominent Albemarle Quakers gradually acquired considerable political influence. Francis Tomes, for example, was a member of the Albemarle Council, deputy collector of customs, and a justice of the peace. The North Carolina Yearly Meeting first met in his home in 1698, and he provided land for three of the meetinghouses. Joseph Scott was a member of the General Assembly, and Gabriel Newby served in the House of Commons. The political influence of Albemarle's most established group of religious dissenters peaked when Proprietor John Archdale, himself a convert of Fox's, became the governor of Carolina in 1694. The following year, for example, the North Carolina assembly passed an act exempting Quakers, who were avowed pacifists, from military service.[48]

Archdale's Anglican successor, Governor Henderson Walker, sought to turn the tide, requesting in 1703 that the Society for the Propagation of the Gospel in Foreign Parts (SPG) send a minister, since "we have been settled near this fifty years in this place, and I may justly say most part of twenty-one years, on my own knowledge, without priest or altar." Reverend John Blair arrived the following year but lasted only six months before he returned to England, impoverished and discouraged. By his account, "the Quakers . . . are the greatest number in the Assembly, and are unanimous, and stand truly to one another in whatsoever be their interests." The next

Figure 6. The Newbold-White House in Perquimans County, built around 1730, was home to many prominent Quakers and may have been used as a meetinghouse. Courtesy of the North Carolina Division of Archives and History.

two SPG missionaries, James Adams and William Gordon, arrived in 1708 and found the Quakers numerous and troublesome. Reverend Adams estimated that Pasquotank, the most densely settled county, had a colonial population of 1,332 that included 900 Anglicans (and a few Presbyterians), 210 Quakers, 11 settlers who professed no religion, and 211 "negroes, some few of which are instructed in the principles of the Christian religion." Reverend Gordon reported that "There are few or no dissenters in this government but Quakers," and these he found "very numerous, extremely ignorant, insufferably proud and ambitious, and consequently ungovernable." Quakers "were made councillors and grew powerful," for the governor's council appointed magistrates to the courts. Furthermore, Friends "were very diligent at the election of members of Assembly." James Adams related that "though not yet the seventh part of the inhabitants, . . . [Quakers] have in a manner the sole management of the country in their hands." Venerable statesmen, Adams charged, had been turned out of the assembly "for no other reason but because they are members of the Church of England." Even worse, "shoemakers and other mechanics" had replaced

them in the assembly, "merely because they are Quaker preachers and notorious blasphemers of the Church."[49]

Friends irritated their non-Quaker neighbors in a number of ways. One
significant conflict centered on Quakers' pacifist refusal to take part in wars
against Native Americans (or to let their servants join the militia), despite
the decree that "all inhabitants and freemen of Carolina" between the ages
of seventeen and sixty "shall be bound to bear arms, and serve as soldiers
whenever the grand council shall find it necessary." Alexander Spotswood,
lieutenant governor of Virginia, complained to the Lords Proprietors of
Carolina that the "Masque of Quakerism" enabled the "lazy or Cowardly"
to use "the pretence of Conscience" to avoid military duty. Nor would Quakers contribute their labor or that of their servants or slaves to the construction of forts, and tensions rose further when Friends refused to pay
the five pound fine for lack of compliance with the law. Their decision may
have been principled, but Quakers who attended muster faced reprimand
and possible disownment from the monthly meeting. Defiance of "worldy"
authority came from compliance with the Society's rules. Yet the penalties
for being a pacifist could be stiff: in 1680, nine Quakers from Perquimans
County (including Hannah Phelps's son, Jonathan) spent six months in jail
for their refusal to attend military exercises, and their property was
confiscated in lieu of fines. For settlers afraid of Indian attacks, Quakers'
refusal to fight represented a profoundly disturbing breach of loyalty to
the colonial enterprise.[50]

Quakers not only practiced pacifism in ways that infuriated their white
neighbors, they also actively cultivated positive relations with those whom
others feared and despised. Henry White, one of the earliest English settlers to Pasquotank, was a Quaker whose "Christian conduct and loving behavior towards the Indians" earned him "great esteem and respect from
them." Nathan Newby, a Quaker blacksmith, mended Indians' guns while
discussing with them the "Sentiments they have about Heaven and heav-
enly Things." White, Newby, and others held fast to the idea that all
people could experience divine inner light. That Quakers would rather
converse with Indians than fight them had already raised the ire of some.
That Newby willingly mended Indian guns when he would not take up arms
against their owners only added to the existing resentment against Friends.
Male Quakers seemed to abrogate their responsibilities as colonial men
when they refused to defend their families as non-Quakers believed effective heads of households must.[51]

In other ways, however, Quakers upheld familiar English norms. In contrast to the Diggers and other radicals of the English Revolution, Quakers
did not advocate a redistribution of property, and many acquired consider-

able holdings in the colonies. Nor did they shy away from acquiring human chattel. By the end of the eighteenth century there was a booming commerce in Indian captives sold as slaves to colonial buyers, and North Carolina Quakers took advantage of the trade to acquire cheap labor. In April 1690, for example, the Perquimans County court forced Alexander, an Indian of unnoted origin, to sign an indenture to wealthy Quaker widow Mary Scott for the unusually long term of eighty years. Alexander had been "imported" into the colony and then sold to Mary's husband, Joseph Scott, who had since died. Aware that justices sometimes freed servants whose masters could not produce the indenture in court, Alexander had "secretly stole away & burnt" the document before running away. Unfortunately for him, however, the court ordered that the recaptured Indian sign a newly drawn indenture that specified he would serve Scott "faithfully and truely in all manner [of] imployment, & labour" and "demeane [him] self [earnestly] and civily." Obviously astute about using the legal system to his advantage, Alexander finally won his freedom in October 1705 when he sued Mary Scott's daughter, Juliana Laker, for detaining him after the expiration of his twelve-year indenture from 1692 (which had apparently replaced the 1690 indenture that called for eighty years of service).[52]

Quakers held African slaves as well. In 1671, George Fox urged Friends to educate their unfree laborers and limit their terms of service, and five years later William Edmundson published a condemnation of the flourishing slave trade in Newport, Rhode Island. Nonetheless, many prominent Quakers continued to hold human chattel, including some of the oldest and most prestigious Quaker families in North Carolina. Henry White owned two men when he died in 1706, and his son Robert divided two women, three boys, and a girl among his children in 1732. Jeremiah Symons owned eight slaves in 1713, while Francis Tomes in 1729 bequeathed to his heirs four male and three female slaves, including a "Negro wench" named Jenney "and all her futer Increes." Hannah Phelps's son Jonathan divided eight Negroes among his wife and children in 1732, Gabriel and Mary Newby owned two slaves in 1733, and Solomon Pool divided up five slaves in 1739.[53]

Antislavery sentiment spread only slowly among southern Friends. English Quaker abolitionists Ralph Sandiford and Benjamin Lay vehemently denounced slavery in the first decades of the eighteenth century, and American-born John Woolman took up the torch after 1754, but the antislavery movement took only gradual hold in the southern colonies. In 1722, the Virginia Yearly Meeting expressed concern about "the importation of slaves or the purchasing them for sale," but it did not prohibit the ownership of slaves. The North Carolina Yearly Meeting recommended in 1740 that slaveholders use their chattel "as fellow-creatures" and not "make too rigorous an exaction of labor from them," and in 1758 asked its members: "Are all that have Negroes careful to use them well and encourage them to come to meetings as much as they possibly can?" But only in 1776 did the Society of Friends officially prohibit slaveholding among their members and threaten to disown Quakers who continued to keep slaves. In terms of human and landed property, then, most Quakers were not radical. Indeed, from the point of view of the Indian Alexander and other servants and slaves, Quakers may have been much like other masters.[54]

Quakers departed most radically from inherited English norms with their perception of gender as irrelevant to spiritual authority. Quakers were the first religious sect in seventeenth-century England to believe that speaking as a messenger for God was not a male privilege. In a break from Pauline tradition, George Fox denounced the presumed spiritual prerogatives of the male sex by asking rhetorically: "may not the spirit of Christ speak in the Female as well as in the Male?" Quakers believed they preached as disembodied spirits. As William Penn put it in 1693, "Sexes made no Difference; since in Souls there is none." The theological tenet of spiritual equality did not have women's liberation as its goal, but in its effects it translated into an expansion of opportunities for women Friends. Quaker women could preach in public, travel as missionaries alone or with female or male companions, publish religious treatises, and organize and run women's meetings. When critics objected to independently traveling women preachers, Fox countered in 1676 with the reminder that "Moses and Aaron, and the seventy elders, did not say to those assemblies of the women, we can do our work ourselves, and you are more fit to be at home to wash the dishes." Rather, "they did encourage them in the work and service of the Lord."[55]

In the last decades of the seventeenth century, the Society of Friends evolved into a highly structured institution with clear disciplinary guidelines and a rigid system of local, monthly, quarterly, and yearly meetings. Quaker women on both sides of the Atlantic conducted monthly meetings (parallel to the monthly men's meeting usually held in the same house) and kept their own records. The women's meetings heard women's requests to travel to other meeting houses, they wrote certificates of permission and recommendation, they organized committees to investigate whether couples were "clear" to marry, and they decided on punishments in disciplinary cases involving women. The women's meeting presented their findings to the men's meeting, which usually endorsed the women's decision. Sometimes a smaller committee of men and women investigated cases of untoward behavior such as bad language, excessive drinking, or "superfluity of apariel," namely "foulds in their coats or any other unnecesary fashons . . . in their dreses." Women's haughty speech or flirtatious demeanor could catch the eye of wary matrons, who subjected the suspect to detailed interrogations. In Pasquotank County, for example, Mary Overman stood accused of "behaving her Self Vane & Loos in her Conversation." Worse, Ann Bundy was engaged to a non-Quaker and "keeps him in her house Contrary to the advise of friends." If the accused confessed and publicly apologized, all was well. If an apology was not forthcoming, the women's and men's meeting conferred over whether the wayward Friend should be disowned. Disowned Quakers could still attend worship, but they could no longer participate in the monthly business meetings where Friends made decisions that affected the whole community. Disowned Quakers achieved readmission only by reading aloud a paper of self-condemnation that persuasively denounced and lamented their trespass against the Friends' moral code. In this tightly structured group, discipline of members was communally enforced. Women's meetings offered both censorship of nonconforming women and a great deal of power to those who complied with the community's moral standards. Within the bounds of conservative sexual mores, women enjoyed authority and influence among Friends. The organization of women as active participants in the community's self-governance marked a departure from other Christian denominations. The Society of Friends was the only Protestant sect in which women met *as women* with a formal collective authority.[56]

Women, like men, played an important role in regulating Quaker marriages. Friends carefully monitored the pacing of courtship and marriage, and they especially tried to prevent marriage "out of Society," which meant either marriage to a non-Quaker or marriage to a Friend in a civil or church ceremony (by which means Quakers ducked court-ordered fines for fornication). Friends believed that marriages to non-Quakers were based on worldly interests and weakened the religious commitment within the community. Pairs of influential (or "weighty") Friends visited those steering toward such a union and tried to persuade them otherwise. When Quaker women insisted on marrying outside of society, the women's meeting often recommended that they be disowned and then sought the men's endorsement of their decision as a final step.[57]

Quaker marriage ideals and practices differed markedly from English norms. Because Quaker spouses were equally subordinate to God, the bride and groom spoke identical nuptial vows that omitted any reference to wives obeying their husbands. Complete submission to God's will modified patriarchal assumptions of a husband's control over his wife, and women ministers were encouraged to pursue their godly calling even at the expense of their domestic duties and their husband's needs. The ideal of spouses as loving and spiritual equals translated into real advantages for women Friends. Despite their strict discipline, Friends remained aware of changes of affection and the need to be flexible in matters of the heart. When Esther Belman and John Turner failed to announced their wedding banns a second time, committees from the men's and women's meetings conducted investigations into the pair and found that they had changed their minds and "Desired that they might be Clear from each other." The meeting allowed the break-up, but "Desired them to be Carefull not to do the Like any more." Friends aspired to loving unions, and if a marriage caused discord, the unhappy spouses could separate (although they could not remarry as long as the spouse still lived). The estranged husband provided an allowance for the woman and, should she move away, a reasonable dowry. Such arrangements differed starkly from the scenarios faced by other unhappy English wives. While both spouses could sue for separation (which was easier to obtain than divorce), men often simply deserted their families. Women who sued for separation usually won their cases only on the grounds of cruelty, and even then they received no financial support. Among Quakers, by contrast, if the relationship soured, disaffection constituted cause enough for untying marriage bonds.[58]

The acceptance of women as authoritative public speakers on matters of religion shaped the Quaker response to outspoken women in general. When Quaker women argued with men, they were chastised for being "unloving" Friends, but not for being unruly women. In 1710, Ann Symons admitted that she "Did Enter into my Cousins Peter Symons house & did Strike him & when I was asked about it by my friends in the Meeting I made Slight of them and gave them Ill Language Not becomeing that holy profession: As Askeing them what Satisfaction they wanted for Strikeing my Lord Mayr." Ann apologized for behavior that was unbecoming of one who should be an example of love and peace. She did not, however, indicate that her behavior was especially unseemly because of her sex. That same year, Mary Tomes hurled "rash words and unseaviery Expressions" at Gabriel Newby. When she apologized later for her "Proud and unstable minde which I doe Condemn as being the fruits of unrighteousness," the women's meeting agreed that she "hath binn to forward in Charging Gabriel with things," but they also advised Newby to be more "Carefull and to not give Agrevation . . . but to Live in younity." The women's meeting reprimanded Tomes for being unloving, but no one described her "rash words" as especially inappropriate because she was a woman. Mary Tomes was the topic of discussion again in 1714 when a Mr. Bundy complained that she was not fit "to preach the gospell" and had given him "bad languig." Tomes told the meeting that Bundy "caled her an oald wicked woman" and said "shee need not be in haist to go to meeting." The meeting sided with Tomes but took the opportunity to admonish her gently to "not take much time on preaching when their is prity large meetings" because people were "not efected theirwith but Rather burthened." The women's meeting thereby reaffirmed Tomes's status as a legitimate (if gregarious) preacher.[59]

To disapproving observers, querulous Quaker women epitomized the dangers of giving women formalized authority. The "uncivil Carriage toward the tithe gatherer" that Elisabeth Tomes flaunted in 1725 exemplified to critics how women's authority within a religious setting could devolve into unruly social behavior. Not that Quaker women were more outspoken than their Anglican counterparts. The level of audacity among different groups of women is impossible to measure, and self-confident women of different backgrounds and persuasions had their day in court. But to Anglican men concerned with their own authority, an opinionated female Friend proved what they feared, namely that religious dissenters promoted social disorder, and that this might first become visible in unorthodox gender relations. Quaker women could be *expected* to insult government officials; that was the logical outcome, critics thought, of letting women preach. And while scolds were offensive, women ministers were blasphemous. Quaker women who abandoned their wifely duties to travel about and speak at different Quaker meetings represented a most appalling inversion of the biblical injunction that women remain submissive to their husbands and silent in matters of scriptural exegesis. From the Anglican perspective, Quaker meetings, female preachers, and marriages that seemed dangerously loose undermined the divinely ordained and socially required patriarchal family. Although Quakers were part of the colonial Christian culture, they overtly defied the government's mandate for militia duty and they opposed the state-supported Anglican Church. In their dress, behavior, language, ideology, and social organization, Quakers stood out as nonconformists. To non-Quakers concerned with the social disorder and lack of deference that marked North Carolina, the Society of Friends was suspect: it seemed to promote behavior that deviated from patriarchal norms and endangered the colony's welfare.[60]

Decades of political tension between Anglicans and Quakers came to a head over the contested deputy governorship of Thomas Cary. Nominated in 1705, Cary began his term in office by strictly enforcing anti-Quaker laws that required an oath of allegiance to serve in the Albemarle assembly. He thereby eliminated Quaker assemblymen (who predictably refused to swear oaths) and replaced them with Anglicans. The dissenters complained to the Proprietors and effected Cary's removal from office, but when Edward

Hyde arrived from England in August 1710 to serve as deputy governor in Cary's place, he also set out to exclude dissenters from the assembly. The Quakers, believing that Cary had been won over to their side, rallied behind him and proclaimed Hyde's commission invalid. Tensions escalated into a rebellion, and supporters on both sides (including some Quakers) took up arms. Only when the Virginia militia arrived to quell the uprising in Hyde's favor did the battles end. In the aftermath of what became known as Cary's Rebellion, the Quaker faction lost power in the assembly. A statute in 1715 allowed "no Quaker or reputed Quaker" to "give evidence in any criminal causes, or to serve on any Jury, or bear any office or place of profit or trust in the government." The Society of Friends had been politically disenfranchised. In the decades after Cary's Rebellion, some Quaker families from Albemarle joined the growing migration of Friends from other colonies into the North Carolina Piedmont and the coastal counties south of Albemarle Sound. Friends also persevered in the older northeastern counties, where Anglican ministers continued to complain about the lack of local support for their endeavors. Nonetheless, the political heyday of Quakers in colonial North Carolina had ended.[61]

Not over, however, were the concerns of Anglican councilmen, magistrates, and ministers that the colony was still a "troublesome and unsettled country," a "barbarous and disorderly place." Half a century after English settlers began to settle in North Carolina, the social order was still in disarray, and disregard for prescribed gender roles contributed to the impression of disorder. In 1711, Reverend Urmston bitterly described the settlement as "a nest of the most notorious profligates upon earth . . . Women forsake their husbands come in here and live with other men." Should the husband follow his wayward spouse to North Carolina, "then a price is given to the husband and madam stays with her Gallant," the lovers spread a rumor that the husband is dead, "become Man and Wife make a figure and pass for people of worth and reputation [and] arrive to be of the first Rank and Dignity." In Urmston's bilious recrimination, gender relations in North Carolina were an inversion of their proper form. The sexually profligate women in his description (real or imagined) embodied the general disorder the discouraged minister saw all around him: settlers did not give enough respect to men of the cloth, they were delinquent in paying his salary, and pridefully contentious in everything else. North Carolina countenanced immorality to the highest degree, Urmston maintained, and one could see it in the fact that adulterous women attained social respectability. For Urmston, the prevalence and acceptance of illicit sex served as a measure of the colony's low moral standing and lack of civility. Unruly and licentious women personified the colony's general social disorder.[62]

Precisely because the image of docile women held such a prominent place in English theories of orderly rule, irreverent women posed a problem for men hoping to establish their authority in an unsettled government. In that context, female defiance, be it adultery and theft, as in Dorothy Steel's case, or public preaching and arrogance toward the tax collector on the part of Quaker women, became part of the struggle for authority. North Carolina's leading men found that to establish a social order, they had to enforce patriarchal gender roles as well. In later years, women's misconduct would seem less threatening to the maturing colony. In the early decades, however, as the colonial outpost grew only slowly amidst tempestuous contests for political control, the social and political conditions in the settlement gave outspoken women particular political resonance. The presence of competing gender norms among Indians and Quakers made the imposition of patriarchal English norms seem all the more imperative. For that reason, the sexual activity of Native American women became a particular focal point for Englishmen concerned with unruly women. Interestingly, not all colonial observers objected to what they saw.

Cross-Cultural Sex in Native North Carolina

On December 28, 1700, surveyor John Lawson departed Charlestown with a small group of men and began a reconnaissance trip that would take him some five hundred miles through the interior of South and North Carolina. Three weeks later, the six Englishmen and their Native American guide stopped at a "pretty big" Waxhaw town in the Carolina Piedmont. The men were "all out, hunting in the Woods, and none but the Women at home." One of Lawson's party, desiring "an Indian Lass, for his Bed-Fellow that Night, spoke to our Guide, who soon got a Couple, reserving one for himself." Though the "pretty young girl" and the eager Englishman "could not understand one Word of what each other spoke," the woman, "being no Novice at her Game," demanded trade goods in exchange for sex. The man "shew'd her all the Treasure he was possess'd of, as Beads, Red Cadis [woven cloth], &tc. which she lik'd very well." The "Match was confirm'd by both Parties, with the Approbation of as many *Indian* Women, as came to the House," and the couple "went to Bed together before us all, and with as little Blushing, as if they had been Man and Wife for 7 Years." In the morning, however, Lawson awoke to find the man pacing the floor in a "deep Melancholy." The woman had "pick'd his Pocket of the Beads, Cadis, and whatever else should have gratified the Indians for the Victuals we receiv'd of them," and she also took the shoes he had made the Night before "of a drest Buck-Skin." With "much ado," Lawson's men "muster'd up another Pair of Shooes, or *Moggisons*" while the women "laugh'd their

Sides sore at the Figure Mr. Bridegroom made." The travelers finally set off again, "the Company (all the way) lifting up their Prayers for the new married Couple, whose Wedding had made away with that, which should have purchas'd our Food."[1]

The misadventure of "Mr. Bridegroom" illustrates the collision of distinct sexual mores in what scholars have alternately called the "middle ground," "contact zone," or "gender frontier" between cultures.[2] Disparate sexual practices prevailed in their respective gender systems—those culturally specific arrangements of gender relations that included the allocation of responsibilities and authority to women and men, conceptions of lineage and customs of family formation, practices of property-holding and inheritance, and related rules concerning women's sexual (and reproductive) behavior. The region's Indians, for example, used sexual liaisons to smooth trade relations: women mediators provided outsiders with language skills and lessons in local customs that facilitated the exchanges. Because these arrangements served an overtly diplomatic function, Indian leaders debated the merits of such associations before giving their assent. To English travelers who viewed chastity as a woman's primary virtue, sexually available Indian women appeared shamelessly promiscuous. Some observers described Indian women as mercenary, while others saw them as innocents in a precivilized Eden. (John Lawson, in turn, did both.) But whether perceived as calculating or naive, women's nonmarital sexual relations appeared to Englishmen as evidence of loose morals that made any serious public discussion preceding the liaison seem absurd. Granted, some colonists enjoyed the commercial and sexual benefits of relations with Indian women, but because those associations were linked to trade (in fact constituted a crucial part of the exchange), they remained tainted and illegitimate to many of the Englishmen involved. From the outset, Lawson's cotraveler and the young Indian woman approached each other with very different ideas about the meaning of their intimacy. They shared an interest in sex for the sake of personal gain, and they both went to bed without "Blushing," but they did not necessarily agree on the rules of conduct, the purpose of the event, or even the price of the exchange.

This chapter examines intercultural sexual encounters from two angles. First, it analyses how colonial depictions of Indian women and their sexual relations became a means of imagining, planning, and explaining colonization. Many colonial writers initially presented Indian women as the eager subjects of cultural assimilation. Both the sexually appealing Indian "maiden" and the overworked "squaw drudge" would presumably prefer Englishmen to their own "savage" husbands. These caricatures constructed racial difference in gendered terms, making clear distinctions between Indian women and men: Indian women were described as more sexually active, attractive, and lighter-skinned than Indian men, suggesting that the descendants of Indian women and colonial men would "blanch" in appearance as they adopted Anglo-American culture. Indian wives would, some writers hoped, be absorbed into patriarchal families and customs, thereby bringing Indian territory into English systems of property and inheritance. Images of native women as sexual agents and sexual objects thus contributed to an ideology of conquest, combining European fantasies of territorial and sexual domination.[3]

Second, the chapter investigates the way Indian-Anglo interactions within Indian villages changed as the balance of power shifted from Native Americans to colonists. As Indian women negotiated intimate aspects of the "middle ground," their experiences of colonialism were shaped by gender relations (both indigenous and intercultural) that changed over time. After the devastating Tuscarora War of 1710–1713, the few colonial leaders who had explicitly promoted intermarriage as a means of assimilation no longer did so. Even as private property and patrilineage altered some Indian ways, English ideas about racial amalgamation and the annexation of Indian land through intermarriage changed. As "race" took on innate physical qualities in the eighteenth century and "redness" came to connote permanent degradation, the promotion of Indian-English marriages waned. Cross-cultural liaisons persisted, of course, especially in the backcountry where Anglo-American traders continued to benefit from liaisons with Indian women and often established permanent families with them. Some of the children of colonial men and Indian women became prominent go-betweens between two cultures. But in general, colonial attitudes about cross-cultural sex reflected changing assumptions about innate difference. Rather than imagine Indians as assimilated and "blanched," the trajectory was now reversed: colonial men were degraded by their intimate relations with Indians and made suspect by the ease with which they apparently moved back and forth between cultures.[4]

Colonial representations of Indians reflected racial attitudes and imperialist aims, but images did not determine social relations as much as socioeconomic, political, and demographic circumstances did. Initially, Europeans seeking inroads into the expansive networks of Indian trade did well to follow local customs of exchange. Vastly outnumbered and far removed from colonial centers on the coast, the first generations of inland traders accepted native terms of trade and the occasional joke at their expense. In 1700, the women in the Piedmont village laughed out loud at Lawson's hapless traveling companion who paid an unexpectedly high price for sex. The joke was hilarious for the women precisely because the man duped was English (nothing befell the Indian guide who also had a bed-fellow that night), and their laughter highlighted both the young woman's control of the situation and the traveler's disappointed expectations. During the eighteenth century, however, colonial encroachment on Indian lands and the devastating impact of wars and disease significantly reduced the ability of Native Americans to determine the course of exchanges—sexual as well as commercial—with Europeans.[5]

Entire Indian communities felt the repercussions of expanding colonial settlement and increased dependence on European manufactures, yet this impact was felt in distinctly gendered ways. The constant hunt for deerskins, chronic wars against other tribes over hunting territory, the sale of Indian captives as slaves to the colonists, the damaging effects of alcohol as a ubiquitous form of currency, the partial adoption of European conceptions of private property and inheritance, the destructive Tuscarora War, and the reconfiguration of authority within native communities—all of these circumstances profoundly altered customary village life in ways that women and men experienced differently. In addition, European gender norms and sexual conventions made inroads into Indian villages along with the metal tools, woven cloth, rum, and a penchant for fencing in land. Over the course of the eighteenth century, native women who had liaisons with English traders went from being cultural negotiators whose sexual relations with unfamiliar outsiders eased relations of diplomacy and trade, to being less prominent go-betweens whose alliances with English husbands no longer afforded them the same kind of diplomatic standing. Native Americans experienced colonialism in distinctly gendered ways, and women's sexual interactions with English men became a signal aspect of their encounter with the newcomers.[6]

This analysis relies on the writings of Anglo-American men whose accounts were strongly shaped by their own cultural bias. (Anglo-Americans, whether born in Virginia, Philadelphia, or Great Britain, penned most of these narratives, but because I use some German and French sources, the writers discussed here are sometimes referred to as "European.") In general, eighteenth-century European writers, whether or not they traveled to the Americas, sought to make sense of American Indians by embedding them in familiar narratives of Greco-Roman or Judeo-Christian history. These authors saw in Native American cultures their own living past: societies at an earlier stage of development. Some writers, envisioning a simpler, nobler antiquity, employed enthusiastic descriptions of naturally generous, honest Indians to critique the growing avarice and corruption they perceived among Europeans. Others described Indians as savages whose presumed idolatry, cannibalism, and nomadism vitiated any claim to the land the Europeans coveted. European images of Indians tended to shift according to expedience, and consistency of representation was not an imperative in these accounts. Indeed, although natural nobility and uncivilized savagery seem at odds with each other, they often appeared together in the same text, albeit under different rubrics of discussion. The "rhetorical bifurcation" of exploration on the one hand (detailed chronological travel narratives) and ethnography on the other (generalized and timeless descriptions of the "manners and customs" of the Indians) allowed lying, lazy, vicious savages to coexist in the same book with courageous, self-possessed, pure Indians.[7]

Descriptions of Native Americans also varied depending on their audience. The Lords Proprietors commissioned John Lawson's surveying expedition, and his *New Voyage to Carolina* was, among other things, a promotional tract. His descriptions of the salubrious climate and its healthy and attractive inhabitants served that end, while anecdotes like that of Mr. Bridegroom's fiasco were meant to amuse readers as well as astonish (and perhaps entice) them with tales of un-self-consciously promiscuous women. The Irish-born James Adair, who spent nearly four decades among the Cherokee and Chickasaw, described his lengthy *History of the American Indians* (1775) as a detailed account of Indians' customs "interspersed with useful Observations relating to the Advantages arising to Britain from her trade with those Indians [and] the best method of managing them, and of conciliating their Affections, and therefore extending the said Trade." Both a profound ethnographic interest and a colonial agenda shaped Adair's book.[8]

Despite bias and occasional polemics, these works provide valuable information about the social relations among Indians and between native women and European men. Some European observers of the American Southeast—notably John Lawson, James Adair, and William Bartram, a Quaker naturalist who traveled extensively in the Southeast in the 1770s—genuinely wanted to understand Native American ways. Curiosity and the desire to promote colonial interests led them to describe the material culture, social arrangements, and belief systems of Indians with the precision of surveyor, social scientist, and naturalist. These observers often misunderstood the cultural meanings of what they saw (James Adair, for example, set out to prove that Native Americans were the lost tribes of Israel), but their detailed ethnographical notes on the customs, attire, architecture, ceremonies, and methods of subsistence of Indians in Carolina provide valuable information about these Native American societies and how they changed with European colonization. By cross-referencing these accounts with each other and with the work of ethnohistorians (who also use archeological and ethnographic sources to interpret written descriptions), one can read eighteenth-century

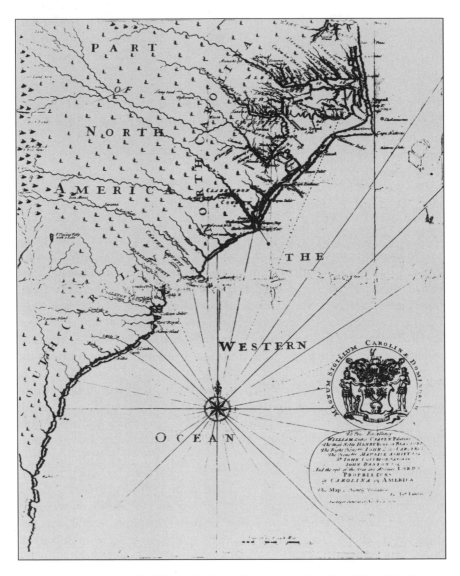

*Figure 7. Surveyor general of North Carolina, John Lawson, drew this "Map of the Caroli-
nas" in 1709 after his five-hundred-mile tour through the region. The most detailed area of
the map is the Pamlico Sound where Lawson purchased land and helped secure the incorpo-
ration of the town of Bath. In the great seal of Carolina, which appears in the lower right
corner of the map, a bare-breasted Indian woman and two children are separated from an
Indian man by two cornucopias. The symbolic conflation of the fertility of the land and its
people was a common trope in colonial images of the New World. Courtesy of the North
Carolina Division of Archives and History.*

sources for what they (often inadvertently) disclose about both the authors and their indigenous subjects. I use these sources, then, to make visible not only English images of Indian women, but also some of the changing choices and constraints faced by the women themselves. Two very different gender systems and culturally distinct ideas about property and race interacted in the eighteenth century, in the process redefining sexual relations between Native American women and European men. In their cross-cultural liaisons, we can see Indian women negotiating some of the dramatic social, economic, and cultural effects of colonization.[9]

"Fine-shap'd Creatures": English Images of Indian Women

European men took great interest in the physical appearance and sexual conduct of Indians, which in turn helped to justify English claims to both the land and its people. Did Indians represent the noble, well-formed figures of an earlier uncorrupted age, or were they hideous and heathen examples of an inferior culture? Did they constitute a civilization with well-ordered social relations and a command of the terrain, or did natives roam the earth like wild animals with as little pretense to mastery over the territory? Europeans looked as much to Indian women as to men for answers to these questions, and descriptions of the appearance, labor, and sexual availability of Native American women often stood in for native culture. Whether depicted as dreary work horses or sensual bedmates, women's bodies served to convey messages about indigenous people and their relationship to the land so coveted by settlers and speculators.[10]

From their first encounters, colonial writers gaped at scantily clad Indians, fantasized about native women as sexual objects, and produced minutely detailed descriptions of their physical appearance. John Lawson, for example, wrote of Indian women that:

> when young, and at Maturity, they are as fine-shap'd Creatures (take them generally) as any in the Universe. They are of a tawny Complexion; their Eyes very brisk and amorous; their Smiles afford the finest Composure a Face can possess; their Hands are of the finest Make, with small long Fingers, and as soft as their Cheeks; and their whole Bodies of a smooth Nature. They are not so uncouth or unlikely, as we suppose them; nor are they Strangers or not Proficients in the soft Passion. They are most of them mercenary, except the married Women, who sometimes bestow their Favours also to some or other, in their Husbands Absence. For which they never ask any Reward.[11]

According to Lawson, these women, whose "Breaths are as sweet as the Air they breathe," were soft, smooth, "proficient" in sexual pleasures, willing (whether married or not), and "of that tender Composition, as if they were design'd rather for the Bed then Bondage." Desirable and available, these imagined women were not sexually aggressive. Although "most extravagant in their Embraces," Lawson said, "yet they retain and possess a Modesty that requires those Passions never to be divulged." The women in Lawson's account remained innocent in their nakedness and bashful in their availability, giving English suitors the pleasure of sexual conquest even as its success was already welcomed and guaranteed. Native women's propensity for sex was further enhanced, Lawson maintained, by the fact that they never went overboard in their passions: none of them "ever runs Mad, or makes away with [kills] themselves on that score." Instead—most conveniently for colonial men interested in multiple sexual opportunities— native women "never love beyond retrieving their first Indifferency, and when slighted, are as ready to untie the Knot at one end, as you are at the other." These non-Christian women were emotionally uncomplicated "Creatures" naturally "design'd" for sex; to ignore this would be to ignore their natural calling. Reports like Lawson's encouraged male readers to fantasize that native women were available to any interested man.[12]

Here in Lawson's account were ideal sexual partners: beautiful, available, silent, and without reproach. They had eloquent ("brisk and amorous") eyes and the "finest Smiles" but reticent tongues. "Amongst Women, it seems impossible to find a Scold; if they are provok'd, or affronted, by their Husbands, or some other, they resent the Indignity offer'd them in silent Tears, or by refusing their Meat." In fact, Indian women's bashfulness was a trope with a long history: in 1584 Arthur Barlowe met a "very bashful" Indian wife, Lawson described "the young Maids" as "generally very bashful," William Byrd saw Indian women with "an Air of Innocence and Bashfulness," William Bartram saw "young, innocent, Cherokee virgins" with "blooming faces" and a "modest maiden blush," James Adair found native women generally "of a mild, amiable, soft disposition: exceedingly modest in their behaviour, and very seldom noisy." Such descriptions of bashful Indian women served to rebuke outspoken English women. "Would some of our *European* Daughters of Thunder set these *Indians* for a Pattern," Lawson said, English families might not be so disrupted "by that unruly Member, the Tongue." Though Native American women—and men—may have customarily expressed themselves in calm and controlled tones that Englishmen found pleasant, the larger point here is that Lawson and others built this observation (or hope) into an already feminized and sexualized version of an ideal Indian woman. Felicity Nussbaum writes that

Figure 8. The transition to a new market economy is suggested in a drawing by John White (ca. 1585) of an Indian woman and young girl. The woman is holding a gourd that had many local uses while the girl is holding a European doll. Copyright the British Museum.

Figure 9. The engraving by Theodor de Bry in 1590 of an Indian woman and girl (based on John White's drawing) shows how Indian figures were Europeanized in features, cloth-ing, and stance, perhaps in part to make them seem more familiar to would-be colonists. Courtesy of the North Carolina Division of Archives and History.

blushing was associated with whiteness in eighteenth-century England. If that is so, then descriptions of blushing (and bashful) Indian women may have served to make them more familiar and less culturally strange to in-terested Englishmen.[13]

European observers commented repeatedly that Indian women were "mistresses of their own bodies" who "manage their persons as they think fit," and a critical component of their sexual autonomy was control over fertility. Lawson found that sexually active unmarried women "scarce ever have a Child; (for they have an Art to destroy the Conception, and she that brings a Child in this Station is accounted a Fool, and her Reputation is lessen'd thereby)." Another traveler to Carolina heard from a "worthy and knowable person" that at about age twenty-seven Indian women ate the root of a certain plant that made them sterile. According to the visitor's anony-mous informant, Indian women had been practicing this form of birth con-trol for generations. This image of women in control of their fertility may have had some basis in fact, but it also allowed European men to believe their sexual capers with Indian women had no consequences and enhanced

The wyfe of an Herowan of Secotan.

Figure 10. John White's drawing of the wife of a Secotan chief shows her in a self-confident pose, adorned with tattoos and gazing directly at the viewer. Copyright The British Museum.

Figure 11. Theodor de Bry's engraving of "A younge gentill woeman doughter of Secota" shows a woman standing with crossed legs and partially covered breasts in a pose Europeans might have identified as bashful. Courtesy of the North Carolina Division of Archives and History.

the image of Indian women as beyond the pale of Eve's curse (as did the commonly held belief that Indian women gave birth without pain). Lascivious women willing to abort potential offspring for the sake of greater sexual pleasure—surely such women were barbaric. Furthermore, if Indian women's experiences of sex, fertility, and childbirth fell outside of biblical accounts, then perhaps Englishmen who had sex with them did so in a state of nature unaffected by Christian rules of matrimony.[14]

Native Carolinian courtship rituals also differed from English prescriptions, adding to the image of Indian promiscuity. Young women might engage in multiple sexual relations before choosing a long-term partner. "The Girls at 12 or 13 Years of Age," Lawson wrote, or "as soon as Nature prompts them, freely bestow their Maidenheads on some Youth about the same Age, continuing her Favours on whom she most affects, changing her Mate very often, few or none of them being constant to one." Apparently, the rules of courtship and consent, at least as Lawson understood them, were straightforward: "The young Men will go in the Night from one House to another, to visit the young Women, in which sort of Rambles they will spend the whole Night. In their Addresses they find no Delays, for if she is willing to entertain the Man, she gives him Encouragement and grants him Admittance; otherwise she withdraws her face from him, and says, I cannot see you, either you or I must leave this Cabin, and sleep somewhere else this Night." Furthermore, Lawson reported, the men "are never to boast of their Intrigues with the Women. If they do, none of the Girls value them ever after, or admit of their Company in their Beds." Lawson was amazed to find that the "Multiplicity of Gallants" was "never . . . a Stain to a Female's Reputation," and that virginity, "so much coveted by the *Europeans,* is never valued by these Savages." In trying to describe the sexual mores of the Indians, Englishmen reached the limits of their vocabulary. Lawson, for example, struggled to explain a different value system when he wrote that "the more Whorish, the more Honourable" the women. Without chastity, Europeans believed, a woman had no honor. The fact that Indian women could enjoy extramarital sex *and* a good reputation attested, in Lawson's mind, to a culture so different it defied all common sense. The disinterest in virginity on the part of both Indian woman and men was part of what made them "savage."[15]

Europeans who fostered images of sexually uninhibited Indian women created a very different portrait of Indian men, choosing to think of them as undersexed and passive, lacking the virility that Englishmen so prized about themselves. When Lawson heard that Indian couples could "lie together under one Covering for several Months" without having sex, he suspected that "Europeans would be apt to break this Custom." Lawson could have depicted native men as self-controlled, not undersexed. After all, Indians' self-possession and self-restraint had frequently impressed English observers. In council meetings, during arduous expeditions of hunting and warfare, and even under torture, Indian men exhibited a fortitude and self-discipline that Englishmen overtly admired. But with regard to sexual activity, Lawson (and others) portrayed Indian men not as self-controlled, but as lacking in manly ardor, with the result that purportedly libidinous Indian women remained unsatisfied. "*Indian* Men are not so vigorous and impatient in their Love as we are," he wrote. "Yet the Women are quite contrary, and those *Indian* Girls that have convers'd with the *English* and other *Europeans,* never care for the Conversation of their own Countrymen afterwards." In this depiction, feminized Indian men could not compete with lusty Englishmen for the sexual interest of native women.[16]

Even favorable depictions of Indian husbands describe them as more tender than ardent. William Bartram reported that he never observed "contention or wrangling" among Cherokee spouses and "never saw an instance of an Indian beating his own wife, or even reproving her in anger." Indian men "are courteous and polite to the women, gentle, tender & fondling even to an appearance of effeminacy, tender & affectionate to their off-spring. An Indian never attempts—nay, he can't use a woman of any de-scription amongst them with indelicacy or indecency, either in action or language." The image of gentle Indian husbands impressed men like Bartram but likely evoked disdain among many other Englishmen who as-sociated effeminacy with feebleness and found sexual reserve toward wives unnecessary if not misplaced. In contrast to Bartram's squeamish allusion to rape, sexual violence seemed to many colonial men entirely per-missible—or not a violation at all—given the presumption of sexually ea-ger and unsatisfied Indian women. In the eyes of many European men, sexual restraint in such circumstances was hardly praiseworthy and may have seemed ludicrous.[17]

Such sentiment was manifest in 1728 when the commissioners and sur-veyors sent from Virginia and North Carolina to chart the disputed colo-nial boundary harassed many of the women they encountered. Colonel William Byrd of Westover, the wealthy Virginia planter who served as chief commissioner of the surveying party, wrote an account of the trip with an eye toward amusing himself and his friends. Byrd's anecdotes are not reli-able as fact, but they describe behavior that would have seemed plausible (and entertaining) to his peers. According to Byrd, the crew offered "sev-eral gross Freedoms" to the sisters and daughters of their hosts along the way. Byrd himself "discharg'd a long score with my Landlord, & a Short one with his Daughter Rachel for some Smiles that were to be paid for in Kisses." Some men became "more boisterous, & employ'd force" when they failed to persuade. When Byrd and John Lovick, commissioner for North Carolina, came across a cottage inhabited by a free black family, "a Dark Angel sur-priz'd us with her Charms." Byrd admired her "deep Copper" complexion and her "fine Shape & regular Features." Lovick, too, examined her "with critical Exactness" and apparently caught hold of the woman because "She struggled just enough to make her Admirer more eager." Byrd claimed that "if I had not been there, he wou'd have been in Danger of carrying his Joke a little too far." Other women were apparently less fortunate. Tongue in cheek, Byrd recounted how, at another household, a woman "to assist in the Kitchen wou'd certainly have been ravish't, if her timely consent had not prevented the Violence." Byrd suspected a man and his servant who had "engag'd in those kinds of Assaults once before." On another occasion, two men "pretended to go a hunting, but their Game was 2 fresh colour'd Wenches, which were not hard to hunt down." Byrd depicted himself as the one who intervened just in time to prevent sexual violence, presenting the image of an appropriately self-restrained overseer of a rambunctious crew. Nonetheless, his jokes about other men's exploits painted the trip as one big sexual caper. Byrd relayed, for example, how the men with "Gaiety" encouraged a "Tallow-faced Wench" to drink with them and then "examined all her hidden Charms, and play'd a great many gay Pranks." Gay pranks could involve the humiliation or exploitation of women through the use of persuasion, liquor, or sheer force, and in many such moments a jovial Byrd did not intervene. Clearly, the surveying crew considered many women they met available for sexual importuning.[18]

Like Anglo-American and African American women, Indian women were also pursued by the surveying team. Byrd himself complained when Nottaway women in southern Virginia "offer'd us no Bedfellows, according to the good Indian fashion, which we had reason to take unkindly." In response, "Our Men . . . were hunting after them all night." Byrd expressed distaste for Indian women, complaining that "the whole Winter's Dirt was so crusted on their Skins, that it requir'd a strong appetite to accost them." But if Byrd's sensibilities were offended, his peers pressed on, some pursuing sex with Indian women more out of curiosity than attraction, others perhaps simply because they could get away with it. William Dandridge, for example, commissioner for Virginia, may have lacked appetite for "these sad-colour'd Ladys, yet curiosity made him try the difference between them & other Women, to the disobligation of his Ruffles, which betray'd what he had been doing." On another occasion Byrd saw "by some of our Gentlemen's Linnen, discolour'd by the Soil of the Indian Ladys, that they had been convincing themselves in the point of their having no furr." Byrd's well-heeled travelers exhibited no squeamishness when it came to intercourse with Indian women, and dirty ruffles represented a trophy of sorts. To others, sexual bravado with Indian women fueled masculine boasting: traders in South Carolina might "brag to each other of debauching" Indian women and "sumtime force them"; one trader reported he "ons see it my self in the Day time Don." Lawson's vision of "Finely shap'd Creatures" slid easily into an image of Indian women ready-made for sexual assault. The perception that Indian women faced no social constraints on their sexuality reinforced the colonial perception of native women as already immoral, degraded, and hence appropriate targets for sexual attack. Men who did not engage in such sex themselves could participate vicariously by watching it "my self in the Day time Don" or by enjoying stories about it afterwards. Byrd's titilating *Secret History* invited his peers to chuckle at the image of ruffled Englishmen in hot pursuit of painted Indian women.[19]

The touted sexual aggression of European men was analogous to the New World takeover that colonizers planned. The trope of rape pertained to

Indian women and virgin soil alike: both were there for the taking by as-
sertive Englishmen. Just as Indian men supposedly lacked sexual ardor for
native women, so too did they presumably lack the enthusiasm and
willpower required to vanquish the untamed wilderness and make the soil
yield its riches. Merely "idle" hunters instead of industrious farmers, native men failed to exploit the natural bounty of the environment that English methods of agriculture would make profitable. Indian men who did
not take full advantage of land and women alike should relinquish their
claims to both and give way to more ambitious settlers. Depictions of sexualized Indian women and undersexed native men played into colonial
appetites for the land and its resources (which seemed to include Indian
women). But while the portrayal of Indian women as available sexual partners appealed to some newcomers, actual cross-cultural liaisons were much
more complicated. Europeans eager for trade found themselves negotiating sexual relationships in the context of long-standing Native American
customs and expectations. From the outset, how those relations would proceed and what obligations they would entail remained uncertain.[20]

"Trading Girls" and "Indian Wives":
Arrangements of Cross-Cultural Sex

By 1700, European traders were accustomed to two formalized types of relationships with native women: long-term marriages or, more commonly,
short-term liaisons with women the Europeans considered prostitutes and
called "Trading Girls." "Trading Girls," Lawson explained, "are those design'd to get Money by their Natural Parts." They could be identified "by
the Cut of their Hair; their Tonsure differing from all others, of that Nation, who are not of their Profession." Lawson perceived such women as
whores with the chief as the pimp: "the greatest Share of the Gain going
to the King's Purse, who is the chief Bawd, exercising his Perogative over
all the Stews of his nation, and his own Cabin (very often) being the chiefest
Brothel-House." Lawson was amused by the seriousness with which his hosts
discussed such arrangements. "When any Addresses are made to one of
these Girls, she immediately acquaints her Parents therewith, and they tell
the King of it (provided he that courts her be a Stranger) his Majesty commonly being the principal Bawd of the Nation he rules over." Elder Indians then "debate the Matter amongst themselves with all the Sobriety and
Seriousness imaginable, every one of the Girl's Relations arguing the Advantage or Detriment that may ensue such a Night's Encounter." The proposed liaison was treated "as if it was the greatest Concern in the World,

and not so much as one Person shall be seen to smile, so long as the Debate holds, making no Difference betwixt an Agreement of this Nature, and a Bargain of any other." In fact, offering a female bedfellow was a traditional gesture of hospitality toward important outsiders. Englishmen who refused such offers displayed poor manners and could incur the wrath of their hosts. One Catawba chief, for example, offered Lawson's company "two or three Trading Girls in his Cabin." When the men "refus'd his Kindness, his Majesty flew into a violent Passion, to be thus slighted, telling the *Englishmen,* they were good for nothing." Englishmen soon embraced these rites of hospitality and felt snubbed when they were not forthcoming.[21]

Indian women did not always comply with the sexual demands of European visitors, however. It is hard to know how much choice Native American women exercised in these diplomatically important liaisons and whether "Trading Girls" were able to refuse those partners who did not appeal to them. But Lawson's men did not always successfully negotiate a trade for sex, especially when women were alone in the village. When Lawson and his fellow travelers arrived at a Congaree town on the Santee River, the men were away on a hunt and the women "very busily engag'd in Gaming." The women made Lawson and his men wait while they finished their game; only at their leisure did they offer the disgruntled travelers some food, which "generally [they do] as soon as you come under their roof." One of Lawson's company propositioned "some of the young Female Fry; but they refus'd him, he having nothing that these Girls esteem'd." These women treated the European traders with nonchalant disinterest, at least when they were alone in the village. Indian men intent on good trade relations may not have appreciated or allowed women's indifference toward these potential trading partners. These particular women, however, felt less inclined to make the visitors feel at home. Whether or not "Trading Girls" determined their involvement in each individual liaison, their status was temporary. Lawson noted that after several years in that role ("in which time they scarce ever have a Child") the women often married, their "Fortunes" not lessened by their sexual history "but rather augment[ed]." Viewing "Trading Girls" as prostitutes, Lawson was surprised to find they were not stigmatized.[22]

In contrast to the temporary liaisons of the "Trading Girls," some Indian women engaged in formalized marriages with European traders that were mutually beneficial. Native Americans used marriages to establish ties with influential outsiders and to ensure good rapport with other groups. The Saponi Indians on the Roanoke River, for example, debated in June 1670 whether they should admit John Lederer "into their nation and councils" and then pressed him (unsuccessfully) to "stay amongst them by a marriage with the kings or some of their great mens daughters." According to custom, conjugal affiliation with an Indian woman implied the husband's acceptance of the trading rules in her village. European men also benefited significantly from such marriages. As Lawson explained, Indian wives helped traders "learn the Indian Tongue [and] keep a Friendship with the Savages." Besides the "Satisfaction of a She-Bed-Fellow," Indian women provided valuable services such as "dressing their Victuals, and instructing 'em in the Affairs and Customs of the Country." More than that, entry into trade relations nearly required a woman's connections. A man who married into a woman's clan was welcomed as kin when he traveled to other villages, where he was hosted by members of that same clan and invited to participate in local trade. Men who did not intermarry remained outsiders. As Lawson put it: "when a Person that lives amongst them, is reserv'd from the Conversation of their Women, 'tis impossible for him ever to accomplish his Designs amongst that People." Clearly, Indian women offered valuable education, labor, and kinship ties to European traders eager to participate in the broad Native American networks of exchange, and such alliances were readily available. "It is the easyest thing in the world, for an English Traveller to procure kindred among the Indians," wrote Thomas Nairne in 1708 (the first Indian agent for South Carolina's Board of Commissioners for the Indian Trade). By "taking a mistress of such a name [or clan]," a trader "has at once relations in each Village, from Charles Town to the Mississippi, and if in travelling he acquants them with what fameily he is incorporated into, those treat, and wait on him as their kinsman." Nairne added wryly that "there are some of our Countryman [sic] of such prudence and forecast, that in case one family should fail them, take care to make themselves akin to severall." Perhaps for this reason, European men made an effort to learn the native translations of phrases like "How d'ye do?" "Will you kiss me?" and "Come to bed."[23]

Nairne's use of the term *mistress* rather than *wife* indicates that he, like Lawson and other European observers, did not ascribe to such relations the same legitimacy they accorded Christian marriages. Some traders who enjoyed sexual relations with Indian women misunderstood or ignored the obligations that such liaisons traditionally incurred among Native Americans. Many European traders never fully shed their notion that sex with an Indian woman was a casual matter, a private indulgence. This misunderstanding may have resulted in part from culturally distinct marriage ceremonies. For Englishmen, marriages were contracted in a number of ways, but they usually involved a repeated public announcement of the pending union, followed by nuptial rites performed by a cleric in front of witnesses. Native American rituals were no less formalized. The pact involved the bride's parents, if not the extended family, and the wedding was often celebrated with a feast of lavish proportions. Not all Europeans recognized the festivity as a marriage celebration, however. Thus one observer made the contradictory statement that Creeks married "without much ceremony, seldom any more than to make some presents to the parents, and to have a feast or hearty regale." English traders often failed to recognize that Indians viewed marriages with Europeans as permanent unions rather than temporary liaisons, and as reciprocal exchanges (and not sexual gifts) that bound new husbands in a web of mutual obligation.[24]

Such behavior could have hurtful effects for the Indian woman involved. Lawson knew one European man, for example, who "had a Child or two by one of these *Indian* Women, and afterwards married a Christian, after which he came to pass away a Night with his *Indian* Mistress; but she made Answer that she then had forgot she ever knew him, and that she never lay with another Woman's Husband, so fell a crying, and took up the Child she had by him, and went out of the Cabin (away from him) in great Disorder." The trader (like Lawson) did not perceive the Indian woman as a legal spouse, and his long-term relationship with her did not hinder him from engaging in another marriage (to a "Christian" woman) that he did consider legally binding. The man's disavowal of any obligation to the Indian woman may have resulted from his unwillingness to acknowledge a non-Christian marriage, but traders were also traversing two worlds and some may have purposefully tried to garner the rewards of both of them.[25]

Other European men remained permanently with the Indians, adapting to matrilineal customs. Like James Adair who spent many decades among the Chickasaw and Cherokee, Indian trader Robert Bunning remained among the Cherokee for thirty-seven years, Cornelius Daugherty for thirty-two, James Beamer for twenty-seven, and Ludovick Grant for twenty-six. Many married Indian women and had children with them. The matrilineal kinship system continued to regulate family life, and Indian women insisted on their traditional right to raise the children. Lawson lamented that most Indian children remained unconverted to Christianity, "for it is a certain Rule and Custom" among Indians "to let the Children always fall to the Woman's Lot." Englishmen found it difficult to send their children away to schools where they might learn "Knowledge of the Christian Principles." Yet others, Lawson noted, did not seem to mind. "*English* Men, and other *Europeans* that have been accustom'd to the Conversation of these savage Women, and their Way of Living, have been so allur'd with that careless sort of Life, as to be constant to their *Indian* Wife, and her Relations, so long as they liv'd, without ever desiring to return again amongst the *English*, although they had very fair Opportunities of Advantages amongst their Countrymen; of which sort I have known several."

Clearly, the image of docile Indian women and converted children remained an elusive goal more than a reality, and intercultural marriage did
not necessarily result in the adoption of colonial customs. Instead, many
Anglo-American husbands adapted to Indian ways.[26]

"Red Copper Tinge": Changing Ideas about Race

While traders took up relations with Indian women for both business and
pleasure, a few colonists promoted intermarriage as a strategy to help establish a permanent English presence in the region. Virginia planter Robert Beverley claimed in 1705 that more intermarriage from the beginning of colonial
settlement would have prevented many wars and enabled the colonial population to grow more rapidly while converting Indians who instead had "fled
to other Parts." Some twenty years later, William Byrd also felt that with intermarriage "Indians would have had less reason to Complain that the English took away their Land" because they would have given it away as their
daughters' dowries. "Had such Affinities been contracted in the Beginning,
how much Bloodshed had been prevented, and how populous would the
Country have been, and, consequently, how considerable?" In North Carolina
at the turn of the century, John Lawson believed it was still "highly necessary" to encourage "ordinary People, and those of a lower Rank" to marry
Indians, because Indians gave newlyweds "Plantations, and Houses, [and] so
many Acres of Land." English spouses of Indians would learn not only "the
Indian Tongue" but also Native American "Medicine and Surgery" as well as
valuable information about the "Rivers, Lakes, and Tracts of Land" colonists
had not yet settled. Indian spouses, Lawson thought, would convert to Christianity and their children would be apprenticed to "proper Masters" and eventually become "Members of the same Ecclesiastical and Civil Government we
are under." In his vision of an ever expanding empire, Lawson imagined that
Indian allies gained through intermarriage would "help civilize a great many
other Nations of the Savages, and daily add to our Strength in Trade" so that
the English "might be sufficiently able to conquer, or maintain our Ground,
against all the Enemies to the Crown of *England* in *America,* both Christian
and Savage." Beverley, Lawson, and Byrd promoted English-Indian marriages
as a cornerstone of conquest: through marriage would come land acquisition,
cultural assimilation, religious conversion, and growth of the colonial population and its Indian allies. In this boldly instrumentalist projection (which
remained a minority view), intermarriage would not lead to the feared disintegration of colonial society's norms of patriarchy and private property.
Rather, intermarriage would eventually strengthen both.[27]

Colonial leaders who discussed the strategic value of cross-cultural unions employed a shifting language of race. By the early eighteenth century, "race" as a means of conceptualizing human differences was an important part of the way colonists understood their relations with Indians, but the development of racial thought and language was neither linear nor uniform across time and place. Initially, those Europeans who promoted intermarriage as a useful colonizing strategy tended to downplay permanent differences between Indians and the English. "All Nations of men have the same Natural Dignity," Byrd claimed in the 1720s, "and we all know that very bright Talents may be lodg'd under a very dark Skin. The principal Difference between one People and another proceeds only from the Different Opportunities of Improvement." Even "very dark skin" was subject to alteration. Had the English intermarried with Native Americans from the beginning of colonial settlement, Byrd argued, "the Infidelity of the Indians had been worn out at this Day, *with their Dark Complexions.*" Indeed, "if a Moor may be washt white in 3 Generations, Surely an Indian might have been blancht in two." Byrd theorized that the descendants of an English-Indian union would not become darker than their European parent. Rather, the grandchildren of an English-Indian union would be racially elevated to approximate the skin color of their white ancestor. This idea of Indian "blanching" was part of Byrd's own answer to an ongoing debate over the origins of Native Americans. The European encounter with people not mentioned in the Bible raised fundamental questions about their place in Genesis. If Native Americans were the offspring of Adam and Eve, when and how had they traveled to the western hemisphere? Were they perhaps descendants of the lost tribes of Israel? As a devout Anglican, Byrd believed in a single origin for all human beings. He also apparently thought that the Native American branch of the family tree was more closely related to the European one than was the African branch, a notion supported by the popular belief that an Indian's skin color was not only lighter than that of an African but also alterable and subject to purposeful manipulation.[28]

No consensus yet prevailed among the English as to the cause, permanence, or even precise shade of Indians' complexions. Europeans had long employed a spectrum of colors to describe Native Americans. Captain Arthur Barlowe reported in 1585 that Indians on the Carolina coast were "of a colour yellowish," while other travelers described natives as tawny, brown, olive, russet, or copper. Many declared that Indians were born white and then purposefully darkened their skin. Indians were "of a tawny" color, Lawson reported, "which would not be so dark, did they not dawb themselves with Bears Oil, and a Colour like burnt Cork. This is begun in their Infancy, and continued for a long time, which fills the Pores, and enables them better to endure the Extremity of the Weather." James Adair agreed "that the Indian colour is not natural": "the external difference between them and the whites, proceeds entirely from their customs and method of living, and not from any inherent spring of nature." The sun and wind "tarnish their skins with the tawny red colour." Furthermore, the constant application of bear's grease "mixt with a certain red root" produces in only a few years "the Indian colour in those who are white born." Adair knew a white man from Pennsylvania who, "by the inclemency of the sun, and his endeavours of improving the red colour, was tarnished as deep an Indian hue, as any of the camp, though they had been in the woods only the space of four years." In these accounts, Indians altered their complexion in accordance with their taste and the practicalities of outdoor living, and whites could undergo the same treatment. Color was only skin deep, the result of exposure to the elements combined with purposeful application of pigment.[29]

For those who still doubted the superficiality of skin color, Indians' admirable physical traits compensated for their darker hue. Beverley found native women "generally Beautiful, possessing an uncommon delicacy of Shape and Features, and wanting no Charm, but that of a fair Complexion." "Indians are generally tall and well-proportion'd," Byrd wrote, "which may make full Amends for the Darkness of their Complexions." Furthermore, "they are healthy & Strong, with Constitutions untainted by Lewdness, and not enfeebled by Luxury." Byrd's reference to lewdness and luxury was a veiled attack on the English elite. After the Restoration of the crown in 1660, critics and satirists targeted the figure of the aristocratic rake as an effeminate fop or "molly" who sought sex with other men in the "molly houses" and masturbation clubs of London. Byrd's Indians, by contrast, had a wholesome and natural strength that made up for the disadvantage of darker skin color and promised (despite the presumed lack of sexual ardor) to produce healthy mixed-race offspring who would carry on the colonial enterprise.[30]

The discussion about mixed unions explicitly addressed concerns about class. None of the promoters of cross-cultural marriage in the colonial Southeast, notably Robert Beverley, John Lawson, and William Byrd, admitted to having intercourse with native women themselves. Such relations were beneath their self-image as dignified men of virtuous self-control, and they described the sexual exploits of their fellow travelers with a mixture of amusement and disdain. But these writers did not object to sex with Indian women per se. After all, even gentlemen in ruffles might enjoy the same sexual prerogatives as robust English adventurers. Cross-cultural *marriage*, on the other hand, must be reserved to the lower orders. Lawson made it clear that only "ordinary People, and those of a lower Rank" should be encouraged to marry Indians. In a culture concerned with dynastic bloodlines, the lower orders could hardly claim purity of blood; elites considered them already closer to a savage state. The Indians that Byrd depicted as, on the one hand, healthier in constitution than an effete aristocracy could, on the other hand, be no worse than the already crude members of the lower ranks. Byrd believed Indian women compared favorably with the English women transported (often from workhouses) to the fledgling Virginia colony, and he supposed "the Indian women would have made altogether as Honest wives for the first Planters, as the Damsels they us'd to purchase from aboard the Ships."[31]

Lawson's account—more a promotional tract than Byrd's tale for the amusement of his peers—focused not on the degraded status of lower-class immigrants but rather on the positive effects the North Carolina climate had on colonial newcomers. Lawson heralded the health enjoyed by people in Carolina. Colonists born there "are a straight, clean-limb'd People" whose children are "seldom or never troubled with Rickets; or those other Distempers, that the *Europeans*" endured. In this environment-induced return to a more natural state, Lawson perceived a distinctly gendered pattern. European American men soon followed in the footsteps of "idle" male Indians (the "plentiful Country, makes a great many Planters very negligent," Lawson explained), while Anglo women, like their Indian counterparts, "are the most Industrious Sex in that Place." But in contrast to the image of the "squaw drudge," transplanted Anglo women represented happy, healthy laborers. According to Lawson, these hardy women marry young, some at thirteen or fourteen, are fruitful, and (like Indian women) "have very easy Travail in their Child-bearing." Even English women who had long been infertile could "become joyful Mothers" in North Carolina. But lest prospective female immigrants worry that along with good health they would acquire darker skin, Lawson added the following reassurance: the "Vicinity of the Sun makes Impression on the Men, who labour out of doors," but Anglo-American women who do not expose themselves to the weather are "often very fair." Lawson anticipated that immigrants would have concerns about the climate that combined issues of reproduction, class, and color.[32]

Other writers claimed Indians already had the complexion of English laborers, but that their sex also determined their hue. William Bartram saw "Indian infants of a few weeks' old" who had the color of a "healthy male European Countryman or Laborer, of middle age," although Indian children did tend more toward a "red copper tinge." At the same time that Bartram found Indian babies as dark as male European laborers, he believed that Cherokee women had a "complexion rather fairer than the men's." Racial difference appears in Bartram's account in gendered form, with men and women racialized differently and in ways expedient to the English vision of themselves and their place in the New World. European men fantasized not only that Indian women were lighter than native men, but also that these women preferred to bear "white" children. Lawson believed the "handsome" Congaree women of South Carolina (with "several fine-finger'd Brounetto's amongst them") "esteem[ed] a white Man's Child much above one of their getting." These Englishmen thus projected a movement toward whiteness among Indian women who allegedly offered themselves as if they wanted to begin the "blanching" process that Byrd predicted. European ideas about racial and sexual difference were melded together in colonial strategies of racial amalgamation.[33]

Notions of race that were blurry for Europeans held even less meaning for Native Americans. Not that Indians were unaware of differences in physical appearance. In their first encounter with the English in 1584, Carolina Indians "wondered marvellously when we were amongst them at the whiteness of our skins, ever coveting to touch our breasts." But the interest in skin color did not translate for Indians into the concept of physically distinct races. Native American identities resided in kinship networks, language, and culture. To them, Africans and Europeans behaved in similar ways and were equally outsiders. In the words of historian James Merrell, "Afro-Americans and Euro-Americans were partners in the invasion of the Southeast. Blacks, like whites, were traders, soldiers, and members of armed gangs who roamed the Carolina upcountry. Blacks, like whites, spoke English or Spanish, sold European goods, and fought Indians when their lowcountry homes were threatened." To native people these were outsiders first, whatever their hair color or skin tone. As with all outsiders, Europeans and Africans might be adopted, driven out, or killed, depending on the circumstances of contact. If they were adopted, however, they became as much a member of a clan as if they had been born into it, regardless of physical appearance.[34]

Because culture and not race distinguished Indian insiders from outsiders, marriages to an English, African, or unfamiliar Indian all represented cross-cultural marriage. Granted, it may have been easier to achieve consensus about the meaning of such a union among Indians who shared a history of conjugal connections. But the purpose of cross-cultural marriage was the same in any case: marriages with outsiders furthered ties of trade and diplomacy. Because kinship was matrilineal, the presence of a foreign husband, whether Native American or not, did not disrupt familial ties. However, other aspects of Native American identity and social cohesion were coming under increasing strain. Social upheavals due to disease, warfare, and the trade in rum and slaves changed familiar patterns of village life and shaped Indian gender relations as well.[35]

"Unjust Dealings": Slaves, Rum, and the Tuscarora War

In the first decade of the eighteenth century, social tensions long in the making developed into a full-blown crisis that would result in the Tuscarora War. The booming trade in Indian captives sold as slaves, the corrosive effects of alcohol on social relations within Indian villages, and the devastation of epidemics and chronic warfare created a growing sense of desperation in North Carolina's Indian communities. These social pressures, while difficult for all, affected Indian women differently than Indian men. Though not immediately related to sexual relations, such developments had long-term repercussions that disrupted the social order and altered gender relations in Indian villages.

Slavery, with which Indians were familiar prior to the arrival of Europeans, took an entirely different form when colonists proved eager to buy Indian captives for the slave trade. Initially, Indian war captives who were not killed or adopted into families worked as slaves. Outsiders in a society where kinship ties were crucial, these unadopted captives (some of whom had their feet mutilated so they could not run away), labored in agriculture and performed other menial tasks. Given the clear separation of responsibilities among Indian women and men, it was a sign of degradation when male slaves tended women's fields. No economic motive promoted the regular use of slaves, however, since Indians did not seek to profit from surplus agricultural produce. Instead, slaves served mostly to symbolize the prestige of their masters. The condition of enslavement was usually neither permanent nor hereditary, and the widespread custom of eventual adoption meant that Indian slaves made up only a tiny portion of the native population. This situation began to change when colonists offered firearms, ammunition, and other commodities in exchange for captives. Beginning in the 1670s, colonists in Charlestown cashed in on the burgeoning trade in Indian slaves, eventually selling tens of thousands of them to plantations in the West Indies and Bermuda. Although most Indian captives were shipped out of the colony (to prevent them from running away and returning home), increasing numbers—and perhaps three to five times more women than men—remained as slaves in South Carolina. By 1682, any Indian brought into Virginia could be legally enslaved as well. With enough wampum, Lawson said, "you may buy Skins, Furs, Slaves, or any thing the *Indians* have." Indians eager to acquire European manufactures found a ready market for prisoners of war, and they began fomenting wars on other groups for the purpose of obtaining captives for sale to the English. Lawson recounted that Machapunga Indians of coastal North Carolina attacked the nearby Coree Indians and sold the prisoners as "Slaves to the English." Dependence on European manufactures ensured that such raids continued. As one Cherokee put it in 1715, if they stopped making war on the Creeks, "they should have no way in geting of Slaves to buy amunition and Clothing."[36]

Alcohol also changed local custom. Lawson reported that Indians had become "much addicted to Drunkenness, a Vice they never were acquainted with, till the Christians came amongst them." The problem was "they are never contented with a little, but when once begun, they must make themselves quite drunk," selling "all they have in the World, rather than not have their full Dose." Excessive consumption was in fact integral to native drinking, as Indians purposefully consumed enough alcohol to be transported into a spiritual realm. If there was not enough alcohol available for everyone present to get completely drunk, Indians would sometimes give it all to one person, preferring that at least one person experience complete inebriation rather than have everyone become only moderately tipsy. Danger arose when intoxicated Indians harmed each other or themselves. Lawson lamented that in their "drunken Frolicks . . . they sometimes murder one another, fall into the Fire, fall down Precipices, and break their Necks, with several other Misfortunes which this drinking of Rum brings upon them; and tho' they are sensible of it, yet they have no power to refrain this Enemy." Imbuing alcohol with its own powers, Indians "never call any Man to account for what he did, when he was drunk; but say, it was the Drink that caused his Misbehaviour, therefore he ought to be forgiven." Despite the policy of forgiveness, lives were ruined through liquor. Lawson recounted that one "Bear-River *Indian,* a very likely young Fellow, about twenty Years of Age" was chided by his mother who "was angry at his drinking too much Rum." The young man, "a Son of the politick King of the Matchapunga," replied that "he would have her satisfied, and he would do the like no more; upon which he made his Words good; for he went aside, and shot himself dead."[37]

Some women bought, sold, and drank liquor, and inebriation made them vulnerable to sexual abuse. Lawson said Indian men who "have a Design to lie with a woman . . . strive to make her drunk," and then "take the Advantage, to do with them what they please, and sometimes in their Drunkenness, cut off their Hair and sell it to the *English,* which is the greatest Affront can be offer'd them." Some Englishmen used alcohol to the same ends. One packhorse rider accompanied a trader to the Cherokee town of Keowee in 1756 and there got a woman drunk and "used her ill." In Williamsburg, William Byrd went with friends "to see some Indian girls, with which we played the wag," and he was amused by "Jenny, an Indian girl, [who] had got drunk and made us good sport." William Bartram was among the Lower Creeks in Florida when the arrival of twenty five-pound kegs from St. Augustine resulted in a drunken fest that lasted ten days. Bartram witnessed "ludicrous bacchanalian scenes" involving "white and red men and women without distinction" taking "liberties with each other" that "they would abhor when sober or in their senses; and would endanger their ears and even their lives." The loss of self-control that came with drinking, and the lack of accountability for acts committed while drunk, resulted in sexual relations that were outside the usual social bounds of conduct. Although Bartram's own disapproval colors the telling of the scene, some of these sexual relations may indeed have been cause for later shame.[38]

Some Indian leaders tried to halt the trade in liquor, but their efforts to stop the influx of alcohol met with resistance, especially among younger men. Although some "*Indian* Rulers desired no Rum might be sold to them," Lawson reported, a law to that effect "was never strictly observ'd." In fact, the "young Indians were so disgusted" at the law penalizing Englishmen who sold them rum "that they threatened to kill the *Indians* that made it, unless it was laid aside." The deterioration of self-restraint and respect in a society otherwise marked by what Lawson called "great Veneration" for "Old Age" led elders to appeal repeatedly to the colonial government, requesting restrictions on the rum trade. The Catawba chief Nopkehe, known to colonists as King Hagler, said that outlawing the sale of liquor to Indians would reduce "those Crimes that is Committed by our young men and will prevent many of the abuses that is done by them thro' the Effects of that Strong Drink." Bartram said some Indians insisted that the "first and most cogent article in all their treaties with the white people, is, that there shall not be any kind of spirituous liquors sold or brought into their towns." Despite these efforts, chief Aucus al Kanigut said that the Tuscarora people "lived but wretchedly being Surrounded by white People, and up to their lips in Rum, so that they cou'd not turn their heads anyway but it rans into their mouths. [T]his made them stupid, so that they neglected Hunting, Planting, &tc."[39]

The growing dependency on European guns, powder, manufactures, and rum affected an entire Indian village, but the social repercussions also had a gendered dimension. Native American reliance on colonial trade goods, together with the unceasing European demand for deerskins, led to an emphasis on Indian men's roles as hunters. The need to expand hunting activities had a number of consequences for village life. Competition for the overhunted deer population led to increased friction between Indian groups, and conflicts over hunting grounds, combined with the inducement to sell Indian captives as slaves to the colonies, resulted in incessant skirmishes. The increased incidence of warfare in turn gave warriors a greater influence in native government, pushing aside more gender-inclusive forms of negotiation in village councils. Since war no longer existed primarily for purposes of blood vengeance and captives could now be sold, women no longer controlled the fate of prisoners or as often played the central roles in torture rituals. Gradually, the male-dominated deer-skin trade became more important to the local economy than the corn women grew. Although women continued to exert authority in traditionally female realms of responsibility such as farming and child raising, they lost some of their influence over traditionally male activities such as warfare, diplomacy, and trade.[40]

Disease also continued to cause massive social dislocation. Epidemic diseases returned again and again, wiping out large segments of Indian villages. Governor John Archdale reported in 1694 that "It pleased Almighty God to send unusual sicknesses amongst them, as the Smallpox." Lawson noted that "Many thousands" had succumbed to the epidemic that swept away "whole Towns, without leaving one *Indian* alive in the village." "Small-Pox and Rum have made such a Destruction amongst them," Lawson wrote, that "there is not the sixth Savage living within two hundred Miles of all our Settlements, as there were fifty years ago." The survivors of the scourge struggled with loss of kin, traditional knowledge, even tribal identity. Grieving and bewildered, they allied themselves with the remaining people of other groups. In the mergers that ensued, people struggled to reconfigure kinship ties, learn new languages, and forge new identities. In this difficult situation, the sharp dealings of English traders did not help matters. Lawson described the Indians as "really better to us, than we are to them; they always give us Victuals at their Quarters, and take care we are arm'd against Hunger and Thirst: We do not so by them (generally speaking) but let them walk by our Doors Hungry, and do not often relieve them." Lawson commented further that "we have abandon'd our own Native Soil, to drive them out, and possess theirs." In return, "we have furnished them with the Vice of Drunkenness, . . . and daily cheat them in every thing we sell." The truth of the matter, Lawson concluded, was that "all the Wars, which we have had with the Savages, were occasion'd by the unjust Dealings of the Christians towards them."[41]

Disease, warfare, and the relentless trade in slaves and rum created a feeling of crisis among coastal and Piedmont Indians. In 1710, the Tuscarora protested the ongoing enslavement of their people in North Carolina and petitioned the Pennsylvania governor for asylum. The Pennsylvania government would not promise refuge, however, and desperation rose among Indians subjected to frequent slaving raids. The spark for revolt came in 1710, when Baron Christoph Von Graffenried, head of a Swiss land company, purchased from the Proprietors 17,500 acres of land along the Neuse and Trent rivers and arrived in September with 100 German and Swiss Protestants (called Palatines) to found the town of New Bern. The site, laid out in plans by surveyor John Lawson, was already inhabited: it was the Neusioc town of Chattooka. Although Von Graffenried apparently made a deal with the Neusioc for the land, the nearby Tuscarora Indians resented the expansion of white settlement so near their towns and made plans for war. Led by a Tuscarora called King Hancock, hundreds of allies including the Coree, Pamlico, Mattamuskeet, Bear River, and Machapunga Indians organized an attack on the English settlement in September 1711.[42]

The first casualties of the war included John Lawson who had persuaded Von Graffenried to join him on a surveying trip up the Neuse River. Von Graffenried, who was kidnapped with Lawson but later released, recalled that a court of forty elders in the Tuscarora town of Catechna initially acquitted the captives. But when Coree Indians from the lower Neuse River arrived and accused Lawson of offenses against them, the surveyor argued with their leader and angered the assembled Indians. A council of war subsequently sentenced the captives to death but then pardoned the baron (whose self-serving account blames Lawson for his own demise). The precise means of Lawson's death remains uncertain. Some Indians told Von Graffenried that Lawson would have his throat cut with the razor that was in his pocket. Other colonists learned from "Indian information" that they "stuck him full of fine small splinters of torch wood like hog's bristles and so set them gradually afire" (see figure 12). Lawson himself had described the "Torments in which thay prolong Life in that miserable state as long as they can" by sticking pitch-pine splinters "into the Prisoner's Body yet alive. Thus they light them which burn like so many Torches; and in this manner they make him dance round a great Fire, every one buffeting and deriding him, till he expires." Whether killed with an English razor or American pine splinters, Lawson's death serves as a symbolic end to a particular kind of Indian-settler interaction in North Carolina. While he had idealized Indian culture in order to promote colonization and criticize European social ills, Lawson had also allowed for the possibility of reciprocal exchange and mutually beneficial coexistence in the Piedmont. Some colonists would continue to value certain aspects of Native American culture, but after the Tuscarora War, the middle ground of constructive interaction in North Carolina diminished.[43]

Lawson's death was just the first stroke in what became a protracted war. In the onslaught that followed, Indians killed about 130 English and German colonists, plundered their houses, and destroyed crops and barns. The Albemarle assembly appealed to its neighboring colonies for military aid,

Figure 12. This image shows the capture of Baron Christoph Von Graffenried, John Lawson, and their black servant by Tuscarora Indians at the outset of the Tuscarora War. Courtesy of the North Carolina Division of Archives and History.

and in January 1712 Governor Gibbes in Charlestown sent Colonel John Barnwell with an expedition of about thirty whites and five hundred Indian soldiers, mostly Yamasee allies and Siouan tribes from eastern South Carolina. Indian allies expected six blankets for every man killed and the going rate in slaves for every captured woman and child. "Tuscarora Jack" Barnwell's forces killed about fifty Indian men and then took some two hundred women and children as slaves. In September, Colonel James Moore, a veteran of slave raids in Spanish Florida, arrived from South Carolina with thirty-three colonials and about nine hundred Indians, including Yamassees, Creeks, Catawbas, and about three hundred Cherokee. Nearly a thousand Tuscarora died during the war, and about seven hundred were enslaved, many of them women and children. Most of the remaining Tuscarora fled north to join the Five Nations of Iroquois. The surviving members of smaller tribes in the coastal region faced the choice of either merging with larger Indian groups or living in the colonial settlements as laborers. With the defeat of the Tuscarora, demographic strength and political power in the Piedmont shifted in favor of the English. In the mountains, the Cherokee (who had sided with the colonists) continued to live in relative autonomy and maintain customary practices of lineage, labor, and authority. But a move was underway in the colonies to define all Indians, even allies, as inherently different from whites. After the war's end in 1713, colonial promotions of intermarriage gave way to official designations of Indians as permanently and racially distinct.[44]

"To the Third Generation": Of Race and Marriage

In a renewed effort to establish social control over a colony marked by a destructive war and political unrest (after Cary's Rebellion in 1711, Quakers were ousted from the North Carolina assembly), the now Anglican-dominated government set out to clarify the racial and social status of the region's inhabitants and to regulate their interactions. The laws of 1715 codified a growing intolerance for cross-cultural unions and strengthened definitions of racial difference—a difference that found its articulation in a concern over intermarriage and mixed-race children. Though aimed primarily at white women and the children they had with black men (as described more fully in the next chapter), these laws also affected relations between colonists and Indians.

The 1715 statute that focused on the crucial question of intermarriage stated that "no White man or woman shall intermarry with any Negro, Mulatto or Indyan Man or Woman," with the penalty placed at fifty pounds for white offenders and for clergymen who performed the ceremony. Although this earliest extant marriage law in North Carolina may have reiterated a previous statute (following Virginia's initial ban on such marriages in 1691), the social climate changed after the Tuscarora War. The prohibition of marriage between Indian women and colonial men theoretically prevented Native American women and their children from inheriting property from Anglo husbands and fathers. Now the long-term liaisons between colonial traders and Indian women were explicitly defined as the illegal union of separate races. In 1723, North Carolina lawmakers levied "an additional Tax on all free Negroes, Mulattoes, Mustees" (the children of Indian-European and Indian-African couples), as well as a tax on anyone, male or female, who was "intermarried with any such Persons." With this tax, white spouses paid an annual financial penalty for having married someone legally defined as not white. The color line remained vague until a statute in 1741 fined white spouses (and officiating clergymen) fifty pounds for marriage to "an Indian, Negro, Mustee, or Mulatto Man or Woman, or *any Person of Mixed Blood to the Third Generation,* bond or free." This strengthened reiteration of the marriage prohibition also added the hostile language of the Virginia law from a half century before that sought to prevent the "abominable Mixture and spurious Issue" born of such a union.[45]

Laws against intermarriage helped define racial boundaries and contributed to the meaning of "race" itself. The expanding scope of the prohibition, which went from banning an "Indyan" spouse to outlawing marriage to someone with even one nonwhite grandparent, made race seem like a physically real and transferable substance, as if some essential "Indianness" coursed through blood lines in diminishing strength with every generation of added "whiteness." Only after three generations would such a mixture be so diluted as not to pose a significant threat of pollution to "white" blood. Marriage laws naturalized the idea that race inhered in the body as something substantive that was passed on to others. Formerly, men like Byrd, Beverley, and Lawson had emphasized the cultural and hence voluntary aspect of Indianness. Culture, like skin color, depended on the environment and was subject to manipulation. But beginning in 1715, the laws in North Carolina made more rigid distinctions between people in ways that overlooked individual appearances and were based on lineage alone. Legal innovations replaced cultural identities with biological ones, and marriage laws helped define the color line as a boundary between white and nonwhite people that suggested a difference much more profound than complexion alone. The marriage prohibition did not specify the precise outlines of different "races"; it mainly determined who was *not* white. Once nonwhiteness had a legal (if catchall) definition, the law could prosecute infractions against the color line as if two inherently different types of humans had crossed over a natural boundary and mingled (in their bodies and in their offspring) what should properly be kept separate. The description of mixed-race children as an "abominable mixture" further construed interracial sex as crossing a natural border as well as a legal one: multiethnic children appeared here as a monstrous amalgam, an unnatural and undesirable product of indeterminable racial status. Marriage prohibitions thus went a long way toward making race seem real. From this point forward in North Carolina, the concept of "interracial sex" (though not yet the term) had a meaning that was supplied by the very law that sought to ban the practice.[46]

This transition in racial thinking occurred unevenly and varied from place to place. In Europe, eighteenth-century naturalists who held (as most did) to the theory of a single origin of all humankind resorted to theories of degeneration to argue that Africans and Native Americans had devolved to a less civilized state than Europeans. In this Enlightenment era, the age-old model of a divinely ordained hierarchy of all life-forms, known as the "Great Chain of Being," gained ranks within its human tier. This distinction among humans received a scientific gloss in 1740 when the Swedish botanist, Carolus Linnaeus, in *A General System of Nature*, categorized humankind into four basic groups: white Europeans, red Americans, yellow Asians, and black Africans. A subsequent edition in 1758 added character traits: Europeans were sanguine, brawny, gentle, and inventive; Americans were choleric and obstinate, but also content and free; Asians were melancholy, haughty, rigid, and covetous; Africans were phlegmatic, crafty, indolent, and negligent.[47]

While European scientists invented fixed and symmetrical categories, colonials rearranged their racial thinking as well, although often less systematically and with a penchant for thinking of Africans and Indians as qualitatively different. As late as 1757, for example, Reverend Peter Fontaine, a Huguenot with relatives in North Carolina, still held that English settlers "ought to have intermarried with" Indians to "become rightful heirs to their lands." Such unions would not have "smutted our blood, for the Indian children when born are as white as Spaniards or Portuguese." Fontaine maintained that Indians' color was self-induced: were it not for their habit of "going naked in the summer and besmearing themselves with bears' grease, &tc., they would continue white." By contrast, Fontaine found it "heinous" and "unjustifiable" that English traders "take up with negro women, by which means the country swarms with mulatto bastards." Worse still, "if but three generations removed from the black father or mother," such mixed-race persons may legally intermarry with whites "and actually do [so] every day." Fontaine believed the negative effects of racial mixture with Africans stained more generations than specified by law, and he abhorred this "abominable practice which hath polluted the blood of many amongst us." In Fontaine's opinion, Native Americans were born white (albeit as swarthy as Iberians), and hence did not have a different kind of "blood" from Europeans. Indians were closer kin who could still be rapidly (and profitably) assimilated. By contrast, even people legally classified as white who had one black great-grandparent had blood so powerfully tainted by an essential blackness that they would transfer this pollution, he thought, to their descendants.[48]

James Adair made similar distinctions between Indians and Africans. After a sympathetic discussion of native women breastfeeding their infants, Adair added this was a good lesson to English mothers who, "as soon as the tender infant sucks in the first breath of air, commit it to the swarthy breasts of a foetid African to graft it on her gross stock." In Adair's telling, race seemed to inhere in bodily fluids (especially female fluids), as if blackness could be transferred through white milk. Like Fontaine, Adair believed that Indians were racially closer to whites than were Africans. But although Native Americans might remain a notch above Africans in the developing model of racialized humanity, both were affected by a hardening color code that did not seek to describe the real and varied complexions of individuals but rather assigned people to crude and nondescriptive categories. By the second half of the eighteenth century, the long favored term for Indians—"tawney"—with its resonance of yellows and browns, was giving way to a fixed flat "red."[49]

How did Native Americans think about differences? "All the Indians are so strongly attached to, and prejudiced in favour of, their own colour," Adair reported, "that they think as meanly of the whites, as we possibly can do of them." Adair found Indians "exceedingly intoxicated with religious pride" and full of "an inexpressible contempt of the white people, unless we except those half-savage Europeans, who are become their proselytes. *Nothings* is the most favourable name they give us, in set speeches." Clearly, Indians could exhibit as much ethnocentrism as the English. But although much of the derogatory language was color-coded (Indians often referred to English colonists as "white dunghill fowl"), such terms did not refer to biological traits or a permanent condition. The chauvinistic "pride" Adair describes was a "religious" one, as converts could be accepted. English traders who were adopted still became Indians. Similarly, Africans and African Americans could be everything from slaves to spouses in an Indian village, and sometimes even both. William Bartram met a Creek chief whose fields were "annually planted & tended by his own private family, which consists of about Thirty People, among which were about 15 Negroes, several of which were married to Indians and enjoy equal priveleges with the Indians, but they are slaves until they marry, when they become Indians, or Free Citizens." The most important distinction remained that of kin; whether one was born or adopted into a family was irrelevant, as was one's "race" as Europeans increasingly understood the term.[50]

Gradually, however, racialist thought developed among Indians as well. As Nancy Shoemaker explains, in the 1720s and 1730s the Cherokee adapted their traditional color symbolism of white (peace) and red (war) clans to develop new categories "that could account for biological, cultural, and political differences." In diplomatic negotiations with self-named "white people," Indians responded by claiming for themselves the term "red." By the 1750s, English officials addressed Indians as "red men" and "red people," although mostly in response to Indian speeches that employed those terms. By the end of the eighteenth century, many Native Americans associated categories of red and white with distinct human origins (as described in creation myths) and with skin color. Precisely what traits these red and white categories denoted and just what relationship they had to one another remained contested, but they had nonetheless become distinctly racial categories that implied innate difference.[51]

As biological categories gained currency, the children of mixed heritage could become a lightning rod for new anxieties. When one Cherokee warrior by the name of Buck died, "none of the warriors would help to bury him," Adair said, "because of the dangerous pollution, they imagined they should necessarily contract from touching such a white corpse; as he was begotten by a white man and a half-breed Cheerake woman." Perhaps it was the mother's status as a "half-breed" that caused the problem. But then this uncertainty about *her* familial and cultural affiliation was new, since traditionally her own mother's Cherokee lineage would have passed onto her and then her children, regardless of paternity. Now, in a break from past assumptions about kinship and identity, a "half-breed" person could have a Cherokee mother and yet not be fully Cherokee. This altered understanding about kinship—that the mother's lineage alone no longer fully determined a child's identity and kin relations—signaled a reevaluation, perhaps also a devaluation, of the Indian women who married English men and of the children born of those liaisons. While the concern with those who crossed cultural boundaries need not have incorporated English conceptions of racial difference, previous Indian assumptions about insiders and outsiders had become unstable, making room for the new category of liminal figures born and raised within Indian communities.[52]

This uncertainty about kinship may have been exacerbated by bicultural children of Indian mothers and Anglo-American fathers, especially the sons who learned to speak, dress, and behave like Englishmen. Some received property from their fathers, together with the desire to establish nuclear and patrilineal families. Others gravitated toward life in the colonial settlements where they could gain status as interpreters and go-betweens. Some bicultural adults achieved political prominence within colonial circles but did not obtain the full support of their Indian community. When these individuals nonetheless acted as representatives in treaties that relinquished land to the colonial government, factions and strife ensued in Native American villages and councils. When Indian women, themselves often of mixed parentage, relayed critical information to their colonial spouses (especially regarding surprise attacks), their allegiance to their own villages seemed uncertain. Contentious circumstances and a growing bicultural population led to new boundaries being drawn between insiders and outsiders, a process that made less clear the position of Indian women married to colonial men.[53]

"All Goods Held in Common":
A Utopian Experiment among the Cherokee

As settlers and Indians increasingly resorted to racialized language to explain cultural divisions, one German immigrant held out hopes to the contrary. Christian Gottlieb Priber planned a community among the Cherokee, in the mountains beyond English settlement, based on equitable relations of gender, property, and race. The fate of his experiment indicates how colonial leaders responded to Native American relations of gender and property, and to sympathetic Europeans, now that the balance of power had shifted to colonial advantage. Born in Zittau, Germany, to a linen merchant and beerhouse owner, Priber became a doctor of jurisprudence at the age of twenty-five and published his thesis (in Latin). While working as an attorney, Priber began developing his ideas for a utopian society, and around 1734 he fled under fear of arrest "for having desired to put his project into execution." Leaving his wife and four children in Saxony, Priber emigrated first to England and then in 1735 traveled to South Carolina. In three December issues of that year's *South Carolina Gazette*, Priber advertised his possessions for sale, including the gentlemanly accoutrements of wigs, guns, a silver watch, a silver-hilted sword, and a "fine chest of drawers." With not more than his precious books, paper, and ink, Priber set out for Great Tellico, chief town of the Over-Hill Cherokee in the southern

Appalachian mountains some five hundred miles from Charlestown. For the next seven years Priber lived among the Cherokee and spoke with them about his plans. To gain their confidence, he "ate, drank, slept, danced, dressed and painted himself, with the Indians, so that it was not easy to distinguish him from the natives,—he married also with them, and being endued with a strong understanding and retentive memory, he soon learned their dialect."[54]

Some Indian traders viewed Priber as a threat to English interests. Adair believed he was a French agent sent to turn the Cherokee against the English by describing the latter as "a fraudulent, avaritious, and encroaching people." Long-time Indian trader Ludovick Grant (who lived among the Cherokee with his Indian wife) accused Priber of inculcating "into the minds of the Indians a great care & Jealousy for their Lands, and that they should keep the English at a distance from them." To prevent traders from taking advantage of them, Priber coached the Indians in "inches and measures" and constructed steelyards. Grant said Priber told the Indians "they had been tricked out of a great part of their Land by the English" and that in the future they should "make no Concession to them of any kind but should profess an equal regard both for the French & English," play one power off the other, and "be courted & caressed & receive presents from both." This was standard foreign policy for Native Americans in many regions, and Priber may have told the Cherokee nothing they did not already know from years of experience. But Adair resented that Priber "inflated the artless savages, with a prodigious high opinion of their own importance in the American scale of power" on account of their geographical location and martial strength. Adair saw in Priber a "philosophic secretary" attempting to build "the new red empire; which he formed by slow, but sure degrees, to the great danger of our southern colonies."[55]

Priber described his ideas for "a new System or plan of Government" in a book that laid down the rules for his proposed town, which he named "Paradice." Even his critics had to admit that "the Book is drawn up very methodically, and full of learned Quotations; it is extreamly wicked, yet has several Flights full of Invention; and it is a Pity so much Wit is applied to so bad Purposes." His contemporaries, whether they liked him or not, conceded that he was "a great Scholar," a man who "had read much, was conversant in most arts and sciences; but in all greatly wedded to systems and hypothesis." Adair corresponded with Priber and found him "learned, and possessed of a very sagacious penetrating judgment, and had every qualification that was requisite for his bold and difficult enterprize." Priber's writings did not survive, but his plans made a deep impression on those who met him. "Paradice" was a multiethnic town based on social equality.

Its inhabitants would welcome "Creeks & Catawbas, French & English, all Colours and Complexions, in short all who were of These principles." Georgia Governor James Oglethorpe, who later spoke with Priber and read his journal, recorded that Priber's town would welcome "Fugitive English, French, Germans and Negroes, and they were to take particularly under protection, the runaway Negroes of the English." There would be asylum for "Debtors, Transport Felons, Servants, and Negroe Slaves in the two Carolina's and Virginia." Organized religion would likely have no place, as Priber spoke out "prophanely against all Religions, but chiefly against the Protestant," and he called himself "a friend to the natural rights of mankind—an enemy to tyranny, usurpation, and oppression." He proclaimed that in his "republic there would be no superiority; that all should be equal there; that he would take the superintendence of it only for the honor of establishing it; that otherwise his condition would not be different from the others." Furthermore, all "lodging, furniture and clothing should be equal and uniform . . . all goods should be held in common, and . . . each should work according to his talents for the good of the republic."[56]

Priber's ideal society would eliminate not only hierarchies of race and class, but of gender as well. The "natural Rights, as he calls them, which his Citizens are to be entitled to, [included] particularly dissolving Marriages and allowing Community of Women." Priber anticipated that "women should live there with the same freedom as men; that there should be no marriage contract, and that they should be free to change husbands every day." Furthermore, the children would be "Children of the public and be taken care of as such & not by their natural parents." They should be "instructed in all things that their genius might be capable of acquiring." In his ideal world, all women, men, and children would develop their talents outside the confines of the nuclear family and with the material support of the community. In Europe, Priber was probably influenced by utopianists such as Sir Thomas More; once in America Priber likely learned a great deal from Native American social customs he witnessed. His suggestion that children be raised by a community of parents, for example, was already customary among the Cherokee, and the notion that women could engage in and break off sexual relations with the same ease as men was commonplace.[57]

The society Priber envisioned, a radical departure from colonial norms of patriarchal families, private property, and a labor system based on racial slavery, could not but disturb colonial officials. To them, Priber's suggestion that people of different cultures and social rank could share property, sexual partners, and authority seemed dangerous anarchy. By the time Priber moved to the mountains in the 1730s, property holders, magistrates, and councilmen in North Carolina were much more established than they had been in the late seventeenth century when the social norms of Quakers and Indians seemed dangerous enough to recently arrived Anglican officials. Nonetheless, Priber's vision proffered such defiance of English norms that it required a forceful response. Likely aware that his plans represented a cultural and political affront of the highest order, Priber informed the colonial government of his intention to create an independent country halfway between the Cherokee and Creek Indians in Alabama. His letters, which he signed as "secretary of state" or "Prime Minister," alarmed officials who in turn commissioned Ludovick Grant to arrest him. Grant recalled that when he arrived to arrest Priber, he "laughed at me desiring me to try in so insolent a manner that I could hardly bear it." Grant retreated in the face of Priber's certainty that his Native American friends would protect him. When Colonel Joseph Fox and two assistants next attempted to apprehend Priber in the central "Townhouse," the Indians indeed "took it very much amiss." They rejected the colonel's gifts and refused to turn Priber over, saying that he "was made a great beloved man, and become one of their own people" and that they would not "allow any of their honest friends to be taken out of their arms, and carried into slavery."[58]

Priber's good luck turned, however, in 1741 during a diplomatic mission to Mobile, Alabama. English traders learned he was staying overnight in "Tallapoose town," a day's journey from the coast. They captured him and sent him, "with a large bundle of manuscripts," to Frederica in Georgia. There Priber was jailed as a political prisoner, apart from other inmates. But his "curious and speculative temper," as Adair called it, did not abandon him inside the cell, and it was in Frederica prison that Priber spoke with Antoine Bonnefoy, Governor Oglethorp, and an unidentified writer whose pen-name was "Americus." "The philosophical ease, with which he bore his confinement," Americus wrote, his "communicative disposition . . . and his politeness, which dress, or imprisonment could not disguise, attracted the notice of every gentleman of Frederica, and gained him the favour of many visits and conversations." Priber sustained his serenity in prison, claiming it "folly . . . to repine at one's lot in life—my mind soars above misfortune—in this cell I can enjoy more real happiness, than it is possible to do in the busy scenes of life." Priber remained in prison for about two years until, as Adair put it, "after bearing his misfortunes a considerable time with great constancy, happily for us, he died in confinement,—though he deserved a much better fate."[59]

Priber had envisioned a new kind of community, one inspired by his own utopian dreams and perhaps by some of the Cherokee customs he observed. He planned a society in which all people produced and shared the material goods they needed, freely chose their intimate relationships, and enjoyed equal inclusion in the community regardless of skin color or sex. But Christian Priber's ideas for equality could not easily coexist with efforts to establish colonial control in the region. His active promotion of Native American independence, his invitation to fugitives of all ethnicities and class backgrounds, and his attack on private property and the sexual control of women directly countered English plans to govern Indian trade and territory and to impose a colonial order onto the region. In the 1740s, this kind of trespass could not be tolerated. As European customs of marriage and inheritance moved westward, Indian women's "promiscuity" was used less as a salacious bonus for traders than as another example of Indian savagery in a colonial rhetoric of dispossession. To expansionist-minded critics who depicted Indians as uncivilized and hence without legitimate claims to the land, Priber's promotion of "Licentiousness" and the disbanding of patriarchal and nuclear families proved the immoral underpinnings of his utopian project. Lone voices of appreciation for Indian ways—opportunistic and romanticizing though they may have been—were being drowned out by the clamor for land.

Change and Continuity

By the time William Bartram traveled through Cherokee country in 1775, he found an entirely different scene than the one Lawson had encountered at the turn of the century. He passed through Keowee, once a large Cherokee town. Some "old traders" described to him how the valley had once been "one continued settlement," the hills "covered with habitations" and the rich level fields by the river "cultivated and planted." What Bartram saw on the eve of the American Revolution was "a very different spectacle, humiliating indeed to the present generation, the posterity and feeble remains of the once potent and renowned Cherokee." During the Seven Years' War, three colonial raids had destroyed Keowee. After the raids, settlers streamed into western Carolina. They traveled down the Great Wagon Road from Pennsylvania and Virginia and occupied the fields of the region's former inhabitants. Although Bartram saw "several Indians mounts or tumuli, and terraces, monuments of the ancients," he found "no Indians habitations at present." Instead, "here are several dwellings inhabited by white people concerned in the Indian trade." After passing abandoned Indian villages and fields, Bartram stopped and ate strawberries and cream with an Englishman and his Cherokee wife. By now her intercultural marriage was markedly different from those of her relatives a few generations before.

Instead of living in a matrilocal village consisting of multigenerational families, Bartram's hostess lived with a husband and perhaps children in a log cabin that by law belonged to him. She may no longer have tended the fields with other women, but she likely cultivated a garden and had mastered dairying, an important skill among English women. Private property prevailed among many Cherokee Indians, who "by the reiterated persuasion of the traders, have entirely left off the custom of burying effects with the dead body" so that "the nearest blood inherits them." English husbands with land titles could will property to their biological descendants. While Indian women who married English men maintained their matrilineal kinship ties and possibly had family members near by, they were no longer diplomats on behalf of an Indian village in which they also lived. Rather, they lived in individual households that, on the surface at least, accommodated colonial family structures.[60]

On the other hand, these marriages did not represent cultural capitulation. Women nurtured social and economic ties with friends and family members, they continued to exert control over the education of their children, and their activities provided cultural continuity, even in the face of change. Adair's recounting of one cross-cultural marriage testifies to the changes that had taken place since Lawson's travels in 1701, but also to the persistence of Indian ways. A Cherokee woman named Dark-lanthorn had married an Englishman "in the Cheeráke fashion," but the husband had insisted on a Christian ceremony as well. Translating for the priest, the bridegroom urged his wife to "use a proper care in domestic life." This irritated his bride. "'You evil spirit, said she, when was I wasteful or careless at home?' 'Never,' he replied. 'Well then, said she, tell him his speech is troublesome and light.—But, first, where are those fine things you promised me?'" Assured she would soon receive them, Dark-lanthorn responded with a smile the clergyman interpreted as amenability to conversion. But when the priest elaborated on the concept of the holy trinity Dark-lanthorn became impatient and asked her husband "the subject of their long and crooked-like discourse." He did not attempt to translate the theological puzzle and instead demanded of the priest "how he could desire him to persuade such a sharp-discerning young woman, that one was three, and three, one?" Afraid his wife would not abide the delay much longer, the anxious groom told the priest that "the bride would take it very kindly, if he shortened his discourse, as nothing can disturb the Indian women so much as long lectures." When the priest baptized Dark-lanthorn her husband explained it "would be a sure pledge of a lasting friendship between her and the English, and intitle her to every thing she liked best." Once they were married, the gratified priest entered her name in his book of converts, but "afterward to his great grief, he was obliged on account of her adulteries, to erase her name from thence, and enter it anew in some of the crowded pages of female delinquents."[61]

The story of Dark-lanthorn, relayed perhaps to amuse readers, expressed the understanding that some intercultural marriages were indeed Christian in name only, and that formal ceremonies could not determine the religious beliefs or the future conduct of the women involved. Like Dark-lanthorn, Indian women with colonial husbands made sense of their unions from within their own cultural framework and may not have felt bound to monogamous behavior. While some aspects of life had changed considerably—many families now lived spread out over the land rather than clustered in villages, for example—Indian women could modify or reject colonial gender roles, even when married to English men. Women insisted on their traditional prerogative to raise their children, for example, and refused to let them attend an English-speaking school. Nonetheless, like Dark-lanthorn, many Indian wives had taken part in two marriages, one Cherokee, the other Christian. If a priest was at hand to perform the second ritual and enter the marriage in his growing records, his presence and his efforts to keep tabs on Indian women attest to cultural changes underway. After the American Revolution, many Cherokee would make a concerted effort to conform to white norms of education, government, land use, slaveholding, family formation, language, and dress. In a sense, Cherokee women who had married colonial men had already begun that process; they were practiced at accommodating multiple and disparate cultural conventions. Like the "settlement Indians" who lived among the colonists and yet maintained distinct social customs, and like the Piedmont peoples who had survived the dislocation and losses of the Tuscarora War to combine with other groups to create a new identity as "Catawba," native women who married colonial men did not abandon familiar ways of growing food, raising children, expressing grief, or celebrating the harvest. The world around them had changed since Lawson's trek at the turn of the century, but older methods of community farming, a kinship-based system of justice, religious beliefs, and strong cultural forms such as music, songs, dance, and stories endured. Indian women's marriages to colonists remained a kind of middle ground in which couples pieced together different aspects of their respective cultures to a create a new form of interaction.[62]

On the whole, however, the context in which relationships between Native American women and English men took place had changed dramatically in the decades since Lawson's journey. Native Americans were tied into a market economy based on European manufactures, and private property was on the rise. Overall, women's status in this new world order had declined. Indian women married to colonial men may still have tended the fields, but laws proscribing interracial marriage jeopardized their inheritance of the land, and the status of their bicultural children remained uncertain. Anglo-Indian conflicts over land had melded with contests over cultural practices and social organization. Challenges to matrilineage, native gender roles, and sexual mores were part of the process of colonization. Women's sexual interactions with English men reflected the shifting balance of power, even as such relations remained an arena in which women contested their own marginalization.[63]

English depictions of Indian women, and actual sexual relations between Indian women and colonial men, serve as a measure of the dynamic power relations between Indians and colonists. Cross-cultural sex was an arena in which cultural distinctions and racial difference were defined and redefined, first in promotional writings, then in social interaction and legal statutes. Colonial concerns about family legitimacy and property ownership resulted in more stringent rules of racial exclusion, but in the relationships themselves, cultural and racial identities remained complicated and contested. As the next chapter shows, social relations, cultural allegiances, and racial identities in colonial settlements were complicated as well. There, the illicit sexual behavior of white and free black women became central to the construction and contestation of a colonial social order.

The Sexual Regulation of Servant Women
and Subcultures of Resistance

At the age of twenty, a white woman named Mary Gorman disguised herself as a man, took the alias of Tom Savage, and hired on board ship as a servant for one Captain Humes. In May 1726, Captain John West of the shallop *Virginity* hired Savage to sail from Currituck to Virginia. Anchored off the Currituck shore in late June, Savage approached West and said "Master I have something to tell you if you will say nothing." Claiming "I am a woman kind," Savage opened her jacket to reveal her breasts. West's response to this revelation is unknown, except that he kept the servant on board. Two weeks later, as West canoed from shore to the boat for the night, he heard a sound like a bleating calf. It was "Thomas" who "said he was very bad with a pain in his Belly." West asked if Thomas had made the beds; Thomas had not but did so and then took West's greatcoat and lay down elsewhere on the boat. Seventeen-year-old Christopher Dawson, also hired for the trip to Virginia, had often heard Thomas complain of "Back Aching," but that night he heard Thomas groan "like a sick man." The next morning West asked Thomas to explain the spots of blood on the "Starn Sheets." Thomas spoke of a nose bleed but West, who "had a Mistrust knowing her to be a Woman," guessed otherwise. (West also noticed that "the Belly of the said man Thomas was very Sank.") West went ashore for milk for Thomas and told one John Ives about the shipmate's "bad Condition," then he sailed for York Town where he sold Gorman's labor (this time as a servant woman) to another master. A month later, Gorman was back in North

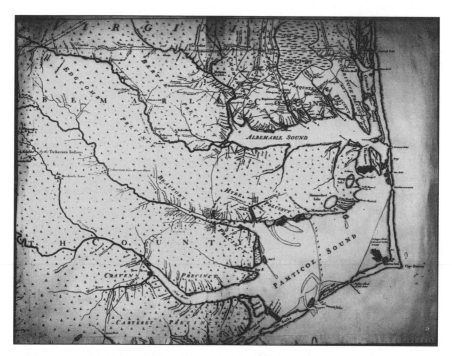

Figure 13. In 1733, Edward Moseley's "A New and Correct Map of the Province of North Carolina" (this is the northeast quadrant) provided the first accurately detailed map of the North Carolina coastal area. Courtesy of the North Carolina Collection, University of North Carolina Library at Chapel Hill.

Carolina and on trial for infanticide. A dead child had washed ashore near the house of Captain Sanderson, justice of the peace in Currituck. A grand jury of twelve men examined the corpse and deposed "all Evidences" (including John Ives), concluding the infant was "Murthered on Board . . . by a Woman Called Tom[,] Servant to the said West Dressed in Mans Apparril." They also believed "West knew she was a Woman" and suspected him as "one of the Murtherers." Gorman explained she had "secretly and privatly Delivered of a *dead* Child" which she "privatly Cast over Board," insisting, "[I] did it myself alone." She pleaded not guilty to the charge of infanticide and the jury acquitted her with court costs.[1]

Mary Gorman went to great lengths to escape her prescribed roles as a domestic servant or as wife and mother, but although she may have gone further than most to avoid domesticity and motherhood, she was not unique. Other women also rejected normative family forms and gender roles, defying sexual mores in an effort to determine their own lives within the restraints placed on their gender, race, and status. As they did so, these women encountered considerable tolerance along the way. In Gorman's case, Captain West accommodated a pregnant, cross-dressing, female runaway, and the jury spared her from hanging for infanticide. Neighbors and relatives often tolerated illegal behavior, including long-standing illicit affairs, without notifying the authorities. Servants especially tended to accept illicit sex among their peers because their inability to marry legally without the master's permission (which was seldom forthcoming) made any sexual relationship by definition illegitimate. The accommodation of illegal behavior also included considerable tolerance for interracial socializing, particularly among the lower orders whose alternative moral codes existed together with, and sometimes in direct contrast to, prescribed mores.[2]

Contesting the law and officially sanctioned moral codes did not necessarily imply empowerment, however, especially for fertile women who engaged in illicit sex. As Mary Gorman's case demonstrates, renegade women faced particular hazards. We don't know by whom Gorman became pregnant, but if her first master, Captain Humes, discovered she was a woman, he may have kept her on board only if she provided him with sexual favors. Unwanted pregnancies placed women in dire situations. Keeping the child would have made Gorman's disguise impossible, while abortion techniques (which she may have tried) were uncertain. Infanticide might result in her execution. Men could avoid the repercussions of illicit sex in ways a pregnant woman could not. Women therefore experienced illicit relationships differently from men: their hopes and fears were shaped by their fertility and by the sexual double standard that punished women more harshly than their male partners. Whether individual women experienced pleasure and self-determination or exploitation and oppression in their illicit liaisons (and the range of experience was broad), illicit sex brought with it special dangers for women.

This chapter explores how sex and fertility shaped the working experiences of servant women, and how women negotiated the complex circumstances of their personal lives. The customary prohibition of marriage for servants, and the penalties for bearing an illegitimate child during the term of indenture, made sexual liaisons (voluntary and involuntary) dangerous for women. But while sexual coercion marked some unlawful relationships, voluntary illicit unions testified to a desire for self-determination. Resistance to legal constraints took place on the most intimate levels of interaction, and patterns of unlawful behavior indicate that some women and men maintained a moral code that differed from mainstream mores. Misconduct involved not only unsanctioned sex, but also other transgressions such as theft, running away, or expressing contempt for men in positions of authority. Illicit transactions of many kinds were part of a culture of resistance that shaped social relations in the colony.[3]

Illicit sex was defined, pursued, and penalized in ways that significantly shaped the colonial social order. When the North Carolina assembly decided in 1715 to curtail the "Great Scandall" they perceived in the colony by prosecuting misdeeds that included "Prophaneness, Immorality, & divers other vicious & Enormous Crimes," their legal codes did not simply reiterate definitions of crime as they existed in England. Rather, the colonial adjudication of morality and immorality supported a labor system based increasingly on racial slavery as well as indentured servitude. Legally innovative definitions of illicit sex and new work arrangements for illegitimate children underscored distinctions of race as well as those of gender and class, turning the control of servants (a long-standing concern for masters in England) into a means of reinforcing racial difference. How women responded to the constraints placed on their personal lives in turn shaped social relations in the colony. Some transgressions of sexual rules, though done for the most personal of reasons, represented a larger challenge to legally prescribed relations of gender, race, and class.[4]

"With a Bastard Child": The Sexual Vulnerability of Servant Women

The regulation of servants' behavior was critical to the social order because servants made up a significant percentage of the European immigrant population to the British colonies. In fact, more than half of all the white immigrants entering ports south of New England before 1776 came as servants. Some were convicts, involuntarily transported to the New World, while others came willingly, pushed to choose the uncertainty of indenture abroad over the hardships created by high unemployment at home. These colonists paid for their passage to America by entering indentures in which they contracted to work for a master or mistress for a certain number of years, usually between four and seven, for room and board (but seldom further wages). During these years, servants performed a wide variety of work: women cared for the garden, dairy, and poultry yard; cured meat and preserved fruits and vegetables; cleaned house, spun thread, washed and mended clothes, looked after children, and prepared meals. Men worked in the fields, cut and stocked firewood, butchered livestock, transported goods to market, and tended the large farm animals.[5]

During their terms of indenture, servants experienced considerable restrictions on their freedom of movement and on their personal lives. Servitude occupied a kind of middle rank on a spectrum of status that ranged from freedom to enslavement. Bound to service for only a limited numbers of years and imbued with rights they could defend in court, indentured servants enjoyed a quasi-freedom that distinguished them from people enslaved for life. Nonetheless, servants could not simply leave an abusive master (although they could bring a court suit against him), nor could they prevent the trade of their labor to others. (In 1695, for example, Thomas White traded a boat in exchange for one year of Catherine Tarkentine's labor.) As part of its regulations, the 1715 "Act Concerning Servants and Slaves" specified the punishment for running away (the court added twice the length of time a servant was gone to the remaining term of indenture, plus more time as reimbursement to the master for the expense of recapture), provided for corporal punishment for violence toward a master ("as an Incouragement for Christian servants to perform their service with Fidelity & cheerfulness"), fined anyone who aided a runaway, rewarded those who apprehended one, and required that servants and slaves have the master's written permission to "buy, sell, Truck, Borrow or Lend" any item. Significantly, masters also controlled whether servants could marry, and those who married without prior permission from the master paid for their unsanctioned union with an extra year of servitude. By forbidding such marriages, masters denied male servants the option of becoming heads of households themselves and prevented servant women from having two competing masters (one being the husband). Masters may also have preferred unmarried servants because they believed that spouses were more likely to encourage each other to leave a bad work situation and start a life as an independent couple, as Henry and Elizabeth Mayer did in 1744. Because servants seldom received permission to marry, any children they had were by definition illegitimate, making the parents subject to penalties for fornication and "bastardy." Unwed servant mothers faced particular penalties. Based on the reasoning that the master lost the servant's services during the time of her pregnancy, the courts extended the mother's term for two years as compensation. She had to serve additional time beyond that if she could not pay the fine for fornication and the court fees.[6]

By the eighteenth century, the court response to fornication and children out of wedlock had changed from a focus on sinful sex to a secular concern with the economics of child support. This change was visible in England and throughout its colonies. Before the Restoration, England's ecclesiastical courts punished fornication and other sexual transgressions as sins that required rituals of public penance from both women and men. Draped in white sheets and holding wands, male and female offenders alike publicly proclaimed their guilt three times. Only such self-abasing public confessions could lead to absolution. After the 1660s, however, magistrates in England and the colonies (which did not have church tribunals) treated fornication and other illicit sexual acts less as sins than as secular crimes, and monetary penalties largely replaced public penance. North Carolina's oldest relevant law in 1715 fined fornicators fifty shillings and adulterers twice that amount (five pounds). Those without access to cash received a public whipping of up to twenty-one lashes. Although whippings were humiliating as well as painful, eighteenth-century court magistrates no longer required a public spectacle of confession and apology. Concerned primarily with the issue of child support, North Carolina courts continued to arraign unwed mothers while prosecution for fornication decreased markedly. In the counties of Pasquotank, Chowan, and Bertie, for example, the courts heard only twenty-one cases of adultery or fornication between 1730 and 1760 although at least ninety-one illegitimate children were conceived in the same time period.[7]

Courts still sought to identify the fathers of illegitimate children in order to procure funds for the child's care. To avoid the use of county taxes for the support of poor children, the court sought a financially solvent man (usually the child's father or the mother's male relatives, but sometimes also a servant's master) to provide for the child. That man then posted bond for child support, which usually covered half of the lying-in costs, half of the annual upkeep of a child for four years, and any "further orders for the maintaining the said Child as the Court shall see convenient and agreeable." Because the courts cared more about securing child support than about identifying the biological father, magistrates usually accepted the mother's identification of the child's father. The law of 1741 stated this approach explicitly: "in case such Woman shall, upon Oath, before the said Justices, accuse *any* Man of being the Father of a Bastard Child or Children, begotten of her Body, such Person so accused shall be adjudged the *reputed* Father of such Child or Children, and stand charged with the Maintenance of the same." The North Carolina law made no legal provisions should the reputed father deny the charges of paternity, further indicating that the court's primary concern was to farm out the financial responsibility for the child, and not to verify the identity of the biological father.[8]

The courts' emphasis on child support has prompted some historians to depict the courts as serving the interests of unmarried mothers. After all, court appearances provided women with the opportunity to lay the financial burden on men, and certainly some mothers welcomed the opportunity to obtain support from their child's father.[9] But financial self-interest could not erase the shame that accompanied a courtroom appearance for nonmarital sex. Given the emphasis on chastity as a female virtue, it is un-likely that a public interrogation regarding illicit sex had lost its power to humiliate the defendant, even if privately a woman felt differently about the transgression. For single women, the appearance before an all-male court on the charge of fornication probably evoked acute embarrassment. Mag-istrates, jurymen, and onlookers would have appraised the defendant while considering her sexual acts, and the language used in court—that the man "had carnal knowledge" of a woman while she remained the body used, known, and acted upon—reinforced hierarchical notions of active men dom-inating passive women. But the judges' assessment was hardly the worst part of the ordeal. Women without access to money suffered public whippings on their bare backs when they could not pay the fines. Men more often had access to cash, but for those who did not, community service could take the place of whippings—an option not open to women. The threat of a public whipping hung over single women who stood before an all-male court, adding further to their sense of powerlessness. For these reasons, women did not usually volunteer to go to court, and they often appeared only after an informer had tipped off a magistrate and effected their arrest.[10]

Some women tried to avoid arrest and extra years of servitude by end-ing their pregnancies. For centuries, women in western societies—as else-where—had used a variety of abortion techniques, including external trauma such as tight binding or punching of the uterus, purposeful falling off chairs and ladders, and deep abdominal massage. Herbal abortifacients such as savin (the berries of juniper or red cedar trees, brewed into a tea) and pennyroyal (an herb also known as squaw mint) could cause uterine contractions and, as a last resort, instruments were inserted into the uterus. Given the generally secret nature of abortion, most remained undetected and documentation of such cases is scant. Nonetheless, men and women alike knew about abortion methods. In July 1750 Mary Davisson sued Abell Bordine for announcing in public that he had "Corpelation" with her daughter "at Sundry Times" and had "boyled Saveren To make her mis-carrey." Whether or not Abell really had sex with Davisson's daughter, he knew about abortion techniques and could refer to the preparation of an abortifacient to make his tale seem more likely.[11]

A case of sheer desperation was that of Ann Sumner of Chowan County in 1744. When her mother referred to her being "with Child" Sumner de-nied it, saying "no for she had been two times in that condition." Appar-ently, Sumner had been pregnant twice before and had both times successfully aborted the fetus. Hoping to succeed a third time, she went to the wheat patch and "got on the top of the fence and jumpt of it" and later "came to the fence and Jumpt of it again." Her mother saw her and said

"Ann youll Kill your Self and your Child to," to which Sumner answered vehemently that "by God she was not with child." After watching her daughter's frenzied and violent efforts to abort, Sumner's mother alerted her husband that their daughter was "With child and she thought it was a gwain to come." When the baby girl was born (probably prematurely), Sumner's sister, Elizabeth Lang, lamented that it was "as weak as any Child as Ever she saw" with "bloody Water" in its mouth. Lang blamed Sumner for the baby's ill-health because "She had tryed to Distroy it" by drinking "a galon of sentry" (apparently an abortifacient). Elizabeth King testified that she had rubbed the child in the mouth (perhaps with a salve), but that Sumner had ordered her to "let it aloan let it die if it [wants] to." Aware that she could be charged with murder if no one else witnessed the baby's death, Sumner told King, "I desire youl stay for I think the Child Will die." Noting that the "blood was settled in the Childs fingers and face," King warmed the baby by the fire until it regained its color, but Sumner adamantly repeated that "she thought that the Child would die that Night." King did not stay the night, and when she returned the next day, the child was indeed dead, with "a froath of Blood at its mouth." Despite the testimony against Sumner, the charge that she had strangled her baby was dismissed.[12]

Ann Sumner expressed anger and defiance about her pregnancy. Her determination to be rid of the fetus differed markedly from the guilt, repentance, and fear experienced by other colonial women.[13] She made no effort to hide her actions: her sister knew about the potion she drank, and her mother watched Sumner fling herself from the fence numerous times. Instead of remorse, Sumner expressed fury at her condition, swearing adamantly that "by God" she was not—or would not remain—"with child." Her two previously successful abortions and her third attempted miscarriage contradict the notion that women accepted all pregnancies as the "natural condition for women" or that they understood possible death in childbirth "as part of the divine plan to which they must bow uncomplainingly." Sumner rejected the legal and cultural injunctions that sex be procreative and confined to marriage, and she refused to accept the pregnancies that resulted from illicit liaisons. Her behavior, like those of other unrepentant fornicators and adulterers, revealed fissures in the family norm.[14]

Infanticide dramatically illustrates both the burden of an undesired pregnancy and a sometimes desperate refusal to accept fertility as fate. The act placed immense strain on the mother, for women could only succeed in secretly killing their babies if their pregnancy and childbirth had gone unnoticed. Hiding a pregnancy and giving birth alone and in silence was difficult given the close quarters in which most settlers lived. Pregnant servant women

had to carry on with the usual chores of domestic service and reveal no unusual hardship or else risk the dangers of absconding during late pregnancy
for a secret childbirth. Few if any servants had their own bedrooms, and they
had to give birth as quickly and quietly as they could, if possible in a private
place outdoors or in the privy. The mother had to cut the umbilical cord,
kill the baby before its cries could give them away, hide its body without being seen, and dispose of the soiled sheets or clothes and the afterbirth. The
trauma, fear, and guilt involved in such actions must have been enormous.
That some women elected this difficult route testifies to the terrible burden
and shame that could accompany illegitimate children.[15]

Courts investigated suspicious infant deaths, but they seldom convicted
women for the capital offense. By law, any woman who concealed the birth
and death of a newborn was tried for murder unless she could prove by at
least one witness that the child had been born dead.[16] Although numbers
of women were charged with infanticide, the only one to die for the crime
in North Carolina was Magdalen Colliar, a poor woman from Chowan
County (she owned no "goods and Chattells"), who was hanged in the spring
of 1720 for killing and burying her child the previous November. Women
sentenced to hang might have their deaths postponed if they were pregnant. When a convicted woman "pleaded the Belly," the court summoned
a jury of matrons with at least one midwife to provide expert opinion on
her condition. For some lucky women a deferred sentence could end in a
pardon; the less fortunate gave birth knowing they would die a few days
later. Overall, however, convictions for infanticide declined in all the
colonies over the eighteenth century as jurors and magistrates proved less
and less willing to execute whites for crimes of a sexual nature. The matrons investigating the case either failed to provide conclusive testimony
of the defendant's guilt, or juries simply dismissed the charges on grounds
the records do not reveal. Martha (also Massey) Musick, for example, housekeeper for Timothy Ryall, appeared in court for infanticide in 1720. Four-
teen-year-old Margaret Ryall said she buried the dead infant at Musick's
request. Despite lack of a witness to confirm that the baby was born dead,
Musick was discharged. Similarly, the court dismissed Rebecca Pritlove in
1723 after a jury of matrons found that she showed "Symptoms of a woman
not long since delivered of a burthen," but whether that burden was a child
carried to term or a premature miscarriage they "can't positively say." Widow
Sarah Lynn found in 1761 that pleading a miscarriage saved her from
charges of infanticide. Margaret Bryan's bill of indictment in 1729 was
also returned "ignoramus," meaning that not all twelve jurymen believed
there was sufficient evidence to support the charge against her. Had the
grand jury returned the indictment as "billa vera" or a "true bill," the crimi-

nal case would have proceeded, brought against Bryan by an appointed prosecutor in the name of the Crown. In a rare criminal trial for infanticide, the General Court in 1735 found Ann Morris not guilty of suffocating her infant son with mud, despite strong evidence of her complicity (she knew where the child was buried).[17]

As capital punishment for infanticide became infrequent, neighbors were given monetary incentive to report pregnant women, perhaps because disclosing a woman's pregnancy prevented a future infanticide attempt, but also because court magistrates sought to procure child support. Informers received half of the resulting court fees (the other half went to the church warden). This incentive fostered sharp scrutiny within the community and played into existing tensions between neighbors. In 1715, for example, David Jones gave "Information against Mary Rivers And reports that she is of a very loose behavior & with . . . a bastard Child." Jones's slight about "loose behavior" suggests that he was already critical of Rivers. If ill will toward Rivers made Jones sensitive to any impropriety on her part, the promise of a monetary reward turned him into an eager tattler of her sexual misdeeds. Peering into windows to catch people in incriminating acts, or attentively watching a woman's belly for signs of pregnancy, was often more than just idle nosiness: it could be a profitable way to harass one's enemies. Lawyer John Luton did not disguise his interest in financial gain. In April 1749, Luton reminded the Chowan County court that the previous August he had reported the pregnancy of widow Susanah Ambros. At the time the court dismissed the warrant for her examination and charged Luton for the court costs. Disappointed that his exposure of Ambros had backfired, Luton smugly announced the following spring that Ambros had in the meantime given birth to an illegitimate child. He hoped that the courts would not only discharge him from the previous court costs but also "order him the usual Reward allowed by Law for such Information." The magistrates granted Luton his petition and made Ambros pay the costs of the first court hearing.[18]

Masters were especially likely to inform the courts when a servant had an illegitimate child since they stood to benefit from lengthened terms of service. When David Jones Sr. announced in court that his unwed servant, Mary Haily, was pregnant, he hoped to gain two extra years of her work. Mistresses also took advantage of this windfall. Widow Rowden charged her servant with having a child out of wedlock and received two more years of Margaret Nowell's unpaid labor. Similarly, Mary Wilson complained to the court that she had been inconvenienced by the birth of her servant's child, and the court ordered Ann Hamon, a free black woman, to make up for her mistress's "Trouble and Expense" by serving two extra years.

When Hamon again became pregnant, she was penalized with two additional years for the second child.[19]

Sometimes the master himself was the father of his servant's illegitimate child. On August 3, 1709, for example, Anne Adams told the magistrates of the Chowan County court that her master, "Mr. William Swann, Gent.," had made her pregnant. The judges cross-examined Adams and then proclaimed Swann guilty of having had "Divers times Bodily & Carnal Knowledge of the said Anne During her being Resident at ye Said Swanns house." Swann had to pay his servant two shillings per week until the child reached eight years of age; at that time the child would be apprenticed to learn a trade. Although Swann was responsible for her pregnancy, Adams had to serve him two extra years, during which time she remained vulnerable to continued sexual involvement with him. Although master-servant relationships were not all equally coercive, the very context in which they took place compromised women's ability to make independent choices. The power relations women servants negotiated in their daily interactions with masters, other men and boys in the household, and male servants led to complicated situations and difficult decisions. Unable to marry, single women remained especially vulnerable to the sexual demands of masters and other men. Although some women may have attained benefits through their sexual relations with masters, the burden of a pregnancy fell on them alone.[20]

Servants had little legal recourse against masters' sexual abuse, since rape charges were likely to fail. Rape was a criminal offense, but accusations against white men did not fare well in the courts. At least fourteen women charged white men with rape in the northeastern counties of colonial North Carolina. The fourteen plaintiffs were white; black women, married or single, free or slave, did not receive a hearing in court for sexual violation, nor did wives of any skin color charge their own husbands with rape. But white women seldom found satisfaction in the courtroom: only two men were tried in a criminal action, and neither of them was convicted. Female plaintiffs had better chances of receiving some kind of redress if they sued for "egregious" or "barbarous" assault without explicit mention of a sexual component. Given the difficulty of proving rape and the likelihood of intimidation by male assailants, most servant women who became pregnant when raped were punished as (voluntary) fornicators. Masters were free, therefore, to have sex with servants with near impunity. Evidence for such liaisons is sparse precisely because servant women could not accuse their masters without harming themselves. Admitting to fornication could bring on a longer term of service (if the woman could not pay the fine) or could cause the master to inflict punishment himself. Occasionally, however, the appraisal of servant women as sexual objects was reflected in newspaper advertisements for runaways. In November 1729, Doctor George Allen of Edenton advertised for his runaway servant Mary Jones, "an Irish woman . . . of Short Stature fresh Colloured, thick Sett has black Hair and Curles very much." James Davis's ad for an Irish runaway described Mary Lambert as "a short, lusty, full faced Woman, very fresh Complexion, wears her Hair down behind, which is very black, and curls handsomely, has a Blemish in one of her Eyes." The ad's description of Lambert went beyond a dry listing of visible details. Davis had looked not only into Lambert's eyes but over her whole body, finding a lusty, fresh-complexioned woman with beautiful hair. A master's sexual advances may have contributed to some women's decision to run away.[21]

Legislators wrote a law to counteract masters' economic incentive to impregnate their servants and gain added years of service, but many masters still took sexual advantage of servant women. A law in 1715 stipulated that if the master was the father of a servant's child, the church wardens would sell the servant to someone else for the remainder of her term and donate the money from this sale to the parish. (The servant woman still served two extra years for the offense of fornication but to a different master.) Even so, sexual vulnerability continued to complicate the daily lives of many servant women. Mary Musick (perhaps the same woman accused of infanticide in 1720), for example, experienced competing forms of coercion when her master, Timothy Ryall, made her pregnant in 1731 and then pressured Musick to keep his name out of the courts. Musick initially "denied to . . . Discover the Father," but she later gave in to the pressure of the courts and admitted that "Timothy Ryall begott of her Body the said Child whereof she is now Pregnant." Two competing male prerogatives were at work: the master's desire to have sexual access to his servant without accountability for the consequences, and the courts' insistence that a father, and not county taxes, provide child support. Musick felt formidable pressure from both sides. The courts represented legal authority and wielded the threat of physical and public punishments, while Timothy Ryall owned her labor and controlled much of her daily life. The difficulty of Musick's choice between two prohibitive options is visible in her court testimony: only after her initial refusal to "Discover the Father" did she reluctantly provide the name of her master.[22]

Many women refused to name the father of their illegitimate child, even when faced with "Corporal or other punishment" for contempt of the court. In 1752, for example, Margaret Ashley, a pregnant single woman, withheld the father's name. Elizabeth Slaughter, Elizabeth Ford, and Rachael Halsey did the same. In such cases, unwed mothers had to pay fines for fornication or undergo a public whipping as well as give security that the child's support would not fall to the parish. If they could not pay the security, they suffered imprisonment. Given the severe punishment for secrecy, the pressures to remain silent exerted by families or sexual partners must have been strong. When a pregnant woman refused to name her sexual partner, the courts expected the midwife to extract the man's identity during childbirth, as it was commonly held that a woman in labor could not tell a lie. Traditionally, midwives threatened to withdraw their aid from the woman in labor unless she named the child's true father. Although this threat may have been part of a formalized ritual of truth-telling, the gravity of the moment underscored the importance ascribed to finding the man responsible for the financial support of the child.[23]

On the whole, the legal constraints on servant women's sexual behavior criminalized their sexual activity (whether voluntary or not) and ensured that resulting pregnancies would not prove disadvantageous for their masters. Sexual rules contributed to the dependence of servants in gendered ways, making sexual vulnerability part of working women's experience. Nonetheless, illicit sex held out multiple possibilities for servant women: not all unlawful unions were coercive, and not all women found illicit sex morally reprehensible. In fact, some women upheld sexual mores that circumvented legal definitions of lawful and appropriate unions, making illicit sex an alternative choice under constrained circumstances.

"Cohabiting Together": Subcultures of Resistance

People found many ways to adopt, adapt, or resist prescribed moral norms. Some flaunted outright disrespect for mainstream mores, while others quietly chose illegal behavior, adjusting their choices to the socioeconomic situation that made compliance with prescriptive morality costly or difficult. Servants who could not marry might run away to do just that, while some well-to-do widows refused to marry when pressed to wed. Each illicit act acquired meaning from its particular context and the social coordinates of the perpetrator: just who transgressed the moral code mattered as much as what was done. Was the offender a woman or a man? A laborer or a landholder? Black or white? Inevitably, relations of gender, class, and race shaped the social meaning of the act as well as local responses to it. Furthermore, what to some seemed an acceptable breach of conduct appeared to others as a threatening sign of social dissolution. Different groups regarded the same act in distinct ways, and sometimes the disagreements produced an open clash of mores.

Lower-class people, in particular, expanded their notions of acceptable sexual behavior to circumvent the legal interventions into their personal lives. Servants unable to marry nonetheless created meaningful partnerships, effectively establishing what the marriage laws proscribed. Jane Warren and carpenter Jacob Tice, for example, both lived on Aaron Blancherd's plantation for several years in the 1730s. Warren and Tice had a child together and lived as a family, laws against fornication notwithstanding. Such couples may have wanted to marry but, denied legal sanction, chose to carry on their relationship and establish families without formal acknowledgement. Social constraints may also explain why servants' sexual transgressions were sometimes overlooked or forgiven by their friends. Indentured women's sexual vulnerability must have been a known fact to everyone in the community, and perhaps for this reason previous sexual experience and childbirth did not necessarily hinder a later marriage. In early 1744, Elizabeth Odum was pregnant by planter Thomas Ward when she married Otho Holland. In October 1745, when Elizabeth's son was a year old, Otho Holland sued Ward for forty pounds for child support. Holland did not try to keep his wife's previous sexual encounters from public view; rather, he took advantage of the opportunity to challenge Ward in court for child support. Had Elizabeth Odum been the daughter of a magistrate intent on marrying a wealthy planter, her premarital pregnancy could have ruined her marriage prospects. But among servants it was understood that pregnancy could occur as the result of coercive circumstances, and an unwed servant mother may have received more understanding from her peers. These long-term relationships and families suggest that people adapted their moral standards to the constraints in their lives. While alternative notions of morality did not exist independent of the colony's normative rules of behavior, morality was also not simply imposed by the law.[24]

Some servants responded to the ban on marriage with outright defiance. In January 1725, Hanah Davis ran away from her master, Dr. George Allen, a man who repeatedly abused his servants. For a whole year Hanah avoided recapture, during which time Dr. Allen invested thirty pounds in a search. His runaway ads described her as having "Black haire black complection . . . Severll Marks in her Arms . . . and a Swarthy Complection." She wore "a red Gown and a Spreckled Lyning Gown." About nine months later, Hanah persuaded Bartholomew McGowan, also a servant and an Irishman with "Much pock gotten in One of his hands," to run away as well. But first, he and Hanah stole many items from Bartholomew's mistress, including a gun, gunpowder, bullets, four petticoats, aprons, many shirts, ribbons and lace, and (from another involuntary donor) silver spurs, all totaling over fifty-four pounds. The two of them either married or pretended they had been married, and Hanah took on the alias of Susanah McGowan. When they were caught three months later, the courts sentenced Hanah and Bartholomew to thirty-nine lashes each for the theft. For running away Hanah received two extra years of labor to Allen (twice the length of time of her absence) and "ffour Years more for his Extraordinary Expences & Charges" in getting her back. Her one year of freedom therefore cost Hanah Davis six added years of servitude to George Allen.[25]

Hanah's rebellion demonstrates that the meaning of marriage depended on one's status in early America. Marriage certainly brought constraints to upper-class women. Under the principle of coverture, married women lost their right to own property, make contracts, and represent themselves in court. But women without property faced different circumstances. Indeed, when servant women were *denied* the right to a legally sanctioned and protected relationship, matrimony gained other, more positive meanings. When Hanah and Bartholomew established a new life as a married couple, their marriage served as a camouflage in their new community, as a marker of freedom and self-determination for themselves, and as a challenge to authority. The prohibition of marriage for servants turned legally unsanctioned unions into an end and a means of servants' resistance.[26]

It is difficult to know what percentage of North Carolina's population actually engaged in illicit sexual relations. Many, perhaps most, white residents shared lawmakers' notions of morality and conformed to widely held expectations of appropriate behavior. Nonetheless, enough women and men in North Carolina lived in nonmarital or extramarital relationships to give the impression that sexual misconduct was not unusual. Approximately one in ten court cases concerned immoral behavior of some kind, and sex-related charges included fornication, adultery, bigamy, interracial sex, homosexuality, prostitution, bestiality, rape, abortion, and infanticide. Of these, fornication and adultery were the most common offenses. In 1715, legislators found that "to the great Scandall of this Government, many persons from Foreign Parts" who lived together "as man and wife" were not only "unmarried to each other, but too often are the husband and wife of others." In an effort to crack down on such couples, North Carolina lawmakers imposed fines of fifty shillings for fornication and twice that amount (five pounds) for adultery. Culprits who could not pay received a public whipping of up to twenty-one lashes. Nonetheless, many white couples endured repeated prosecution rather than give up their unlawful bedfellows. Some offenses, such as bigamy, were hard to detect in a mobile society of migrants, and only a few cases of multiple marriages appeared in the North Carolina courts. One surfaced in 1727 when "Severall" people testified that John Brown had left one wife and "cohabits with another which he acknowledges to be his lawfull Wife both of the Sayd Women Within this Government." Shrewder bigamists put a greater distance between wives, as did John Diall from Maryland, who had a wife named Sarah Shirley in his former home, as well as a new spouse, Diana West, in Pasquotank County. Although many sexual transgressions remained invisible to the law, the statutes attest to the perception among legislators and court magistrates that persistent immoral behavior plagued the colony.[27]

Sexual misconduct was certainly not unique to North Carolina. In New England's county courts, for example, by far the largest category of criminal cases prosecuted between the 1690s and 1770 involved extramarital sex (most commonly fornication or adultery). In Virginia, sexual offenses also constituted the most common criminal prosecutions in the county courts, and the Virginia assembly passed more laws pertaining to public morality (sexuality, blasphemy, and drunkenness) than statutes to protect the state, persons, or property. North Carolina's newer and less efficient court system did not prosecute moral offenses to the same degree as did colonial courts elsewhere, exacerbating critics' concern about levels of lawlessness in the colony. At any rate, the appearance of repeat offenders in court, many of whom were related to one another, suggests that certain groups of people did not hold to officially sanctioned standards of behavior, and they formed a distinct and persistent presence in colonial North Carolina.[28]

Often members of a single family engaged in similar kinds of misconduct. The Sikes family, for example, displayed a penchant for unlawful behavior: William Sikes lived "in baudry" with Mary Clenny and kept her "as a Concubine," Joseph Sikes did the same with a woman named Lurany Rose, and Ben Sikes was arrested for adultery as well. In Pasquotank County, Alexander Jack and Ann Cartwright, Thomas Cartwright and Mary Roads, Daniel Roads and Elizabeth Burnham, John Burnham and Sarah Sawyer, Joseph Sawyer and Dorothy Hastings were among the illicit couples whose family ties linked them in a mesh of unlawful relationships. Free black couples engaged in unsanctioned relations as well. John Lett lived with Mary Butler (alias Johnson) from July 1746 through the following May. Elizabeth Butler and planter Arthur Williams (a white man) lived together for years, and Jane Mitchell and Robert Butler had established a family by the time they were arrested in April 1758 for "Cohabiting Together and Begetting Bastard Children." Similarly, brothers Gabriel Manley and Solomon Manley of Bertie County had long-term illicit relationships with their live-in partners. To some, having partners and children out of wedlock may have been a conscious act of resistance to authority, a specialized form of nose-thumbing. But even for those who did not perceive their own intimate behavior as overtly political, feelings of humiliation did not necessarily accompany unlawful relationships to the degree hoped for by government officials. It was not that misbehaving Carolinians cared nothing for the opinions of others, or that they were completely free from the social restraints that existed in the larger colonial society. Within the larger culture, however, people created spaces for alternative standards of acceptable conduct. These coexisting moral codes found some of their most concrete expressions in intimate relationships that clearly disregarded state and church definitions of appropriate unions.[29]

Many unlawful partners may have considered themselves as good as married even without the legal formalities; for them, long-term relationships constituted common-law marriages. Mary Hudson, for example, lived with Thomas Holladay on his plantation for a number of years and had several children by him. After Holladay's death some time in 1745, Hudson became the sole executrix of his estate. Others chose to put off official marriage for economic reasons. Widows, especially those with property, stood to lose their wealth to new husbands if they remarried. This may explain why widow Elizabeth Braizer shared her house with planter William Barker but did not marry him even though they had two children together. Similarly, widow Martha Godwin did not marry until she was prosecuted in April 1757 for living in adultery with Samuel Hollamon since the previous December. Godwin's reluctance to marry Hollamon may have been due to a discrepancy in wealth and status. When her previous husband died in 1753, Godwin inherited a four-hundred-acre plantation and two slaves. Hollamon, on the other hand, was probably less well-to-do: in 1753 he was described as a "laborer" in a suit accusing him of assaulting Isaac Middleton, a servant. In her decision to marry Hollamon, Godwin must have weighed the costs of further prosecution against the transference of her property to a new husband. Such cases suggest that unsanctioned liaisons could attain social legitimacy outside the aegis of legal authority. Unlawful couples did appear in court eventually, but the time lag between the beginning of an illegal relationship and its prosecution in court suggests that neighbors were not so shocked by the phenomenon that they felt called on to root out adulterous couples with particular vigilance. Clearly not everyone imbued illicit relationships, be they casual or committed, with the shame that ecclesiastical or civil authorities ascribed to extramarital sex.[30]

Sometimes servants expressed explicit disdain for local magistrates and their ability to enforce the law. Others doubted or ignored the legitimacy of the law itself. Servants could feign deference to prescribed norms when necessary but hold all the while to a different moral standard. In November 1723, for example, Martha Morris decided to run away from the household of magistrate Roger Kenyon where she was indentured to work for another two years. Eleanor Clerk, another servant, and Mary Cotton, a single woman, were planning to leave the small town of Bath to start a new life in Virginia. In preparation for the trip, Morris furtively placed a stolen linen sheet by the Kenyons' back door so Cotton could take it and "Cutt it up & make it into a gown." Morris was nervous about the theft but Cotton reassured her: if anybody found the sheet in her house, Cotton "would Swear Damned to her own Soul if She knew how it came there." Morris continued to pilfer sheets, some of Kenyon's shirts, and a window curtain. Emboldened by their success, Cotton persuaded Morris to leave the back door open so Cotton herself could "go into the Bedroom & Steal out of Mr. Kenyon's Trunk what Cloaths She Could find." Cotton also wanted to take Kenyon's money box, "tear of the hinges & take out the mony & thro the rest into the Creek," but Morris, made skittish by Cotton's audacity, persuaded Cotton to leave the box and take only a money bill for "provisions to go to Virginia." Morris herself took a five-pound bill and gave it to Cotton "to buy a boat as She Said." Afraid of being discovered, Morris asked Cotton what she would do if "Called to Accounts." Cotton didn't hesitate. If she were sworn in court she would "Kiss the book & then Say what Come next in her head & tale a hundred Lyes." Besides, "no Justice in the County knew how to give an oath." Cotton also boasted of her success in helping other runaways, namely "Mr Paytons maide & Mr Murphes man." Before the women could leave for Virginia, however, they were caught. Standing before the court, Cotton did indeed "tale a Hundred Lyes" as she had planned, but she found her partner in crime worse than useless: Morris confessed to the theft. Outside the courtroom, Cotton was furious with her. "Dam you, you have ruined me & your Self too," Cotton fumed, "I put words in your mouth and you would not Swear them." In fact, Martha Morris had already cut a deal with Roger Kenyon. She would pay him thirty-eight pounds to replace the stolen goods if he would drop his charges against her. Mary Cotton (who pleaded "not guilty") was convicted of petty larceny and received thirty-one lashes on her bare back at the whipping post. Cotton also had to post one hundred pounds sterling as security for her good behavior and all the court fees and costs.[31]

Mary Cotton's statements show clear disrespect for authority figures in the colony. Declaring that "no Justice in the County knew how to give an oath," she implied they were inept and not worthy of respect. Her willingness to "Swear Damned to her own Soul" if she knew about the theft and her plan to kiss the Bible and "tale a hundred Lyes" combined blasphemy with perjury. Clearly, Cotton held the court and its magistrates in low regard. Cotton also demonstrated an unconflicted attitude about stealing from a justice of the peace, an ongoing (and illegal) commitment to aiding runaways, and an uncomplicated willingness to lie in court. Her attitude indicates a general disdain for church, court, and government institutions, their representatives, and the social mores they stood for. Mary Cotton demonstrated what colonial officials surmised: that irreverent thought and illegal acts fueled each other, appearing together as linked assaults on norms of deference. Given North Carolina's reputation as an unruly settlement that harbored people of dubious character, evidence of such disrespect confirmed suspicions among prominent men that their social status did not evoke the reverence they desired. They repeatedly lamented their relative lack of wealth and status. In 1754, for example, Governor Arthur Dobbs described North Carolina as "scarcely arrived at the state of Manhood our neighbouring Colonies have attained to either in wealth or number." A decade later a Frenchman admired the "very great Estates" in Virginia but disparaged North Carolina with its "very few if any rich people" as "a fine Country for poor people, but not for the rich." Disrespectful words uttered by servant women like Mary Cotton confirmed the perception of disorder. When cases like these did come to light, they suggested that the lower classes routinely broke the law in ways that evaded surveillance and regulation, and that acts of deference covered a wellspring of disrespect.[32]

Even if servants disdained magistrates, they found ways to use the courts to their advantage. Mary Collins, for example, was both smart and bold when she ran away in February 1743. She began by taunting her master, Robert Parks, in front of a witness, saying she doubted he even had an indenture for her. He replied that he did indeed have written proof of her servitude, and on her goading he retrieved it. When he reappeared with the two halves of the indenture, Collins "Snatched them out of his hands and ran away." Parks was put "to great Expence in following her and haveing her taken up" and did not succeed until November. At that point Collins petitioned the court and brought witnesses. She won her case in July 1745 when the court ruled that Robert Parks "had Voluntarily Delivered up to the said Mary Collins Her Indenture and her Servitude." The court dismissed the complaint, discharged Collins, and left Robert Parks with the court costs. Due to her gumption and her ability to use the court system to her advantage, Collins was free.[33]

The absence of respect could be deeply galling to men in positions of authority. Katherine Jolley, for example, refused to show contrition for her illicit behavior. In August 1749, justice of the peace John Harvey encountered Jolley, an unwed mother, at a blacksmith's shop. He asked her when she planned to pay the court-ordered security for support of her illegitimate child. Jolley did not take kindly to Harvey's question, and she retorted, as he later said, "in a most Gross, & Scandelous maner" that Harvey and

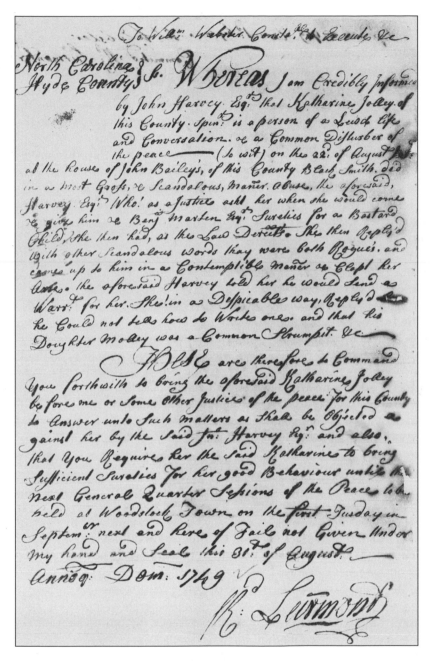

Figure 14. The arrest warrant for Katherine Jolley reiterates her insulting language toward justice of the peace, John Harvey. Courtesy of the North Carolina Division of Archives and History.

another magistrate "were both Rogues." She then "came up to him in as Contemptible maner & Clapt her Arse." Harvey responded to the disrespectful words and gesture by threatening to make out a warrant for Jolley's arrest. Undaunted, Jolley responded again "in a Despicable way," saying that "he Could not tell how to write one." Having openly challenged Harvey's ability to perform his duties as justice of the peace, Jolley then topped off her insults with the proclamation that Harvey's "Doughter Molley was a Common Strumpit." Resentful of the magistrate's allusion to her debt for an illegitimate child, Jolley turned the barb of his question around to accuse the women in his own family of promiscuity. Harvey complained to the Hyde County court that Katherine Jolley was "a person of Lewd life and Conversation & a Common Disturber of the peace." Despite Jolley's protests the court agreed with him, and she was fined fifteen shillings for her audacity.[34]

When Jolley smacked her behind in a provocative gesture and called Harvey a "Rogue," her "Despicable" words and suggestive body language displayed not only her disrespect for Harvey as an individual, but also her disregard for the larger authority he represented. As a justice of the peace, John Harvey held multiple offices in the colony. He acted as a judge of the precinct court, an examining officer, and the head of law enforcement in his county. In effect, Harvey embodied the local government and the law enforcement system in colonial North Carolina. Jolley's slur against Molly Harvey targeted the magistrate's authority as well. The commonplace analogy between patriarchal families and governmental rule held that if Harvey could not control his daughter's sexual behavior, as Jolley implied, then he hardly deserved respect from the public at large. In a culture that prescribed deference for authority figures, especially from women, rude behavior toward a government official took on political connotations. Harvey had to retaliate, not only to avenge himself of a personal insult, but also to reassert the larger authority he represented.[35]

Such misconduct troubled especially those who lamented the lack of a powerful church presence in North Carolina. The Anglican church had not become a particularly forceful institution in the colony, even after Quakers were disenfranchised in 1715. Missionaries complained for decades that North Carolinians were disinterested at best. Even if disaffected preachers exaggerated North Carolinians' lack of piety or disregarded altogether the scattered Baptist, Methodist, and Presbyterian worshippers, the fact that most people lived spread out on small farms did make regular weekly church attendance more difficult. Many had strong religious faith without attending church, but the perception remained that "too many," as James Reed said in 1760, "can hardly be said to be members of any particular Christian society."[36]

Given the assumption that irreverence was contagious by bad example and that it revealed a weakness in the social order, some prominent citizens found lower-class misconduct distressing even when it was not aimed at them. On a hot July day in 1737, an indignant Edenton resident saw Hannah Nugent, Frances Tool, Jeremiah Vail, and William Bailey (all of them probably white laborers) "striping themselves Naked and going into the water togather in the face of the Town." The affronted citizen informed a magistrate of the impromptu swim, and he, in turn, ordered the sheriff to summon the four culprits to court. Having heard the case, the presiding judges ordered that the men give bond for good behavior in the future, while the two women, Hannah and Frances, received ten lashes each on their bare backs at the "publick Whiping post." The women suffered whippings because they could not afford to pay bond for good behavior; access to cash could have staved off the pain and humiliation of the public thrashing. But the outraged informer and other like-minded spectators may have felt that the public humiliation was an appropriate reprimand for the transgression of female modesty. If women who were properly meek, submissive, and above all chaste began to strip shamelessly "in the face of the town," who could answer for the consequences? Their own naked swim was replaced with an involuntary stripping meant to shame the women and reassert rules of proper behavior. Men and women who socialized together in such openly physical and "promiscuous" ways showed a disregard for propriety that demanded punishment lest such irreverence spread and weaken the constraints placed on other forms of conduct.[37]

Taverns, also called tippling houses or "ordinaries," provided a common target for legal regulation. Misconduct flourished in such gathering places and included gambling, prostitution, interracial socializing, brawling, and thieving. In 1715 an exasperated North Carolina assembly had declared that the "loathsome Sin of Drunkeness is of late grown into common Use within this Province & [is] the Root & Foundation of many Enormous Sins." Henceforth, the lawmakers decreed, "for the Better prevention of Riots and disorders in Ordinarys," innkeepers had to obtain a license, renew it annually, and post a bond "for the due Observance" of the law. Widowed women were likely petitioners for a tavern license, and between 1741 and 1753 eight women received licenses to keep ordinaries in Edenton. Twenty percent of all tavern licenses in colonial Chowan and Pasquotank counties, and 10 percent in Perquimans County, were issued to women, and several were innkeepers of long standing. Dorothy Sherwin, Mary Wallace, and Elizabeth Wallace, for example, each kept a tavern in Edenton for over twelve years. In addition to providing "good Wholesome, and cleanly Lodging and Dyet for Travellers," innkeepers were not to permit unlawful gaming nor "on the Sabbath Day, suffer any Person to Tipple and drink more than is necessary." Just as importantly, the legislature sought to prevent lower-class people from congregating without permission from their superiors. Innkeepers who harbored any sailor, servant, or slave without the master's consent could lose their license, and anyone operating an unlicensed tavern had to pay a five-dollar fine or suffer thirty lashes at the whipping post.[38]

Despite these legislative efforts, people often ignored the law. In 1731, when an unnamed women was ordered to the stocks "for appearing drunk in the publick Street in Edenton," her husband and a bystander refused to help the marshal, so she went free that day. Some taverns were especially rife with illicit activity. Ordinaries provided a place where commoners could meet and talk, and some suspected that sharing grievances along with a few pints might lead to trouble. Certainly everyone knew that interracial networks of theft and illegal exchange persisted despite the injunction that trade with any servant or slave required the master's written consent. Taverns provided a place where schemers could plan such ventures of trade or theft, and there was plenty of evidence for both. Indeed, some taverns became centers of routine and perhaps organized robbery. In the 1720s and 1730s, Margaret and Robert Kingham ran a tippling house in Bertie without a license, and they appeared in court at different times charged with theft, assault, murder, and aid to three prisoners escaping from jail. In 1736 Mary and William Waltham were punished for harboring burglars at their ordinary, using foul language repeatedly, and for being thieves themselves.[39]

Other illicit exchanges included sex, which could range from sexual barter for goods or favors to the outright sale of sexual services. While the colonies did not have the equivalent of London's long-standing neighborhoods of ill repute, "lewd and disorderly houses" probably existed in every larger town. Prostitutes were especially available in places like New York, Boston, Philadelphia, and Williamsburg, but women sold sexual services in smaller communities as well. Colonial women worked as prostitutes on their own or in brothels for a number of reasons. Some women were pushed to the trade by the loss of a husband's financial support, or because they were orphaned at an early age and left vulnerable to male seduction and violence. Girls kidnapped or "spirited" from England sometimes became prostitutes. Others continued the trade they had begun in England, where they had been imprisoned and then transported to the colonies as convicted felons. Sometimes these women were not banished from England so much as bribed to the colonies: ships' captains on their way to southern plantations stopped by houses of correction, handed out liquor to the women there, and cajoled them into moving overseas.[40]

Prostitution had long been considered a moral debasement of women, but in the context of England's colonial wars, prostitutes received heightened attention. Reformers feared that the spread of immorality and disease would cause soldiers and sailors to lose their strength. "If this Lustful Fire be not quench'd, or else be timely restrained," one forecaster wrote, " 'twill soon emasculate the Age, consume the Strength, and melt down the Courage of the Nation. . . . If we design to maintain our Martial Vigour, for which we are now renown'd thr' the World, we must keep at a Distance from Venus' tents." To combat the negative effects associated with prostitution, eighteenth-century English reformers launched sustained efforts to regulate sexual commerce.[41]

In the southern colonies, efforts to curb prostitution were fueled by concerns about illicit lower-class behavior and interracial socializing. Widow Elizabeth Marston, for example, a tavern-keeper in Edenton in the 1720s, was allegedly "a common Bawd" who allowed "the persons that frequent her house" to commit "great disorders to the disturbance and annoyance . . . of the neighbourhood." James Trotter accused Marston in 1728 of being "a Bawd to Your own Daughters," claiming she had "putt two of Your own daughters to Bed with two Men in Virginia and received a pistole of the Sayd Men" in return. Trotter added that "One of Your Daughters had a Mollatta Bastard in Virginia and he would prove it." Trotter's words may have been spurious slander as Marston claimed, but if she did indeed run a "disorderly house," chances were that it was not an establishment for whites only.[42]

Edmund Gale, one of the wealthiest men in Edenton, had a similar concern about a white woman named Elizabeth Abell. In July 1737 he accused Abell of keeping a "disorderly house without any Lycense" and entertaining other people's servants. Although Abell gave bond for good behavior and promised that in the future she would not "sell any more Liquor as a tipling house," the trade in liquor, while offensive to Gale, was not foremost on his mind. He appeared again before the bench later that month and this time "duly proved to this Court" that Abell not only operated a "Tippleing house" without a license, but that her house was "Lew'd and disorderly" and contrary to law. If not a prostitute herself, Gale implied, Abell kept a brothel or at the very least countenanced unlawful activities in her home. She may have entertained servants, slaves, or sailors. Her clientele was not limited to white men, because in 1737 and then again in 1745 and 1750 Abell gave birth to mulatto children. For her "Lewd and Vile actions" Abell received the traditional public punishment of whores: she was "tyed to a Carts tayl and . . . whipt out of the Town by receiving Thirty Lashes on her bare Back well laid on." In response to Abell's illicit socializing, the court-ordered spectacle of her debasement theatrically reasserted government authority.[43]

Abell's example illustrates that the symbolic importance of sexual and social misconduct often eclipsed the impact or intent of the original misdeed. Even when transgressive acts were not necessarily intended as a self-conscious display of resistance to sexual norms, white women's illicit behavior represented a symbolic challenge to the ability of lawmakers and court judges to enforce their notions of order and good government. In a world where the personal and political realms overlapped, sexually misbehaving women became "common disturbers of the peace" whose actions undermined norms of female deference and highlighted the limits of state authority. Fornication, adultery, prostitution, even skinny-dipping, defied norms of appropriate female conduct, and the response to these infractions could be a forceful display of state power that retraced the limits of personal autonomy.

Illicit social and sexual exchanges among the laboring classes unnerved wealthier Carolinians because such activity, be it theft, aid to runaways, or illicit sex, took on aspects of politically subversive behavior and portended other forms of lower-class collaboration. Indeed, these multiple and often simultaneous forms of social and sexual misconduct posed a threat precisely because they were perpetrated by the "poorer sort." Court magistrates could more easily tolerate fornication, adultery, and sex with prostitutes as lapses of elite men, but they vigorously prosecuted the same infractions if the offenders came from the lower ranks of society. In other words, the political impact of any given transgression hinged more on *who* was breaking the law than on what actually transpired. Increasingly, the race as well as class of the offender would determine social and judicial repercussions.

"Fitting for Mallatoes": Racial Legislation and the Struggles of Free Black Families

As slavery spread in eighteenth-century North Carolina, legislators and court magistrates criminalized interracial sex in ways that greatly affected the free black population. Lawmakers wrote increasingly detailed statutes that adjudicated race relations and prohibited interracial interactions of all kinds, including sex and (more especially) marriage. With increasing clarity, such statutes defined acceptable marriage partners in racial terms and determined punishments for unlawful spouses and for officiating clergymen who defied the law. Chapter 2 described the growing specificity of those marriage laws and the way in which they aided the "naturalization" of racial difference: marriage prohibitions delineated boundaries of race in ways that made racial categories seem obvious and based on natural "fact." Just as important to the construction of racial difference were the long-term social implications of these marriage laws. Especially critical in this regard were the legal provisions for the apprenticeships of free black children born to white and free black mothers. Longer terms of indenture for children of color had severe repercussions for the free black community. The relationship between race and social status often remained unclear, however, and free blacks used moments of legal uncertainty to their best advantage, struggling against a conflation of blackness with servitude. The inconsistent application of these longer terms of service attests to the halting and uncertain process by which race was constructed in everyday life.[44]

Statutes that outlawed certain unions could not deter them entirely. Virginia first banned interracial marriages in 1691, and by 1715 the North Carolina legislature had followed suit, prohibiting the marriage of a white person to "any Negro, Mulatto or indyan Man or Woman." In 1723, North Carolina lawmakers levied an additional tax on free people of color and on any white person who married a nonwhite spouse. A statute in 1741 fined white spouses fifty pounds for marriage to "an Indian, Negro, Mustee, or Mulatto Man or Woman, or any Person of Mixed Blood to the Third Generation, bond or free." Unable to marry their partners had they wanted to, white mothers continued to give birth to mixed-race children. A white woman named Sarah Williamson, for example, appeared before the General Court in July 1716 after the birth of her mulatto son. Amy Demsey, the mulatto daughter of a white women, was born in Bertie County in 1723. In July 1727 there were "Severall persons" in Edenton who knew that Elizabeth Puckett, a white woman, had "left her husband and hath for Some Years cohabited with a Negro Man of Capt. Simon Jeffries." Despite the legal prohibitions, some couples even married. In 1725, John Cotton officiated at the marriage of Margaret MacCarty, a white woman, to Ed Burkitt, a free black man. That same year Martha Paul, a free black woman, and Thomas Spencer, a white man, married "according to ye form prescribed by ye Church of England." The Women's Meeting of the Pasquotank Society of Friends denounced Damaris Symons in 1749 for "Lewdness in whoredom with a negro man." In 1754, Jemima Griffin, a white woman, named her newborn "Mulato daughter" Patience. Clearly, some intimate relationships crossed a legal boundary that was relatively new and not yet firmly institutionalized in the colony.[45]

In its effects, if not in its letter, the law of 1715 targeted both white and black families. Only white women, however, were punished explicitly for interracial sex. A white woman, whether indentured or not, who gave birth to a mulatto child paid a fine of six pounds or worked two years as a servant. Unwed mothers who were already servants had the usual two years added onto their indentures for childbirth and two more for having a "Bastard child by a Negro, Mullatto or Indyan." By contrast, white men did not suffer penalties for sex with a black partner. The courts ignored liaisons between white men and slaves, and although interracial *marriage* was prohibited, *nonmarital* sex between white men and free black women—even when an illegitimate child resulted—went unpunished. The illegitimate children of free black women did not receive child support from public funds as the children of white mothers did, so courts did not seek a man to take on that financial responsibility. Black mothers virtually never appeared in court on charges of interracial sex, while white women with black partners found themselves the focus of much legislative attention. But despite the law's explicit focus on whites, the long-term repercussions affected free black families as well. Free people of color found their marriage options sharply limited: they could not legally marry a white person, and no law recognized the marriage of a slave. Furthermore, manumitted slaves who did not leave the colony within six months could be enslaved again, further curtailing the size of the colony's free black population and restricting the pool of eligible spouses. Free people of color were thus constrained in their ability to establish legal families. In the small free black community in early North Carolina, these restrictions would have been keenly felt.[46]

Furthermore, the free black children of unlawful couples were greatly affected by these marriage laws. The prohibition of intermarriage dovetailed with the remarkable stipulation (first passed in Virginia in 1662 and then adopted by other colonies) that a child's status as slave or free followed that of the mother. This extraordinary departure from English customs of patrilineage ensured that the children of enslaved women would be slaves even if their father was free, and it made the fertility of enslaved women a means by which slave owners increased their human property. But this legal innovation also meant that the mixed-race children born to white women inherited both their mothers' free status as well as their father's racial affiliation, augmenting the free black population at a time when legislators wanted to reserve free status for whites only. The same law also provided that the children of free black women were free, even if their father was a slave. The response to growing numbers of free black children took the form of extended indentures for them. The children of poor or unwed parents were routinely bound out as apprentices to learn a specific trade and literacy skills. But while the usual terms lasted until the ages of twenty-one and eighteen for white boys and girls respectively, the mixed-race children of white mothers were by law bound out until the age of thirty-one. The law thus made a clear legal distinction between the "white" and "black" children born to white women (sometimes the same white mother), with the result that mixed-race children, though nominally free, effectively spent their most productive and reproductive years as servants.[47]

Not only did free black children serve longer terms than whites, but they often had only the minimal rights of indentured servants. Court clerks who wrote generic apprenticeship contracts, leaving spaces for names to be filled in later, often crossed out the master's obligation to teach reading and writing if the would-be apprentice was a free person of color. For example, white Jemima Griffin's "Mulato daughter" Patience, born in Pasquotank County in 1754, was indentured at age five for thirty-one years, and the line that she be taught to read, write, and cipher, was crossed out. Very revealing was a second copy of the contract for Patience Griffin. In addition to deleting the literacy stipulation, the court clerk crossed out the word "apprentice" and replaced it with the word "servant," indicating that Patience was not to have the status and benefits of other white apprentices.[48]

There are other indications that free blacks did not receive the same treatment as white apprentices and that inequities were written into the contract from the start. Two-year-old Delaney Bright (the daughter of a white woman killed by a falling tree) was bound out in 1746 for thirty one years with the stipulation that she receive "Meat Drink Washing Lodging and Apperrele *fitting for Mallatoe's.*" With insistent repetition, the court clerk added the words "the mulatto" throughout the contract to describe the child. Sometimes the daughters of free women of color found their terms lengthened to that of boys: instead of being bound out until age eighteen, like white girls, some black girls were apprenticed until age twenty-one, the same age as (black and white) male apprentices. This happened to the three daughters of Doll, a free woman of color. Such changes in standard work contracts show discrimination against people of color, with more years of labor demanded in exchange for fewer obligations on the part of the master. This lengthened indenture also withheld from black girls the younger marital age allowed white girls, who could earlier assume the domestic duties that defined white femininity and womanhood. Even when longer terms of service were not written into the contract, some masters tried to take advantage of free blacks by holding them beyond their time of indenture. Joseph Williamson, for example, was bound out until the age of twenty-one but appeared in court in 1747, still seeking his freedom at the age of thirty-two. Similarly, one Olson petitioned in 1756 that as the son of a "Free White Woman" he was being illegally "detained in Bondage."

Some white apprentices also appeared in court to complain that they were held beyond their time of service, but free people of color had an added burden of proof: they had to persuade the court of their status as free-born.[49]

Free black women found various means of resisting the effects of discrimination. Whenever possible, free black mothers tried to keep their families together by apprenticing their children to the same household in which they, too, worked. Amy Demsey, for example, apprenticed her three sons to Margaret Duckenfield in 1756. That year Sarah Pugh apprenticed her two children to Margaret Duckenfield as well: her son Isaac until age twenty-one and her daughter Pen until age eighteen. Pen was to learn to read and write (like her brother), in addition to "the art of Spinning and other Household Business." The Demsey and Pugh children grew up together on the Duckenfield plantation, where their mothers probably also worked as servants. But mothers did not always succeed in keeping their children together; in 1759 Sarah Pugh apprenticed another son and a daughter to James Jones.[50]

Free blacks without family or friends to vouch for their status were especially vulnerable to being kidnapped and enslaved. In 1726 one Peter Van Trump from New York petitioned the North Carolina court. He claimed he was a free man who routinely hired himself out as a sailor, but that one captain, promising to set sail for Europe, landed in North Carolina instead. Van Trump was put ashore and sold and since then had been "held & used" as a slave by Edmund Porter (one of the colony's wealthiest men). The court dismissed Van Trumps's petition the following year and he remained the property of Porter. Similarly, William Derry complained that he had been freed by his former master's will in Virginia, but in 1737 one Godfrey Hunt had "come in the night" and "in a Barbarous manner Seized [Derry] in his own dwelling House" and then sold him to a William Taylor who transported Derry to North Carolina and held him there as a slave. Given the chronic danger of enslavement, free blacks who were separated from their families carefully preserved knowledge of their genealogy. Ruth Tillett, for example, committed to memory the story of her mother, Ann Tillett, a free woman who bore Ruth in 1743 at the house of one Timothy Mead. Ruth stayed in the Mead household until he died, after which she was unlawfully sold to a "distant Merchant" and then to many different masters, each, she said, "getting rid of her, as soon as they could, on hearing of her Story and Resolution to regain her Liberty." Tillett eventually "made her Escape and came [back] to her Native Country," but a previous master caught up with her and sold her again. Undaunted, Tillett managed to find "reputable and honest Evidence still alive," now some forty years later, who could vouch for "her Birth, and of her Civil and Social Rights." With her evidence carefully assembled, and arguing that her complexion was "an Art of the Almighty God, Not her Crime," Tillett finally succeeded in obtaining her freedom in 1783.[51]

The courts could not always be counted on to provide redress, and indeed, sometimes court magistrates were themselves responsible for the unlawful treatment of free people. In 1733, "divers free people Negros & Mollattoes residing in this province" were "taken up" by order of justices of the peace and bound out until the age of thirty-one, "Contrary to the Consent of the parties bound out." A committee of unnamed white inhabitants protested to the General Assembly that such unlawful practices— "well known" in the settlement—must be stopped. Under pressure from other whites, the General Assembly agreed that the children illegally bound out should be returned to their parents or guardians. Precariously positioned between slavery and freedom, free blacks vigilantly guarded their legal status in the courts and in the larger community.[52]

Women were central to the maintenance of a small but resilient core of free black families who, by learning how to use the courts, and by carefully preserving genealogical knowledge for future generations, proved essential for the freedom struggles of African Americans. A case in point is that of the Boe family of Pasquotank County. Sarah Boe (also known as Sarah Overton) was born in about 1700 to a white mother and indentured to a wealthy Quaker named Edmund Chancey until the age of thirty-one. As an indentured servant she was probably prevented from marrying the father of her children (perhaps a man surnamed Boe), and her children were in turn illegitimate. Sarah apprenticed her children to the man she worked for in order to maintain as much influence as she could over their lives. In April 1742, Edmund Chancey appeared in court to obtain the apprenticeships of "a Mallatto Boy Bob Boe aged Twelve years" and his two younger brothers, Jack Spaniard Boe and Spanyoll Boe. As Chancey put it, he had "this Several Years past raised a percell of Mallatto Children born of [one] Sarah Boe A Mallatto Servant wench belonging to [him]." At the time of his petition, Edmund Chancey had already benefited from a number of years of Bob Boe's work. With prospects of additional labor soon to come from the younger siblings as well, Chancey paid the fines for Sarah and received the indentures for her sons.[53]

Sarah's three sons were apprenticed to Chancey until the age of thirty-one, even though such long terms were explicitly meant for the mixed-race children of white mothers, and not for the children born to free black mothers like Sarah Boe. This was a point of legal inconsistency: sometimes the courts bound out the illegitimate children of free black mothers the same length of time as white children (twenty-one years for boys, eighteen for girls), and sometimes for thirty-one years. These inconsistencies reveal the confusion that accompanied efforts to create differentiated legal treatment for people in various racial groups. The transition to a racial caste system was neither smooth nor sudden, and legal arrangements pertaining to free black children were shaped by judges' own uncertainties about the relationship between racial definitions and legal status. This legal uncertainty affected the Boe children adversely: in 1738 the court had indentured Sarah's children until they "Arive to the Age of Twenty One Years," but four years later Chancey returned to the courts and acquired lengthier indentures of the Boe children, namely until they turned thirty-one.[54]

Chancey was not a slaveholder, yet he and his family benefited from decades of the Boe family's indentures. Certainly Chancey did not willingly free Sarah Boe from her servitude. In 1745, at the late age of forty-five, Sarah petitioned the courts for her freedom and received it only after the courts allowed her to "go up the river to see for her age in a Bible there." Furthermore, Chancey continued to benefit from the labor of Sarah's family. In July 1748, he petitioned for the indenture of Sue Boe, the "Mullatto Daughter" of Sarah's daughter, Frank, who was already "a Negro Mallatto Servt. to Edmund Chancey." Sarah's granddaughter, Sue, was the third generation of Boes to give years of unpaid servitude to the Chancey family. When Chancey made his will in 1753, he passed on to the next generation the labor of the Boe children. To one heir Chancey gave the time remaining on the indentures of Jack Spaniard Boe and Spanyoll Boe, and to another heir he gave Bob Boe, Rachel Boe, Frank Boe, and Frank's two children "Durin the time of their Indenters." At that time Bob Boe was already twenty-four years old, and his niece, Sue, was but an infant. [55]

The Boe family's experience shows the ripple effect of the criminalization of sex between white women and black men. Laws against interracial sex made possible the thirty-one-year indentures prescribed for the free black children of white mothers, punishing not only the white woman involved in the initial interracial liaison, but her posterity for generations to come. As servants, these mixed-race children of white mothers were in turn prohibited from marrying without permission, so that any children they had during this time were by definition illegitimate and bound out as well. Long terms of service thus had the dual effect of hindering legal marriage and then binding out the illegitimate children of parents who were not allowed to marry. Marriage laws therefore resulted in generations of African Americans who spent much of their lives working as unpaid laborers despite the fact that they were nominally free. Free black women and their children became the long-term victims of laws that explicitly targeted only white people for punishment. Although seldom punished by the courts for fornication, black women and their children endured the long-term effects of laws that banned interracial sex.[56]

Despite her limited powers, Sarah Boe must have carefully instilled into her children an identity of themselves as free-born as well as her own hard-won knowledge about how to petition the courts. Shortly after Chancey's death in 1753, Bob Boe appeared before the magistrates requesting his freedom. Bob Boe complained that Chancey had kept him "in servitude he being of the age of Twenty one & Restrained of his Liberty in his Lifetime." Furthermore, Chancey's executors "since his decease have done the same; and held unlawfully & illegally restrain'd of his Liberty, in Bondage & slavery; which your Petition[er] Apprehends they have no right to do." Bob was determined to end his indentured status, even if it meant biding his time until a strategic moment offered itself (such as the death of his master) to plead his case before the court. The records do not reveal the immediate outcome of Bob Boe's petition, but in 1790 he was head of a Pasquotank County household of five "other free" persons, presumably his wife Sarah and their children.[57]

As legal and social constraints continued to tighten around the free black community, free black women drew on a variety of strategies in their struggle to remain free. They tried to maintain influence over their children by apprenticing them to the same master, and they carefully passed on to their children the precious genealogical knowledge on which their status depended. They learned to use the courts, carefully marshaling their evidence and convincing whites to testify in their behalf. The need to provide evidence of a free maternal ancestor made familial relationships a source of resistance against encroachments on their freedom. Women persevered in their efforts to create partnerships and familial bonds, and as they coped with, adapted to, and rebelled against the constraints that shaped their personal lives, they challenged the racial order. Nonetheless, in the long run, the prohibition of interracial marriage and the lengthy apprenticeships for African American children had a negative impact on the free black community. The laws did more than restrict the autonomy of individual black households: they made marriage and the control over one's children a privilege of race as well as status, reinforcing the fact that even free African Americans did not have the same entitlements as free whites. Illegitimacy was thus institutionalized in ways that reinforced the racial hierarchy.

As the institution of slavery grew in North Carolina, so did whites' fears of repercussions. As early as 1715, some expressed alarm at the prospect of armed slaves, advising that "great Caution [be] used, lest our Slaves when arm'd might become our Masters." During the Stono Rebellion of 1739, roughly one hundred slaves outside of Charlestown attempted to flee to freedom in Spanish Florida. The insurgents were caught, executed, and had their heads impaled on pikes, but not before they had killed some twenty whites. Slaveholders in North Carolina shuddered at the news and scanned the faces of their slaves for signs of rebellion. Along with slave resistance came the backlash. In 1741, newly restrictive laws in North Carolina cracked down on human chattel. They enforced the pass system and encouraged whites to arrest slaves traveling without a "Ticket" from their master; permitted whites to kill runaways who had been absent for two months; prohibited slaves from trading, borrowing, or selling goods without the master's permission; created separate "slave courts" that dispensed swift punishment and reimbursed owners for executed slaves; disallowed unsupervised meetings of slaves; mandated that masters obtain a license to free a slave and that manumitted persons leave the colony within six months or face renewed enslavement; and forbade slaves to carry firearms without a court-approved "Certificate" from the master.[58]

The law did much to create a racial caste system, but how did people think about race? To whites, the rights and privileges that inhered in white skin seemed increasingly indicative of an immutable distinction between owners and slaves, an indelible difference that could account not only for racial slavery, but also for the hostility whites encountered in some of the people they owned. Ideas about racial difference, long present in inchoate form, were articulated quite explicitly by the mid eighteenth century and gained wider currency than before. The insulting rumors that white colonists spread about one another provide clues about their racial thinking. Sexual slander, in particular, marked the limits of acceptable intimacy within the context of deepening social divisions. As the next chapter shows, racial slurs left traces of changing perceptions of race.

4

White Reputations
"Blacken'd & Made Loose"

In June 1747, planter Thomas Partree complained to a Hyde County magistrate that Katherine Jolley had spread "Malicious tales" about his wife and daughter by announcing to Isaac Jackson and Lamb Harvey that "Jefferey a mulato Keeps Company" with the two Partree women. Jolley's insinuation of unseemly familiarity between Jefferey and the Partree mother and daughter raised doubts about the women's moral standing and questioned Thomas Partree's ability to control the members of his household. Furthermore, the innuendo played on a growing concern among the region's white inhabitants that their reputations could be compromised by the appearance of unacceptable socializing across racial lines. Whether or not the Partree women actually visited with Jefferey is unknown, but the initiation of a slander suit against Jolley served as a public denial of behavior considered inappropriate for the female relatives of a property-holding white man. The court agreed that "Spinster" Jolley's slur was harmful, and for being a "Common Disturber of the Peace" (Jolley had also assaulted one Elizabeth Marten the week before), she had to give bond for good behavior in the future. With that result, Thomas Partree had reasserted his reputation as a man in charge of an orderly household, and his wife and daughter could reclaim their good standing not only as chaste women, but also as virtuous *white* women who did not socialize with black men. Jolley's insult and its courtroom rebuttal suggests that, by the mid eighteenth century, class-related notions of honor for white women and men had become

131

entwined with assumptions of racial difference. The restoration of tarnished honor required the assertion of racial identity in public performances of "whiteness."[1]

Defamation cases preserved the words of people who seldom left behind other written evidence of their racial ideas, providing unique insight into the way ordinary whites contributed to the idea of race as a physical fact. While colonial statutes chart *legal* definitions of race and legislators' assumptions about difference, insults show how common whites, in their informal interactions with each other, also participated in the construction of race. (All the plaintiffs in North Carolina defamation suits were white, as African Americans could not defend their reputations in court, although one defendant was black.) Especially with the increase in slave importations to the colony after around 1730 and the concurrent rise in the number of immigrants from Europe and Great Britain, white North Carolinians became increasingly sensitive about their own racial (and ethnic) status. Slanderers who spread tales of interracial sex, and plaintiffs who heatedly denied such allegations, negotiated their reputations in racial terms: plaintiffs reasserted their claims to a race-based virtue while accepting the slanderer's implication that interracial sex (which they denied having) would debase a white person. Arguments over white reputations therefore also invoked "blackness" as something different and inferior. In formulating and refuting rumors of intimacy with African Americans, slanderers and their targets reinforced the idea that blacks and whites were inherently and naturally distinct, and that sexual mingling degraded a white person. By linking interracial sex to loss of white virtue, slanderers and their victims contributed to notions of race as a physical reality.[2]

Insults shored up ideas about racial difference, whether or not the offending allegations were based on fact. Indeed, the veracity of the slur is not at issue here (and can hardly be determined). A guilty person might initiate a slander suit preemptively to curb harmful gossip and ward off a larger investigation. In such cases, words prosecuted as slander sometimes proved true reports when the plaintiff was later convicted for the behavior they had disavowed as defamation—when, for example, a single woman who brought suit against rumors of fornication soon proved to be pregnant. At other times slander was just the mean-spirited fabrication the plaintiff claimed it to be. Most often the court records do not disclose whether an alleged transgression actually occurred. Therefore, I neither assume that stories prosecuted as slander were true (i.e., not slander at all but a factual report), nor that the behavior imputed to the plaintiff did not happen. Instead, I focus here on the words and social effects of racial insults and on what their refutation suggests about racial ideology among whites in mid-eighteenth-century North Carolina. Without conflating public self-representation with inner identity, both are at issue here: what do public contests over reputation suggest about whites' ideas of whiteness? Insults, reiterated before a magistrate as a source of harm, reveal what kinds of behavior were publicly unacceptable and therefore in need of a rebuttal (even if the plaintiff was guilty of that behavior). While defamation cases do not reliably describe actual sexual behavior, they do show links between sexual honor (in its gendered forms) and a racialized self-image among European Americans.

Often the only remaining document in a slander suit is the arrest warrant, drawn up by a court clerk with instructions to the sheriff after a magistrate heard a complaint. The warrants commonly included the offending words and their audience, the plaintiff's defensive self-portrait as a virtuous man or woman who was innocent of the slanderous allegation, a (generally formulaic) account of the harm done by the slander, and the amount of payment the plaintiff wanted from the defendant (called "damages"). Sometimes information about the disposition of the case was noted on the back side of the warrant, for example, whether the sheriff found the defendant and received a recognizance for appearance at the next court session, or whether a jury dismissed the charges for lack of sufficient evidence or instead considered the bill of indictment a "true bill," in which case the defendant was brought to trial. Unfortunately, it is harder to track the outcomes of trials, as they were seldom noted on the warrant and the lower court records are incomplete. I have provided what information I found about court decisions in slander suits, but the focus here is less on the adjudication of defamation suits and more on what the insults themselves reveal about ordinary whites' ideas about honor, gender, class, and race.[3]

On the whole, slander suits reveal tensions in mid-eighteenth-century conceptions of race. On the one hand, sexual slurs increasingly implied an innate and permanent difference between white and black bodies that made sexual intercourse unnatural (and therefore degrading to whites). On the other hand, the very need for whites to refute such an insult called into question the obviousness of racial identity and its guarantee of other qualities (such as moral superiority). A white person's honor was not assured by virtue of their "race," and whiteness seemed both obvious and elusive at the same time. Left unaddressed, an insult might compromise the qualities associated with whiteness. In other words, at the same time that race was being construed as inherent, whiteness needed to be performed in order to be persuasive. For these litigants, then, whiteness existed as much in behavior (sexual choices, for example) as it did in some biological truth that was beyond contamination. Furthermore, ideas about race had a gendered dimension, and sexual slurs worked differently for men than for women. Gender, like class, determined the constituent parts of a person's honor and mediated the impact of an affront. Although allegations of interracial sex could effectively target both men and women, the slights and their implications were different, depending on the target's sex and status. Drawing on gendered notions of honor among white women and men, slurs about interracial sex tapped into familiar notions of femininity and masculinity, reinforcing ideas about gender difference at the same time that they underlined notions of race. Performances of gender—visible in verbal and physical fights over reputation—also helped naturalize concepts of race.[4]

Gender, Status, and Speech Crimes: Sedition, Swearing, and Scolding

The first half of this chapter discusses words that did not explicitly invoke racial difference at all: it explores the social construction of an insult and the role that gender and status played in forming the reputations of white women and men. Words had long served as indicators of a person's place in the social hierarchy. Social rules about who could legitimately author certain kinds of speech, and court-ordered punishments for transgressive talk that took the speaker's sex and rank into account, reinforced a social order that required displays of deference to superiors and respect toward one's peers. The importance of reputation in a largely oral culture and a credit-based economy pushed white women and men to prosecute insults, and these courtroom contests over honor in turn shored up ideas about distinctions of gender and class. These conflicts over reputation were already implicitly about whiteness, but only eventually would blackness be explicitly invoked as a contrast to white virtue. Just how racial slurs fit into (and in some ways altered) the construction of white virtue based on gender and class, and how they encouraged ideas about racial difference, is treated in the second half of the chapter.

The legal treatment of misspeaking women and men in North Carolina stemmed from English jurisprudence regarding speech crimes. Early-modern English law gave the state the power to punish unruly speech to protect the social order. In their verbal exchanges, people either reenacted or disrupted prescribed relations of deference, and the truth itself was no defense for uttering disrespectful words about the crown and its officials. Language that threatened the orderly functioning of the state, such as sedition, was prosecuted in the name of the monarch as a criminal breach of the peace. (By contrast, speech that harmed a private individual, such as slander, constituted a civil matter.) As in England and its other colonies, the most serious speech offense in North Carolina was sedition.

Seditious speech could sound like ordinary slander (calling the colonial governor a "cheating Rogue," for example), but it was punished more severely than slander because it targeted the crown via its high-ranking representatives. "Contempt" for courts and magistrates was usually considered less serious than sedition, but in either case, those found guilty suffered public whippings or fines (or both). Seditious speech included criticism of the government in general (its laws, practices, and policies), and it could involve the spreading of "false news" that might incite people to rebellion. The first constitution of North Carolina, written in 1669 by John Locke, specified that "No person whatsoever, shall speak any thing [in their religious assembly] irreverently or seditiously of the government or governors, or of state matters." In 1715, North Carolina lawmakers responded to political upheavals in the colony with a statute that prohibited "any seditious Words or Speeches, or . . . false News . . . against the present Government." Anyone who tried to "disturb or obstruct, any lawful Officer in the executing of his Office" or who sought to "incite rebellious Conspiracies, Misdemeanors, Riots, or any Manner of unlawful Feuds or Differences" shall be punished "by Fine, Imprisonment, Pillory, or otherwise, at the Discretion of the Justices of the General Court."[5]

Despite these penalties, some women and men expressed their disdain for government officials and court magistrates. In November 1695, for example, Elinor Moline was arrested and brought to court for her "Contemptious Words" against Thomas Harvey, the deputy governor of North Carolina. While aboard ship, Moline had "uttered abusive Words" against Harvey "to the Honorable deputy Governors Face." The court ordered "fifteen stripes upon her bare back" at the public whipping post and made her husband Robert pay a security for her good behavior in the future. In an effort to appease the court and avoid the whipping, Elinor Moline submitted a lengthy petition that "humbly acknowledgeth her Contemptious and abusive words" for which she was "heartily sorrowful." She went on to beg the pardon of the deputy governor and the court and, "confessing her selfe unworthy of the least favor[,] Wholy submitteth her selfe to the Honorable Court earnestly craving to be pardoned for this her Crime." Although Moline's petition delayed the punishment until the next court meeting, her apology did not sufficiently appease the magistrates, and in February 1696 Moline received the fifteen lashes.[6]

The symbolic impact of Moline's insulting speech hinged on her own social position and that of the person she maligned. Harvey represented the local government and law enforcement system in colonial North Carolina and, by extension, the English crown. Whether so intended or not, when Moline spoke out of turn, dramatizing her disregard for Harvey in colorful, contemptuous language, she symbolically undid (or unsaid) proper relations of deference. Rude behavior toward a government official was a political act, and her personal antipathy represented a seditious offense. The fact that Moline was a woman further exacerbated the insult. Her prosecution stands out amid the vast majority of suits brought against male offenders for sedition, many of whom were from the upper ranks of society themselves. As historian Jane Kamensky put it, "speech against authority was a crime of social proximity." Most of the 160 defendants on trial in the North Carolina higher courts for contempt of authority between 1670 and 1776 were men. When "Contemptious and abusive words" came from a woman, their impact was shaped by prescriptions for female speech. Sermons and prescriptive literature extolled the feminine virtues of humility and compliance, and they championed the ideal woman's submission to male authority. One primer advised women that "such ought thy modesty to be that thou shouldest scarce speak but when thou answereth." In reality, however, unruly women spoke out with rash words and unsavory expressions, giving men "bad languig." Often, women's talk was ignored by men, whose reputations were not sufficiently harmed by female speech to warrant a lawsuit. Occasionally, however, women's words proved damaging enough to prompt legal retaliation. In such cases, Moline's being an example, the transgression of gender norms exacerbated the verbal offense, adding to the impression of social disorder.[7]

Court-ordered punishments for sedition often took the speaker's gender and class into account. Although whippings chastised women and men unable to pay a fine, men of better standing could avoid the whipping with a public display of remorse that was not as effective for women of the same rank. These men could undo their transgressive speech by speaking *more:* a public apology on bent knee before the court effectively unsaid the harmful words and reestablished relations of deference at the same time that it reasserted the apologizing man's authority to speak in public. In 1737, for example, Patrick Dalton was in trouble for "haveing offered an Insult to this Court" by mistreating a magistrate. On hearing that he was to be committed to the stocks for his "Contempt and Insolent beehavior," Dalton "went down on his knees to the Court and beged pardon." This show of deference undid the initial damage and restored order in the eyes of the court, and Dalton was discharged with fees. Similarly, one year before Moline received fifteen lashes for haranguing Thomas Harvey, Jonathan Clapper was arrested for seditious words against the same deputy governor. In Clapper's case, the court made him "publickly upon his knees" beg the deputy governor's pardon and give bond for good behavior. Clapper redeemed himself by offering a symbolic annulment of his social disrespect. Such a public apology did not work for Elinor Moline. When Moline insulted Harvey to his face in 1695, she had crossed too many boundaries of deference, including prescriptions of silence for women, to allow a retraction of the offending words. The court took her bond for good behavior but refused to accept her apology in lieu of a public whipping.[8]

Such apologies did not always work for men either, and the status of offender and offended (and the defendant's ability to pay the fine) were decisive in this regard. In February 1724, for example, Joseph Castleton, a "Labourer," called Governor George Burrington a "damn'd Rogue and a Villain" because when a man he knew went to Burrington for justice, the governor "beat him and made him kneel down on his knees and begg his life." Castleton threatened to report this misuse of power to the Proprietors in England. Finding himself prosecuted by the crown's attorney, Castleton pleaded not guilty at first, but when the grand jury indicted him, he withdrew that plea and "Humbly moved the Court for mercy." Castleton's apology did nothing for him, however, and lacking "visible effects whereon to levy a fine," he stood for two hours in Edenton's pillory "on the public parade." By contrast, when planter Robert Atkins of Bath County declared that same month in 1724 that the government's authority was "good for nothing" and that the government as well as its justice of the peace, Joseph Bell, Esquire, "might kiss his own Arse," Atkins was released with an (admittedly hefty) fine of forty pounds plus a hundred-pound bond for good behavior. These cases exemplify the importance of status and property in determining punishments. They also suggest that, like laboring men, women (even those with access to funds) did not have the power to unsay transgressive words with more words. That privilege was reserved for men of higher status who rightfully had a public voice. Rebellious women like Moline, and laboring men like Castleton, suffered public humiliation instead, enduring physical punishments that reduced them in stature and elicited cries of pain rather than scripted apologies.[9]

Over time, the impact of verbal attacks on men in positions of authority in North Carolina diminished in inverse proportion to the strength of the colonial social order. The declining power of words to harm is mirrored in the reduced punishments for such talk. In 1697, when Zachary Keeton spread "false and Scandalous reports" about the daughter of a propriety deputy, the court ordered thirty stripes on Keeton's bare back and insisted that he "openly acknowledge his fault." Increasingly, however, the courts ordered mild punishments for speech offenses or none at all. In 1749, for example, Katherine Jolley (with whom this chapter began) called justice of the peace John Harvey a "Rogue" and his daughter, Molly, "a Common Strumpit." Jolley had accused Harvey of ineptitude on two counts: he was morally unfit for his position as court magistrate, and he was unable to control the women in his household. Though Harvey pursued Jolley in court for two years, her eventual penalty was a mere fifteen shillings rather than the fifteen lashes Elinor Moline suffered for her insult to another Harvey a half century before. The impact of words still hinged, however, on who spoke to whom, and men's disparagement of ruling men likely still mattered more than women's slights. When laborer John Lackey, for example, pronounced "God Damn King George" in 1728 and toasted the health of "King James the third," saying "let him reign for ever," he was punished with twenty-one lashes at the public whipping post.[10]

Gender continued to shape the penalties for two other kinds of speech: swearing (or blasphemy) and scolding, both of which constituted a criminal breach of the peace. Outspoken women, the most obstreperous of whom were known as "scolds," had long been considered a social menace. In seventeenth-century England, a scold was defined as "a troublesome and angry woman, who by her brawling and wrangling amongst her Neighbours, doth break the publick Peace." Scolding women could receive a punishment reserved for them alone: a drenching in the ducking stool. Culprits were tied to a board or a chair and then lowered repeatedly into a pond, river, or big barrel of water. This practice was imported into the colonies, where brazen women were also ducked. In 1738, for example, foul-mouthed Mary Waltham, a tavern keeper in Edenton, stood in the stocks for three hours and was "Ducket in the publick Ducking pool" for her "profane Swearing 163 Oaths." Who kept such precise count is unknown, but that Waltham's verbal transgressions were compounded by her sex would have been clear to all onlookers who knew that the ducking stool was for unruly women and was not inflicted on misspeaking men. Ducking, because it served as punishment for women only, became a particular form of degradation. The physical silencing of women, who were rendered speechless under water and came up spluttering and gasping for air, represented the female nature of the transgression: women were not meant to speak out, and those who did were reminded of their place in ways that outspoken men were not.[11]

Another gender-specific punishment was that of being "carted" or drawn about town in a cart and exposed to public ridicule, as was commonly done in England and the colonies to women accused of prostitution. In 1765, North Carolina blasphemer Mary Sylvia was "Carted about town with labells on her back & breast espressing her crime, for one hour, and afterwards stand in the Pillory for one hour more." Not only did the punishment carry the innuendo of a promiscuous woman, it also replaced her own unruly speech with that on the "labell," which likely denied her the ability to speak with any authority. Ducking and carting humiliated women in ways that reinforced the gendered rules of speech: women's punishment was as

*Figure 15. Ducking stools, which took different forms, punished women for unruly speech.
From G. F. Townsend,* The Town and Burough of Leominster *(Leominster [1863]),
p. 317, originally printed c. 1700 in* A Strange and Wonderful relation of the old
Woman who was Drowned at Ratcliffe-highway *(London, n.d.).*

distinctive as their verbal transgression against norms of female virtue. By
contrast, men who were physically chastised for swearing received the
gender-neutral and standard punishment of a whipping. John Hassell, for
example, another inveterate curser, paid multiple fines for his "Blasphemous words and Discorses" (as well as for adultery) until finally, in 1722,
he received thirty-nine lashes for pronouncing one Sunday after a sermon
that even "If an Angell should come down from Heaven and tell him face
to face that he should Dye and be Damned to all Eternity he would not
forbear Swearing at Some times." Hassell's punishment was severe, as blasphemy was forbidden by both scripture and North Carolina statute, but like
other male swearers he was whipped and not ducked or carted. The point
is not that one punishment was worse than another, but rather that misspeaking women received a special punishment, indicating that unruly
speech had a different meaning for women speakers than for men. Scolds
merited special forms of humiliation as women who transgressed gender
roles as well as rules of proper speech.[12]

Sedition, swearing, and scolding all reveal the importance of gender and
class to the impact of unruly talk. The meaning of speech was situational in

nature and depended on the context and the players involved. Slander cases also hinged on who was speaking to whom, although in contrast to criminal cases, slander suits were civil actions brought most often by plaintiffs against their social equals. Gender still mattered enormously in the motivation, prosecution, and outcome of these cases, however, and class continued to shape the power of an insult. Eventually, racialized insults were introduced into this nexus of gender, status, and speech, contributing to racial "knowledge" even as they melded with existing ideas about social status and gender roles. In this way, contests over slander became multifaceted performances of white, gendered, class-based honor.

"Whoores and Theives": Slander and Sexual Honor

Reputations were a crucial asset in North Carolina's credit-based economy, yet only certain kinds of insults could be brought to court. Seventeenth-century English legislative reforms sought to relieve overloaded court dockets by limiting the kinds of injurious words plaintiffs could prosecute. In England and its colonies, three categories of slanderous speech remained actionable: allegations of unlawful behavior, claims of professional dishonesty or incompetence, and rumors of a condition, such as an infectious disease, that could result in social ostracism. To win a suit, the plaintiff had to demonstrate that the slander caused economic harm, not just hurt feelings. For that reason, plaintiffs in North Carolina (as elsewhere) typically stated in formulaic language that because they had been "damnified in their good name," suitors had broken off their courtship or neighbors did "more and more withdraw" from relations of sociability and commerce. Tales of wrongdoing, be they whispered innuendo or trumpeted claims of misconduct, had led to shunning and financial loss or to ruined marriage prospects (which injured women's means of livelihood especially). Plaintiffs sought a public retraction of the harmful words as well as monetary "damages" from the defendant. Soon after the General Court for Albemarle County opened for business in January 1670 (with the governor and his Council serving as magistrates), plaintiffs initiated defamation suits along with actions for debt, theft, and other infractions.[13]

Despite the drama of individual cases, slander suits made up only a tiny part of the overall caseload in colonial courts, both in numerical terms as well as in proportion to the growing colonial population. The small number of defamation cases may have resulted from the restrictions placed on actionable words, but more importantly, trespasses against property (especially debt and theft) took center stage in eighteenth-century civil suits.

Successful slander suits resulted more often in monetary recompense than in the elaborately staged public apologies so coveted by seventeenth-century plaintiffs. The changing manner in which courts dealt with defamation did not mean that insults had lost their power to wound, however. Court restrictions on actionable words did not necessarily overlap with ordinary understandings of honor, and insulted people may have been unable to bring viable suits against slights they resented. The vast majority of insults remain irretrievable to us now, but words that survived in a written complaint reveal which slights were damaging enough to make court-ordered redress seem feasible.[14]

Like sedition and swearing, slanderous talk and its legal redress had a gendered dimension. Eighteenth-century assumptions about the honor of women and men determined which insults plaintiffs could and wanted to bring to court. While both women and men were harmed by allegations of dishonesty, a woman's "honesty" depended on her chastity, as a woman with "loose" morals could not qualify as honest in any case. Women's social standing resided first and foremost in their sexual reputations, and so the most effective (and common) insult involved claims of sexual misconduct. Sexual slurs against women became an easy way to antagonize men as well, escalating arguments that were initially not about sex at all. For example, the same year that Elinor Moline vexed Thomas Harvey (in 1697), her husband Robert tangled with one Captain John Hunt over the inheritance of another man's plantation. In a fury, Robert said Hunt was an "old Cheating Rogue" who "got his Estate by Cheating" and that Hunt, a "stump handed Dog," could "kis my arse." For good measure, Moline added that Hunt's "old Cuckoldy rogue for his wife . . . played the whore with one Samuel Woodward for a stuf Gowne." Robert Moline hurled gender-specific insults against husband and wife, first denouncing John Hunt with allegations of financial corruption and then accusing Elizabeth Hunt of bartering sexual favors. Although Moline may not have held a grudge against Elizabeth Hunt, slandering her as a whore proved an effective means of irritating John Hunt, because his wife's reputation reflected on his own. Hunt demanded five hundred pounds for each instance of damage done to himself and his wife, but the jury ordered that Moline pay only fifty and twenty shillings respectively for his slurs, suggesting that the captain's reputation was not nearly as valuable as he thought, and that his wife's reputation was worth less than half of his own.[15]

The sexual double standard decisively shaped slander litigation: it determined which insults male and female plaintiffs brought to court. By the eighteenth century, male plaintiffs no longer prosecuted allegations of sex with a white woman. This marked a change, because earlier in the seventeenth century both women and men argued that slurs of "whore" and "whore-monger" (respectively) had ruined their good names. By 1700, such stories had lost their power to damage a white man's reputation, which depended instead on honesty and reliability in commercial transactions. By contrast, white women's virtue continued to reside primarily in their chaste behavior, making them easy targets for sexual innuendo. Of seventy-seven suits for defamation initiated in the lower courts of North Carolina's northeastern counties before 1765, the content of the slander is known for sixty-five of them. Of the forty-one cases involving insults of a sexual kind, thirty-two slurs targeted a woman. Furthermore, none of the suits brought by men for sexual defamation refuted allegations of sex with a white woman.[16]

In fact, in the eighteenth century white men could openly brag about real or invented sexual exploits with a white woman, thus defiling her reputation without harming their own (and perhaps even gaining esteem among their male peers). In 1700, for example, William Reed boasted that Bartholomew Hewitt was a cuckold and his wife Ann a whore because Reed "had Fuckt her Fourteen or Fifteen times." Similarly, in 1735 single woman Ann Hosey defended her reputation against Thomas Stafford Jr., who bruited about the neighborhood that he had "lain with & knock't her Several times." When several witnesses testified in court that they, too, heard Stafford's claim, he confessed to the slander, saying "that it was false." In fact, Stafford conceded, "he had no Carnal Knowledge of hir Body Neither knoweth whether She . . . be man or woman." Stafford invented his sexual exploits and falsely advertised them without fear of punishment. When the distressed Ann Hosey sued in her own defense, Stafford simply retracted his statement. While Stafford could easily withdraw his insult when necessary, Hosey could not afford to let his story go unchallenged lest she suffer serious damage to her reputation and her marriage prospects. Not only did gender determine the parameters of acceptable sexual behavior, it also shaped one's relationship to language. Ann Hosey feared the impact of Stafford's words and brought an immediate countercharge of slander. Stafford, on the other hand, enjoyed much more flexibility in his use of language: he could issue and retract statements with an ease that mocked the urgency with which Hosey felt forced to respond to them. Like Thomas Stafford, Robert Hill had no qualms announcing in 1750 that Hepsebeth Minshew, a single woman "within the age of twenty One years," had "Came in to bed to me . . . with only her shift on." He described her as "a whore," saying: "I . . . have layn with her." By this account Minshew was a "whore" for sleeping with Hill, while his reputation remained unaffected by his having "layn with her." White men's reputations resided now in their standing as honest trading partners, and their sexual behavior became a secondary (even unremarkable) aspect of their honor. The persistence of chastity as the main element of white female virtue, together with the fading attention given to white men's sexual behavior, is a reflection of the sexual double standard.[17]

One unusual case between two men further illustrates that double standard. When two white men accused each other of illicit sex with a white woman, a suit arose over who was lying rather than over the issue of sexual misconduct. In 1758, Thomas Perry, a laborer in Bertie County, posted a written "Advertisement" declaring that he had not made Martha Goodin pregnant six years earlier and that William Rice, also a laborer, was really the father of her child. Perry said he was about sixteen years old in 1752 when William Rice fetched Martha Goodin from Perry's father's house (where she may have been a servant) because William's wife was about to have a baby. On the way home with Goodin, Rice "set her & himself Down on the way," and there Perry and another (unnamed) person saw Rice "with the Remainder of the Instrument which out of many Chances the Pox had left him . . . hard at Work on the Body of the said Martha Goodin on April 29, 1752." Martha delivered her child just above nine months after that event, Perry continued, and since his own "Dealings" with Martha were "not till a Good While after that Time," the case was obvious and "Everyone may Judge who is the Real Father" of Goodin's child. The advertisement denounced Rice as "a Lyar & so not Worth Regarding the Business of." It is unclear why Perry chose the moment he did to make his announcement. The issue was no longer one of child support, because by that time Goodin's six-year-old child would have been bound out to someone else. Perry claimed that Rice, in "a mean Spirit of Revenge," tried to identify Perry as the father, perhaps raising the old issue in retaliation for a more recent grievance. At any rate, when Rice sued Perry for "Gross & Scandelous Libel," he responded to Perry's charge that Rice was a "Lyar" and not to the alleged fornication. Neither man denied his "Dealings" with Martha Goodin. The issue of unlawful sex (including Perry's claim that Rice was pox-ridden) simply provided the backdrop to Perry's more harmful charge that Rice was a "Lyar" whose business was "not Worth Regarding."[18]

Women, by contrast, remained vulnerable to rumors of licentiousness and guarded their reputations with great care, yet they seldom received satisfaction in the courtroom. Elizabeth Hacket, for example, self-described as "a pious chast & honest Virgin never known by any Man whatsoever," sued bricklayer John Nichols for slander in 1744. Hacket was being courted by "Several Young men of Good name Character & Credit" who "with great fervancy and protestations of Love & Sincerity Sollicited [her hand in] in marriage." But John Nichols, she complained, sought to deprive her of a

happy marriage with the lie that she was the "damn'd whore" of lawyer John
Hull. Hacket sued the day after the slander, but with poor results. Nichols
pleaded not guilty (whether he denied saying the words or claimed they
were true remains unclear), and the case dragged on for a year until Hacket
discontinued the suit in July 1745. Single woman Sarah White was similarly frustrated when she sued Samuel Commander in June 1755 for saying she was "a Damned Whore, and Run about the County a whoring, and
got [her] Living by whoring and are the Damnest Whore in the Government." Commander pleaded not guilty and White dropped her suit in September. Tamar Jones fared no better when she sued Joseph Ferrill in 1754
for proclaiming that "he Knew a man that fuckt her twice one Night." The
case dragged on into the next year when Jones lost the case and paid nearly
two pounds in court costs. Other slander victims maintained that even a
successful suit did not always quell persistent rumors. In June 1743, Samuel
Cook spread the word that Hannah Lowry, a single woman, was pregnant.
Arrested and brought before a justice of the peace, Lowry was examined
and found not pregnant. But she remained unwed, and in January 1749
she sued Cook for ninety-nine pounds, certain that suitors were put off by
her sullied reputation.[19]

Married women, who often sued together with their husbands, had
higher success rates. Of the thirty-two sexually maligned women in this study,
fourteen were married, fifteen were single, and three were widows. Married women typically charged that malicious utterances ruined not only
their own reputation, but their husband's as well. In July 1744, for example, Elizabeth Ward and her husband sued Edward Whorton for declaring in a loud voice that Ward "is a whore a Publick whore and . . . he
would prove it." Ward lamented that the slander "greatly Hurt and
damnified" her good name, but "more especially," she argued, Whorton's
"false feigned & Scandelous Words" angered her husband William, who
"the bed & Company of the Said Elizabeth hath refused." This formulaic
wording protected William Ward who publicly eschewed his wife until she
cleared her name, since her reputation reflected his own. Elizabeth Ward
sued for ninety-nine pounds in damages, upon which Whorton retracted
his story and paid the court costs. By clearing her name, Elizabeth Ward
had restored her husband's reputation as well.[20]

While both married and single women brought slander suits, they did so
against different kinds of defendants. Married women sued both male and
female defendants in roughly equal numbers; unwed female plaintiffs
brought slander suits only against men. Though women likely slandered unwed women as well, single women apparently found that only the weightier
words of men required that they risk the court costs in hopes of a courtroom

rebuttal. Married men, by contrast, found it worthwhile to pursue women as well as men who had slandered their wives, and the courts did sometimes award considerable damages for the harmed reputation of a wife and her vicariously slighted husband. Thomas Garrett, for example, paid eight pounds plus court costs for announcing in 1762 that he saw "the Prick of one James Mason . . . in Mary Aires's Cock" (paraphrased by the court clerk as meaning that Garrett saw Mason have "carnal Knowledge" of Mary Aires). Garrett also stated that if Mary "will not be easy, I . . . will raise a greater Scandal of some of the Family," implying that he could blackmail Mary into having sex with him. The relatively high damages suggest that David Aires suffered significant harm to his reputation. Although Mary was the subject of the slander, the case was actually one between men. While women made easy slander targets, the courts generally allotted greater value to men's speech and their reputations than to those of women.[21]

The power of slanderous words, then, depended on the status of both the speaker and the intended victim. Damage to men's reputations received greatest recompense in court, while women's words against men seldom resulted in a lawsuit. Not a single male plaintiff sued a woman for tales of fornication. Instead, women found themselves scurrying to deflect sexual insults, especially those issued by men. But in a few cases, men did find themselves refuting stories of illicit sex, even when spoken by a woman. These were tales of sex that were outside the bounds of the acceptable, even for white men unharmed by charges of fornication with white women.

"Against the Order of Nature": Of Beasts and Men

White men sued for only a few kinds of sexual slander: sex with other men, sex with animals, and sex with black women. The numbers, admittedly, are minuscule. Before 1765, male plaintiffs refuted one allegation of sodomy, four accusations of bestiality, and five charges of sex with a "Negro" or "Mulatto." But that these cases were brought at all reveals the limits of acceptable behavior for white men. Furthermore, these particular slurs about acts considered "unnatural" give a glimpse into ideas about race and interracial sex in the context of slavery.

Accusations of sex between men resonated with a density of cultural meanings rooted in the Bible and English society and law. The Bible decried "sodomy" as "abominable" and "Odious," in part because it involved "spilled" or "wasted seed." Exactly how that seed was wasted was a secondary aspect of the offense, and seventeenth-century definitions of sodomy included not only sex between men but also anal intercourse between a man and a woman, intercourse with young (premenstrual) girls, and sex with animals. The offense resided in nonprocreative sex, not in non-heterosexual sex. English law did not list sexual acts between women as part of the definition of sodomy. The emphasis on penetration and emission, both required as proof of the crime, made women's sexuality less visible, and because the concept of men as "seeders" allocated procreative powers to men, sexual acts between women were not thought to "waste" seed in that way. Although sexual relationships between women troubled some New England ministers, such acts remained nearly invisible to the colonial courts.[22]

In the second half of the seventeenth century, sodomy in England acquired particular political and cultural meanings as its allegation served to malign the English aristocracy. The older image of the aristocratic rake who had sex with both women and boys as a sign of his masculinity gave way to a new stereotype of the effeminate fop or "molly" who sought sex only with other men. The public outrage against the new "molly houses" and masturbation clubs of London incorporated an array of criticisms against an aristocracy perceived as degenerate and unduly privileged. Mollyphobia harnessed xenophobic hostility as well. Anglicans disdainful of the Roman Catholic church linked sodomy with Italians and insulted the papacy as a "second Sodom," "new Sodom," and "Sodom Fair." In London, "Italian" served as a synonym for sodomite, and eighteenth-century British moralists blamed the proliferation of sodomy on the Italian opera. By associating sexual transgressions with national and religious differences, sexual norms became a form of patriotism.[23]

The colonies prosecuted sodomy as well. This was especially true in New England where Puritans wrote new laws for themselves and grounded their statute against sodomy in biblical passages. The southern colonies simply regarded the English statute on "buggery" (the secular term for sodomy) as in force. But despite their ideological differences, colonists in both North and South viewed sodomy as a detestable vice and listed it as a capital offense together with witchcraft, theft, arson, treason, adultery, bestiality, rape, and fornication. At least four men were executed for sodomy in the British colonies in the seventeenth century: one in New Haven, two in New York, and one in Virginia. More often, however, the accused were whipped, branded, and exiled, and after the turn of the century, whites no longer received capital punishment for the crime.[24]

No trial for sodomy took place in colonial North Carolina, but one plaintiff did deny such behavior. In March 1718, John Clark, Esquire, captain of a militia company, justice of the peace, and assemblyman in Hyde County, sued brothers William and Edward Winn for slander. Clark complained that two years prior, William Winn announced in public that Clark "would have Buggered me and use[d] divers ways to seduce and perswade me to it." Winn apparently called Clark a "nasty fellow" who "used his Endeavor to Bugger me as he hath done Severall times for many months past." Clark also sued William's brother, Edward, for saying that Clark "wanted to buggar my brother and I, and often perswaded me to lett him do it." Clark not only "hath Buggared me," Edward continued, but he also "endeavored . . . Severall others (meaning young men in the Neighbourhood)" as well. These public charges, Clark declared, caused him "great Disgrace, Trouble, Shame, Scandal, Injury, Scorn, [and] hatred amongst his Neighbors" and hurt his "Trade and Commerce" with them. Besides harming Clark's reputation in the neighborhood, the allegations also brought him "into very Great and apparent Dangers of Prosecution . . . for that most Notorious abominable, Odious, Shameful, and most hated Sins of Buggery and Sodomy, whereby he may undergo the disgrace and trouble of . . . Imprisonment, Trial for his Life, and the Danger of losing all his Estate."[25]

At this distance it is hard to know what actually occurred between John Clark and the Winn brothers. William and Edward Winn may have falsely accused Clark of "buggery" in an effort to sully his reputation, perhaps in retribution for other conflicts. John Clark owned an estate in Perquimans County and held multiple government positions. The defamation may have been a way for men of lower social standing to harm the well-connected Clark in response to other social frictions. Or perhaps the accusations were not false at all, and Clark had indeed sought sexual relations with men "in the Neighbourhood," with varying degrees of success. If the charge was true, Clark may have spent the two years between the slander and the suit trying to diffuse the conflict out of court; only when the rumors persisted did Clark see the need to clear his name officially. For unknown reasons, Clark failed to appear in court in July 1718, and the defendants were discharged.[26]

What had been a xenophobic understanding of sodomy in England may have acquired racial overtones in North Carolina's slave society: a sodomized white man had apparently lost (or relinquished) mastery over his own body and hence also an important aspect of white male privilege. As discussed in the next chapter, black men were emasculated in physical and symbolic ways that legislators considered inappropriate for whites. Both demasculinized "blackness" and "female" passivity represented inappropriate uses of white men's bodies, and sodomy symbolically combined aspects of "femininity" and "blackness" in ways that blurred the distinctions between white men and black men.[27]

While fornication between men seemed sinful in part because it did not occur for the sake of procreation, people abhorred intercourse with animals precisely because they commonly believed the act could produce progeny. Many believed that men could impregnate female animals and that male animals could impregnate women, leading in both cases to the creation of deformed offspring, part human and part animal. Given the fear of producing such monsters (an event known to be impossible between two men), bestiality may have seemed more "dehumanizing" an act than sodomy. In the seventeenth century, bestiality was punished with the death penalty more often than sodomy, although the standards of evidence (proof of penetration, requirement of two witnesses) were the same for both crimes.[28]

Men no longer suffered death for bestiality in the eighteenth century, but the accusation retained its power to harm a white man's reputation. In July 1724, for example, Thomas Handcock sued Solomon Hughes, a carpenter, for saying in February to Handcock's face and in the presence of others: "You . . . are a Cow buggering Son of a bitch and I will prove it." Handcock demanded fifty pounds as recompense. What he received we do not know, but in March 1725 he declared himself "Satisfyed of the Damages" he received from Hughes and dropped the case. Similarly, Augustin Wright was "greatly Scandaliz'd" when Sarah Barnett contended in 1734 that he "did Committ Buggery" with his father's cow. Wright claimed that neighbors who "us'd to buy sell & deal" with him now "desist to meddle or to have any Commerce" with him, and "daily do more & more with draw," for which reason he "is extreamly impoverished defamed & discredited." The outcome of the case is unknown, but Barnett's accusation of bestiality was both plausible and derogatory enough to propel Wright to court to clear his name. White women (whose allegations of heterosexual fornication did not prompt men to bring a court suit) found themselves defendants when they alleged "buggery," indicating that such words had the power to wound, even when spoken by a woman.[29]

Barnett's words may not have been slander at all, but based on fact; certainly some men who sued for slander soon found themselves defendants accused of the crime. John Everet, for example, found that his preemptive slander suit did not protect him from becoming the defendant in a bestiality case. In 1762, Everet sued Thomas Garrett for saying that he saw Everet "frig a Mare," and Garrett was fined one hundred pounds plus court costs. By 1764, however, the tables had turned, and Everet stood charged with "a venereal affair" with "a Certain Black Mare." The grand jury dismissed the bill (probably on a technicality), but people may still have believed Garrett's gossip. Robert Johnston, a hatter in Salisbury, was accused in 1765 of "feloniously wickedly diabolically and against the order of Nature" engaging in "a veneral affair" with a black cow, "that detestable and abominable Crime of Buggery (not to be named among Christians) to the great displeasure of Almighty God, to the great Scandal of all human kind, against the form of the Statute in such case made." This case, like the one brought against James Patrick the same year, was dismissed by the grand juries, perhaps because bestiality was a capital offense for which no one wanted a neighbor hanged. Sometimes the charge seems more obviously invented. When David Davis announced that Shadrick Taylor "had fucked his Mare and also his Bitch," he was imputing to Taylor an indiscriminate and degraded sexuality that lowered him symbolically to the level of beasts. Davis could probably have continued his list of animals with which Taylor had purportedly copulated, in order to demean him.[30]

In the context of slavery, allegations of sex with animals may have resonated with racial meanings. For Anglo-Americans who viewed slaves as beasts of burden, as closer to nature and the animal world than to (white) culture and sensibility, white men thought to have copulated with animals may have been symbolically lowered to the level of slaves whom whites imagined as already more beast-like. Such imaginative links between bestiality and whites' ideas about race remain conjecture, at this point, but the conception of interracial sex as itself unnatural stands out more clearly. White men prosecuted only slander that implied especially heinous, "unnatural" sex, namely sex with other men, with animals, and, as we shall see, with black women. Slander suits reinforced simultaneously definitions of sexual "normalcy" and notions of racial difference. As sexual slurs became racialized, white men found that their reputations had become vulnerable to a new form of attack: rumors of sex with a black woman.[31]

Sex, Race, and White Men's Honor

White men, although unharmed by claims of fornication with white women, did, on occasion, sue against allegations of sex with a black woman. Such cases were rare, yet they suggest that white men's sexual prerogatives were mediated by racial concerns: despite the sexual double standard, some allegations of interracial sex were harmful enough to prosecute. With so few slander cases it is difficult to chart change over time, but all five of the suits in which white male plaintiffs denied interracial sex occurred after the 1739 slave uprising in Stono, South Carolina. As North Carolina's black population grew from about one thousand in 1705 to roughly six thousand in 1730 and then more than tripled to about nineteen thousand by 1755 (when African Americans comprised approximately one third of the colony's population excluding Indians), whites' concern with defining and maintaining the racial distinctions that underlay slavery grew as well. Anxiety about slave rebellions may have exacerbated whites' apprehension about interracial sex, especially since mixed-race children, free and enslaved, defied simple racial categories and challenged justifications of racial slavery. A consensus about the immorality of interracial sex was never hegemonic, however, and long-term unions persisted. (In 1755, inhabitants in several counties petitioned for repeal of a law that "free Negroes and Mulatto's Intermarrying with white women are obliged to pay taxes for their wives and families.") Nonetheless, some white women and men felt compelled to redeem their reputations with courtroom denials of interracial sex, which had acquired a tinge of degradation. Regardless of white men's actual behavior, certain sexual crossings of the color line had become at least publicly inadmissible. That fact turned tales of sex into an effective weapon against white men otherwise inured to sexual slander.[32]

In 1745, for example, Dr. Josiah Hart sued planter George Leaden for asserting that Hart "was no Doctor" because when William Burges hired Hart to "Cure his Negro Whench's Sore Eyes," the doctor "began at the wrong end." Hart had "knockt Mr Burges' Negro Whench," Leaden continued, and was "Guilty of whoredom" with her. These accusations, Hart complained, had "hurt, Blacken'd & made loose" his "Name, fame, & Credit." As a result of this deleterious "Blackening" of his reputation, Hart "lost the opportunity & advantage of advancing his fortune by Marriage, & also much of his Bussiness and his Practice." Whether or not Hart took sexual advantage of the enslaved patient, he was scandalized by the accusations of "whoredom" with a black woman and sued to clear his name.[33]

The insult was effective in part because the slave belonged to someone else: unauthorized sex with another man's slave represented a transgression of the slave owner's property rights.[34] No men brought suit against allegations of intercourse with their *own* slaves. If gossip about the sexual exploits of slave owners circulated (as is likely), it did not injure its object effectively enough to prompt a suit. Instead, such slander was made harmless by the widely shared (if unspoken) assumption that a male slave owner's control over his slaves included sexual access to them. But the allegation of unauthorized sex with another man's slave was a different matter. The rumor against Dr. Hart implicitly brought slave owner William Burges into the story as the wronged party. (Certainly the slave woman herself had no recognized right to control her body.) The doctor's business was in jeopardy not so much because his peers expressed objection to sex with a slave, but more likely because he stood accused of a trespass against another man's property.

The language in this case suggests that even more was at stake than property rights. By the eighteenth century, as we know, the accusation of "whoredom" was generally used only against women. White women labeled as whores had lost (but could regain) the honor that resided in their chaste reputations, while black women were assumed to be lascivious by nature, hence naturally whores and always without honor. When Leaden claimed Hart was "Guilty of whoredom" with a slave, he ascribed to the doctor an immorality commonly associated with white and black women. The insult implied that interracial sex was more than a transgression of property rights, it also degraded the white man involved. The woman's blackness, and not just her status as another man's property, shaped the moral implications of the act. Not only Hart's professional reputation, but also his image as an honorable (white) man, had been tarnished by the allegation, as if during physical intimacy the woman's "blackness" had rubbed off, tainting his whiteness and making him susceptible to a "whoredom" not otherwise associated with men. Conceptions of morality, race, and manhood worked together in this insult, and for Hart to regain his status as an honorable man, he had to untangle himself from the implications of a feminized, sexualized, racialized dishonor.

Leaden's slur and Hart's suit illustrate a duality in the conceptualization of race: on one hand, race had become a physical matter that inhered in the black and amoral bodies of slaves. On the other hand, blackness, like immorality (and sexual disease), could spread, staining the reputation of a person whose claim to white virtue was not guaranteed by the body alone but required performances of whiteness (in this case: abstinence from sex with blacks). Reputations could be "made loose"; virtue could come free from the white body. The case also exemplifies the close ties between black debasement and white honor. In rumors of interracial sex, white gossips marked their own racialized virtue (*they* did not have sex with a black person) while asserting black inferiority and degrading the implicated white person at the same time. Black degradation was assumed in order to show the loss of a white man's honor by intimate association. Slanderous words were reiterated in court, of course, but because they were first spoken in backrooms, taverns, and fields, they reveal some of the informal, everyday means by which whites asserted racial difference.[35]

Hart and Leaden were probably social peers, but men of lower rank could also effectively slander the well-to-do with charges of sex with a black woman. Richard Towers was a servant when he spread the news in August 1749 that he saw Samuel Overman, the eldest son of a wealthy slave-owning Quaker, "between the Thighs of Negro Hester a Negro woman belonging to Henry Dedon." (Here, too, the woman in the story belonged to another man.) Apparently unwilling or unable to claim financial loss due to the story, yet requiring evidence of damages to make the lawsuit stick, Overman employed

the formulaic language of slander-induced marital harm commonly used
by female plaintiffs. In response to the rumor, Overman said, his wife had
"altogether forsaken" his bed. That claim may have been merely a front, as
Overman did not bother to sue until the following April, and then perhaps
to harass or intimidate Towers as part of another dispute. Just as possibly,
however, the rumor may have persistently goaded Overman or his wife, leading Overman to seek its end in court. Either way, the image of Overman between the legs of another man's slave was one that Overman, at least, found
worthy of legal redress. He did not receive satisfaction, however, and in 1752
dropped the charges and paid the accrued court costs. Towers had gotten
away with a slur of interracial sex against a social superior whose reputation
proved vulnerable to such an allegation, even when spoken by a servant.[36]

The third court-recorded accusation of interracial sex against a white
man was especially blunt, and it, too, involved men of unequal rank. Henry
Horah, who owned a number of town lots and a tavern in Salisbury Town,
sued Barnaby Bower, a laborer, in 1763 for saying "[You] are a Negro Fucker.
I never fucked a negroe." While Horah enjoyed considerably more wealth
and status than Bower, the latter implied that he was superior to Horah in
other ways. Bower's words suggested that at least he had never degraded
himself as Horah had by having sex with a "Negro." Bower insinuated moral
inferiority on the part of a man whose elevated social status was supposed
to imply a higher moral standing as well. In Bower's telling, illicit sex became a moral equalizer of sorts, reducing the landowner to a commoner
who fornicated without (racial) distinction. In this case, Bower did not specify that Horah had sex with another man's slave (nor did he specify gender). The insult was more general, implying a general inclination on
Horah's part, perhaps even a regular activity, rather than a specific incident.
Horah sued to reestablish his moral standing as a man who acknowledged
racial distinctions as a proper sexual divide.[37]

While these suits do not indicate whether the plaintiff really objected to
or abstained from interracial sex, they do demonstrate that the charge was
harmful enough to provoke a lawsuit, even in an era when white men generally refrained from prosecuting for sexual slander and could brag with
impunity about having "knock't" a white woman. By the mid eighteenth
century, white men in North Carolina did not go to court to deny extramarital sex with a woman *unless she was black*. Although untold numbers of
white men had interracial sex with impunity, public allegations of such
sexual intimacy could occasionally (if rarely) result in a courtroom refutation. Stories of interracial sex could nettle established men, even if the
tale came from a man of lower status, and especially if the transgression
was tied to the infringement of another white man's property rights. The

fact that even a few white men felt compelled to refute allegations of interracial sex (whether true or false) is remarkable, given the sexual prerogatives usually accorded white men of their rank. While the infraction of another man's property rights is central in two of these three cases, the insults gained their power from the racial innuendo. Since no cases exist of white men refuting in court that they had sex with another man's white servant, it would appear that slander alleging sex with slaves stung not only because of the status of the woman involved (another man's dependent), but also because of her race. The slur was insulting in part because the alleged partner was black, suggesting that the slanderer's target had degraded himself with the act of interracial sex.

The notion that interracial sex degraded the white person involved was not new. As early as 1630 the Virginia courts ordered that one Hugh Davis be "soundly whipt before an assembly of negroes & others for abusing himself to the dishonor of God and shame of Christianity by defiling his body in lying with a negro." But evidence that ordinary whites considered interracial sex degrading is harder to come by, especially since it was a pervasive prerogative of slave owners as well as matter of choice among some lower-class people. These slander cases point to unresolved tensions in racial thinking. On the one hand (as discussed at greater length in the next chapter), coerced sex demonstrated the owner's power over his slaves and contributed to his sense of mastery. In the words of Winthrop Jordan, "the sex act itself served as ritual re-enactment of the daily pattern of social dominance." On the other hand, the fact that white men sometimes refuted insulting allegations of interracial sex suggests that they considered such liaisons beneath them. Their honor was reasserted in public claims to the contrary and in efforts to force a retraction of the offensive story.[38]

Because interracial sex could degrade a white man's honor, another effective slur asserted that a white man's sexual partner was neither entirely free nor fully white. In 1747, for example, Joseph Parsons sued William Brounin for saying that "Izbel Goldsmith was a melato . . . and a sarvent to John West" and that Parsons had "run a way with hir." Parsons sued to defend his reputation and, if Brounin's tale was true, to ward off an investigation into Izbel's status that could have brought charges against Parsons for aiding a runaway. Men also defended the white status of their female kin. John Adams Fisher of Currituck sued Spence Hall in 1767 for saying that John's wife Mary was a "damned Mullato Whore." Someone (perhaps also Spence Hall) called George Fisher (maybe Mary Fisher's son) "a Dam'd mulatto Son of a bitch & your mother was *deemed a Mullato* where she came from . . . & if your father had not a come a way he must have paid Double levys." In the mobile society of North Carolina, it was hard to keep track of newcomers and their racial status. That made it easy to question another's racial background, compelling plaintiffs to assert their white status and deny that they (or a family member) had crossed the sexual color line.[39]

With a boom in immigration at mid-century that brought Irish, Welsh, Scottish, Scots-Irish, and German settlers into the colony, ethnic slurs increased. White men sued for slights against their place of origin and ethnic identity. In 1755, for example, William Caron sued Thomas Gidings for saying Caron was "a dam Irish man and Damb the Scotch and Irish." In 1750, Isaac Ratliffe and John Edwards came to blows over Edwards's calling Ratliffe a "New England Man." Ratliffe responded with violence and eventually choked Edwards to death. Clearly, more than a simple dichotomy of white and black was operative. Ethnicity made whiteness more complicated, creating a hierarchy within the category of "white" that was contested in physical confrontations. But even as white men retaliated for slights to their ethnic background, their inclusion into the larger category of whiteness was made more clear by the exclusion of "blacks." As men fought over their honor as Irishmen and New Englanders, they assumed a shared whiteness on which that honor was ultimately based. Blacks could have no honor, but all "white" men potentially did.[40]

The presumption that honor resided partly in "whiteness" meant that unfavorable comparisons to black men could start a scuffle. In 1743, for example, a white man named James Parrum attended a social gathering where "one John Higdon was dancing with a woman which James Parrum keeps company with." The jealous Parrum said "he had a Negro that could dance better than" Higdon. Joseph McKeel heard the comment and "reprimanded the said Parrum for the comparison," suggesting it was inappropriate and insulting. McKeel's reply only irritated Parrum further, who cursed McKeel and said "a Negro he had was better or as good as" he, to which McKeel answered that "he or any man who would compare a Negro to a white man was no better than a Negro himself." At this, Parrum "fell into a great rage, and expressed himself in very base Language." When McKeel left the gathering, James Parrum and John Rickson followed him, threw him to the ground, and then beat and kicked him. Sparked by sexual rivalry between white men, racialized insults—first the comparison of a white man's dancing to that of a black man, and then a comparison of white and black men in general—escalated into a brawl. Both Parrum and McKeel knew these were fighting words; the claim that a black man was as good or better than a white man, whether as a dancer or simply in general, was both insult and challenge. Parrum was enraged by McKeel's insinuation that he was "no better than a Negro himself," and both Parrum and McKeel agreed that to be judged "beneath a Negro" offended their honor as white men. Neither man used the term *slave*. They reiterated the word *Negro* instead, which suggests that blackness, and not enslaved status, served as the insult. Linked with blackness in this insult was African-style dance, which many whites commented on as unseemly (because of strong pelvic motions) or ungraceful and wild (because of polyrhythmic movements and angular motions). In contrast to the carefully controlled motions which mid-eighteenth-century whites found graceful and genteel, the rhythmic exuberance that characterized much African American dance may have seemed to white observers linked to brute force and crude sensibilities—qualities they attributed to slaves. Because dancing was a performance of race as well as class, the insult of dancing worse than a Negro more than ridiculed the dancer's coordination or style; it challenged his performance of whiteness as well.[41]

What, more precisely, were the images of blacks that whites held in mid-eighteenth-century North Carolina? It is hard to say. We know much more about how European scholars imagined human "races" and the physical, moral, and mental attributes they ascribed to "species" of humans. Scientists laid out elaborate musings, for example, on whether Africans were really apes. But white settlers in America knew better. They had no doubts about the humanity of the people with whom they lived, worked, fought, slept, stole, and ran away. Nonetheless, as ideas about difference were reinforced through legal regulation of behavior, marriage, and (as discussed in the next chapter) physical punishments, whites distanced themselves from "blackness." As whites fought with each other over their honorable reputations, they contributed to notions of racial difference. The most harmful insults whites hurled at each other included claims of sex with black people, with animals, and with members of the same sex. These most "unnatural" sexual acts had the power to mar white reputations. They also contributed to the ideological blurring of blackness, sin, and bestiality.[42]

Racial Slander Against White Women

Though white men could be harmed by sexual slander involving black women, the racialized slurs that targeted white women were even more malignant, implying that sexually transgressive white women were more depraved than misbehaving white men. The most vicious allegations of interracial sex targeted white women in part because the double standard made illicit sex a greater offense for women than for men, but also because the mixed-race children born to white mothers increased the free black population and challenged ideas about racial difference and innate white superiority. In the context of increased anxiety over racial distinctions, the accusation of interracial sex symbolically reduced a white woman to the status of blacks, imputing to her the base sexual drives assigned to African Americans. Such a woman,

the slander implied, had engaged in cultural and racial treason: she had voluntarily lowered herself to the level of slaves and "blackened" her name.

In May 1732, for example, two Quakers exchanged bitter words involving sexual degradation. William Symons publicly accused Mary Low of being "a Negro whore" (i.e., a whore with Negro men), describing her further
as "a proud Bitch with a Pack [of] Dogs after her." Four days later, his wrath
unabated, Symons declared that Low "was a hore & Robert Davis['s] Negro could not satisfie her & [Symons] Desired her not to send for his Negro Till she had wore out the said Davis['s] Negro." Symons also announced
that Thomas Stafford (the slanderer who tormented Ann Hosey) "puled a
Negro fellow . . . out of Bed from the said Mary." Low denied the accusations, pleaded chastity, and said she was "Extreemly hurt & Damnified in
her good name." The implication that Low's sexual cravings could not be
satisfied by numbers of black men was a stunning degradation that suggested she had a sex drive as beastlike as that imputed to black men
("Dogs"), one that might even "wear out" her black partners. By her an-
tagonist's account, Low's insatiable lust made her a promiscuous, irrational
being. The stereotype of animalistic black male virility—a theme that would
resonate in later eras as well—combined with an image of white female
sexual depravity to form a nearly inhuman union.[43]

Mary Willabe's slanderer went a step further. William Clerk, a laborer,
declared "openly and publickly" in September 1755 that Willabe, an unmarried woman, was "a whore and the widow Godwins Negro-boy has kept
her Company all this Summer, and fuck't her." Not only that, Clerk continued, "My Dog . . . us'd to go this Summer to Elizabeth Vise's, and fuck
Mary Willabe and Loin her." Clerk ascribed to Willabe a raging sexuality
that led her to fornicate indiscriminately with men and animals. In the
process, Clerk equated black men's sexuality with that of beasts, making
men and dogs appear interchangeable in the accusation that Willabe had
intercourse with both.[44]

These most graphic and degrading slurs against white women described
interracial sex as not only illegal and immoral, but as unnatural as well.
Scandalous accounts linked the concept of gender difference (the idea that
chastity was crucial for women though not for men) with that of race (the
belief that blacks and whites were inherently different and properly separate) to compound the insult: if a virtuous woman was chaste, and blacks
and whites were naturally distinct, then a white woman who fornicated
with a black man had abrogated her privileged status on two counts. She
had disavowed what made her virtuous as a woman and what made her
racially superior as a white person. In slanderous tales of racialized immorality, concepts of race and gender mutually reinforced each other, each

building on the other's apparently biological essence. Interracial sex for white women, like sodomy and bestiality for white men, represented unnatural intercourse and a forfeiture of the moral superiority that presumably inhered in whiteness. Both forms of slander, albeit in gendered terms, suggested a degradation to the level of beasts at the same time that they invoked racial difference.

White women believed to have had sex with black men had shamefully abandoned their racial privilege, but they were assumed to have done so of their own volition. The burden was on the slandered woman to repudiate such charges, even in one extraordinary case when the slanderer was himself a male slave. In May 1756, a slave named Ned made sexual boasts involving Elizabeth Flimm, an unmarried white woman. To defend herself, Flimm sued for slander. She reported to a court magistrate that on the previous Saturday night Ned "Did *Attempt* to go to bed" with her and that now, "out of Spite And malice in his heart," he "Degraded and Scandelously told Lyes of one Elizabeth Flimm." For this breach of the peace Ned was arrested and brought to court to explain himself. Ned's testimony was not recorded, but his pronouncements (as Flimm recounted them) may or may not have reflected what actually happened. Flimm may have voluntarily slept with Ned and then felt dismayed by his boasts in the days that followed. To defend herself, she reduced the encounter to an "Attempt" and called Ned a liar for claiming more. On the other hand, if Ned had sex with Flimm by force, she had at least two (very different) reasons not to charge him with rape. The North Carolina courts rarely heard charges of rape brought against slaves; only two cases before 1765. Perhaps Flimm did not expect the court to indict a valuable male slave for the sake of an unwed woman's reputation. But slaves who *were* convicted of rape suffered execution. If Flimm and Ned were in fact sexual partners, she may have wanted to avoid this fate for Ned and chose instead to represent his bragging as malicious fabrication. Another possibility is that Ned did indeed invent his exploits with Flimm, and that his talk was the slanderous fiction she claimed it to be. Finally, Ned may have said nothing at all, and Flimm may have invented the whole tale to get him into trouble.[45]

The outcome of Flimm's suit is unknown, but it is significant that in 1756, such words by a slave (real or fabricated) did not mean Ned's life. Had Flimm accused Ned of rape, she could have sent him to the gallows. But at issue was consensual sex, and the white woman, Flimm, claimed to suffer from the story. In a later era, North Carolina's white male community would not have tolerated such (real or imagined) sexual bravado by a black man about even a lower-class white woman. But in the mid eighteenth century, allegations of interracial sex targeted whites rather than blacks. The use of sexual insinuation to malign and then murder African Americans would wait another century.[46]

Some slanderers doubled up on insults, accusing white women of multiple transgressions. During a financial dispute between her husband and Robert Gibbs, for example, Mary Hall told Sarah Phips in 1760 that Robert Gibbs was a rogue because he testified in a suit against Hall's husband "for a great deal of money when there was none due." When Sarah replied that Gibbs "did not look to be such a man for he seemed to be very civil and his wife too," Mary replied that Judith Gibbs "was as scandalous as him for she had a negro bastard" which, on her sea voyage from Virginia, "she threw over board." The accusation that Gibbs bore and then murdered a Negro child served as a highly charged insult, for which the Halls had to pay Robert and Judith Gibbs (who sued together) six pounds plus court costs. Mary Hall's slur merited such recompense because she had combined charges of perjury with the potent taboos of interracial sex and infanticide. In so doing, her tale implied that sex with a black man was so degrading that evidence of the liaison had to be (literally) washed away. By implication, sex with a black man was nearly as wicked as murdering one's own child. A woman degenerate enough for one misdeed, Hall insinuated, might well perform the other.[47]

Slanderous rumors and their courtroom rebuttal reinforced the notion that racial difference was as self-evident as interracial sex was unnatural. While legislators ensured that slavery would be permanent and hereditary, writing laws that defined racial categories, ordinary white people conceptualized and fought over their own ideas of race. Slanderers who implied that interracial sex was disgusting as well as illegal, and plaintiffs who heatedly disavowed having sex with a black person, reinforced the perception of "natural" racial difference. Insults among whites constituted a social practice, a commonplace exchange, that hardened racial barriers and made some sexual liaisons publicly indefensible. As ideas of African American inferiority became entrenched, even elite men could feel the sting inherent in allegations of interracial sex. Nonetheless, the slander that targeted white women employed generally more excessive and debasing images than slurs against men. Insults of interracial sex braided together assumptions about the naturalness of gender and race, conveying the message that some hierarchies were based on inherent and immutable differences.[48]

Hostile language between whites served as one powerful means of demarcating a racial divide. Even more vivid than verbal insults among whites were the markings inflicted by slave owners and the courts directly onto slaves' bodies. The next chapter explores how violence inscribed slaves' bodies with a racial status, marking them as physically, and so racially, distinct.

5

Sexualized Violence
and the Embodiment of Race

On September 29, 1729, Judith Spellman fled Joseph Stoakley's plantation in Pasquotank County on an urgent errand to the court house on Newbegun Creek. Before she could reach a court magistrate "to make her Complaint, and to seek Wayes to dispute her freedom," Stoakley overtook her and "with strong hand" forced her back to the plantation. He proceeded to "Tye up & with Cords & whips Lay on [her] Naked Body . . . Sundry Blows So that Her Body was all over Bloody, and then put Irons on Boath [her] leggs and the same Doth keep on, so that her ffett are Greviously Swollen." A few days later Spellman successfully escaped and testified before a justice of the peace that Stoakley wrongly held her as a slave. She was a free-born woman of color, an "Orphan Child," she explained, "Boarne of the Body of a Christian white woman, and so ffree to all Constructions in law without any order of Court, Indenture or other Agreement of her own or parents." To support herself, Spellman had chosen to work for Stoakley for "Some time," but now he "pretends To Hold" her as a slave and would "Not Suffer her to [go at] Large or Liberty, as of right she Ought." The General Court in Edenton requested that Stoakley appear before the bench, but before he could answer Spellman's charges of "Trespass assault Battery wounding and ffalse Imprisonment," he took ill. On December 12 he made his will, and by January 3 he had died, leaving over five hundred acres and seven slaves to his wife and children. Stoakley's will did not list Judith Spellman as a slave, but she appeared in court again in late January, this time "to Dispute her freedom" against Joseph Stoakley Jr.[1]

When Stoakley applied whips and shackles to Spellman, he did more than try to ensure her continued service: he participated, even if inadvertently, in eighteenth-century constructions of race. Brutality of the kind Stoakley inflicted was endemic to slavery. Only coercion made slaves toil to enrich their owners, and the law placed no limits on the violence slaveholders could use against their human chattel. But different rules applied to free-born servants like Judith Spellman. Though servants also suffered corporal punishment, by law masters and mistresses "shall not exceed the Bounds of moderation in correcting" their indentured or apprenticed laborers. In cases of exceptionally harsh punishment, servants could appeal to a magistrate for redress. Stoakley and Spellman disagreed over whether she was indentured to him (she thought not, though as the free black daughter of a white mother she could have been indentured until age thirty-one), but Stoakley most certainly knew she was not a slave. (His will did not list her as a slave, the courts proceeded as though she was a servant, and Judith later acquired freedom papers for her daughter Milly, whose free status hinged on that of her mother.) Stoakley's violence against Spellman exceeded the bounds of moderate "correction" for a servant; the brutality with which he prevented her from appealing to a magistrate was of the kind most commonly applied to slaves. In effect, Stoakley behaved as if Spellman's race was more important than her free status in determining what level of violence against her was acceptable.[2]

Violence shaped racial ideology in profound ways. The brutal treatment of slaves, in particular those forms of violence that left permanent traces such as brandings, whiplashes, and amputations, supported whites' growing sense that race was a physical quality, inherent to the body and visible at the same time. As statutes increasingly limited violence against whites, the restriction of lawful uses of violence against European servants, combined with the continued sanction of force against slaves, shored up whites' ideas of physical differences between them. The visible marks that corporal coercion imprinted on the bodies of slaves came to connote to whites an underlying physical difference in the victims—a nonwhiteness—that in turn served to justify the violence perpetrated against them. The point here is not that violence against African Americans increased over the course of the eighteenth century, nor that violence against European Americans ceased altogether. Rather, the divergence in legally acceptable forms of violence reinforced the idea that the bodies of African Americans were innately different and inherently "black." Violence was a social practice, another performance of race, that transformed official categories of race into a physical relationship: some people had rights to freedom from violation while others did not. The growing protection of even lower-class white bodies from violence made the marks of officially condoned brutality against blacks into an insignia of inferiority.

Much of this violence had a sexual dimension. The slave system institutionalized the sexual exploitation of enslaved women by making access to their bodies a prerogative of male slaveholders that the courts consistently ignored. (One result was a growing slave population of multiracial heritage.) But other acts of sexual violence that did not involve intercourse also reinforced social relations of slavery and ideas about race. Spellman may not have experienced rape, for example, but Stoakley's flogging of her "Naked Body" exemplified her physical and sexual vulnerability. Other forms of violence that targeted the sexual agency of the victim—the court-ordered castration of male slaves, for example—served as a sexualized marker of the victim's racial identity and slave status. It is in this sense that violence could be sexualized (and not just sexual): the brutality may not have involved sexual intercourse or have aroused sexual feelings on the part of either victim or perpetrator, but the violence nonetheless had a sexual dimension, often one that involved a person's capacity to behave in a sexual manner. The ability to engage in voluntary sexual activity, to enforce the use of another person's body in a sexual act, or to obliterate another person's sexual agency, had long been privileges of power. In the context of slavery, sexualized violence also served to mark a body as "raced"—as black or as white. As violence inscribed a racial identity onto the body, it also contributed to racialized understandings of masculinity and femininity. White manhood resided in sexual agency and sexual prerogatives that were withheld from black men (and white and black women), while white and black women (and some black men) were subjected to sexual exploitation, albeit in distinctly different ways. As sexualized violence enacted relations of power that were infused with ideas about masculinity and femininity, definitions of manhood and womanhood came to depend on race as well as on gender and social status.[3]

"Nakedness Expos'd": Sex and Violence against Slaves

Sexualized power relations took a variety of forms, and some—like nakedness—were at once more subtle and pervasive than others. While Africans, who appeared "naked" to European slave traders, had different sensibilities about how much of the body should be covered, the meaning of their physical exposure changed dramatically in the context of slavery. Stripped at the auction block, poked and prodded by buyers who examined human merchandise for strength, defects, and breeding potential, the nakedness of enslaved Africans now signaled lack of control over their bodies, their labor, and their fate. As white buyers tried to "read" black bodies for their profitability, they projected ideas about racial difference onto the physical traits they perceived. Gradations of skin color, for example, were associated with different levels of strength, intelligence, health, and the propensity to run away. Slaves' inability to prevent such readings, their chronic exposure to the gaze of others, white and black alike, indicated their lowly status. Over the eighteenth century, this exposure, which made visible slaves' vulnerability to physical and sexual exploitation, became associated with racial identity as well as social status.[4]

Slaves' nakedness acquired social meaning in connection with the long-standing English assumption that clothing reflected social rank. Sumptuary laws, first enacted in the thirteenth century, were no longer strictly in force by the eighteenth, but tailored cuts, rich colors, and soft, smooth material such as fine linen, velvet, and silk were still reserved for people of higher status. Colonial North Carolina's wealthiest inhabitants wore many layers of imported finery, donning different garments to suit the occasion. More ordinary folk, including artisans, farmers, and middling professionals, owned fewer items of clothing, mostly looser-fitting clothes made from osnaburg (a course linen), homespun wool, or rough fustian (a mixture of linen and cotton), which they wore and mended for as long as the fabric would last. Most humble of all was the attire of servants and slaves who received apparel from their master; they might have only one set of clothes and shabby ones at that. The clothes of slaves, in particular, tended to be simple and without much variation. One owner could expect his readers to know what he meant when he advertised for a runaway clad in "Negro Cottons."[5]

In contrast to slaves, servants could at least insist on a minimum of coverage and warmth. By law, masters had to provide servants with "Competent Dyet, Clothing & Lodging." White indentured servants often wore simple, course garb, but it generally sufficed to shield their bodies from probing glances, protecting their dignity with layers of clothing. When John Pearson kept the "three poor and helpless young Children" of a white woman "altogether unclothed and naked and exposed to great Hardships," she took him to court for "barbarous & inhuman Treatment." By contrast, slaves had no legal recourse when owners kept them ill-clad. An observer in North Carolina noted in 1737 that enslaved children "of both Sexes wear little or no Cloaths, except in the *Winter,* and many of the young Men and Women work stark naked in the Plantations in the hot Season, except a piece of Cloath (out of decency) to cover their Nakedness; upon which Account they are not very expensive to the Planters for their Cloathing." Slaves were kept underclad even in the winter, for one December another visitor saw "a Negroe in only his shirt bringing a horse from the fields, he shook with cold." The same chronicler also noticed "five Negroe Children every one dress'd in a Shirt Only—Clothes are not bestowed on these Animals with much profusion—," and "in Newbern I saw a boy thro' the Street with only a Jacket on, and that unbuttoned." The generally scant clothing allotted to slaves was one immediately visible emblem of their degraded status: as human chattel without any rights, they could not insist on any particular standard of physical comfort.[6]

The practice of keeping slaves ill-clad encouraged slaveholders to believe that African Americans as a group had intrinsically different physical needs and sensibilities than even lower-class whites. Although cost was a consideration (many slave owners spent only a minimum on the necessities of their human property), the exposure of poorly dressed slaves also provided a constant reminder of their vulnerability and of the power that slave owners wielded over them. Physical exposure contributed to the imaginative link in whites' minds between slaves and animals. Whites well knew that slaves were human, but the deprivation of clothing underlined the association of slaves with animals; as crude beasts of burden, both were supposed to submit mutely to physical discomfort. Exposed European American children were thought to suffer "inhuman Treatment" while African American children who shook with cold were not. To whites, the double standard in clothing reinforced the notion that African Americans could better tolerate harsh living conditions and hard labor than their European counterparts. They could, it seemed, because they already did.[7]

The near nakedness of some slaves allowed whites to believe that the emotional sensitivity of enslaved workers was blunted as well. A traveler in Virginia "frequently [saw] young negroes and negresses running about or basking in the court-yard naked as they came into the world, with well characterized marks of perfect puberty; and young negroes from sixteen to twenty years old, with not an article of clothing, but a loose shirt, descending half way down their thighs, waiting at table where were ladies, without any apparent embarrassment on one side, or the slightest attempt at concealment on the other." Believing that slaves were unfazed by their exposure to whites and to each other, white observers saw slaves' near nakedness as a sign of their unrefined sensibilities, their proximity to "nature" and hence distance from white "culture." Whites' ability to scrutinize naked black bodies and imagine them engaged in sexual acts reinforced the link in their minds between blackness and baseness. When an officer from Pennsylvania dined at a Virginia plantation he was served by boys about fourteen and fifteen years old, their "whole nakedness Expos'd." The officer insisted that "It would Surprize a person to see these d—d black boys how well they are hung." Reminiscent of slander cases that imagined the sexual prowess of black men as akin to that of beasts, this comment reveals the officer's interest in "black" sexuality. Though it was he who stared at the genitals of others, the boys subjected to his gaze were the ones presumed lacking in civilized modesty and, by extension, sexual restraint. The exposure of slaves signified to white viewers a combination of powerlessness, physical hardiness, and moral degradation that, whites believed, made them well suited for slave labor.[8]

Slaves' nakedness did more than support racist assumptions; it reinscribed relations between whites as well. The Pennsylvania officer was "surprized" that it "does not hurt the feelings of [the] fair Sex to see these young boys," but in fact the real or feigned disinterest on the part of white women played an important role in maintaining the social relations of slavery. On one hand, elite women's blasé demeanor about the exposure of enslaved boys' genitals during dinner played to the idea that slaves were so obviously inferior (and physically different) as to make their near nakedness entirely unremarkable, even to an upper-class woman of presumably tender disposition. On the other hand, white women's apparent disinterest retraced the constraints inherent in elite prescriptions of female propriety. A proper plantation mistress could, in theory, never desire a black man. Because elite women could pursue sexual relations with black men only at great risk to themselves (and their partners), they kept such desires (and relationships, if they had them) hidden. Masters, by contrast, could ogle naked slaves and know—as their wives also did—that they had the power to enact their sexual desires with impunity if they so chose. The nakedness of slaves thus conveyed multiple meanings: it served as an external sign of the physical difference and moral degradation that presumably separated blacks from even lower-class whites, it served as a reminder of the patriarchal relations between plantation masters and their wives, and it exemplified the control slave owners exerted over black bodies.[9]

Although the threat of sexual violence pervaded the master-slave relationship, written traces from the eighteenth century are sparse. Slave owners' sexual access to their human property was a prerogative that remained socially unremarkable to whites (at least stories of illicit sex with slaves were not damaging enough to provoke defensive slander suits) and legally invisible at the same time: African Americans could not testify in court against whites, and slave owners were not prosecuted for illicit sex or for having illegitimate children who, as their father's slaves, did not tap into public funds for their upkeep. The sexual exploitation of slaves by whites does, occasionally, appear in the writings of the slaveholders themselves. Virginia planter William Byrd, inclined to take advantage of women servants and slaves he encountered during his travels, kept a regular diary that offers a rare glimpse into one man's sexual activities. Byrd noted in his diary that in October 1709, while in Williamsburg, "I sent for the wench to clean my room and when I came I kissed her and felt her." Two years later, Byrd wrote that while visiting Colonel Harrison, "At night I asked a negro girl to kiss me." In December 1720 Byrd reported that he "felt the breasts of the negro girl which she resisted a little." In these encounters, Byrd elicited sexual favors that underscored his status as a white male planter. Certainly his power would have been clear to the women he felt and kissed; they risked retaliation if they rebuffed him. Perhaps in his own mind as well, Byrd's ability to engage in sexual transgressions with impunity reinforced his high-status masculine whiteness. Elite women could not do the same without forfeiting their claim to virtuous white womanhood.[10]

In addition to sexual gratification, men who had sex with women they owned could hope for economic benefits. Because the children of enslaved women inherited their mother's unfree status, slave women's reproductive capacities became a means by which slaveholders increased their property. Masters in North Carolina as elsewhere took advantage of this legal provision. In 1737, naturalist John Brickell observed that slave owners encouraged enslaved women to procreate and, if conception was slow to occur, might enforce sexual relations with different men. "It frequently happens," Brickell commented, "when these Women have no Children by the first Husband, after being a Year or two cohabiting together, the Planters oblige them to take a second, third, fourth, fifth, or more Husbands or Bedfellows; a fruitful Woman amongst them being very much valued by the Planters, and a numerous Issue esteemed the greatest Riches in this Country. The Children all go with the Mother, and are the Property of the Planter to whom she belongs." Such purposeful breeding was likely less the norm than encouragement of whatever sexual relations arose among slaves, but all owners hoped for "increase." In his will of November 17, 1749, William Houghton optimistically divvied up not only his existing slaves, but also the children not yet born of his "wenches." Hester Gerbo, a white woman whose son was indentured to Quaker Francis Tomes, complained to the court that Tomes "doth unlawfully use your Petitioners Son . . . to lye with his negro woman." Tomes may have been tolerating a voluntary liaison, but Hester Gerbo had clearly identified the economic benefit that accrued to slave owners whose slaves had children. Viewed by owners as human property, likened to animals and listed in plantation records along with cattle, pigs, and horses, many enslaved women found their sexual liaisons encouraged, if not coerced, to increase the master's holdings in slaves. Slave women's sexuality and reproductive capacity became a means of oppression that women suffered in addition to the labor exploitation endured by both enslaved women and men. As Harriet Jacobs, a fugitive slave from Edenton in the nineteenth century, expressed it: "Slavery is terrible for men; but it is far more terrible for women. Superadded to the burden common to all, *they* have wrongs, and sufferings, and mortifications peculiarly their own." Clearly, sexual exploitation haunted enslaved women's experiences of bondage.[11]

The sexual coercion of enslaved women had broad repercussions in the slave community. It affected not only the victim, but also the victim's family and friends who were unable to prevent the violation. Because male slaves and servants could not well protect female family members from sexual abuse, the effects of sexualized violence were multiply gendered, marking the female victim as an object of domination while symbolically undermining the manhood of the woman's male kin. Sexual violence showcased enslaved men's inability to protect their wives, mothers, sisters, and daughters from sexual abuse and to prevent the master's prurient intervention into their family relationships.[12]

The sexual prerogatives of masters also affected their own wives. Forced to countenance illicit liaisons between the men in their family and slave women, some mistresses vented their anger and frustration by brutalizing slaves. While many a husband may have looked on (or the other way), William Byrd engaged in a power struggle with his wife, Lucy, over her tendency to lash out at slaves. In July 1710, William Byrd wrote in his diary that Lucy "against my will caused little Jenny to be burned with a hot iron, for which I quarreled with her." On New Year's eve, 1711, "My wife and I had a terrible quarrel about whipping Eugene while Mr. Mumford was there but she had a mind to show her authority before company but I would not suffer it, which she took very ill." On March 2, 1712, Byrd again "had a terrible quarrel with my wife concerning Jenny that I took away from her when she was beating her with the tongs. She lifted up her hands to strike me but forbore to do it. She gave me abundance of bad words and endeavored to strangle herself, but I believe in jest only. However after acting a mad woman a long time she was passive again." The power to punish slaves became a source of conflict between these slave-owning spouses. In his efforts to monopolize the punishments of Jenny and Eugene, Byrd also exerted control over his wife, who chafed at the restrictions and wanted badly to "show her authority" over the slaves, perhaps to compensate for her relative lack of social and sexual power vis-à-vis her husband.[13]

Whippings and mutilations were meant for a black audience as well as a white one. In some cases slaves were forced to witness and even participate in the torture of others. In 1743, for example, Doctor Matthew Hardy tied a "Negro girle" named Lucy to a ladder, ordered several slaves to whip her, made Lucy's mother bring straw, then set fire to Lucy and roasted her. On Hardy's order another slave "drew [Lucy] through the fire" so that she was "very much burned." She died some days later. In this cruel display, Hardy demonstrated his own power and his slaves' lack of power by forcing the mother and friends of Lucy to torture her with lethal violence. Hardy made himself into a master of ceremonies in this pageant of brutality in which he, like his forced accomplices, were both actors and spectators. His graphic assertion of control revealed a combined need and hatred for the slave community he owned. His orchestration of his slaves' anguish implicitly acknowledged his dependence on them: his mastery turned not only on his ability to kill Lucy but on his power to force others to watch and even to participate in her death. Perhaps Hardy knew that his ability to brutalize his slaves did not, however, give him real authority in their eyes. A tyrant and a sadist, he could force actions but not emotions from his human property. The inner world of the slaves on whom his mastery depended remained ultimately outside of Hardy's control, and that fact may have fueled the rage that led to his exhibition of brute force. While evidence of slaves' responses is hard to come by, they likely judged their assailants by their own standards of morality. Another slave once recalled how two white men "beat and mangled me in a shameful manner, leaving me near dead." The abuse was not only awful, it was also immoral. The sadistic practices of slave owners and overseers may have contributed to racial ideas for blacks as well as whites, albeit in distinct ways. While some white colonists viewed black bodies as appropriate targets of violence, African Americans saw whites as cruel oppressors, sadistic and self-deluded at the same time.[14]

A similar rift in perception accompanied whippings, which for some assailants induced or resulted from a sexual desire that was likely absent for the victim. Some owners and overseers experienced sexual pleasure in the act of whipping, mingling voyeurism with a lust for blood in the floggings of naked or scantily clad slaves. It is perhaps not coincidental that flagellation became widespread in the pornographic fantasies of eighteenth-century Europe; Europeans may have found their sexual imaginations stimulated by the conditions of slavery in the American colonies. Certainly images of voluptuous, bare-breasted African women, bound and stretched in defenseless anticipation of assault, presented a sexualized image of an exotic and violable body that titillated some viewers. Whippings merged sexual and racial meanings in another way as well. The sexual desire of white men for slave women implicitly acknowledged a shared humanity, and sexual liaisons might undermine whites' notions of racial difference. But

Flagellation of a Female Samboe Slave.

Figure 16. Titled "Flagellation of a female Samboe Slave," this etching from Surinam depicts the punishment of a woman in ways some viewers may have found erotic. This image suggests that African men were made to inflict the whipping. Courtesy of the John Ford Bell Library, University of Minnesota.

the brutal floggings of slaves reasserted the racial hierarchy, upholding racial divisions even as elite men exploited the porous sexual boundaries between themselves and enslaved women.[15]

"Exceeding the Bounds": Violence against White Servants

In contrast to the unregulated flogging of slaves, the legal regulation of the punishment of servants underscored whites' perception that African Americans and Europeans had inherently different physical sensibilities. The statutory limits placed on the "correction" of servants did not halt excessive violence against them, but it did mean that masters had to be more circumspect in their application of force or risk a fine. The ability to summon courtroom protection against excessive violence was a privilege of free status, but it was also increasingly connected with the idea that some bodies were inherently more valuable than others. Defining some kinds of violence against servants as transgressive implied that white bodies were inappropriate targets of certain types of abuse.

Servants could sue masters for corporal punishment that overstepped the legally acceptable yet unclearly defined "Bounds of moderation." In January 20, 1732, for example, Mathilda Sherriff complained that her master, Dr. George Allen, had treated her "barbarously." The magistrates placed her in overnight protection with the court marshal in Edenton but returned her to Allen's household when he posted a fifty-pound bond that he would not "Exceed the bound of moderation in correcting her." When Sherriff appealed to the court again the following July, the justices agreed that Dr. Allen had so "barbarously" abused his servant that Sherriff should be sold "at a Publick Vendue to the highest Bidder" for the remainder of her indenture. (Allen received the money from the sale of Sherriff's remaining time of indenture minus the court costs.) By curtailing one master's "excessive" use of force against a white servant, the court upheld the image of indentured servitude as an orderly and legitimate labor system.[16]

When masters did inflict unlawful degrees of violence, they tried to keep the marks concealed. On March 20, 1735, after a prolonged period of suffering, a white servant named Judith died in the household of Reverend John Garzia. Uncertainty as to the cause of Judith's death led to a court investigation three years later. It is not clear who initiated the suit, or why, but four men and two women came forward to testify. One Richard Rigby reported that a year before Judith's death he attended a wedding on the Garzia plantation and noticed Judith's bruised arm. When Rigby asked about the bruise, Judith "reply'd that her master had lick't her, & shew'd a bruise from her elbow to her shoulder & down her shoulder as far as [he] would see." Ann Collier, the wife of a local sawyer, recounted that Judith had shown her the "bruises on her thigh and arms" which Judith said "her master had given her with the Mill Stick." Mrs. Jane McWilliams, who often did wash at the Garzia household, said that although Judith was "good temper'd & never refused . . . to obey her master & mistress's orders," she showed McWilliams "severall bruises on her arms thighs & back at Several times" that Judith said her master had inflicted with a stick. Judith also told McWilliams that the Garzias would not let her "paddle to town for fear she would complain when they used her ill," and she begged McWilliams "not to let her Master know that she had shew'd her bruises to her, for said she, her Master would kill her if He should come to hear of it." Three or four weeks prior to her death, Judith showed McWilliams the injuries on her "Groin & small of her Back" and expressed the fear that the "bruises given her by her master would be the cause of her death." McWilliams noticed that Judith "could not walk upright by reason of such bruises but that she would often cry bitterly as she went along." Despite the abuse taking place in the Garzia household, no one acted to help Judith. Jane McWilliams admitted that she "did not know how to go about discovering this affair" to the authorities. Richard Rigby said that he once "heard the Cry of murder" coming from the Garzia plantation and "believes it was Judith's voice," but it is not clear that he told anyone else about it at the time. No one challenged the power of the master over his servant.[17]

The situation went from bad to worse, yet no one halted the violence. When Judith first took ill, she was placed on a bed in the hall until she recovered, but when she became sick again, she was "turn'd to the Kitchin and laid on a coarse rug." Jane McWilliams was at the Garzia household the last two nights of Judith's life, during which time Judith asked for nothing and was offered nothing; she was "senceless." On the night that Judith died, McWilliams took a candle and went upstairs with one of the Garzia daughters to see the corpse, but she "did not see any marks of violence upon her because she was not stript." Perhaps in an effort to see the body for herself, McWilliams asked Mrs. Garzia if Judith's body would be stripped and wrapped in linen for the burial, but Mary Garzia responded that she could not afford linen, and that Judith would be buried the way she was. McWilliams felt certain that Judith died of the beatings and that Mary Garzia's claim that Judith died of "the pox" only hid the real cause of the servant's death. Ann Collier heard the same thing but testified that she "never saw any Sores about her, nor heard Judith complain that she had the pox." Those who had known Judith and seen her bruises remained unconvinced that venereal disease had killed her.

Before Judith's death, as well, the Garzias tried to conceal the violence. John Garzia beat Judith often, but not in the company of outsiders, nor in ways that would be readily visible. The minister thrashed Judith with some self-control, aiming his blows towards parts of her body—her "groin," "lower back," and down her shoulders—that would not show when she was dressed, and he avoided her face and hands where bruises would be conspicuous. His careful aim suggests an effort to avoid detection. Although Garzia's reasons for inflicting frequent and vicious beatings on Judith remain unknown, his violence may have been entangled with sexuality. Mary Garzia's efforts to conceal the violence and her insinuation that Judith's death resulted from her own lascivious behavior may have been motivated not only by a concern about the legal repercussions of Judith's death, but also by discomfort about the violent relationship between her husband and the abused servant woman. But whatever the motives behind the secret beatings, Judith was at pains to reveal her wounds. Perhaps hoping for help, Judith undressed partially so Richard Rigsby could see down her shoulder, and perhaps completely so Jane McWilliams could examine the bruises on her groin and lower back. By unveiling these marks of brutality, Judith refused to aid in the literal cover-up of her abuse. Her death eventually elicited a response from the white community, although the three-year delay is hard to explain. Perhaps the investigation served as a way to harass the unpopular minister. Or maybe it took that long for one of the deponents to decide to bring a suit. At any rate, in March 1738 John Garzia was charged with inflicting on Judith "Several mortal bruises and wounds," but in the following court session, for reasons the documents do not explain, the jury acquitted him. The decision may have rested on a technicality, a frequent end to criminal suits brought against established white men.[18]

The corporal punishment of servants, commonplace in England and its colonies, became more complicated in the context of racial slavery. "Appropriate" levels of violence were reassessed, since excessive punishment of white bodies blurred the distinctions between indentured servants and slaves. When Garzia treated Judith as a slave, that is, in a way that would have been legal had she been a slave, he exceeded the "Bounds of moderation" precisely because he transgressed the bounds of race and ignored the privilege of whiteness (which included not being abused to death). But while Garzia overstepped the racialized boundary of violence, his abuse of Judith did not render her "black." Rather, his violence against a white servant remained legally unacceptable, and the transgressive nature of the beatings therefore reinscribed her whiteness. The law allowed or prohibited brutality, depending on the victim, and thereby distinguished not only who was free and slave, but also who was white, and therefore "properly" exempt from certain kinds of abuse. The ability to seek redress for certain levels of violence (even after death, in Judith's case) was increasingly a privilege of whiteness as well as of free status. Perhaps Garzia understood this. The inappropriate nature of his mistreatment of a white servant in a slave society may have prompted him to flog Judith in ways that would remain invisible as long as she was dressed. Garzia's efforts at secrecy contrasted starkly with Joseph Stoakley's attacks on Judith Spellman just a few years prior. Whereas Garzia struck his white servant only where the bruises would not show, Stoakley did not try to hide his brutal treatment of Spellman. He kept her altogether "Naked," beat her until she was "all over Bloody," and shackled her in irons. Both Garzia and Stoakley inflicted violence on free servant women, but the secrecy and openness, respectively, with which they did so suggests that they viewed the racial identity of their servant as more important than her free status in determining whether such violence was publicly acceptable. What could be openly done to one free woman had to be inflicted secretly on another; the deciding factor was race.

Tarring bodies, like the flogging of servants, was another custom that acquired new meaning in the context of racial slavery. As early as the twelfth century, English sailors had inflicted and endured tarrings and featherings as a form of public humiliation (because tar looked like excrement) and punishment. Tarring appeared only sporadically in the seventeenth and eighteenth centuries, although it sometimes targeted English women. (In England in 1722, for example, a woman was tarred and then hanged and burned for murdering her husband.) Colonial women could also suffer the disgrace, as one did for prostitution and another for disguising herself as a seaman. In North Carolina, too, women's sexual transgressions might bring on molten retribution. On July 8, 1734, a white woman named Mary Reed was attacked by two white men, Thomas Jones and John Robinson, and a mulatto man named Winslow. The three men beat her and stole clothes and shoes from her house. The next day, with the aid of Sarah, John Robinson's wife, the assailants threw Mary Reed "on the Ground and Spread her Leggs abroad & took burning Tarr and threw it on her Private parts and all about her Limbs and Body & Violently beat and abused her." Reed's complaint does not indicate the motive for the attack, but the exposure and tarring of Reed's "Private parts" suggests her assailants believed her guilty of sexual misconduct. Perhaps Reed was accused of lewd conduct with an African American man, and Winslow's involvement in the assault was not incidental. The humiliation of having her sexual organs exposed and burned was probably exacerbated by the fact that an African-American man took part in the exercise.[19]

The racial implications of this assault were twofold. For an African American man to look at the blackened genitals of a white woman was to invert the gaze of racial privilege, namely white men's intrepid stare at exposed black bodies (and elite women's averted eyes), both of which represented key performances of "whiteness." In the context of slavery, a white woman's name (and body) could be symbolically blackened in ways that undermined ideas about natural racial difference, making her claims to an inherent whiteness less fixed, more precarious. Reed was forced into a momentary abrogation of her racial privilege as apart from and above African Americans. (Indeed, the punishment may have been meant to demonstrate that she had done just that by engaging in inappropriate and perhaps interracial sex.) On the other hand, however, because such violence remained illegal and transgressive, it reinscribed Reed's status as white. We do not know the outcome of her complaint, but that she could bring a suit and hope for redress reasserted her racial privilege. Violence, like slander, was a transgression that could reinscribe the whiteness it seemed to undo.

Tarring was a weapon available to women as well. In 1747, Hannah Luton suspected her husband, a lawyer named Thomas, had sex with Sarah Ricket, a single white woman who was probably a servant for Jane and Joseph Champion. In her husband's absence, Hannah Luton choreographed a gruesome inquisition. She tied Ricket to a stair post and then, under the pretense of being ill, summoned to her house three women who became witnesses and jurors in the trial that followed. With Jane Champion, Sarah Howcott, and Deborah Thompson assembled, Luton untied Ricket and questioned her "concerning her being carnally familiar with [her] husband." When Ricket denied any such intimacy Luton had her rebound "tho' the Said Sarah begged on her knees not to be tyed again for she would tell her the whole truth without it." Luton "Order[ed] a knife to be brought, & Swore She would cut her" with it. Faced with these threats, Ricket confessed that "Thomas Luten had laid with her three nights." Hannah Luton "gave Sarah some stripes with a horse whip" and "Called for a Skillet of Tar," saying that "She was Galled" and that "she must anoint the bitch." Deborah Thompson watched Luton "with one hand hold up the tail of the Coat of the Said Sarah and with the other hand apply the Mop of Tar under the Cloaths of the Said Sarah to her naked body." Sarah Howcott also described how Luton applied the tar to Ricket's head, "legs, and Thighs." None of the witnesses apparently demurred at the scene or attempted to intervene—perhaps one of them fetched the skillet of tar. Not content with the tarring and whipping, the next day Luton marched with her husband to Jane and Joseph Champion's house to see Sarah Ricket again. In a belated effort to prevent Ricket's incriminating confession, Thomas Luton greeted her with a raised

switch saying "don't belye me for if you do I'le give you a whipping."
Hannah Luton asked Ricket if it was "not true that he came to bed to you."
Caught between a whipping from Thomas Luton and more violence from
his wife, the unhappy Ricket replied "no it was not true," sending Hannah
Luton into a fit of rage. She lunged to strike Ricket with a stick but when
Joseph Champion caught the weapon she grabbed Ricket's ear and "Caused
blood to flow therefrom and likewise Said to her if she did not Soon re-
move out of the place She would be her butcher, or be the Death of her."[20]

Ricket's ordeal reveals a community of women engaged in a drama of
revenge. Hannah Luton staged a semipublic ritual of punishment, creating a spectacle of the servant woman's torture and debasement. The fact
that Luton did so in the presence of other women, but not in the presence
of men, suggests the limits of her power: her "courtroom" of inquisition
and torture could only be a partial one. But it also suggests that when women
could not bring a case of sexual misconduct to court (as wives could not
against philandering husbands) they could enact an unofficial trial amongst
themselves. Hannah Luton could not directly punish her husband for
sexual infidelity, but she could summon her neighbors to participate in
the interrogation and torture of the servant woman. As witnesses, judges,
and even executioners in this "case," Luton and her cohorts took into their
own hands the "trial" and punishment of the servant. The physical vulnerability and relative powerlessness that both Ricket and Luton experienced vis-à-vis Thomas Luton did not bind the two women together,
mediated as their positions were by class and marital status. Both experienced the vulnerabilities of their gender and social position very differently.
Ricket posed a threat to Hannah Luton, appearing as a sexual competitor
and challenging Luton's efforts to control the goings-on in her household.
Luton could not stop her husband's infidelity, but by burning Ricket's genitalia, she symbolically (if not actually) put Ricket in her sexual place: the
tarring reminded her and all onlookers that no sex the servant woman
had could be legitimate, and it rendered her sexually unavailable to Thomas
Luton and any other man. Luton punished Ricket in ways meant to destroy (or at least impede) Ricket's ability to have sex in the future. As in
the tarring of Mary Reed, Hannah Luton's attack on Ricket's genitalia sur-
passed legally acceptable forms of punishment of whites. In targeting
Ricket's sexual organs, Luton mistreated Ricket in ways that would have
been acceptable had she been a slave. But because the violence was illegal,
Luton's actions actually reinforced Ricket's status as white.

Increasingly, legislators sought to constrain the kinds of violence that
whites could inflict on one another. After 1741, a servant in North Carolina
who laid "violent hands on his or her Master or Mistress or Overseer" could

receive no more than twenty-one lashes, and a penal offense resulted in a maximum of thirty-nine stripes. Servants could avoid these punishments by paying a fine. Significantly, the 1741 statute also stipulated that masters "shall not, at any Time, give immoderate Correction, neither shall [they] at any Time whip a Christian servant *naked,* without an Order from the Justice of the Peace." Statutes regarding the treatment of servants reflected the concern that the bodies of whites not be exposed, whipped, and degraded in the way that black bodies were. Over time, the laws defined more explicitly the limits of acceptable violence against servants. Slaves, by contrast, remained at the mercy of their masters, who could torture them until they died. This contrast in lawfully condoned levels of violence was enacted in gruesome ways that shaped whites' ideas about race.[21]

"Malicious Maiming and Wounding":
The Racial Divergence of Punishment

Statutes detailing the punishment of slaves were written to control unwilling laborers, yet the violence these laws endorsed did more than repress rebellion: they created slaves as a different, degraded category of worker. As slaves continued to resist their owners, legislators wrote increasingly severe laws that allowed—even demanded—that whites employ force (which could include death) in chastising rebels and capturing runaways. In 1715, the North Carolina assembly created a pass system requiring written certificates of permission for slaves found off their owner's land and a special allowance for carrying a gun. Owners could be fined for allowing their slaves to travel without a pass, whites were paid to apprehend such slaves, and magistrates could order punishment of the slave as they saw fit before returning the renegade property to his or her owner. Slaves who had been "outliers" for more than two months, living as best they could off the land and with surreptitious help from other slaves, could be killed; the owners were reimbursed for their loss. With the growth of the slave population and especially in response to the 1739 Stono Rebellion in South Carolina, anxious assemblymen in North Carolina elaborated on the slave law. Twenty-two of the fifty-eight articles in the 1741 code dealt with runaways, ordering twenty lashes for a slave carrying an unauthorized gun and execution for those conspiring to rebel. The law aimed to reduce the possibility of an armed uprising or the ability of slaves to hold out in furtive freedom in places like the Great Dismal Swamp that stretched from Norfolk, Virginia, nearly to Edenton, North Carolina. But these statutes, devised as rational and expedient measures to control bondspeople, contained symbolic messages as well.

Especially as certain punishments no longer applied to whites or were inflicted only in exceptional circumstances to mark extreme degradation, the corporal punishments of slaves came to connote more than enslaved status: the violence left marks that signaled racial debasement.[22]

African Americans understood the degradation that whipping scars represented. In August 1766, just a month after one man had finally purchased his freedom, he was threatened in Savannah with a whipping for fighting with another man's slave. "I dreaded, of all things," Olaudah Equiano later wrote, "the thoughts of being striped, as I never in my life had the marks of any violence of that kind. At that instant a rage seized my soul." Marks of violence, Equiano and others knew, made permanently visible a moment of subjugation at the hands of a white person (even, of course, when whites forced African American slaves or overseers to do the whipping). It was a mark that could never be erased, becoming a part of the life story a body told. But such marks revealed different histories to different readers. As slave buyers looked at scars to gauge a slave's character and determine docility, so slaves could read scars as evidence of resistance and courage that had resulted in punishment. Scars also reflected on the perpetrator in ways read differently by whites and blacks. While slave owners viewed crisscrossing lashmarks as a signature of mastery, written directly onto the bound bodies of their human property, slaves saw open welts and raised scar tissue as evidence of the callousness of whites. To the victims of violence, corporal traces of sadism did not reflect on black character so much as on the assailant's own, contributing to African American understandings of racial difference. Equiano, for example, expressed contempt for those who would whip him as well as a keen understanding of disempowerment, preferring to "die like a free man, than suffer myself to be scourged by the hands of ruffians, and my blood drawn like a slave."[23]

The gradual reservation of certain markings for African Americans pertained especially to brandmarks seared directly onto the skin. In March 1752, for example, Samuel Johnston placed an advertisement in the *North Carolina Gazette* for a runaway named Frank, a "sensible Negro" who was branded on the buttock with the letter "P." In November 1753, William Brothers identified a twenty-eight-year-old runaway named Ruth "by a Burn upon one of her Breasts." The Society for the Propagation of the Gospel marked their human property by branding the letters "S-O-C-I-E-T-Y" onto the chests of their newly purchased slave women and men. Some men believed their branding techniques took the slave's gender into account. William Bosman, a Dutch slaver, described how French, English, and Dutch traders applied a red-hot iron with their company's mark to the breast of every African captive, but "we yet take all possible care that they are not burned too hard, especially the women, who are more tender than the men." Whether done with "care" or not, brandings crudely marked slaves' bodies as property, creating "a kind of hieroglyphics of the flesh" that told of their subjugation. Using a technique of identification commonly applied to livestock, owners forced slaves to advertise their own degraded status as human chattel.[24]

Brandmarks and whipping scars competed with the "country marks" or ritual scarification that often adorned the bodies of African-born slaves. In the 1750s, as many as two thirds of the slaves in North Carolina were born in Africa, and perhaps a third of the slave population was African-born in the following decade. Whites heard an array of African and pidgin-creole languages, they witnessed unfamiliar dances, funeral rites, and celebrations, and they noticed that Africans decorated their bodies with sometimes elaborate designs. Jack, for example, who fled with his wife and two friends in 1769, had "country marks on his face," purposeful cuts that scarred, creating a pattern that marked him as a member of a certain tribe. All four runaways were "outlandish" (recently arrived) Africans. In August 1774, a "new Negro fellow" named Quamino escaped. He was about thirty years old, "has a Scar above his right eye, his Teeth are filed, and is marked with his Country marks." By the following April, Quamino had not been recaptured, despite the fact that he fled wearing "a Collar about his Neck with two Prongs, marked G P, and an Iron on each leg." Quamino's "scar" may have been like the "weal" that distinguished the forehead of some African elders, and his teeth were filed as a mark of beauty. When Europeans encountered Africans with country marks, they may have sought to overwrite this evidence of tribal identification and ethnic pride with their own proof of purchase. Lashes symbolically erased a particular African past, replacing it with crude and generic marks of degradation. Unable to make sense of the meaning of distinctive country marks, whites disfigured them with new marks that they, the white viewers, associated not only with servility, but also with an ahistorical, perpetual, uprooted "blackness."[25]

Like slave owners, colonial courts also participated in the marking of bodies. The North Carolina laws did not mandate specific punishments for convicted slaves and instead provided for "Special Courts" to convene when slaves were accused of "any Crime or Offence whatsoever." With a simple majority of its three justices and at least three or four (usually slave owning) freeholders, the court could "pass Judgment for life or Member or any other Corporal Punishment" of the convicted slave. Should a slave be "publickly executed to the Terror of other Slaves," the owner would receive compensation from local taxes. Although slaves could bring their testimony before the special court, they received neither legal counsel nor a jury. The special court acted rapidly, and the trial, conviction, and punishment usually occurred on the same day.[26]

Slave tribunals favored the severing of ears, a visible mark that did not impede a slave's ability to work, and many convicted slaves suffered that particular amputation. In 1745, for example, a slave named Chance admitted (perhaps with a mixture of pride and terror) that he struck his master, for which he received a hundred lashes at the public whipping post and lost an ear. In March 1754, a slave named Judeth was arrested for "Attempting to have Killed Judeth Boyce . . . with an ax on Sunday." The court ordered that Judeth have "her Right Ear Nailed to the Whiping post and to Stand Ten minutes and then to have the Said Ear Cut [off] and then to have forty Lashes well Laid on her Bare Back." For stealing "Two Pockett Books and Papers and . . . some ribbons and a pen knife" in 1764, both Bob and Simon received 150 lashes (spread out over three days), and Simon had both his ears nailed to the whipping post and hacked off. In 1766, Charles Jordan sought reimbursement for runaway Sesor, a nineteen-year-old with "both his years Cropt" who was apprehended and hanged. For the years between 1715 and 1785, we know the court-ordered punishments of fifty-four slaves in North Carolina. Of these fifty-four, twenty were flogged and eighteen others lost one or both ears in addition to being whipped. Whipping scars, brandmarks, and amputated ears served to punish acts of resistance and to terrorize other slaves, but they also became labels that forever advertised the slave's low social status and the concurrent lack of control over his or her body.[27]

In significant contrast to the treatment of slaves, eighteenth-century courts rarely ordered brandmarks or amputations for convicted European Americans. Previously, some colonial statutes had called for the branding of servants: in 1622, for example, a Virginia law provided that incorrigible servants be burned in the tongue with a red-hot iron. In 1643 Virginia legislators mandated that for a second runaway attempt servants be branded with an "R" on the cheek or shoulder. By the early eighteenth century, however, the law books no longer specified branding as a penalty for indentured Europeans. The only exception to the rule appears to have been a South Carolina statute in 1735 that imposed a fine of five hundred pounds on whites who aided slave runaways. Whites who could not pay the fine were whipped and branded instead. In this unusual case, a white person who undermined the property rights of slaveholders was symbolically reduced to the level of the slave they tried to help. Interacting with slaves in subversive ways merited the visual association with slavery that a brandmark invoked. In North Carolina, magistrates inflicted only a small number of brandings on whites, and these were mostly in lieu of capital punishment.

Between 1670 and 1776, the higher courts sentenced twelve whites to brandmarks in the hand (usually on the thumb) for theft or manslaughter, and at least one such sentence was remitted. Court-ordered amputations for whites also fell out of favor. Samuel Pricklove lost an ear at the pillory for theft in 1680, and Stephen Manwaring had an ear severed in 1698 for counterfeiting money, but after 1700 few if any whites suffered amputation as a court-ordered penalty.[28]

Precisely because courts ordered amputations mostly for convicted slaves, the loss of an ear, long the mark of a criminal, was now also associated with the extreme degradation of enslavement. In 1726, Thomas Spires, a planter and deputy marshal, sued William Daniel (a tavernkeeper) for saying Spires was a "Rogue" and if he tried to serve a writ in Bertie County, Daniel would "cutt of[f] his Ears." Daniel, who the month before had been humiliated when Spires and Francis Pugh assaulted him and clapped him in jail for twelve hours, retaliated verbally by threatening to treat Spires in a way reserved for slaves. Daniel's boast promised to inflict an indignity increasingly associated with blackness, and Spires dropped his suit only when Daniel countersued for assault and won five pounds in damages. In 1736, doctor John Stuart sought to ensure that no one would see his lopped ear as a sign of a criminal past. Lest people "should imagin" that Stuart lost the ear due to some "fellonious Act," he had two magistrates attest in writing that Stuart had a "difference and being engaged with a Gentleman" lost his ear in the process. Transforming the amputated ear from a sign of degradation to one of high status (dueling was the recourse of elite men), Stuart tried to make the missing ear into a badge of honor.[29]

The disinclination to brand or mutilate European Americans was the result of a number of different impulses that came together in the eighteenth century. After the Great Awakening, a move away from orthodox Calvinist ideas about human depravity and the inevitability of suffering meant that physical pain—once viewed as an opportunity to test one's religious fervor—now seemed unnecessary and even abhorrent. Within the bourgeoisie, a new "culture of sensibility" celebrated the expression of finer feelings and deplored the spectacle of public torture. Reformers advocated regulation and moderation of corporal punishment, which dove-tailed with a shift in the expression of state power: traditional forms of public punishment were replaced by privatized penalties and by a "fixed and graduated scale of more lenient but more certain punishments." Courts in Europe and its colonies increasingly preferred the imposition of fines or extended terms of service over violent punishments in public spaces, and legislators wrote laws in an effort to curtail interpersonal violence. In North Carolina, lawmakers sought to hinder whites from mutilating one another in ways that seemed excessive. In response to fights that humiliated by leaving a mark or lopping off a facial feature, legislators wrote an act in 1754 "to Prevent Malicious Maiming and Wounding," making it a felony to "cut out, or disable the Tongue, put out an Eye, slit the Nose, bite or cut off a Nose or Lip, bite or cut off or disable, any Limb or Member of any Subject of his Majesty." The disfiguring of bodies, while acceptable when it involved human chattel, was no longer appropriate for free subjects of the crown.[30]

While some bodies received legal protection from violent treatment, others did not. Brandings, whippings, and amputations were diminished or discontinued altogether as lawful penalties for whites, but these punishments continued to mark the bodies of slaves. This divergence in the corporal treatment of European Americans and African Americans became part of what made bodies identifiable as white or black. The distinction between those bodies that should remain free of permanent markings and those that could be seared and amputated was becoming a distinction of "race": what could be done to a particular person was both a result and a symbol of their body's racial status. The fact that the bodies of slaves *could* be branded, amputated, and kept naked (even when many individuals were not) reinforced whites' notion that slaves had a physically "different" body, and that this "natural difference" justified further violence. "Blackness" itself came to mean the very violability of a black person's body, whether or not it was actually so marked.

In stark contrast to legislative efforts to ease bodily harm done to whites and to protect their corporal autonomy, lawmakers prescribed dismemberment for slaves. In 1758, during the costly Seven Years' War, North Carolina lawmakers sought to reduce the "many great Charges" incurred when masters received the customary compensation from tax funds for executed slaves. (As John Brickell explained in 1737, "When any of these *Negroes* are put to death by the Laws of the Country, the Planters suffer little or nothing by it, for the Province is obliged to pay the full value they judge them worth to the Owner." This prevented "the Planters being ruined by the loss of their Slaves, whom they have purchased at so dear a rate.") As a replacement for the death penalty, North Carolina lawmakers institutionalized the castration of male slaves convicted for the first time of a criminal offence (except for murder or rape, which still received capital punishment). Jailers received twenty shillings to perform the deed, and masters received up to sixty pounds if the slave did not survive the amputation. Between 1759 and the law's repeal in 1764, the courts ordered the castration of at least sixteen men, at least two of whom died from the mutilation. Some examples of castration as a punishment preceded the law. In 1755 a slave named Tom broke into a white man's house and stole rice, for which he had "both his Stones Cut out." Tom died from the "Opparation," and his owner received seventy pounds as compensation. The legislature reasserted the death penalty in place of castration in 1764, mostly because the fiscal crisis due to the Seven Years' War had passed, and perhaps also because owners preferred compensation for executed slaves over the abiding bitterness of castrated workers. But castration remained a humiliation that was associated with the punishment of slaves, and especially with the ritual of their execution. In 1764, for example, a slave named Isaac was first castrated and then hanged for house burning.[31]

Castration as a punishment contributed to the sexualization of mastery. It linked sexuality and masculinity, purposefully annihilating in slaves the sexual agency that whites asserted as part of their manhood. By emasculating enslaved men, slave owners and courts made literal the (social) impotence of enslaved men, destroying the victims' sexual agency and ability to have children, even as white men continued to impregnate enslaved women. White men's sexual self-determination contrasted with (and perhaps, on some psychological level, offset) their dependence on black labor. Only black men, purchased and prized for strength and stamina, suffered lawfully mandated castration, and amputated slaves (whose mutilation did not, when they survived it, impede their productivity) seemed all the more different, "lacking," and—ultimately—black. As masculinity was racially defined, so was race defined in sexual terms.[32]

Yet the "neuterings" by which slave men were punished and presumably tamed were done not because the perpetrators believed slaves were animals, but precisely because they knew of their victims' humanity. No animals were *punished* with castration and branding, and such standard acts of animal husbandry, when applied to defiant slaves, implicitly acknowledged the difference between beasts and men, forcing recognition of the humanity of slaves even as it was degraded. Castration marked black men as "different" precisely because whites understood that they were, fundamentally, not very different at all. The dialectic between a recognition and then symbolic denial of slaves' humanity was deeply intrinsic to the process of debasement that fueled racism.[33]

Rape, Race, and Retaliation

The rape of a white woman was a capital crime, but the diverging outcomes of cases involving white and black defendants contributed in powerful ways to the sense that sexual crimes meant different things, depending on the race of the accused man. The process by which white and black men were brought to trial, the evidence required for a successful suit, and the conviction rates and court-ordered punishments differed markedly, depending on the race of the defendant. Of fourteen complaints of rape or attempted rape made against white men in colonial North Carolina, seven became criminal actions, two of these came to trial, and neither defendant was found guilty. By contrast, all twelve enslaved men accused of rape in the colony were convicted and executed for the crime. The racial adjudication of rape charges contributed to the strong sense that the social meaning of a sexual transgression hinged on the race of those involved.

In general, juries were reluctant to indict white defendants. When Mary Haughton, a married woman, charged mariner Christopher Buttler with rape in 1721, her complaint was dismissed. Haughton's accusation could have failed for a number of reasons. Only certain kinds of evidence sufficed to show that a rape, and not consensual sex, had occurred. Lacking witnesses of the assault, a woman had to demonstrate she had resisted to the best of her ability by crying out for help. She had to report the incident quickly to someone and show signs of a struggle (bruises or torn and dirty clothing). Furthermore, she had to be of a "reputable" character, someone considered above reproach for unchaste behavior or "licentious carriage," since it was not clear to juries why a woman who had previously volunteered for illicit sex had not simply done so again with the defendant. The need to assert irreproachable purity made it especially difficult for single women to prove that a rape, and not voluntary illicit sex, had occurred, since their behavior was easily suspect. Jurors tended to sympathize more with married women (whose husbands they considered vicariously injured) and with girls at or near the age of consent (ten years). Elizabeth Hassell, "about the age of fifteen," fit into neither category in 1728 when she charged David Oliver with rape. The sparse documentation provides no further detail, but perhaps Hassell waited too long to report the incident or could not prove her resistance. Or maybe she did not have supporters who could testify to her good character.[34]

Another hindrance to the successful prosecution of white men for rape lay in the penalty: convictions brought the death sentence. The evidence is only circumstantial (namely that no white man received the death penalty for rape in the colony), yet it appears that jurors and magistrates were unwilling to put white men to death for sexual crimes. This was part of a general secularization of sexual misconduct in the eighteenth century, manifested in the preference for fines over capital punishment and in an emphasis on crime rather than sin. (By contrast, theft, murder, treason, and counterfeiting could still lead to the noose.) In one of the colony's rare trials for rape involving a white defendant, planter Joseph Pye of Bladen

County was acquitted in 1736 for the rape of Mary Brady, an eleven-year-old. Some twenty years later, in 1757, Robert Boyd and Henry Howard, planters, and William Hurst, "Gentleman," each gave one hundred pounds recognizance to appear at the Supreme Court to answer charges of rape brought by widow Leah Davis, but the paper trail ends there. Clearly, white women did not succeed in the courts when they accused white men of rape.[35]

Three accusations of attempted rape failed in court as well, even though an attempted crime was actionable in English common law and convictions would not mean the death penalty. In the first of these, in May 1733, Robert Kingham, a tavernkeeper in Edenton, tried to coerce Elizabeth Montgomery, a "child" of unspecified age. Kingham and a servant named Ambrose had come to Montgomery's house to get passage across a creek, and Elizabeth's mother had bid her go with the men and paddle the canoe back. On the way across, Kingham "talkt very rudely" to Montgomery, saying "she should be his Housekeeper." He "Sayed he would Lye with her," and when she refused, he "threatnd he would force her & went about to heave her overboard if she would not Comply." Ambrose told Kingham to stop, saying "it was a Shame to use any young Child so." Nonetheless, when the canoe reached the shore, Kingham "tooke violent hold of her & attempted by force to [haul] her out of the Canoe & Sayed he would lay her down on the bank and lye with her whether She would or no." Montgomery resisted and Ambrose told Kingham to let her go. The frightened girl returned home safely, but when she told her mother about the incident she "Cryed & Seemed in great fear and dread about it." The next day she refused to go into town because she was "afrayed" of Kingham. Upon the complaints of the mother and daughter, Kingham was apprehended and gave one hundred pounds security to appear at the next General Court, but there the case was apparently dropped. Other cases of attempted rape were simply ignored. In 1746, Mrs. Ann Carter charged planters James Pritchard and James Ruffin with an attempted rape, but as late as April 1749, the sheriff had not yet arrested Pritchard for the charge, and no punishment for Pritchard or Ruffin appears in the records. Samuel McCleneham was tried for the attempted rape of Jemima Phillips in 1775, but again there is no record that he was convicted or punished.[36]

Perhaps because criminal charges of rape had a low rate of success, six plaintiffs brought civil cases instead. Four were brought by husbands and two by fathers of the women in question. John Campell, for example, complained that in August 1759, Robert Lenox "Ravished, compressed Debauched and Carnally knew" John's wife, Mary, "whereby the said John lost and was deprived of the Comfort and Society of his Wife." John valued the damage at five thousand pounds. Lenox pleaded not guilty, but in

1762 the jury found for the plaintiff and ordered a payment to Campbell of 1,333 pounds, six shillings, and eight pence, plus court costs. Lenox appealed, but the judgment was affirmed. Civil suits for rape may have been more successful because a conviction did not mean the death penalty and because juries agreed that a man of good standing suffered measurable harm as the head of his household when his female relatives were sexually exploited and dishonored.[37]

Men understood that the rape of another man's wife was also an attack on the husband. In 1739, an argument between William Odanell and one Fardengle escalated into violence against Fardengle's wife. Demanding rum, Odanell began beating Fardengle in the yard until Fardengle's wife came out of the house and asked Odanell "what he beat here husband fore and tuck a stick" to threaten Odanell. Odanell forced Mrs. Fardengle into the house. An eyewitness "heard a racket" and saw Odanell reappear with a "goun" (gown?) and "sware that he had fuckt fardengle's wife." Whether a rape occurred is unknown, but the claim was meant to insult and humiliate Mr. Fardengle.[38]

Some fathers brought suit on behalf of their daughters. In 1757, John Turner claimed Benjamin Miller, "Gentleman," assaulted and impregnated Turner's seventeen-year-old "Daughter and Servant," Ellinor. By claiming Ellinor as his servant, Turner could assess the economic harm to himself as the loss of her labor for nine months, but he also included in the two hundred pounds damages the "Scandal [and] Infamy" done to Turner and his family. Miller appeared in court, but the outcome is unknown. Other cases of "ravishment" clearly differed from the "rape" that was defined as a violent act imposed on an unwilling woman. In one case, the father's claim of "ravishment" came only after his daughter had unsuccessfully prosecuted a suitor for failing to fulfill his promise of marriage. In May 1762, Mary Leary (under the age of twenty-one) sued planter John Hall for one hundred pounds in damages for reneging on his last year's marriage proposal. Her suit made no mention of pregnancy, but in May 1763 her father took action, suing Hall for "ravishing" his daughter and making her pregnant. The loss of her labor due to pregnancy for "six months and upward" he placed at one hundred pounds. Thomas Leary's complaint used the same formulaic language of assault cases, claiming that Hall with "force & arms" made assault upon Mary, but because the courts knew of Mary's failed courtship and assumed she voluntarily engaged in what she thought was premarital sex, Leary requested one hundred pounds in damages and not more.[39]

On the whole, white women faced an uphill battle when they charged white men with rape. No white North Carolinian was put to death for the crime, and whites were seldom punished in other ways. By contrast, rape charges had different results when they targeted slaves. In such cases, even single women's words carried much weight, and the plaintiff did not face stringent requirements regarding evidence of resistance or even, necessarily, "good character." Clearly, their honor as women was of relative value, depending in part on the race of the man they accused. Slaves faced charges of rape more often than whites and their trials had starkly different outcomes. Although African Americans made up about one third of the population in the second half of the eighteenth century, more black than white defendants appeared in court on criminal charges (namely twelve slaves, compared with seven white men). The guilt or innocence of the accused is impossible to know, as "confessions" were often extracted under torture, but in contrast to the white men charged, each of the black defendants was quickly convicted and sentenced to death.[40]

Although most rape charges against slaves were brought in the 1760s and 1770s, two earlier cases show what could happen to the accused. On July 15, 1740, sixteen-year-old Mary Busby testified that Harry, a slave belonging to John Turner in Edgecombe County, did "commit a Rape on her Body." Harry, "being asked whither he Lay with the said Mary Declared he Did." The court ordered the county sheriff to bring Harry "immediately . . . to the next convenient Tree and cause him to be hung up by the neck untill he be Dead." In 1743, a slave named Phill was charged with raping Mrs. Sarah Baucom. Phill, upon "being Examined," confessed to the act and was hanged. In addition to this standard execution, the court ordered that after his death "his private parts [be] Cut off & thrown in his face." The postmortem castration of Phill added physical and symbolic retaliation for a crime the court perceived as especially heinous when committed by a black man upon a white woman. Because rape represented a trespass against a man's property and also the disintegration of his mastery as head of a household, the (real or imagined) rape of a white woman by a black man represented an inversion of the patriarchal order of racial slavery. Throwing Phill's genitals in his face symbolically annulled his act of sexual violence with sexualized violence against him.[41]

By the 1760s, various forms of torture and dismemberment had become rituals in the executions of male slaves accused of raping white women. In 1766, for example, a slave named Cato, convicted of raping Elizabeth Hallaw, was ordered "fastened to a Stake" at noon one Monday and "there burnt until he be dead." In 1770, George, convicted of raping Jane Ryncky, was hanged and then had his head "Severed from his Body and Stuck up at the Forks of the Road." In April 1775, Jem pleaded not guilty to raping Sarah Langly but he was convicted and hanged that afternoon, then his

*Figure 17. The Chowan County Courthouse, begun in 1767 and overlooking Edenton
Bay, was designed to convey sturdy serenity and judicious balance. Its brick structure likely
held different meanings for lower-class men and women brought before the magistrates.
Courtesy of the North Carolina Division of Archives and History.*

head was cut off and "Placed on a Pole 16 feet High." In September 1775,
Ben pleaded not guilty to the charge of raping Christianna Atwater, but
because she "positively swore" that "he actually did by violence commit a
Rape on [her] Body," the court unanimously found Ben guilty. The following Saturday Ben was hanged, his head was "Severed from his Body" and
"put upon a pole" at the fork of Neuse and Trent roads, "and afterwards
his Body [was] Burn't."[42]

More than a hundred slaves were executed by the authorities in North
Carolina between 1748 and 1772, and more than fifty after 1764. One gets
the impression that in the 1760s, especially, the public display of mutilated
and rotting corpses had become a rather common sight, contributing to the
horror of those who knew the victims and to the complacent prejudice of
those who saw them as less than fully human. In England, the "lower sort"
had long been terrorized by the spiked display of convicts' severed heads,
but this practice ceased for whites in eighteenth-century North Carolina.
Death by hanging remained the standard form of capital punishment for
white felons, but in no instance did a white man suffer court-ordered cas-

tration or death by burning or have his head stuck on a pole as a warning to his friends. Furthermore, by the 1760s and 1770s, the death penalty was reserved mostly for slaves and for those considered enemies of the state, such as the Regulators, whose movement in the backcountry for fair taxation created the largest armed rebellion in the colonies prior to the American Revolution. The crackdown of eastern merchants and politicians on the farmers' efforts to regulate taxation and the debtors' courts resulted in a battle in Hillsboro in 1771 and the public trial and hanging of seven of the movement's leaders. Perhaps the images of hanging men, black and white, were linked in the minds of those who saw the Regulators as base criminals, giving added meaning to rural rebellion within the context of slavery.[43]

Overall, however, slaves were singled out for the most atrocious displays of power, and their dismembered and charred bodies and impaled heads signaled their "difference" from whites. The sight of mutilated, scorched, decaying bodies led some white viewers to distance themselves emotionally from the victims, confirming their perception of blacks as degraded and different, as sometimes *appropriately* mangled. This display of white power and black difference occurred routinely in response to the alleged rape of a white woman, making the sexual intimacy of white women and black men into a powerful symbol of racial transgression. Just as black women could be flogged to reassert racial difference in the face of white men's desires for them, so were black men castrated for having (purportedly) asserted their own manhood by dominating the bodies of white women. The diverging treatment of white and black men, seen most starkly in charges of the rape of a white woman, shored up the notion that sexual dominance was the purview of white men only, making sex between black men and white women into a terrible test of the color line.

Despite the gruesome punishments meted out to slaves, whites' participation in racist practices was not monolithic. There was no sudden or absolute switch from mutual cooperation in matters of theft, running away, or sex to an alienation so deep that it hindered cooperative, pleasant, even loving interracial interaction. It is true that slanderers used allegations of interracial sex to dishonor whites, implying that whites who had black partners were more degraded than other white fornicators. Nonetheless, interracial liaisons, some of them voluntary, persisted. Martha Hodes found that in nineteenth-century North Carolina the social and legal treatment of such unions hinged on the status and reputation of the white person involved. In other words, race relations remained unfixed, negotiable, and dependent on the specific context, even as ideas about racial difference were gradually reformulated into scientific terms of biological essence. Whites did not all become suddenly, equally, or unequivocally racist.[44]

In the last decades of the eighteenth century, increasing numbers of re-formers in Europe and America defended the humanity of slaves. Essays in the French *Encyclopédie* of 1765 decared that Negroes could not be di-vested of their natural right to enjoy freedom. In 1774, John Wesley, the English founder of Methodism, chastised Europeans involved in the slave trade. As tensions mounted between England and its colonies, some Ameri-can patriots commented on the irony of agitating for freedom while hold-ing human chattel. The Philadelphia physician Benjamin Rush, for example, found it "useless for us to denounce the servitude to which the Parliament of Great Britain wishes to reduce us, while we continue to keep our fellow creatures in slavery just because their color is different from ours." In North Carolina, chief justice Martin Howard deplored the legal distinction between killing a white person and killing a slave, and in 1771 he lectured a grand jury that "all men are by nature equal and by nature free," and that "the souls and bodies of negroes are the same quality with ours." In 1774, the killing of a slave was redefined as murder. Throughout the 1760s and 1770s, university students in England and the colonies de-bated the legality and morality of slavery.[45]

But discussions of slaves' humanity found counterbalance in the idea that blacks were indeed physically different from whites. The development of racial distinctions made possible the (admittedly uncomfortable) coexis-tence of Enlightenment rhetoric of liberty with the ongoing torture of slaves. The scientific racism that sought to "prove" African inferiority developed in conjunction with (and perhaps in response to) Enlightenment ideas of equality, and it helped Enlightenment thinkers like Thomas Jefferson tol-erate the slavery they deplored on principle. The perception of African Americans as physically different—as biologically "raced"—came to the aid of European Americans who considered themselves reasonable, en-lightened, and humane, but who continued to enslave and brutalize blacks, or at the very least, wanted to avoid conflict with those who did so. Only the belief in innate inferiority could placate slaveholders who otherwise held to a rhetoric of human equality.[46]

Repeated practices, such as the violent marking and dismemberment of slaves, contributed to ideas of black inferiority and racial difference. Some-where within the body, it seemed, was the racial essence that brutality made plain. Bodies opened up—cut, dismembered, and displayed—appeared now to reveal racial selves, perversely confirming the suspicion that they had already been somehow deformed and different. As the body in gen-eral became increasingly subject to scientific scrutiny and taxonomies of difference, it seemed less fluid and alterable than it had before, and race, too, as an aspect of the body, appeared increasingly corporeal. In fact, racial thinking would continue to be remarkably malleable, shifting according to expediency and making exceptions at every turn. But "race" itself, thought now to reside in the body, seemed as real as flesh and blood. Ordinary whites participated in myriad social acts that made this idea commonplace. Not all did so, and certainly not all at once, but observers and participants in the brutalization of slaves must have been in some way altered by the violent performances of white privilege that wrote blackness onto the bodies of persons, making their disempowered status into a sign of racial difference.

Scottish traveler Janet Schaw, who eventually visited North Carolina, provides an example of how this ideological process worked. Self-described as a "lady of quality," Schaw was shocked when she first saw the scarred backs of whipped slaves in the West Indies in 1774. But she soon made peace with the sight, choosing to believe that Africans' "Natures seem made to bear it, . . . whose sufferings are not attended with shame or pain beyond the present moment." Schaw winced when she first imagined the painful whippings, but the lack of shame and emotional pain she projected onto the slaves became part of the mark of their difference: the slaves' "shameless" exhibition of their scars somehow proved to Schaw that Africans experienced pain differently. In a twist of logic, the brandmarks and whiplashes that whites inflicted on blacks allowed the perpetrators to believe that blacks could tolerate such pain more easily than they, and that Africans' supposed insensitivity toward physical and emotional pain (such as separation from family members) made them better suited for grueling physical labor. Schaw defined the experience of pain "proper" as a capacity reserved for whites. In her construction, slaves' experience of pain was of limited duration, a brief physical sensation without deeper emotional impact or meaning. For Schaw, physical markings pointed to innate physical characteristics that in turn enabled her to make peace with the cruelty and exploitation inherent in slavery.[47]

The broad spectrum of violence used against slaves, which ranged from the withholding of sufficient clothing to whipping, branding, rape, castration, and execution, reinforced this kind of racialist thought. The courts' tolerance of, and participation in, the brutalizing of slaves, together with the legal prohibitions against this kind of treatment for European Americans, formed a critical part of the larger system of racial distinction that marked slave society. But even without court sanction, as in the case of Joseph Stoakley's abuse of Judith Spellman, European Americans who brutalized African Americans did so in the growing conviction that blacks were innately and permanently distinct and inferior to themselves. As skin color and other phenotypic qualities failed to provide reliable markers of "race," whites inscribed difference directly onto the bodies of slaves. Evincing circular logic, the violence that whites inflicted on blacks seemed to prove that scarred, branded, and amputated bodies were appropriate targets of such abuse. John Brickell demonstrated this logic perfectly when he commented on the punishment of slaves: "I have frequently seen them whipt to that degree, that large pieces of their Skin have been hanging down their Backs; yet I never observed one of them shed a Tear, which plainly shews them to be a People of very harsh and stubborn Dispositions."[48]

Deeply implicated in the social practices of slavery were sexualized forms of violence. In their intimate lives, people expressed and experienced the power relations that inhered in slavery. Sexual agency and sexual privilege became both indication and effect of one's place in the hierarchy of the household and in the larger social order. Sexualized violence had long served as an indicator of status; now it outlined boundaries of race as well. Persons who could be flogged naked without end, raped with impunity, and legally castrated were defined as members of a different, lower race. Those so treated, no doubt, had their own ideas about the inherent qualities of their tormentors. Perhaps acts of brutality were so drastic and desperate because no violence could eradicate the shared humanity of all involved. Violence reasserted claims to a fundamental difference, even as sexual liaisons belied racial boundaries.

Epilogue: Dangerous Liaisons

In 1799, the well-known Philadelphia physician Benjamin Rush published his "Observations intended to favor a supposition that the Black Color (as it is called) of the Negroes is derived from the LEPROSY." The doctor marshaled his arguments: leprosy causes the skin of afflicted whites to turn black; both the breath of lepers and the bodies of Africans smell like mortified limbs; leprosy induces an "insensibility in the nerves" fully apparent in the ability of Negroes to endure pain much better than whites; lepers, like Negroes, show "strong venereal desires"; leprosy causes big lips, flat noses, and (perhaps) also "woolly" hair. To the objection that leprosy was contagious but that "no infectious quality exists in the skin of the negro," Rush countered with an anecdote from North Carolina. "A white woman in North Carolina," he claimed, "not only acquired a dark color, but several of the features of a negro, by marrying and living with a black husband." A "similar change in the color and features" of a white woman had occurred in Pennsylvania, "and from a similar cause." In both cases, Rush added, "the women bore children by their black husbands." In his description, white women acquired the "features of a negro" as one would a contagious disease; living in intimacy with a black husband could bring on the deformation. Sex and pregnancy may have hastened the transition, changing women's bodies from the inside out. In fact, Rush was unclear about the relationship between cohabitation, sexual intimacy, and the acquisition of "negro" features. Had cohabitation alone brought on the

change? Or did sex and procreation prompt the staining of skin and warp-
ing of lineaments?[1]

Precise answers to questions regarding the constitution and transference
of racial "features" proved elusive. The conceptual link between sex and
race had been in place at least as long as marriage laws defined and pa-
trolled racial boundaries—over a century by the time Rush published his
tract—yet just how the process of "mixing" occurred (not only in the second generation but now also, apparently, in the first), was still a matter of
debate. Thirty years before, Rush had denounced the practice of keeping
"our fellow creatures in slavery just because their color is different from
ours," but the question remained unanswered: was color only skin deep?
If so, and if a person's race was alterable within a single lifetime, as Rush's
example from North Carolina suggests, how could whites be sure of their
whiteness and of the superiority it supposedly entailed? Rush himself dismissed the belief in white superiority as based on "ignorance and inhu-
manity." Indeed, "if the color of the negroes be the effect of a disease,"
then the only appropriate responses were compassion and medical efforts
to extirpate the malady (Rush suggested "bleeding, purging, or abstinence,"
as well as chemical bleaches). For now, whites should avoid contact with
infectious blacks, but eventually, Rush maintained, curing Negroes of their
blackness would prove beneficial. The blanching of dark skin would destroy
one of the main arguments for slavery, it would please Negroes who only
"appear to be satisfied with their color" but in fact prefer white complexions, and it would prove that all humans descended from Adam and Eve,
thus supporting "Christian revelation" and the "universal benevolence" it
promoted. Rush held clear convictions on the benefits of homogeneous
whiteness, but his comments could not sweep away uncertainties over the
composition of "race" and just how it was acquired, altered, or maintained.[2]

What "race" meant was determined only partly by statutes, medical tracts,
and the writings of educated men. It acquired the status of reality not so
much on paper as in social exchanges that often belied the neat racial divisions created by law. Statutes could specify how many generations it took
for blood to be cleansed of polluting influences, but the law was applied
inconsistently, and other concerns could take priority over racial categories.
For example, Jeremiah and Henry Bunch in Bertie County, North Carolina,
themselves descendants of free black slaveholders (since at least 1725),
were taxed as "free male Molattors" in 1764, as whites the following year,
and again as "free Molatoes" in 1766. In 1800, Henry Bunch headed a
household that included his wife and two children, one white servant
woman, and three slaves. By the racial logic of a slave society, African American men were not supposed to have authority over white women or over

slaves, but in the Bunch family, they did. For members of property-owning free black families, social and even racial status fluctuated, depending on the specifics of local circumstances: social and economic relations with neighbors, the value of one's land, the inclination of the tax collector—all of these conditions and more could amend if not rewrite racial labels. Race attained meanings—multiple, fluctuating, and contradictory meanings—in the interactions of people whose behavior made it seem real.[3]

Most women and men did not engage in scientific debates over human origins or taxonomies of racial difference, but in their everyday relations with each other, ordinary people participated in changing ideas about race. White women and their cuckolded husbands, backcountry traders and their Cherokee wives, runaway servants, promiscuous masters and angry mistresses, free black families, and enslaved African Americans all took part in the daily contests over power and order, race and status. Native Americans and African Americans struggled against tightening restrictions and racist violence, keeping as much control as possible over intimate relationships, family ties, cultural expressions, and labor arrangements. Native Americans began to develop a shared "Indian" identity that coexisted with tribal affiliations, while African Americans created Creole cultures that preserved aspects of African ethnicities within a newly configured black racial identity. While racial definitions of "self" and "other" remained complicated, people of different backgrounds increasingly understood "race" to be a matter of inherent physical difference. Whatever the assumption—that Indians were savage, Africans beastlike, or whites sadistic—,what had been understood as the result of religious or cultural differences had, in the eighteenth century, acquired the status of an inherited trait. This trend was most pronounced among Anglo-Americans who viewed the black body itself as vile. Benjamin Rush opposed slavery, but he also objected to "blackness." Yet race as a concept remained malleable and unevenly applied; not all people of color appeared equally "nonwhite." At the turn of the nineteenth century, Thomas Jefferson still imagined the eventual assimilation of Indians into American society, albeit with a mutation on their part, a blanching process, an absorption into whiteness. Race would be reinvented over and over again, but an important shift in racial thinking had transpired: by the end of the eighteenth century, race was insistently about the body.[4]

Sexual relations played an important role in this transition. As race came to reside in the body, sexual acts acquired racial significance as well. Acts of physical intimacy, together with the legal retribution or informal license that gave them social meaning, conveyed strong messages about bodily difference. Even as sexual liaisons bespoke the shared humanity of those involved, they occurred within personalized relations of power—those of colonialism, slavery, gender, and class—that ascribed racial traits in different and unequal measure. In illicit encounters, voluntary or coerced, in the changing balance of power in intercultural unions, in conversations about transgressive behavior, in acts of violence and in efforts to resist coercion, women and men defined, defied, and reasserted boundaries of race. As a result, unlawful sexual exchanges had repercussions as political as they were personal. These suspect relations contributed to the idea of race as a fixed reality, even as that sense of permanence required continual rearticulation in the social and sexual practices of everyday life.

Notes

Introduction

1. For the insight that racial ideology cannot simply be handed down but must be "constantly created and verified in social life," see Barbara Jeanne Fields, "Slavery, Race and Ideology in the United States of America," *New Left Review* 181 (May/June 1990): 95–118; Colette Guillaumin, "The Idea of Race and Its Elevation to Autonomous Scientific and Legal Status" (1980), reprinted in Colette Guillaumin, *Racism, Sexism, Power, and Ideology* (London: Routledge, 1995).

2. Europeans had for centuries represented Africans and Native Americans as savages, noble or otherwise. See Winthrop D. Jordan, *White over Black: American Attitudes toward the Negro, 1550–1812* (Chapel Hill: University of North Carolina Press, 1968); Margaret T. Hodgen, *Early Anthropology in the Sixteenth and Seventeenth Centuries* (Philadelphia: University of Pennsylvania Press, 1964). But these earlier descriptions of physical difference were, in the words of one historian, "not yet racist in the nineteenth-century sense of the term because they were not based on an explicit doctrine of genetic or biological inequality." George M. Fredrickson, *White Supremacy: A Comparative Study in American and South African History* (New York: Oxford University Press, 1981), 7. On fears that Europeans in America would "go native," see Bernard Sheehan, *Savagism and Civility: Indians and Englishmen in Colonial Virginia* (Cambridge: Cambridge University Press, 1980), 63; Alden T. Vaughan, "From White Man to Redskin: Changing Anglo-American Perceptions of the American Indian," *American Historical Review* 87, no. 4 (October 1982): 917–53, especially 953, n. 97; David D. Smits, "'Abominable Mixture': Toward the Repudiation of Anglo-Indian Intermarriage in Seventeenth-Century Virginia," *Virginia Magazine of History and Biography* 95, no. 2 (April 1987): 157–92.

3. This paragraph properly pertains only to northern Europeans, since Spain had already developed forms of biological racism by the sixteenth century—ideas that did not take hold in Britain and northern Europe until the eighteenth century. See Jorge Cañizares Esguerra, "New World, New Stars: Patriotic Astrology and the Invention of Indian and Creole Bodies in Colonial Spanish America, 1600–1650," *American Historical Review* 104, no. 1 (February 1999): 33–68; Verena Stolcke, "Invaded Women: Gender, Race, and Class in the Formation of Colonial

Society," in *Women, "Race," and Writing in the Early Modern Period,* ed. Margo Hendricks and Patricia Parker (London: Routledge, 1994), 272–86.

4. On Sir William Petty, see Loren Goldner, "Race and the Enlightenment: From Anti-Semitism to White Supremacy, 1492–1676," *Race Traitor* 7 (winter/spring 1997): 32–49. On Bernier, see Jordan, *White over Black,* 217–18. David Hume, *Of National Characters,* is cited in Emmanuel Chukwudi Eze, ed., *Race and the Enlightenment: A Reader* (Cambridge, Mass.: Blackwell, 1997), 33. On the introduction of the word *biology* into scientific discourse, see Nancy Leys Stepan, *The Idea of Race in Science: Great Britain, 1800–1960* (Hamden, Conn.: Archon Books, 1982), 5. The Bible posited one human family, but the story of Noah served to justify racial slavery. See William McKee Evans, "From the Land of Canaan to the Land of Guinea: The Strange Odyssey of the 'Sons of Ham,'" *American Historical Review* 85, no. 1 (February 1980): 15–43; Benjamin Braude, "The Sons of Noah and the Construction of Ethnic and Geographical Identities in the Medieval and Early Modern Periods," *William and Mary Quarterly,* 3d ser., 54, no. 1 (January 1997): 103–42.

5. As nicely exemplified in the forum on "Constructing Race" in the *William and Mary Quarterly,* 3d ser., 54, no. 1 (January 1997), colonial historians use a variety of theoretical frameworks and linguistic terms to come to grips with what some do, and others do not, call racism. See also Hannah Arendt, who distinguishes eighteenth-century "race-thinking" from the racism that she says arose in conjunction with nineteenth-century imperialism. Hannah Arendt, *Origins of Totalitarianism,* 2d ed. (New York: World Publishing, 1969), chap. 6. Similarly, Kwame Anthony Appiah uses the term *racialism* to avoid the anachronistic projection of current-day conceptions of race and racism onto the past. Appiah, "Race," in *Critical Terms for Literary Study,* ed. Frank Lentricchia and Thomas McLaughlin (Chicago: University of Chicago Press, 1990), 274–87.

6. On the history of the idea that women were inside-out versions of men, see Thomas Laqueur, *Making Sex: Body and Gender from the Greeks to Freud* (Cambridge, Mass.: Harvard University Press, 1990); Anthony Fletcher, *Gender, Sex, and Subordination in England, 1500–1800* (New Haven, Conn.: Yale University Press, 1995), chap. 2; Tim Hitchcock, *English Sexualities, 1700–1800* (New York: St. Martin's Press, 1997). For European accounts of male genitalia descending in unsuspecting women, see Ann Rosalind Jones and Peter Stallybrass, "Fetishizing Gender: Constructing the Hermaphrodite in Renaissance Europe," in *Body Guards: The Cultural Politics of Gender Ambiguity,* ed. Julia Epstein and Kristina Straub (London: Routledge, 1991), 80–111. See also Randolph Trumbach, "London's Sapphists: From Three Sexes to Four Genders in the Making of Modern Culture," in ibid., 112–166. For an example of shifting gender identity in Virginia, see Kathleen M. Brown, "'Changed . . . Into the Fashion of a Man': The Politics of Sexual Difference in a Seventeenth-Century Anglo-American Settlement," in *The Devil's Lane: Sex and Race in the Early South,* ed. Catherine Clinton and Michele Gillespie (New York: Oxford University Press, 1997), 39–56; Mary Beth Norton, "Communal Definitions of Gendered Identity in Seventeenth-Century English America," in *Through a Glass Darkly: Reflections on Personal Identity in Early America,* ed. Ronald Hoffman, Mechal Sobel, and Fredrika Teute (Chapel Hill: University of North Carolina Press, 1997), 40–66. Other historians question the extent to which the medical and scientific espousal of a "one sex model" gained credence in popular culture. Lyndal Roper argues that early modern English culture "rested on a very deep apprehension of sexual difference as an organizing principle of culture," even if medical literature described gender as fluid and nonbinary. See Lyndal Roper, *Oedipus and the Devil: Witchcraft, Sexuality, and Religion in Early Modern Europe* (London: Routledge, 1994), 16. See also Laura Gowing, *Domestic Dangers: Women, Words, and Sex in Early Modern London* (New York: Oxford University Press, 1996), 6–7.

7. For an overview of the expansive literature on "bawdy" women in early modern England, see Fletcher, *Gender, Sex, and Subordination,* chaps. 1–5.

8. On the shift from a one-sex to a two-sex model, see Laqueur, *Making Sex,* and Fletcher, *Gender, Sex, and Subordination.*

9. On ideas about race in the eighteenth century, see David Brion Davis, *The Problem of Slavery in Western Culture* (Ithaca, N.Y.: Cornell University Press, 1966), chap. 15; Jordan,

White over Black, chap. 6; Peter Fryer, *Staying Power: The History of Black People in Britain* (London: Pluto Press, 1984), chap. 7; Thomas Gossett, *Race: The History of an Idea in America* (Dallas, Texas: Southern Methodist University Press, 1963), chap. 3; Audrey Smedley, *Race in North America: Origin and Evolution of a Worldview* (Boulder: Westview Press, 1993), chap. 7–8; Ivan Hannaford, *Race: The History of an Idea in the West* (Baltimore, Md.: Johns Hopkins University Press, 1997), chap. 7. Much of the work on eighteenth-century sexuality focuses on England (London in particular). Henry Abelove, for example, argues that as a consequence of industrial work regimes, sex in eighteenth-century England was redefined to mean only heterosexual and reproductive intercourse, while a wide range of previously accepted but nonprocreative sexual acts (such as mutual masturbation, oral sex, anal sex, and same-sex activity) were reformulated as merely foreplay. Abelove, "Some Speculations on the History of Sexual Intercourse during the Long Eighteenth Century in England," *Genders,* no. 6 (fall 1989): 125–30. See also, Roy Porter and Mikulá Teich, eds., *Sexual Knowledge, Sexual Science: The History of Attitudes to Sexuality* (Cambridge: Cambridge University Press, 1994); Thomas DiPiero and Pat Gill, eds., *Illicit Sex: Identity Poli-tics in Early Modern Culture* (Athens: The University of Georgia Press, 1997); Paul-Gabriel Bouçe, ed., *Sexuality in Eighteenth-Century Britain* (Totowa, N.J.: Manchester University Press, 1982); Hitchcock, *English Sexualities;* Randolph Trumbach, *Sex and the Gender Revolution,* Vol. 1., *Heterosexuality and the Third Gender in Enlightenment London* (Chicago: University of Chicago Press, 1998). My concern here is less with changing forms of sexuality (difficult to draw out of court records) and more with the social repercussions of sexual acts. Most scholarship on sexuality in colonial North America has not discussed race. See, for example, Peter C. Hoffer and N. E. H. Hull, *Murdering Mothers: Infanticide in England and New England, 1558–1803* (New York: New York University Press, 1981); Roger Thompson, *Sex in Middlesex: Popular Mores in a Massachusetts County, 1649–1699* (Amherst: University of Massachusetts Press, 1986). This is changing, however. See Kathleen M. Brown, *Good Wives, Nasty Wenches, and Anxious Patriarchs: Gender, Race, and Power in Colonial Virginia* (Chapel Hill: University of North Carolina Press, 1996); Ann Marie Plane, *Colonial Intimacies: Indian Marriage in Early New England* (Ithaca, N.Y.: Cornell University Press, 2000); Sharon Block, *He Said I Must: Coerced Sex in Early America* (Chapel Hill: University of North Carolina Press, forthcoming); Jennifer L. Morgan, "Laboring Women: Enslaved Women, Reproduction, and Slavery in Barbados and South Carolina, 1650–1750" (Ph.D. diss., Duke University, 1996); Jennifer M. Spear, "'Whiteness and the Purity of Blood': Race, Sexuality, and Cultural Identity in Colonial Louisiana, 1699–1795" (Ph.D. diss., University of Minnesota, 1999). The links between sexual regulation and racial categories in the nineteenth century have received much more historical analysis, and I have benefited from these works. See Verena Martinez-Alier, *Marriage, Class, and Colour in Nineteenth-Century Cuba: A Study of Racial Attitudes and Sexual Values in a Slave Society* (Cambridge: Cambridge University Press, 1974); Victoria E. Bynum, *Unruly Women: The Politics of Social and Sexual Control in the Old South* (Chapel Hill: University of North Carolina Press, 1992); Ann Laura Stoler, *Race and the Education of Desire: Foucault's History of Sexuality and the Colonial Order of Things* (Durham, N.C.: Duke University Press, 1995); Peter Bardaglio, *Reconstructing the Household: Families, Sex, and the Law in the Nineteenth-Century South* (Chapel Hill: University of North Carolina Press, 1995); Laura Edwards, *Gendered Strife and Confusion: The Political Culture of Reconstruction* (Urbana: University of Illinois Press, 1997); Martha Hodes, *White Women, Black Men: Illicit Sex in the Nineteenth-Century South* (New Haven, Conn.: Yale University Press, 1997).

10. The scholarship on women and gender in early America is too vast to itemize here, but my thinking about the role of gender in structuring the colonial social order is especially indebted to the extensive discussions in Carol F. Karlsen, *The Devil in the Shape of a Woman: Witchcraft in Colonial New England* (New York: Vintage Books, 1989); Cornelia Hughes Dayton, *Women before the Bar: Gender, Law, and Society in Connecticut, 1639–1789* (Chapel Hill: University of North Carolina Press, 1995); Brown, *Good Wives, Nasty Wenches;* Mary Beth Norton, *Founding Mothers and Fathers: Gendered Power and the Forming of American Society* (New York: Knopf, 1996); and Jane Kamensky, *Governing the Tongue: The Politics of Speech in Early New England* (New York: Oxford University Press, 1997). See also Carole Shammas, "Anglo-American

Household Government in Perspective," *William and Mary Quarterly,* 3d ser., 52, no. 1 (January 1995): 104–44. On the historiography of gender in colonial American history, see Kathleen M. Brown, "Beyond the Great Debates: Gender and Race in Early America," *Reviews in American History* 26, no. 1 (March 1998): 96–123.

11. Brown, *Good Wives, Nasty Wenches.* On the way legislation defined race, see also A. Leon Higginbotham, *In the Matter of Color: Race and the American Legal Process: The Colonial Period* (Oxford: Oxford University Press, 1978); A. Leon Higginbotham and Barbara K. Kopytoff, "Racial Purity and Interracial Sex in the Law of Colonial and Antebellum Virginia," *The Georgetown Law Journal* 77, no. 6 (August 1989): 1967–2029.

12. Kathleen Brown argues, for example, that gender in early modern England was the model for other relations of inequality, but that in mid eighteenth-century Virginia the "political uses" of gender "had been equaled, perhaps even supplanted, by race," *Good Wives, Nasty Wenches,* 1 (Brown states elsewhere, however, that social categories "intersect and mutually shape one another," 4). Cynthia Kierner, by contrast, argues that "class distinctions gradually were overshadowed by those based on sex in a society in which race was consistently the most salient category." Cynthia A. Kierner, *Beyond the Household: Women's Place in the Early South, 1700–1835* (Ithaca, N.Y.: Cornell University Press, 1998), 4. Although historians generally agree that "scientific racism" budded in the late eighteenth century and became full blown in the nineteenth, the debate over what came first, racism or slavery, remains controversial. Two historiographical essays that take different positions on this issue are Alden T. Vaughan, "The Origins Debate: Slavery and Racism in Seventeenth-Century Virginia," *Virginia Magazine of History and Biography* 97, no. 3 (July 1989): 311–54, and Theodore W. Allen, *The Invention of the White Race,* Vol. 1, *Racial Oppression and Social Control* (London: Verso Press, 1994), 1–24.

13. I draw here on Nancy Hewitt's idea of identities as "compounds" of gender, race, class, and sexuality (among other things), from which one aspect cannot be isolated without affecting the whole. Nancy A. Hewitt, "Compounding Differences," *Feminist Studies* 18 (summer 1992): 313–26. On the simultaneity of categories of analysis, see also Barbara J. Fields, "Ideology and Race in American History," in *Region, Race, and Reconstruction,* ed. J. Morgan Kousser and James M. McPherson (New York: Oxford University Press, 1982), 143–77. For the instability of categories of both race and gender, see Karen Ordahl Kupperman, "Presentment of Civility: English Reading of American Self-Presentation in the Early Years of Colonization," *William and Mary Quarterly,* 3d ser., 54, no. 1 (January 1997): 193–228.

14. Feminist scholars have argued that sex (in the sense of anatomical distinctions of male and female as well as in the sense of sexual activity) is as socially constructed as gender (the social definitions of masculinity and femininity). While I agree that there is no transhistorical meaning of "sex," I use the term to refer to gendered distinctions of anatomy as well as to sexual activity, realizing that both were understood within historically specific contexts. See Gisela Bock, "Women's History and Gender History: Aspects of an International Debate," *Gender & History* 1 (1989): 7–30, and Bock, "Challenging Dichotomies: Perspectives on Women's History," in *Writing Women's History: International Perspectives,* ed. Karen Offen et al. (Bloomington: Indiana University Press, 1991), 1–23. My understanding of gender as an empty conceptual category that is continually refilled with historically specific meanings comes from Denise Riley, *"Am I That Name?": Feminism and the Category of "Women" in History* (Minneapolis: University of Minnesota Press, 1988). See also Judith Butler, *Gender Trouble: Feminism and the Subversion of Identity* (London: Routledge, 1990) on the "performativity" of gender.

15. Michel Foucault, *History of Sexuality, An Introduction,* Vol. 1 (New York: Vintage Books, 1990), 141. See also 116, 140, 149.

16. On the "backwardness" of North Carolina, see A. Roger Ekirch, *"Poor Carolina": Politics and Society in Colonial North Carolina, 1729–1776* (Chapel Hill: University of North Carolina Press, 1981), and Donna J. Spindel, *Crime and Society in North Carolina, 1663–1776* (Baton Rouge: Louisiana State University Press, 1989). Reevaluations of colonial North Carolina include Elizabeth A. Fenn and Peter H. Wood, *Natives and Newcomers: The Way We Lived in North*

Carolina before 1770 (Chapel Hill: University of North Carolina Press, 1983); James H. Merrell, *The Indians' New World: Catawbas and their Neighbors from European Contact through the Era of Removal* (Chapel Hill: University of North Carolina Press, 1989); Jon F. Sensbach, *A Separate Canaan: The Making of an Afro-Moravian World in North Carolina, 1763–1840* (Chapel Hill: University of North Carolina Press, 1998); Marjoleine Kars, *Breaking Loose Together: How Colonial North Carolina Farmers Came to Fight the War of the Regulation* (Chapel Hill: University of North Carolina Press, forthcoming).

17. Indeed, only by looking at lower class women can we comprehend the exercise of power in all its complexity. Feminists scholars have reframed historical interpretations by placing people previously cast as peripheral into the center of their analyses. One of their discoveries has been the extent to which political centers of power have defined themselves by their margins. See, for example, Joan Kelly-Gadol, "Did Women Have a Renaissance?" in *Becoming Visible: Women in European History,* ed. Renate Bridenthal and Claudia Koonz (Boston: Houghton Mifflin, 1977); Nancy A. Hewitt, "Reflections from a Departing Editor: Recasting Issues of Marginality," *Gender and History* 4 (summer 1992): 3–9.

Chapter 1

1. *Crown v. Lee and Spelman,* depositions of William Lee, John Spellman, James Seserson, and Elizabeth Vina, August 24, 1697, Colonial Court Papers—Civil and Criminal, North Carolina State Archives, Division of Archives and History (hereafter cited as NCSA). Jury's presentments, October 9, 1697, in *North Carolina Higher-Court Records, 1670–1696,* ed. Mattie Erma Edwards Parker, vol. 2 of *The Colonial Records of North Carolina* [Second Series], ed. Parker et al. (Raleigh: Division of Archives and History, 1963–), 90 (hereafter cited as Parker, NCHCR, vol. 2). Fornication and adultery were usually punished with twenty-one lashes at the public whipping post or a fine of fifty shillings or five pounds respectively. *Laws of North Carolina,* ed. Walter Clark, vol. 23 of *The State Records of North Carolina,* ed. Clark, 16 vols. numbered 11–26 (Winston and Goldsboro: State of North Carolina, 1895–1906), 5 (hereafter cited as LNC). Although *ravishment* was a term that could mean "rape," it did not in this instance imply rape (which was a capital offense). The court understood Steel's adultery to be voluntary. (Rape charges are discussed in chapters 3 and 5.) Elizabeth Vina was probably a servant, and Seserson, Hardy, and Hayes may have been servants as well. The runaways were likely white, as the court clerk did not mention their race, while Manuel and Tom Andover were identified as Negroes. On Manuel and Thomas Andover, see Susan Brinn, "Blacks in Colonial North Carolina, 1660–1723" (M.A. thesis, University of North Carolina, 1978), 33–35, 44–45. William Steel may have entered the colony as a servant for John Sanderson, who claimed headrights for Steel in February 1696. (There was no mention of Dorothy at the time.) Weynette Parks Haun, *Old Albemarle County North Carolina, Book of Land Warrants and Surveys, 1681–1706* (Durham, N.C.: for the author, 1984), 117–18.

2. Patriarchy is the institutionalized dominance of men over women and children in the family and in society in general. On patriarchal households as foundational to the English social order, see Susan Dwyer Amussen, *An Ordered Society: Gender and Class in Early Modern England* (Oxford: Blackwell, 1988), especially chaps. 2–3; Anthony Fletcher and John Stevenson, eds., *Order and Disorder in Early Modern England* (Cambridge: Cambridge University Press, 1985); Martin Ingram, *Church Courts, Sex, and Marriage in England, 1570–1640* (Cambridge: Cambridge University Press, 1987); Gordon J. Schochet, *Patriarchalism in Political Thought: The Authoritarian Family and Political Speculation and Attitudes Especially in Seventeenth-Century England* (Oxford: Blackwell, 1975); Lawrence Stone, *The Family, Sex, and Marriage in England, 1500–1800,* abridged ed. (New York: Harper Torchbooks, 1979).

3. I am elaborating on the concept of the "gender frontier" as a place where different gender systems collide. See Kathleen M. Brown, "Brave New Worlds: Women's and Gender History," *William and Mary Quarterly,* 3d ser., 50, no. 2 (April 1993): 310–28.

4. William Gouge, *Of Domesticall Duties: Eight Treatises,* 3d ed. (London, 1634), 17, quoted in Amussen, *An Ordered Society,* 37. Sir William Blackstone, *Commentaries on the Laws of England*

in Four Books [1753], 4 vols. (London, 1793), vol. 1, 441. See Janelle Greenberg, "The Legal Status of the English Woman in Early Eighteenth-Century Common Law and Equity," *Studies in Eighteenth-Century Culture* 4 (1975): 171–81; Bridget Hill, *Women, Work, and Sexual Politics in Eighteenth-Century England* (Oxford: Blackwell, 1989), chap. 11. Marylynn Salmon explains the legal restraints on a married woman's right to own and convey property in *Women and the Law of Property in Early America* (Chapel Hill: University of North Carolina Press, 1986). Unlike colonial New England, where divorces were granted, the southern colonies followed the Church of England in allowing only separations (an exception was Maryland, which had a statute for divorce as early as 1720). North Carolina first permitted divorce in 1814. See Roderick Phillips, *Putting Asunder: A History of Divorce in Western Society* (Cambridge: Cambridge University Press, 1988), 143.

5. On women's work in eighteenth-century England, see Ann Kussmaul, *Servants in Husbandry in Early Modern England* (Cambridge: Cambridge University Press, 1981); Mary Prior, ed., *Women in English Society, 1500–1800* (London: Methuen, 1985); Hill, *Women, Work, and Sexual Politics;* Bridget Hill, *Servants: English Domestics in the Eighteenth Century* (Oxford: Clarendon Press, 1996).

6. On prescriptive literature about women's roles and female chastity, see Anthony Fletcher, *Gender, Sex, and Subordination in England, 1500–1800* (New Haven, Conn.: Yale University Press, 1995). On courtship and marriage in England, see John R. Gillis, *For Better, For Worse: British Marriages, 1600 to the Present* (New York: Oxford University Press, 1985); Stone, *Family, Sex, and Marriage;* Amussen, *An Ordered Society,* chap. 2; Ingram, *Church Courts, Sex, and Marriage,* chap. 4; Alan Macfarlane, *Marriage and Love in England, 1300–1840* (Oxford: Blackwell, 1986), chap. 13; David Cressy, *Birth, Marriage, and Death: Ritual, Religion, and the Life-Cycle in Tudor and Stuart England* (Oxford: Oxford University Press, 1997).

7. On common-law marriages in England, see John R. Gillis, "Married but Not Churched: Plebeian Sexual Relations and Marital Nonconformity in Eighteenth-Century Britain," in *'Tis Nature's Fault: Unauthorized Sexuality during the Enlightenment,* ed. Robert Purks Maccubbin (Cambridge: Cambridge University Press, 1987), 31–42. On the high incidence of nonmarital sex and pregnancy in England, see Keith Wrightson, *English Society, 1580–1680* (London: Hutchinson, 1982), 85; Peter Laslett, *Family Life and Illicit Love in Earlier Generations: Essays in Historical Sociology* (Cambridge: Cambridge University Press, 1977); Peter Laslett, Karla Oosterveen, and Richard M. Smith, eds., *Bastardy and Its Comparative History: Studies in the History of Illegitimacy and Marital Nonconformism in Britain, France, Germany, Sweden, North America, Jamaica, and Japan* (Cambridge, Mass.: Harvard University Press, 1980). For disorderly gender relations in the early modern period, see Natalie Zemon Davis, "Women on Top: Symbolic Sexual Inversion and Political Disorder in Early Modern Europe, in *Society and Culture in Early Modern Europe* (Stanford, Calif.: Stanford University Press, 1975); David Underdown, "The Taming of the Scold: The Enforcement of Patriarchal Authority in Early Modern England," in Fletcher and Stevenson, eds., *Order and Disorder in Early Modern England;* Anna Clark, *The Struggle for the Breeches: Gender and the Making of the British Working Class* (Berkeley: University of California Press, 1995); Laura Gowing, *Domestic Dangers: Women, Words, and Sex in Early Modern London* (New York: Oxford University Press, 1996).

8. Laws quoted in Edmund S. Morgan, *The Puritan Family: Religion and Domestic Relations in Seventeenth-Century New England,* rev. ed. (New York: Harper and Row, 1966), 145. The *Virginia Gazette* is cited in Julia Cherry Spruill, *Women's Life and Work in the Southern Colonies* (reprint ed., New York: Norton, 1972), 164. On the fear of "masterless men" in England, see A. L. Beier, *Masterless Men: The Vagrancy Problem in England, 1560–1640* (London: Methuen, 1985). On community surveillance of and intervention into colonial family life, see Helena M. Wall, *Fierce Communion: Family and Community in Early America* (Cambridge, Mass.: Harvard University Press, 1990).

9. Philip Ludwell, "Boundary Line Proceedings, 1710," *Virginia Magazine of History and Biography* 5, no. 1 (July 1897): 10. On discrepancies between legal definitions of marriage and colonists' understanding of a legitimate union, see Mary Beth Norton, *Founding Mothers and Fathers: Gendered Power and the Forming of American Society* (New York: Knopf, 1996), 66–69.

Conflicting notions of immorality and illegitimacy are discussed further in chapter 3, below. On the (often foiled) efforts to transplant English norms of sex and marriage into Maryland and Virginia, see James Horn, *Adapting to a New World: English Society in the Seventeenth-Century Chesapeake* (Chapel Hill: University of North Carolina Press, 1996), chap. 5.

10. For more examples of the way the "small politics" of the neighborhood often became "enmeshed in the larger politics of the colonial legal system," see Norton, *Founding Mothers and Fathers*, chap. 5 (this quote on p. 243).

11. On the grant to Heath, see William S. Powell, ed., *Ye Countie of Albemarle in Carolina* (Raleigh: State Department of Archives and History, 1958), xvi, xxiv, and John Spencer Bassett, "The Naming of the Carolinas," in Bassett, *Slavery and Servitude in the Colony of North Carolina* (Baltimore, Md.: Johns Hopkins University Press, 1896), 343–52. Shaftesbury Papers [1665], in *Colonial Records of North Carolina*, ed. William L. Saunders, 10 vols. (Raleigh: State of North Carolina, 1886–90), vol. 1, 87 (hereafter cited as CRNC). Harry Roy Merrens, *Colonial North Carolina in the Eighteenth Century: A Study in Historical Geography* (Chapel Hill: University of North Carolina Press, 1964), chap. 2. For a detailed analysis of the workings of the headright system in Virginia, see Anthony S. Parent Jr., "'Either a Fool or a Fury': The Emergence of Paternalism in Colonial Virginia Slave Society" (Ph.D. diss., University of California, Los Angeles, 1982); Edmund S. Morgan, "Headrights and Headcounts: A Review Article," *Virginia Magazine of History and Biography* 80, no. 3 (July 1972): 361–71.

12. Patrick Copeland, *Virginia's God be Thanked* (London: Printed by I. D. for William Sheffard and John Bellamie, 1622), 13, quoted in Powell, ed., *Ye Countie of Albemarle*, p. xv (Pory). Edward Williams, *Virginia: More Especially the South Part thereof . . .* (London, 1650), cited in ibid., xix–xx.

13. Proprietors to Philipp Ludwell, December 5, 1689, CRNC, vol. 1, 360–63. Proprietors to Edward Hyde, January 24, 1712, ibid., 844. On the Albemarle assembly (first convened in 1665), see ibid., 48–50, 79–92, 101, and Paul M. McCain, *The County Court in North Carolina Before 1750* (Durham, N.C.: Duke University Press, 1954), 4. A second county, Bath, was founded in 1696. In 1739, Albemarle and Bath counties were disbanded and their precincts became counties. At that time, the precinct courts were also renamed county courts. The North Carolina State Archives has filed all colonial court records as "County Court Records," even when they dated from before 1739 and were still precinct court records, and I have kept this designation in my citations.

14. Thomas Woodward to Sir John Colleton, June 2, 1665, CRNC, vol. 1, 100. On landholding in Virginia, see Parent, "'Either a Fool or a Fury,'" 16–26. On the small clusters of non-English Europeans in North Carolina before 1730 (Welsh, French, German Palatines, and Scots-Irish), see Merrens, *Colonial North Carolina*, 21–23. On migration as families and the sex ratio (139 men to every 100 women for seventeenth-century Perquimans), see James M. Gallman, "Determinants of Age at Marriage in Colonial Perquimans County, North Carolina," *William and Mary Quarterly*, 3d ser., 39, no. 1 (January 1982): 176–91, esp. 178.

15. Colonel Jenings to the Lords of Trade, November 27, 1708, CRNC, vol. 1, 692 (poorer sort). Letter from the Virginia Council, October 19, 1708, ibid., 690–91 (easier Termes). Colonel Seymour to the Lords of Trade, June 10, 1707, ibid., 664–65. Virginia Council, October 19, 1708, ibid., 691 (no settled Government). The following year Seymour wrote: "Wee are dayly made sencible of the loss and removall of divers Inhabitants and residents in this Province to our neighbouring Colonys of Pensilvania & Carolina." Colonel Seymour to the Lords of Trade, June 23, 1708, ibid., 682–83. Lord Culpeper to the Board of Trade, December 12, 1681, British Public Record Office, class 1, piece 47, folio 261, photocopy filed as 70.507.1–4, NCSA. Letter from Captain Burrington, Governor of North Carolina, 20th February, 1731/2, CRNC, vol. 3, 332–33. To encourage immigration to North Carolina, the Albemarle assembly passed an act in January 1670 prohibiting suits for debt for five years after a person's arrival in the colony. See Clark, ed., *The State Records of North Carolina*, vol. 25, 119. Virginia did not give freed servants land; they had to buy or rent it from those who had received the headright bounties. See Parent, "'Either a Fool or a Fury,'" 22. On land in North Carolina that was "readily available at low prices" see Gallman, "Determinants of Age at

Marriage in Colonial Perquimans County," 190 and n. 29. In 1754 Governor Arthur Dobbs described North Carolina as "one of the latest Colonies, and scarcely arrived at the state of Manhood our neighbouring Colonies have attained to either in wealth or number." Upper House Journals, December 18, 1754, CRNC, vol. 5, 224. On the social status of early white North Carolinians, see Jacquelyn H. Wolf, "The Proud and the Poor: The Social Organization of Leadership in Proprietary North Carolina, 1663–1729" (Ph.D. diss., University of Pennsylvania, 1977); Hugh T. Lefler and William S. Powell, *Colonial North Carolina: A History* (New York: Scribner's Sons, 1973), chap. 7; Charles B. Lowry, "Class, Politics, Rebellion, and Regional Development in Proprietary North Carolina, 1697–1720" (Ph.D. diss., University of Florida, 1979).

16. "Affidavit of Thomas Miller Concerning the Rebellion of Carolina," January 31, 1679/80, CRNC, vol. 1, 281. "Representation to the Lords Proprietors of Carolina Concerning the Rebellion in that Country," ibid., 261. A narrative of the rebellion (without endnotes) is in Hugh F. Rankin, *Upheaval in Albemarle: The Story of Culpeper's Rebellion, 1675–1689* (Raleigh: Carolina Charter Tercentenary Commission, 1962). See also Lindley S. Butler, "Life in Albemarle County, Carolina, 1663–1689" (M.A. thesis, University of North Carolina, 1964), 73–101; Lindley S. Butler and Alan D. Watson, eds., *The North Carolina Experience: An Interpretive and Documentary History* (Chapel Hill: University of North Carolina Press, 1984), 53–78; Mattie Erma E. Parker, "Legal Aspects of 'Culpeper's Rebellion,'" *North Carolina Historical Review* 45 (April 1968): 111–27. Letter from Captain Burrington, governor of North Carolina, February 20, 1731–32, in CRNC, vol. 3, 338. On Sothell, see John Spencer Bassett, *The Constitutional Beginnings of North Carolina* (Baltimore, Md.: Johns Hopkins University Press, 1894), 12. Culpeper's Rebellion was not explicitly linked to the more famous rebellion in Virginia led by Nathaniel Bacon the year before, although settlers in both places resented colonial leaders who did not, in their opinion, merit positions of authority and respect. Susan Westbury and Kathleen M. Brown emphasize the real and symbolic importance of women's involvement in the revolt. See Susan Westbury, "Women in Bacon's Rebellion," in *Southern Women: Histories and Identities,* ed. Virginia Bernhard et al. (Columbia: University of Missouri Press, 1992), 30–46; Kathleen M. Brown, *Good Wives, Nasty Wenches, and Anxious Patriarchs: Gender, Race, and Power in Colonial Virginia* (Chapel Hill: University of North Carolina Press, 1996), 162–67. The documentary evidence about Culpeper's Rebellion and women's involvement in it is sparse, but my argument here is that the general political turbulence in early North Carolina politicized women's misconduct and made would-be leaders sensitive to challenges to their authority.

17. Quote on Edenton from William Byrd II, *Histories of the Dividing Line Betwixt Virginia and North Carolina,* ed. William K. Boyd (New York: Dover, 1967), 96. On landholding, see A. Roger Ekirch, *"Poor Carolina": Politics and Society in Colonial North Carolina, 1729–1776* (Chapel Hill: University of North Carolina Press, 1981), 20–22, 222–23; Gallman, "Determinants of Age at Marriage," 177. On early southern architecture, see Carl Lounsbury, "The Development of Domestic Architecture in the Albemarle Region," in *Carolina Dwelling: Towards Preservation of Place,* ed. Doug Swaim (Raleigh: North Carolina State University, 1978), 46–61; Cary Carson et al., "Impermanent Architecture in the Southern Colonies," *Winterthur Portfolio* 16, nos. 2/3 (summer/autumn 1981): 135–96; Catherine W. Bishir and Michael T. Southern, *A Guide to the Historic Architecture of Eastern North Carolina* (Chapel Hill: University of North Carolina Press, 1996). Slave cabins were a nineteenth-century phenomenon; in the eighteenth-century, most slaves lived in their owners' houses. See Edward A. Chappell, "Housing a Nation: The Transformation of Living Standards in Early America," in *Of Consuming Interests: The Style of Life in the Eighteenth Century,* ed. Cary Carson, Ronald Hoffman, and Peter J. Albert (Charlottesville: University Press of Virginia, 1994), 191–93, 199–200 (North Carolina). On rituals of respect in Virginia, see Rhys Isaac, *The Transformation of Virginia, 1740–1790* (New York: Norton, 1988).

18. George Burrington to Board of Trade, January 1, 1733, CRNC, vol. 3, 433. Mr. Adams to the Secretary, October 4, 1709, ibid., vol. 1, 720 (1709 tally of Pasquotank). Pasquotank and Perquimans were the most densely settled counties at that time. There is no such head-

count for Perquimans or Chowan, but in Currituck Reverend James Adams counted 97 blacks, 442 whites, and "about seventy or eighty Indians, many of which understand English tolerably well." Mr. Adams to the Secretary, March 27, 1710; September 4, 1710, ibid., vol. 1, 721, 734 (quote on Indians). On earliest slaveholders, see Hugh Talmage Lefler and Albert Ray Newsome, *North Carolina: The History of a Southern State* (Chapel Hill: University of North Carolina Press, 1954), 16. On Pasquotank's 283 households, see Wolf, "The Proud and the Poor," 156. Tithables (taxable workers) were defined in 1715 as either free male servants over the age of sixteen, or enslaved men or women over the age of twelve. LNC, 72. On slaveholding in Pasquotank, see Ekirch, "*Poor Carolina*," 20–22. Ekirch's analysis of Perquimans County in 1740 shows that of 323 households, 295 claimed between one and five taxable workers (black and/or white), 24 claimed between six and ten, 3 claimed between eleven and twenty, and one household (that of James Henby Jr.) claimed more than twenty-one. On the population in Virginia, South Carolina, and North Carolina in 1730, see Peter H. Wood, "The Changing Population of the Colonial South: An Overview by Race and Region, 1685–1790," in *Powhatan's Mantle: Indians in the Colonial Southeast*, ed. Wood, Gregory A. Waselkov, and M. Thomas Hatley (Lincoln: University of Nebraska Press, 1989), 38. Figures for 1705, 1748, and 1763 are in Marvin L. Michael Kay and Lorin Lee Cary, "A Demographic Analysis of Colonial North Carolina with Special Emphasis upon the Slave and Black Populations," in *Black Americans in North Carolina and the South*, ed. Jeffrey J. Crow and Flora J. Hatley (Chapel Hill: University of North Carolina Press, 1984), 112–13. See also Kay and Cary, *Slavery in North Carolina, 1748–1775* (Chapel Hill: University of North Carolina Press, 1995), appendix, 221.

19. Spruill, *Women's Life and Work*, 28 (Bird). Haun, *Book of Land Warrants*, 8 (Esau Albertson), 16 (Francis Tomes). Records of Perquimans Precinct Court, CRNC, vol. 1, 394 (John Bentley), 650 (Isaac Wilson). Colonial Court Records, Miscellaneous Papers, 1677–1775, 192, Folder: "Slaves pertaining to runaways, sale and trade, ownership, etc.," NCSA (James Cole). Perquimans Precinct Court Records, January 6, 1706, CRNC, vol. 1, 650 (Rebekah Baily). Although blacks and whites cooperated in many ventures, they could suffer different forms of punishment when caught. The court ordered that Baily receive five lashes on her bare back, but upon her "Submission" the order was rescinded. The slave woman belonging to William Glover was most likely not spared the whipping.

20. This paragraph is based on Nicholas P. Canny, *The Elizabethan Conquest of Ireland: A Pattern Established, 1565–76* (New York: Barnes and Noble, 1976), 123–36; Anne Laurence, "The Cradle to the Grave: English Observations of Irish Social Customs in the Seventeenth Century," *Seventeenth Century* 3, no. 1 (spring 1988): 63–84. Historians have argued that English prejudice against the Irish, with its rhetorical construction of savage and inherently degraded "others," not only justified colonization but also became a template for racism against other peoples as well. See, for example, Laurence, "The Cradle to the Grave," 81; Canny, *Elizabethan Conquest of Ireland*; Arthur H. Williamson, "Scots, Indians, and Empire: The Scottish Politics of Civilization, 1519–1609," *Past and Present* 150 (February 1996): 46–83.

21. This paragraph is indebted to Jennifer L. Morgan, "'Some Could Suckle over Their Shoulder': Male Travelers, Female Bodies, and the Gendering of Racial Ideology, 1500–1770," *William and Mary Quarterly*, 3d ser., 54, no. 1 (January 1997): 167–92. It is also informed by Alden T. Vaughan and Virginia Mason Vaughan, "Before Othello: Elizabethan Representations of Sub-Saharan Africans," *William and Mary Quarterly*, 3d ser., 54, no. 1 (January 1997): 19–44; Kim F. Hall, *Things of Darkness: Economies of Race and Gender in Early Modern England* (Ithaca, N.Y.: Cornell University Press, 1995); Emily Bartels, "Imperialist Beginnings: Richard Hakluyt and the Construction of Africa," *Criticism* 34, no. 4 (fall 1992): 517–38; Peter Erickson, "Representations of Blacks and Blackness in the Renaissance," *Criticism* 35, no. 4 (fall 1993): 499–527. For European views of Africans generally, see Winthrop D. Jordan, *White over Black: American Attitudes toward the Negro, 1550–1812* (Chapel Hill: University of North Carolina Press, 1968).

22. On the rough equality that frontier conditions promoted, see Peter H. Wood, *Black Majority: Negroes in Colonial South Carolina from 1670 through the Stono Rebellion* (New York: Norton, 1974), chap. 4. On the necessity of creating a functional "middle ground" of interaction

through cultural accommodation, see Richard White, *The Middle Ground: Indians, Empires, and Republics in the Great Lakes Region, 1650–1815* (Cambridge: Cambridge University Press, 1991), especially 50–93. On whites' understanding that Africans were human, see Jordan, *White over Black*, 232–34. On the fluidity of race relations and racial prejudice in seventeenth century Virginia, see David D. Smits, "'Abominable Mixture': Toward the Repudiation of Anglo-Indian Intermarriage in Seventeenth-Century Virginia," *Virginia Magazine of History and Biography* 95, no. 2 (April 1987): 157–92; T. H. Breen and Stephen Innes, *"Myne Owne Ground": Race and Freedom on Virginia's Eastern Shore, 1640–1676* (Oxford: Oxford University Press, 1980); George M. Fredrickson, "Social Origins of American Racism," in *The Arrogance of Race: Historical Perspectives on Slavery, Racism, and Social Inequality* (Middletown, Conn.: Wesleyan University Press, 1988), 189–205. With the growth of slavery came increasing legal and social restrictions for free blacks. See Michael L. Nicholls, "Passing through This Troublesome World: Free Blacks in the Early Southside," *Virginia Magazine of History and Biography* 92, no. 1 (January 1984): 50–70; Douglas Deal, "A Constricted World: Free Blacks on Virginia's Eastern Shore, 1680–1750," in *Colonial Chesapeake Society*, ed. Lois Green Carr, Philip D. Morgan, and Jean B. Russo (Chapel Hill: University of North Carolina Press, 1988), 275–305; Brown, *Good Wives, Nasty Wenches*, chap. 4.

23. John Lawson, *A New Voyage to Carolina* [1709], edited, with an introduction, and notes by Hugh Talmage Lefler (Chapel Hill: University of North Carolina Press, 1984), 242 (Tuscarora in 1700). E. Lawrence Lee, *Indian Wars in North Carolina, 1663–1763* (Raleigh: Carolina Charter Tercentenary Commission, 1963), 3 (on Tuscarora and Algonquians); Peter H. Wood, "North America in the Era of Captain Cook: Three Glimpses of Indian-European Contact in the Age of the American Revolution," in *Implicit Understandings: Observing, Reporting, and Reflecting on the Encounters Between Europeans and Other Peoples in the Early Modern Era*, ed. Stuart B. Schwartz (Cambridge: Cambridge University Press, 1994), 493–94 (on Cherokee). For the history of the Siouan-speaking peoples in the Piedmont before 1700 and the immense changes wrought by European contact and trade, see James H. Merrell, *The Indians' New World: Catawbas and Their Neighbors from European Contact through the Era of Removal* (New York: Norton, 1989), 8–48. On the demographic changes wrought by disease and warfare, see Peter H. Wood, "The Impact of Smallpox on the Native Population in the 18th Century South," *New York State Journal of Medicine* 87 (January 1987): 30–36, and Wood, "The Changing Population of the Colonial South," 38, 43–46. Merrell notes that epidemics struck Indians in the Carolina piedmont in 1698, 1718, 1738, and 1759, reducing the Catawba population from around 5,000 to only 500. See James H. Merrell, "The Indians' New World: The Catawba Experience," *William and Mary Quarterly*, 3d ser., 41, no. 4 (October 1984): 542.

24. Lawson, *A New Voyage*, 35. Lawson's expedition began at the mouth of the Santee River in South Carolina, followed the Santee and the Wateree River northwest to present-day Charlotte, North Carolina, then traveled the well-worn Indian trading path northeast to what is now High Point, passed north of present-day Durham, and headed southeast, past modern-day Greenville, to end the trek in what would eventually become the town of Washington. Lawson encountered nineteen tribes in the coastal plain alone, and numerous other tribes in the interior, but unfortunately he does not always specify the groups he mentions.

25. Lawson, *A New Voyage*, 57. Englishmen may have been ethnocentric "in that they saw their own system as the standard by which all others should be judged, but this did not prevent them from attempting to understand an alien system." See Karen Ordahl Kupperman, *Settling with the Indians: The Meeting of English and Indian Cultures in America* (London: Dent, 1980), 62. For a lengthier discussion of these sources, see chapter 2, below. The silence in the court records about sexual relations between Indians and white colonists may be the kind of purposeful judicial oversight of Indian marriages, families, and kinship relations that Ann Plane found in New England. See Ann Marie Plane, *Colonial Intimacies: Indian Marriage in Early New England* (Ithaca, N.Y.: Cornell University Press, 2000), chap. 3, esp. 69, 80–81.

26. On clans and matrilineage, see Theda Perdue, *Cherokee Women: Gender and Culture Change, 1700–1835* (Lincoln: University of Nebraska Press, 1998), 42–47. Lawson, *A New Voyage*, 193 (marrying sisters). On incest prohibitions, see John Lederer, *The Discoveries of*

John Lederer, In three several Marches from Virginia, to the West of Carolina and other parts of the Continent (London: Printed by J.C. for Samuel Heyrick, at Grays-Inne-gate in Holbourn, 1672), 8; Lawson, *A New Voyage,* 193; Thomas Nairne, *Nairne's Muskhogean Journals: The 1708 Expedition to the Mississippi River,* ed. Alexander Moore (Jackson: University Press of Mississippi, 1988), 61. David H. Corkran, ed., "Alexander Longe's 'A Small Postscript,'" *Southern Indian Studies* 21 (October 1969): 33–35. Longe described Indian gender relations as aberrant: "the woman rules the roost and wears the breeches and sometimes will beat their husbands within an inch of their lives. The man will not resist their power if the woman was to beat his brains out," ibid., 30. Most Southeastern tribes were organized into matrilineal clans, although matrilineage also existed among groups without clans, such as the Siouans. See Frank G. Speck, "The Question of Matrilineal Descent in the Southeastern Siouan Area," *American Anthropologist,* n.s., 40 (January 1938): 1–12.

27. On the importance of separating lineage from gendered relations of power and authority, see Eleanor Leacock, "Women's Status in Egalitarian Society: Implications for Social Evolution," *Current Anthropology* 19, no. 2 (June 1978): 254–55, and Plane, *Colonial Intimacies,* 21–22. Indians told Adair that "formerly they never waged war, but in revenge of blood." Samuel Cole Williams, *Adair's History of the American Indians* (New York: Promontory Press, 1930), 161; see also 157–58 (blood vengeance), 417–20 (torture). Lawson, *A New Voyage,* 205–8. This paragraph is indebted to Perdue's *Cherokee Women,* 53–55; John P. Reid, *A Law of Blood: The Primitive Law of the Cherokee Nation* (New York: New York University Press, 1970); Tom Hatley, *The Dividing Paths: Cherokees and South Carolinians through the Era of the Revolution* (New York: Oxford University Press, 1993), 56–57. On the wartime activities of "Beloved Women" or "War Women," see Perdue, *Cherokee Women,* 38–39.

28. Adair, *History,* 462 (Indian law), 437 (cheerfulness). Charles M. Hudson explains that "agricultural land was, in effect, privately controlled but communally owned." *The Southeastern Indians* (Knoxville: University of Tennessee Press, 1976), 313. On different kinds of property among the Cherokee, see Theda Perdue, *Slavery and the Evolution of Cherokee Society, 1540–1966* (Knoxville: University of Tennessee Press, 1979), 33–35. For an extensive discussion of Native American conceptions of property in New England, see William Cronon, *Changes in the Land: Indians, Colonists, and the Ecology of New England* (New York: Hill and Wang, 1983), chap. 4, especially 62–65. On gender divisions of agricultural labor among the Cherokee, see Perdue, *Cherokee Women,* 18–20; Thomas Hatley, "Cherokee Women Farmers Hold Their Ground," in *Appalachian Frontiers: Settlement, Society, and Development in the Preindustrial Era,* ed. Robert D. Mitchell (Lexington: University Press of Kentucky, 1991), 37–51.

29. Adair, *History,* 438–39. On food production, see Perdue, *Cherokee Women,* 20–22.

30. On powers of the blood, see Adair, *History,* 130–31; Perdue, *Cherokee Women,* chap. 1, esp. 29–36; Raymond D. Fogelson, "On the 'Petticoat Government' of the Eighteenth-Century Cherokee," in *Personality and the Cultural Construction of Society: Papers in Honor of Melford E. Spiro,* ed. David K. Jordan and Marc J. Swartz (Tuscaloosa: University of Alabama Press, 1990), 161–81, esp. 172–75. On gendered divisions of labor, see Hudson, *The Southeastern Indians,* 264–69. An extensive discussion of distinct but complementary gender roles among the Cherokee is in Perdue, *Cherokee Women,* chaps. 1–2. See also the introduction in Nancy Shoemaker, ed., *Negotiators of Change: Historical Perspectives on Native American Women* (New York: Routledge, 1995), 5. Shoemaker is careful to note that gender divisions were ubiquitous in native societies but that the specific divisions of labor and authority varied considerably among different tribes.

31. George Percy, "A Discourse of the Plantation of the Southern Colonie in Virginia" [1606–1607], quoted in *Envisioning America: English Plans for the Colonization of North America, 1580–1640,* edited and with an introduction by Peter C. Mancall (New York: Bedford Books of St. Martin's Press, 1995), 123. John Smith echoed this opinion in 1612, see David D. Smits, "The 'Squaw Drudge': A Prime Index of Savagism," *Ethnohistory* 29 (1982): 281–306. W. Byrd II, *Histories of the Dividing Line,* 116. See also Karen Ordahl Kupperman, *Indians and English: Facing Off in Early America* (Ithaca: Cornell University Press, 2000), 148–53. On white men's concern that contact with Indians might alter colonial gender roles, see Kupperman, *Settling*

with the Indians, 155–58. On English and Indian work patterns and allocations of time, and on colonists' views of "lazy" Indians, see Edmund S. Morgan, *American Slavery, American Freedom: The Ordeal of Colonial Virginia* (New York: Norton, 1975), 44–70. On the colonial assumption that Indian hunting practices were a form of leisure, see James Axtell, *The European and the Indian: Essays in the Ethnohistory of Colonial North America* (New York: Oxford University Press, 1980), 50, 52–54; Kupperman, "Presentment of Civility: English Reading of American Self-Presentation in the Early Years of Colonization," *William and Mary Quarterly,* 3d ser., 54, no. 1 (January 1997): 226–28. On the endless chores of colonial women, including innumerable hours spent spinning, weaving, sewing, and mending clothes, see Spruill, *Women's Life and Work,* chap. 1; Laurel Thatcher Ulrich, *Good Wives: Image and Reality in the Lives of Women in Northern New England, 1650–1750* (New York: Oxford University Press, 1983), chap. 1.

32. For the argument that native women worked willingly because they controlled the fruits of their labor, and for Butrick's quote, see Perdue, *Cherokee Women,* 24.

33. Gregory A. Waselkov and Kathryn E. Holland Braund, eds., *William Bartram on the Southeastern Indians* (Lincoln: University of Nebraska Press, 1995), 127 (public granary). Adair, *History,* 18 (community of goods; generous temper), 462 (hospitality). Lawson, *A New Voyage,* 176 (never work), 178 (gambling), 185 (fire), 175 (Loss and Gain), 206 (natural Vertues). On the Green Corn Ceremony, see Adair, *History,* 105–17. Adair said Indians called the English "covetous, because we do not give our poor relations such a share of our possessions, as would keep them from want." Ibid., 462–63. The giving of gifts could become a ritual of power in itself, and among some Indian groups the ability to redistribute wealth became an important mark of leadership. See Richard White, *Roots of Dependency: Subsistence, Environment, and Social Change among the Choctaws, Pawnees, and Navajos* (Lincoln: University of Nebraska Press, 1983), chap. 3, esp. 40–45.

34. Adair, *History,* 480 (virtue to part), 153 (petticoat-government). Lawson, *A New Voyage,* 192–93 (divorce), 41 (adultery). Alexander Longe said of the Cherokee: "I have seen Them leave one the other in 8 or 10 dayes with as litell Consearen as if they never had known one the other . . . the man gone and tooke another wife and the women another husband . . . the prestt giving for Resone that they had better be asonder then together if they doe nott love one and other." Longe's "A Small Postscript," 31.

35. Lawson, *A New Voyage,* 42 (several Couples). Native American courtship and marriage are discussed in greater detail in chapter 2. On different kinds of Indian marriages in New England, see Plane, *Colonial Intimacies,* 24–26, 132. Among Southeastern Indians, Cherokee women apparently enjoyed the most sexual self-determination. Adair believed the Cherokee did not punish women's extramarital relationships, see Adair, *History,* 152–53. Although Muskogee (Creek) Indians also had a matrilineal kinship structure, Creek women had less economic and sexual autonomy than Cherokee women. Creek men controlled their wives' agricultural produce, and Creek women were excluded from political affairs. Although Creek women could experiment sexually before marriage, adultery was punished with divorce and the cropping off of hair and ears. See Richard A. Sattler, "Women's Status among the Muskogee and Cherokee," in *Women and Power in Native North America,* ed. Laura F. Klein and Lillian A. Ackerman (Norman: University of Oklahoma Press, 1995), 214–29; Kathryn E. Holland Braund, "Guardians of Tradition and Handmaidens to Change: Women's Roles in Creek Economic and Social Life during the Eighteenth Century," *American Indian Quarterly* 14, no. 3 (summer 1990): 239–58; Claudio Saunt, *A New Order of Things: Property, Power, and the Transformation of the Creek Indians, 1733–1816* (Cambridge: Cambridge University Press, 1999). On Creek adulterers (men and women) who had their ears cut off, see Waselkov and Braund, eds., *William Bartram,* 58; Adair, *History,* 151.

36. On the enclosure movement, see Beier, *Masterless Men.* On the Diggers, see Christopher Hill, *The World Turned Upside Down: Radical Ideas during the English Revolution* (London: Penguin, 1975). The persistent struggle over the commons is described in E. P. Thompson, *Whigs and Hunters: The Origin of the Black Act* (New York: Pantheon, 1975). On descriptions that linked Indians and English noblemen, see Karen Kupperman, "Presentment of Civility," 193–228.

37. Nathaniel Batts Papers, PC 1293, NCSA; Proprietors to Sir William Berkeley, September 8, 1663, CRNC, vol. 1, 53–54; "Fundamental Constitutions of Carolina," drawn up by John Locke, March 1, 1669, ibid., vol. 1, 199. Locke was part of the intellectual circle of proprietor Anthony Ashley Cooper, Lord Shaftesbury, in London. On the proprietors, see William S. Powell, *The Proprietors of Carolina* (Raleigh: State Department of Archives and History, 1968). In 1648 Henry Pumpton of Nansemond County, Virginia, Thomas Tuke, and others bought land from the Indians on the Morratuck River. William S. Powell, ed., *Ye Countie of Albemarle in Carolina* (Raleigh: State Department of Archives and History, 1958), 81. See also Elizabeth Gregory McPherson, ed., "Nathaniell Batts, Landholder on Pasquotank River, 1660," *North Carolina Historical Review* 43, no. 1 (1966): 72–81; Lawrence N. Morgan, "Land Tenure in Proprietary North Carolina," *James Sprunt Historical Publications* 12 (1912): 41–63; William S. Powell, "Carolana and the Incomparable Roanoke: Explorations and Attempted Settlements, 1620–1663," *North Carolina Historical Review* 51 (January 1974): 1–22. On the English assumption that possession of "new" lands depended on the creation of English-style houses and gardens, see Patricia Seed, *Ceremonies of Possession: Europe's Conquest of the New World, 1492–1640* (New York: Cambridge University Press, 1995), chap. 1.

38. CRNC, vol. 1, 153 (1666 attack). Flor O'Sullivan to Lord Ashley, September 10, 1670, ibid., vol. 1, 207. Accounts of early Indian–colonial clashes are in Lee, *Indian Wars in North Carolina, 1663–1763,* 14–20, and scattered throughout CRNC, vol. 1.

39. Parker, NCHCR, vol. 2, 95 (Chowan, 1694), 178, 207 (John King). A report from 1754 still mentioned two men and five women in Chowan County, but by 1820 whites believed the Chowan were extinct. See William S. Powell, *North Carolina: The Story of a Special Kind of Place* (Chapel Hill: Algonquin, 1987), 32–33. See also Patrick H. Garrow, *The Mattamuskeet Documents: A Study in Social History* (Raleigh: Archeology Branch, Division of Archives and History, Department of Cultural Resources, January 1979); Maurice A. Mook, "Algonkian Ethnohistory of the Carolina Sound," *Journal of the Washington Academy of Sciences* 34, no. 6 (June 1944): 181–97; Douglas L. Rights, *The American Indian in North Carolina* (Winston-Salem: Blair, 1957), 33–36. On the perseverance of Indians in New England despite colonial myths of their "extinction," see Jean M. O'Brien, *Dispossession by Degrees: Indian Land and Identity in Natick, Massachusetts, 1650–1790* (Cambridge: Cambridge University Press, 1997).

40. Edward Moseley, William Glover, Francis Foster, Samuel Swann to the Virginia Council, June 17, 1707, CRNC, vol. 1, 657–63. On colonial attempts to pressure Indian households to exert more authority over young men, see Richard White, "What Chigabe Knew: Indians, Household Government, and the State," *William and Mary Quarterly,* 3d ser., 52, no. 1 (January 1995): 151–61.

41. Adair, *History,* 66 (satyr), 461 (jesting). Carole Shammas argues persuasively that the importance of collateral kin in Native American societies rather than the authority of male heads of households (as in the English system) led Europeans to wonder "how stable societies could be fashioned from such unstable household units," though she also notes that individual male settlers may have appreciated what colonial leaders did not. See Carole Shammas, "Anglo-American Household Government in Comparative Perspective," *William and Mary Quarterly,* 3d ser., 52, no. 1 (January 1995): 104–44, esp. 112–13. On the "fluidity of native household composition," see Plane, *Colonial Intimacies,* 98.

42. For a discussion of the convergence of property-holding patterns with gender roles among Native Americans, see Coontz, *The Social Origins of Private Life,* chap. 2; Theda Perdue, "Southern Indians and the Cult of True Womanhood," in *Web of Southern Relations: Women, Family, and Education,* ed. Walter J. Fraser Jr., R. Frank Saunders Jr., and Jon L. Waeklyn (Athens: University of Georgia Press, 1985), 35–52, and Perdue, "The Traditional Status of Cherokee Women," *Furman Studies,* n.s., 26 (December 1980): 19–25.

43. For Quaker women preachers and Friends' gender norms, see Phyllis Mack, *Visionary Women: Ecstatic Prophecy in Seventeenth-Century England* (Berkeley: University of California Press, 1992); Rebecca Larson, *Daughters of Light: Quaker Women Preaching and Prophesying in the Colonies and Abroad, 1700–1775* (New York: Knopf, 1999); Mary Maples Dunn, "Saints and Sisters: Congregational and Quaker Women in the Early Colonial Period," *American Quarterly* 30 (winter

1978): 27–46; Mary Maples Dunn, "Women of Light," in *Women of America: A History*, ed. Carol Ruth Berkin and Mary Beth Norton (Boston: Houghton Mifflin, 1979), 114–36; Margaret Hope Bacon, *Mothers of Feminism: The Story of Quaker Women in America* (San Francisco: Harper and Row, 1986); Jean R. Soderlund, "Women's Authority in Pennsylvania and New Jersey Quaker Meetings, 1680–1760," *William and Mary Quarterly*, 3d ser., 44, no. 4 (October 1987): 722–49. As early as the 1690s, women missionaries traveled to North Carolina, and women's meetings in the colony wrote out certificates for local members to travel as well. On women missionaries in North Carolina, see Spruill, *Women's Life and Work*, 251, n. 67; Larson, *Daughters of Light*, 4, 93, 112. On the virulent reaction, generally, to women preachers, see Bacon, *Mothers of Feminism*, 6; Larson, *Daughters of Light*. For the Apostle Paul's prescription of silence and subjection for women, see I Corinthians 14:34–35 and I Timothy 2:11–12.

44. Mack, *Visionary Women*, 241–42.

45. This paragraph is based on Howard Beeth, "Outside Agitators in Southern History: The Society of Friends, 1656–1800" (Ph.D. dissertation, University of Houston, 1984), 294–306. See also Robert J. Brugger, *Maryland: A Middle Temperament, 1634–1980* (Baltimore, Md.: Johns Hopkins University Press, 1988), 29. The laws are in William Hand Brown et al., eds., *Archives of Maryland*, 72 vols. (Baltimore: Maryland Historical Society, 1883–1972), vol. 3, 352; William Waller Hening, *Statutes at Large: Being a Collection of all the laws of Virginia from the First Session of the Legislature in the Year 1619*, 13 vols. (Richmond, Va., 1809–23), vol. 1, 532–33; vol. 2, 48, 165, 180–83. The last quote (from Governor Berkeley) is in Edward W. James, *The Lower Norfolk County Virginia Antiquary*, vol. 4 (Richmond, Va.: Whittet and Shepperson, 1895–1906), part 2, 78.

46. "A Declaration and Proposals to All that will Plant in Carolina," August 25, 1663, CRNC, vol. 1, 45 (liberty of conscience). "Fundamental Constitutions," ibid., vol. 1, 202–3. Jonathan M. Chu, *Neighbors, Friends, or Madmen: The Puritan Adjustment to Quakerism in Seventeenth-Century Massachusetts Bay* (Westport: Greenwood, 1985); Carla Gardina Pestana, *Quakers and Baptists in Colonial Massachusetts* (Cambridge: Cambridge University Press, 1991).

47. William Edmundson, *A Journal of the Life, Travels, Sufferings, and Labour in the Work of the Ministry of That Worthy Elder, and Faithful Servant of Jesus Christ, William Edmundson* (Dublin: Printed by Samuel Fairbrother, 1715), 58–59. Edmundson (1676) quoted in Rufus M. Jones, *The Quakers in the American Colonies* (New York: Russell and Russell, 1962), 290. Gwen Boyer Bjorkman, "Hannah (Baskel) Phelps Hill: A Quaker Woman and Her Offspring," *Southern Friend* 11, no. 1 (spring 1989): 10–30. The Phelpses' neighbors, Christopher and Hannah Nicholson and Isaac and Damaris Page, had also been persecuted as Quakers in Massachusetts and had moved to Albemarle Sound around 1663 (16–17). On the treatment of Friends in New England, see Mack, *Visionary Women*, 256–60.

48. On early meeting houses, see Seth B. Hinshaw and Mary Edith Hinshaw, eds., *Carolina Quakers: Our Heritage, Our Hope. Tercentenary, 1672–1972* (Greensboro: North Carolina Yearly Meeting, 1972), 12. Quakers did not keep membership lists, so historians must rely on Meeting Minutes to ascertain the names of members. See also William Wade Hinshaw, *Encyclopedia of American Quaker Genealogy*, 6 vols. (Baltimore, Md.: Genealogical Publishing, 1973). Archdale spent only six weeks in Albemarle and was based in Charlestown, but his deputy governor in Albemarle, Thomas Harvey, extended tolerance to Quakers and may have been a Quaker himself. See Jones, *The Quakers in the American Colonies*, 344. For the act of March 16, 1695, see Stephen B. Weeks, *Southern Quakers and Slavery: A Study in Institutional History* (Baltimore, Md.: Johns Hopkins University Press, 1896), 59.

49. Henderson Walker to the Bishop of London, October 21, 1703, CRNC, vol. 1, 571–72. Mr. Blair's Mission to North Carolina, no date [1704], ibid., vol. 1, 601. Mr. Adams to the Secretary, October 4, 1709, ibid., vol. 1, 720. Mr. Gordon to the Secretary, May 13, 1709, ibid., vol. 1, 708, 713. Gordon provides a detailed (albeit hostile) history of Quakers in the colony in ibid., vol. 1, 708–15. Mr. Adams to the Secretary, September 18, 1708, ibid., vol. 1, 686–87 (shoemakers). The ministers felt almost as much disgust for their Anglican parishioners. Adams complained that the twelve vestrymen in Perquimans were "most, if not all of them, very ignorant, loose in their lives, and unconcerned as to religion." During a communion

service, "the looser sort at their drunken reveling spared not to give about their bread and drink in the words of administration, to bring into contempt that most holy sacrament, and in derision of those few persons who then received it." Despite his complaint to magistrates, the culprits went "unpunished and unregarded." Ibid., vol. 1, 713–14, 719–20. For a detailed account of the personalities and experiences of SPG ministers, see Charles B. Hirsch, "The Experiences of the S.P.G. in Eighteenth-Century North Carolina" (Ph.D. diss., Indiana University, 1954).

50. "Fundamental Constitutions," CRNC, vol. 1, 204 (militia duty). Robert A. Brock, *The Official Letters of Alexander Spotswood* (Richmond, Va.: Virginia Historical Society, 1882–85), vol. 1, 121 (October 15, 1711), vol. 2, 4 (February 11, 1712). October 22, 1681, Piney Woods Monthly Meeting Minutes (Perquimans), Friends Historical Collection, Guilford College, Greensboro, North Carolina (hereafter referred to as the Friends Historical Collection).

51. Weeks, *Southern Quakers and Slavery*, 133–34 (White). Typescript copy from *A Journal of the Life of Thomas Story (Being an account of his travels and labors in the Quaker ministry from 1699 to 1708)* (New-Castle-Upon-Tyne: Printed by Isaac Thompson, at the New Printing Office on the Side, 1747), 155, filed as Thomas Story Paper, PC 967.1, NCSA (Newby). On Quakers' appreciation for Native American ways, see Robert Daiutolo Jr., "The Early Quaker Perception of the Indian," *Quaker History* 72, no. 2 (fall 1983): 103–19.

52. *Old Albemarle County, North Carolina: Perquimans Precinct Court Minutes, 1688 through 1738*, transcribed by Weynette Parks Haun (Durham, N.C.: for the author, 1980), 7–8 (Alexander). "Records of Perquimans Precinct Court," CRNC, vol. 1, 626–27 (Alexander's suit against Laker). Prior to the 1716 initiation of the courthouse on Queen Anne's Creek (incorporated as Edenton in 1722), the court sessions convened in private houses. One of these, the Scott house, was rebuilt in 1730 and still exists (see figure 6, the Newbold-White House). See also Elizabeth A. Fenn and Peter H. Wood, *Natives and Newcomers: The Way We Lived in North Carolina before 1770* (Chapel Hill: University of North Carolina Press, 1983), 28–31. Gary B. Nash describes Quakers' accumulation of wealth in *Quakers and Politics: Pennsylvania, 1681–1726* (Princeton, N.J.: Princeton University Press, 1968), 56–67.

53. Secretary of State Papers, will of Henry White, Sr., September 19, 1706; will of Robert White, January 1, 1732; will of Jeremiah Symons, March 30, 1713; will of Francis Tomes, [proved October 7] 1729; will of Jonathan Phelps, December 4, 1732; will of Gabriel Newby, March 26, 1733; will of Solomon Pool, July 30, 1739, NCSA. Quakers fought among themselves over the ownership of individual slaves. See, for example, *Jeremiah Symons v. James Took* and *Thomas Bundy v. John Bundy*, January 10, 1708, and June 4, 1730, Eastern Quarter Symons Creek Monthly Meeting Minutes (Pasquotank), Friends Historical Collection. This is a sampling and not an exhaustive list of Quaker slaveholders. Some Quakers migrated from Rhode Island to North Carolina to continue holding slaves. See Neva Jean Specht, "Mixed Blessing: Trans Appalachian Settlement and the Society of Friends, 1780–1813" (Ph.D. diss., University of Delaware, 1997), 62, n. 6.

54. Weeks, *Southern Quakers and Slavery*, 201 (1722, 1740), 208 (1776). North Carolina Yearly Meeting Minutes, 1758, Friends Historical Collection. Thomas Newby of Perquimans County was apparently the first North Carolina Quaker to seek manumission for his slaves (in 1774). On Quaker manumissions in North Carolina, see Kathryn Renee Dungy, "Life on a Tightrope: The Problems of Becoming Free in Perquimans County, North Carolina, 1775–1800" (M.A. thesis, Duke University, 1993), 32–34; Hiram H. Hilty, *Toward Freedom for All: North Carolina Quakers and Slavery* (Richmond, Ind.: Friends United Press, 1984); Donald Vernon Dowless, "The Quakers of Colonial North Carolina, 1672–1789" (Ph.D. diss., Baylor University, 1989), 233–71. For Quakers' conflicted positions on slaveholding, see David Brion Davis, *The Problem of Slavery in Western Culture* (Ithaca, N.Y.: Cornell University Press, 1966), 291–332; Jean R. Soderlund, *Quakers and Slavery: A Divided Spirit* (Princeton, N.J.: Princeton University Press, 1985); Herbert Aptheker, "The Quakers and Negro Slavery," *Journal of Negro History* 25 (July 1940): 331–62.

55. George Fox, *Concerning Sons and Daughters, and Prophetesses Speaking and Prophecying, in the Law and in the Gospel* (London: MW, n.d.), 9, quoted in Dunn, "Saints and Sisters," 596.

William Penn, *Fruits of Solitude* (London: Northcott, 1693), 33, quoted in Bacon, *Mothers of Feminism*, 251, n. 2. George Fox, "An Encouragement to All the Faithful Women's Meetings" (letter 320), in *The Works of George Fox* (New York: Isaac Hopper, 1831), vol. 8, 93, quoted in Bacon, *Mothers of Feminism*, 22. For a discussion about Quakers as fundamentally bourgeois regarding property ownership and yet radical in their affirmation of Quaker women's authority, see Mack, *Visionary Women*, especially 246, 408–11. Mack notes that two of Fox's most important early converts were Elizabeth Hooten and Margaret Fell, who significantly shaped the sect and provided role models for other women. On Quaker women as transatlantic missionaries, see Larson, *Daughters of Light.*

56. October 6, 1716 (on apparel), North Carolina Yearly Meeting: Standing Committee Minutes, 1704–93, Friends Historical Collection. April 3, 1746 (Overman), December 1, 1743 (Bundy), Symons Creek Women's Minutes, 1715–68, Friends Historical Collection. In 1708, for example, Edward Mayo had to "publickly Condemn his unseemly Action" by writing a letter of self-condemnation that was read aloud in the meeting. Mayo's apology read: "Dear Friends, thro' the Instigation of the Enemy & for want of watchfullness I Did left my mind & made Sute to the widdow Gormack by way of Courship Contrary to the good & wholesome ordeer Settled amongst friends it being too Soon after the Death of my Wife therefore I am heartily Sorry." July 8, August 12 (Mayo), 1708, Minutes of Eastern Quarter Symons Creek Monthly Meeting, 1699–1785, Friends Historical Collection. See also Mack, *Visionary Women*, 344–46. On the structure of and different positions within the Quaker meeting, see Sydney V. James, *A People among Peoples: Quaker Benevolence in Eighteenth-Century America* (Cambridge, Mass.: Harvard University Press, 1963), chap. 1, and Jack Eckert, *Guide to the Records of Philadelphia Yearly Meeting* (Philadelphia: Records Committee of Philadelphia Yearly Meeting, 1989). On women's meetings, see Soderlund, "Women's Authority in Pennsylvania and New Jersey Quaker Meetings, 1680–1760," 722–49. My understanding of Quaker women's collective authority is indebted to Mack, *Visionary Women*, 284–85, 346. See also Larson, *Daughters of Light*, 303–4.

57. On marriage out of society, see Jack D. Marietta, *The Reformation of American Quakerism, 1748–1783* (Philadelphia: University of Pennsylvania Press, 1984), chap. 3. See, for examples, the cases of Esther Belman and John Turner and the marriages of Elizabeth and Cathern Cartwright, August 1715–June 1716, Women's Monthly Meeting Minutes, Friends Historical Collection.

58. January 15, February 12, 1712, Minutes of Eastern Quarter Symons Creek Monthly Meeting, Friends Historical Collection. On gender relations within Quaker marriages, see Larson, *Daughters of Light*, chap. 4, esp. 143–55. On Quaker separations, see William J. Frost, *The Quaker Family in Colonial America: A Portrait of the Society of Friends* (New York: St. Martin's, 1973), 181–82. The Society of Friends punished men more than women for fornication and required less evidence to prove a man's guilt. See Marietta, *Reformation of American Quakerism*, 15–16. On separations in England, see Amussen, *An Ordered Society*, 123–29, and Lawrence Stone, *Broken Lives: Separation and Divorce in England, 1660–1857* (Oxford: Oxford University Press, 1993). On divorce in the colonies, see Merril D. Smith, *Breaking the Bonds: Marital Discord in Pennsylvania, 1730–1830* (New York: New York University Press); Cornelia Hughes Dayton, *Women before the Bar: Gender, Law, and Society in Connecticut, 1639–1789* (Chapel Hill: University of North Carolina Press, 1995), chap. 3.

59. March 16 (Scurrilous), June 15 (Ill Language), 1710, Minutes of Eastern Quarter Symons Creek (Pasquotank) Monthly Meeting, Friends Historical Collection. August 2, September 5 (rash words), November 1 (unstable minde), November (date torn) (younity), 1710, Piney Woods (Perquimans) Monthly Meeting Minutes, Friends Historical Collection. Mary Tomes and Gabriel Newby, both from prominent, landholding families, may have been the Tomes and Newby who married in 1689. June 26, 1714, Eastern Quarterly (Perquimans and Little River) Meeting Minutes, Friends Historical Collection. The page containing Mr. Bundy's first name is torn. For more on gendered rules of speech, see chapter 4.

60. August 4, 1725, Eastern Quarter Symons Creek (Pasquotank) Women's Minutes, Friends Historical Collection. On Southern Quakers as an "organized" and highly visible

"counter-culture," see Beeth, "Outside Agitators," 275. But for confrontational Anglican women, see Joan R. Gundersen, "The Non-institutional Church: The Religious Role of Women in Eighteenth-Century Virginia," *Historical Magazine of the Protestant Episcopal Church* 51 (1982): 347–57.

61. The Vestry Act in 1704 demanded an oath of allegiance to Queen Anne and disenfranchised noncompliant dissenters. On Quaker migration to and within North Carolina, see Weeks, *Southern Quakers and Slavery*, 77–91. For a detailed account of Cary's Rebellion, see Gloria Beth Baker, "Dissenters in Colonial North Carolina" (Ph.D. diss., University of North Carolina, 1970), 103–19.

62. Mr. Adams to the Secretary, October 4, 1709, in CRNC, vol. 1, 721 (troublesome); Mr. Adams to the Secretary, March 27, 1710, in ibid., vol. 1, 722. Mr. Urmston's Letter, July 7, 1711, ibid., vol. 1, 767. Urmston complained for over a decade about the people and circumstances in North Carolina. See Hirsch, "The Experiences of the S.P.G.," 99–166.

Chapter 2

1. John Lawson, *A New Voyage to Carolina* [1709], edited with an introduction and notes by Hugh Talmage Lefler (Chapel Hill: University of North Carolina Press, 1984), 46–47 (emphasis in the original). It is often difficult to know which Indian tribes Lawson refers to, in part because he was not sure himself. Many of the Siouan-speaking tribes of the Piedmont (although not the Waxhaw) eventually became known as the Catawba Indians. See James H. Merrell, *The Indians' New World: Catawbas and Their Neighbors from European Contact through the Era of Removal* (New York: Norton, 1989), 47–48, 102-6, 287, n. 4.

2. Many scholars now avoid the term *frontier* because it presents the longtime homelands of native peoples as peripheral regions located at the outer edges of European knowledge and settlement. Pratt defines contact zones as "social spaces where disparate cultures meet, clash, and grapple with each other, often in highly asymmetrical relations of domination and subordination." Mary Louise Pratt, *Imperial Eyes: Travel Writing and Transculturation* (London: Routledge, 1992), 4. Richard White describes a "middle ground" that lies in between cultures and in which people create "new systems of meaning and exchange." Richard White, *The Middle Ground: Indians, Empires, and Republics in the Great Lakes Region, 1650–1815* (Cambridge: Cambridge University Press, 1991), x. White notes that the middle ground served as a place to resolve problems that occurred in daily intercultural encounters, and that "[m]any of these problems revolved around basic issues of sex, violence, and material exchange. . . . Sex and violence are thus important not only in their own right but also as avenues for understanding how cultural accommodation on the middle ground, in fact, worked." Ibid., 56, 60. Kathleen M. Brown describes the "gender frontier" as a place where different gender systems collide. See Brown, "Brave New Worlds: Women's and Gender History," *William and Mary Quarterly*, 3d ser., 50, no. 2 (April 1993): 310–328. Richard Godbeer, whose "Eroticizing the Middle Ground: Anglo-Indian Sexual Relations along the Eighteenth-Century Frontier," in *Sex, Love, Race: Crossing Boundaries in North American History*, ed. Martha Hodes (New York: New York University Press, 1999), 91–111, draws on many of the same primary sources as this chapter, argues that sex "had an important role to play in Anglo-Indian relations" and that the "sexual middle ground bore witness to the many possibilities of intercultural contact," from "violent coercion to respectful coexistence," 92, 105.

3. I am building on a large body of scholarship that has explored the colonial uses of sexualized images of indigenous women. These works include Rayna Green, "The Pocahontas Perplex: The Image of Indian Women in American Culture," *Massachusetts Review* 16, no. 4 (autumn 1975): 698–714; Louis Montrose, "The Work of Gender and Sexuality in the Elizabethan Discourse of Discovery," in *Discourses of Sexuality: From Aristotle to AIDS*, ed. Domna C. Stanton (Ann Arbor: University of Michigan Press, 1992), 138–84; Peter Hulme, *Colonial Encounters: Europe and the Native Caribbean, 1492–1797* (London: Methuen, 1986); Ann Laura Stoler, *Race and the Education of Desire: Foucault's History of Sexuality and the Colonial Order of Things* (Durham, N.C.: Duke University Press, 1995); Karen O. Kupperman, "Presentment of Civility: English

Reading of American Self-Presentation in the Early Years of Colonization," *William and Mary Quarterly,* 3d ser., 54, no. 1 (January 1997): 193–228. For an overview of the literature, see Kirsten Fischer, "The Imperial Gaze: Native American, African American, and Colonial Women in European Eyes," in *The Blackwell Companion to American Women's History,* ed. Nancy Hewitt (Oxford: Blackwell Publishers, forthcoming).

4. Thomas Jefferson remained a prominent exception with regard to the declining enthusiasm for Indian-white marriage, which he supported as late as 1808 as a means of assimilation. See Winthrop D. Jordan, *White over Black: American Attitudes toward the Negro, 1550–1812* (Chapel Hill: University of North Carolina Press, 1968), 480; Peter S. Onuf, *Jefferson's Empire: The Language of American Nationhood* (Charlottesville: University Press of Virginia, 2000), 49–52. The focus in this chapter on Indian women in Native American villages rather than in colonial settlements is due to the paucity of North Carolina court records that mention intimate relations between Indians and colonists in the Albemarle counties. See chapter 1 and also Merrell, *The Indians' New World,* 99–102, 106–9. Studies of "settlement Indians" include Sylvia Van Kirk, *"Many Tender Ties": Women in Fur Trade Society, 1670–1870* (Norman: University of Oklahoma Press, 1980); Jean M. O'Brien, *Dispossession by Degrees: Indian Land and Identity in Natick, Massachusetts, 1650–1790* (Cambridge: Cambridge University Press, 1997); Ann Marie Plane, *Colonial Intimacies: Indian Marriage in Early New England* (Ithaca, N.Y.: Cornell University Press, 2000). Much of this chapter focuses on the Piedmont peoples and the Cherokee in the region that is now North Carolina, but it also draws on the writings of eighteenth-century Virginians such as Robert Beverley and William Byrd II when their comments pertain to Indians along the border between Virginia and North Carolina.

5. James Merrell shows how trade relations gradually shifted the balance of cultural and political power in the Piedmont. See Merrell, *The Indians' New World.* On the initial imperative for colonists to follow native rules of conduct and trade, see ibid., 29–34. For the way growing native dependence on European trade goods altered relations of diplomacy and commerce, see ibid., 59–65. Laughter serves as an indicator of power relationships "because in intercultural contacts whoever made fun of the other generally was in control of the situation." James H. Merrell, "'The Customes of Our Countrey': Indians and Colonists in Early America," in *Strangers Within the Realm: Cultural Margins of the First British Empire,* ed. Bernard Bailyn and Philip D. Morgan (Chapel Hill: University of North Carolina Press, 1991), 117–156, quote on 120.

6. These themes are also addressed in studies of the relations between Native American women and fur-trading Anglo-American men. These include Jennifer S. H. Brown, *Strangers in Blood: Fur Trade Company Families in Indian Country* (Norman: University of Oklahoma Press, 1996) and Van Kirk, *"Many Tender Ties."*

7. On the "rhetorical bifurcation" of travel literature, see Gordon M. Sayre, *Les Sauvages Américains: Representations of Native Americans in French and English Colonial Literature* (Chapel Hill: University of North Carolina Press, 1997), 80–81, 126–29. On early modern uses of Eurocentric models for understanding American Indians, see David Armitage, "The New World and British Historical Thought: From Richard Hakluyt to William Robertson" in *America in European Consciousness, 1493–1750,* ed. Karen Ordahl Kupperman (Chapel Hill: University of North Carolina Press, 1995), 52–75, and Sabine MacCormack, "Limits of Understanding: Perceptions of Greco-Roman and Amerindian Paganism in Early Modern Europe," ibid., 79–129. Anthony Pagden explains that sixteenth-century Spanish ethnologists in the Americas "had to be able to classify *before* they could properly see" and therefore "had no alternative but to appeal to a system which was already in use." Anthony Pagden, *The Fall of Natural Man: The American Indian and the Origins of Comparative Ethnology* (Cambridge: Cambridge University Press, 1982), 2. But on the explosive discovery that the "ancients" were wrong about some things, and hence perhaps wrong about many more, see Anthony Pagden, *European Encounters with the New World: From Renaissance to Romanticism* (New Haven, Conn.: Yale University Press, 1993), chap. 3, esp. 91–96, and Anthony Grafton, *New Worlds, Ancient Texts: The Power of Tradition and the Shock of Discovery* (Cambridge, Mass.: Belknap, 1992), introduction. On the way the language of natural science aided colonizing efforts by encompassing new

lands and peoples within a homogenizing scientific framework, see Pratt, *Imperial Eyes,* especially chaps. 2–3.

8 Samuel Cole Williams, *Adair's History of the American Indians* (New York: Promontory Press, 1930), xxii, hereafter cited as Adair, *History.* This chapter relies heavily on Lawson, *A New Voyage;* Adair, *History;* Gregory A. Waselkov and Kathryn E. Holland Braund, eds., *William Bartram on the Southeastern Indians* (Lincoln: University of Nebraska Press, 1995). I have omitted John Brickell's *The Natural History of North Carolina,* ed. J. Bryan Grimes (1737; reprint, Raleigh: Authority of the Trustees of the Public Libraries, 1911) because much of it was plagiarized from Lawson's *A New Voyage* (although, as Gordon Sayre points out, the concept of plagiarism as we understand it today was not operative among travel writers in the eighteenth-century. See, Sayre, *Les Sauvages Américains,* 122). On Brickell's borrowings from Lawson, see Percy G. Adams, "John Lawson's Alter-Ego," *North Carolina Historical Review* 34 (July 1957): 313–26. Mark Catesby also borrowed much from Lawson for his *Natural History of Carolina, Florida, and the Bahama Islands,* 2 vols. (London, 1731–1743).

9. Steven Greenblatt says "we can be certain only that European representations of the New World tell us something about the European practice of representation." See Greenblatt, *Marvelous Possessions: The Wonder of the New World* (Chicago: University of Chicago Press, 1991), 7. But on the value of eighteenth-century texts as ethnographic sources, see Karen Ordahl Kupperman, *Settling with the Indians: The Meeting of English and Indian Cultures in America* (London: J. M. Dent, 1980), 62, 105–106; Ann Marie Plane, *Colonial Intimacies: Indian Marriage in Early New England* (Ithaca, N.Y.: Cornell University Press, 2000), chap. 1, esp. 15–18, 27–32.

10. For conflicting images of Indians, see Gary B. Nash, "The Image of the Indian in the Southern Colonial Mind," *William and Mary Quarterly,* 3d ser., 29 (1972): 197–230; Robert Berkhofer Jr., *The White Man's Indian: Images of the American Indian from Columbus to the Present* (New York: Knopf, 1978). Mutual fear and curiosity are described in Karen Ordahl Kupperman, *Indians and English: Facing Off in Early America* (Ithaca, N.Y.: Cornell University Press, 2000).

11. Lawson, *A New Voyage,* 189–90. Robert Beverley commented in ethnographic detail on the size and shape of Indian women's breasts in Robert Beverley, *The History and Present State of Virginia* [1705], ed. Louis B. Wright (Chapel Hill: University of North Carolina Press, 1947), 166.

12. Lawson, *A New Voyage,* 194–95.

13. Arthur Barlowe, "A New Land like unto That of the Golden Age (1584–85)," quoted in Louis B. Wright, *The Elizabethans' America: A Collection of Early Reports by Englishmen on the New World* (London: Edward Arnold, 1965), 107. Lawson, *A New Voyage,* 43. William Byrd, *William Byrd's Histories of the Dividing Line Betwixt Virginia and North Carolina,* intro. and notes by William K. Boyd (Raleigh: North Carolina Historical Commission, 1929), 114, cited hereafter as Byrd, *Dividing Line.* Byrd met Saponi women "so bashfull they wou'd not mount their Ponys til they were quite out of Sight." Ibid., 311. Waselkov and Braund, *William Bartram,* 81, see also 111. Adair, *History,* 6. Adair made a similar comment about men: "they never scold each other when sober." ibid., 461. See also Lawson, *A New Voyage,* 210. Felicity A. Nussbaum, *Torrid Zones: Maternity, Sexuality, and Empire in Eighteenth-Century English Narratives* (Baltimore, Md.: Johns Hopkins University Press, 1995), 122–23.

14. "Journal of Diron D'Artaguiette, 1722–1723," in *Travels in the American Colonies: 1697–1774,* ed. Newton D. Mereness (New York: Macmillan, 1910), 73 (mistresses). Beverley, *History,* 170–71 (manage their persons). Lawson, *A New Voyage,* 194. R.F., "The Present State of Carolina, With Advice to the Settlers." Transcript cited in J. Ralph Randolph, *British Travelers Among the Southern Indians, 1660–1763* (Norman: University of Oklahoma Press, 1973), 38–39 (knowable person). Indian women used abstinence and breastfeeding to space births. One observer noted that Cherokee women abstained from sex while breastfeeding and that "from the time she begins to suckeel [the child] for the speace of one yeare she will nott lett her husband bed with her for feare that itt should spoyle the childs milke and Cause itt to day [die]." David H. Corkran, ed., Alexander Longe's "A Small Postscript," *Southern Indian*

Studies 21 (October 1969): 33–35 (quote on 35). On Native American practices of birth control and abortion, see Ann Marie Plane, "Putting a Face on Colonization: Factionalism and Gender Politics in the Life History of Awashunkes, the 'Squaw Sachem' of Saconet," in *Northeastern Indian Lives, 1632–1816,* ed. Robert S. Grumet (Amherst: University of Massachusetts Press, 1996), 140–65.

15. Lawson, *A New Voyage,* 40 (Maidenheads), 194 (Intrigues), 40–41 (Gallants), 40 (the more Whorish).

16. Lawson, *A New Voyage,* 193. (Lawson's account contradicts itself: elsewhere, he notes Indian men's lack of sexual restraint after a dance, 45.) Adair was impressed with Indians' self-control in council debates: "They reason in a very orderly manner, with much coolness and good-natured language, though they may differ widely in their opinions." Adair, *History,* 460. Conversely, the Indians "never frequent a Christian's House that is given to Passion . . . for they say, such Men are mad Wolves, and no more Men." Lawson, *A New Voyage,* 210. On the patience and self-control of Indian men, see also ibid., 205–6, 243. Native custom involved the stoic forbearance of torture: captives mocked their captors with songs of their own heroic exploits while being flayed or burned alive. Indians laughed when tortured Europeans begged for mercy and derisively called them "women." Adair, *History,* 419. Eighteenth-century European scientists argued over whether American Indian men had beards and whether beardlessness signalled an underdeveloped or effeminate man. See Londa Schiebinger, "The Anatomy of Difference: Race and Sex in Eighteenth-Century Science," *Eighteenth-Century Studies* 23, no. 4 (summer 1990): 387–405, esp. 391–92, and Sayre, *Les Sauvages Américains,* 156. The eighteenth-century French naturalist, George Louis Leclerc, comte de Buffon, argued that "in the savage, the organs of generation are small and feeble. He has no hair, no beard, no ardour for the female." Cited in Berkhofer Jr., *The White Man's Indian,* 42–43. On feminized images of Indian men in Virginia, see Kathleen Brown, "The Anglo-Algonquian Gender Frontier," in *Negotiators of Change: Historical Perspectives on Native American Women,* ed. Nancy Shoemaker (New York: Routledge, 1995), 26–48.

17. Waselkov and Braund, *William Bartram,* 114 (no wrangling), 152. While Bartram likely idealized Indian marriages, it appears that coerced sex was rare among many Indian groups in the Southeast. Even captured women were rarely raped, in part because they might be adopted as family members, making intercourse with them retroactively incestuous. Adair relayed that the Indians "are said not to have deflowered any of our young women they captivated, while at war with us; . . . they would think such actions defiling, and what must bring fatal consequences on their own heads." Adair, *History,* 172. On warriors' ritual abstinence before, during, and after warfare, see Perdue, *Cherokee Women,* 35. Perhaps, too, warriors' rituals of abstinence and purification after battle merely postponed the violation. Adair said he knew Choctaw Indians who took "several female prisoners without offering the least violence to their virtue, till the time of purgation was expired;—then some of them forced their captives, notwithstanding their pressing entreaties and tears." Adair, *History,* 172. Adair also recounts one case of a Cherokee woman gang-raped for adultery. Adair, *History,* 153.

18. Byrd, *Dividing Line,* 53 (gross Freedoms), 105 (Rachel), 91 (boisterous), 56–57 (Dark Angel), 149 (ravish't), 151 (Wenches), 59 (Tallow-faced). The survey team consisted of seven commissioners, four surveyors, one chaplain, one Indian guide, and some dozen male laborers. On the intended audience of the *Secret History,* see Richard Beale Davis, *Intellectual Life in the Colonial South, 1585–1763,* vol. 3 (Knoxville: University of Tennessee Press, 1978), 1371. Byrd's sex life and self-image have received much attention. On Byrd as an anxiety-ridden misogynist, see Kenneth A. Lockridge, *On the Sources of Patriarchal Rage: The Commonplace Books of William Byrd and Thomas Jefferson and the Gendering of Power in the Eighteenth Century* (New York: New York University Press, 1992). On Byrd as a man in unceasing pursuit of mastery, over himself and others, see Lockridge, *The Diary, and Life, of William Byrd II of Virginia, 1674–1744* (Chapel Hill: University of North Carolina Press, 1987), and Kathleen M. Brown, *Good Wives, Nasty Wenches, and Anxious Patriarchs: Gender, Race, and Power in Colonial Virginia* (Chapel Hill: University of North Carolina Press, 1996), 324–28. On Byrd's sexual exploits as an enactment of his gentility and power, see Brown, *Good Wives, Nasty Wenches,* 328–34; Richard Godbeer,

"William Byrd's 'Flourish': The Sexual Cosmos of a Southern Planter," in *Sex and Sexuality in Early America*, ed. Merril D. Smith (New York: New York University Press, 1998), 135–62.

19. Byrd, *Dividing Line*, 115, (sad-colour'd), 123 (Linnen). The quote on South Carolina traders is from David Crawley's letter to William Byrd, dated July 30, 1715 in Marion Tinling, ed., *The Correspondence of the Three William Byrds of Westover, Virginia, 1684–1776*, vol. 1 (Charlottesville: University Press of Virginia, 1977), 289. Byrd's concern with the personal hygiene of Indian women is interesting given that he washed his feet only every few weeks and rarely bathed. See Lawrence Stone, *The Family, Sex, and Marriage in England, 1500–1800* (New York: Harper and Row, 1977), 485 (and on English hygiene generally, 485–88). Native people, by contrast, bathed after using "sweating houses," and "they frequent the Rivers in Summertime very much, where both Men and Women very often in a day go in naked to wash themselves, though not both Sexes together." Lawson, *A New Voyage*, 48, 55, 226 (sweating houses), 200 (Rivers).

20. On the gendering of the New World as "virgin" land that was female and violable, see Annette Kolodny, *The Lay of the Land: Metaphor as Experience and History in American Life and Letters* (Chapel Hill: University of North Carolina Press, 1975); Montrose, "The Work of Gender and Sexuality in the Elizabethan Discourse of Discovery," 154, 158.

21. Lawson, *A New Voyage*, 41 (chief Bawd), 190 (Adresses), 50 (good for nothing). Diplomatic sex with outsiders ("Strangers") was different from personal relations within the village. Only the former required public discussion, for "If it be an *Indian* of their own Town or Neighbourhood, that wants a Mistress, he comes to none but the Girl, who receives what she thinks fit to ask him, and so lies all Night with him, without the Consent of her Parents." Ibid., 190.

22. Lawson, *A New Voyage*, 34 (busily engag'd), 36 (Female Fry), 194 (Fortunes).

23. John Lederer, *The Discoveries of John Lederer, In three several Marches from Virginia, to the West of Carolina and other parts of the Continent* (London: printed by J.C. for Samuel Heyrick, at Grays-Inne-gate in Holbourn, 1672), 15. Lawson, *A New Voyage*, 192. Thomas Nairne, *Nairne's Muskhogean Journals: The 1708 Expedition to the Mississippi River*, ed. Alexander Moore (Jackson: University Press of Mississippi, 1988), 60–61. Phrases quoted in Edward Porter Alexander ed., *The Journal of John Fontaine. An Irish Huguenot Son in Spain and Virginia, 1710–1719* (Charlottesville: University of Virginia Press, 1972), 95.

24. Bernard Romans, *A Concise Natural History of East and West Florida*, ed. Rembert W. Patrick (Gainesville: University of Florida Press, 1962), 97. See also Merrell, *The Indians' New World*, 63–64.

25. Lawson, *A New Voyage*, 195. On eighteenth-century English traders in the Hudson Bay region who married both Indian and English wives, see Brown, *Strangers in Blood*, 52–55, 89–90.

26. Lawson, *A New Voyage*, 192. On long-time traders, see Michael D. Roethler, "Negro Slavery Among the Cherokee Indians, 1540–1866," (Ph.D. diss., Fordham University, 1964), chap. 2. On Europeans who joined Indian society, see James Axtell, "The White Indians of Colonial America," *William and Mary Quarterly*, 3d ser., 32 (1975): 55–88; James Axtell, *The Invasion Within: The Contest of Cultures in Colonial North America* (New York: Oxford University Press, 1985), 302–27.

27. Beverley, *History*, 38–39. Lawson, *A New Voyage*, 244–45. Byrd, *Dividing Line*, 3–4, 120. See also Axtell, *The Invasion Within*, for different approaches among the French and the English regarding intermarriage.

28. Byrd, *Dividing Line*, 120 (emphasis added), 3–4. For European debates over Native American origins, see Kupperman, *Settling with the Indians*, chap. 6; Margaret T. Hodgen, *Early Anthropology in the Sixteenth and Seventeenth Centuries* (Philadelphia: University of Pennsylvania Press, 1964), chap. 7; Lee Eldridge Huddleston, *Origins of the American Indians: European Concepts, 1492–1729* (Austin: University of Texas Press, 1967); Berkhofer Jr., *The White Man's Indian*, part 2; William G. McLoughlin and Walter H. Conser Jr., "'The First Man Was Red': Cherokee Responses to the Debate over Indian Origins, 1760–1860," *American Quarterly* 41, no. 2 (June 1989): 243–64.

29. Arthur Barlowe, "A New Land like unto That of the Golden Age (1584–85)," quoted in Wright, ed., *The Elizabethans' America*, 107. Lawson, *New Voyage*, 174. Adair, *History*, 4. Adair

postulated that purposefully darkened skin color became transgenerationally "fix't" because, "the colour being once thoroughly established, nature would, as it were, forget herself not to beget her own likeness." His theory combined an environmental explanation of appearance with an inherited one: the effects of sun and ointments were transferred to the next generations. See Alden T. Vaughan, "From White Man to Redskin: Changing Anglo-American Perceptions of the American Indian," *American Historical Review* 87, no. 4 (October 1982): 917–53, esp. 930. For a catalog of English descriptions of Indian skin color, see ibid., 921–27. For colonial concerns with Indians' appearance, see Kupperman, "Presentment of Civility"; Joyce E. Chaplin, "Natural Philosophy and an Early Racial Idiom in North America: Comparing English and Indian Bodies," *William and Mary Quarterly*, 3d ser., 54, no. 1 (January 1997): 229–52. On the prevalence of the term *tawny* to describe Indians (which was later replaced with "redskin"), see Jack D. Forbes, *Africans and Native Americans: The Language of Race and the Evolution of Red-Black Peoples* (Urbana: University of Illinois Press, 1993), 123–24. For similar concerns in New France about color as inherited or acquired, see Olive Patricia Dickason, *The Myth of the Savage and the Beginnings of French Colonialism in the Americas* (Edmonton: University of Alberta Press, 1984), 143–46.

30. Beverley, *History,* 159; Byrd, *Dividing Line,* 3. On concerns with an effete English aristocracy, see Alan Bray, *Homosexuality in Renaissance England* (London: Gay Men's Press, 1982), chap. 4.

31. Lawson, *A New Voyage,* 244–45. Byrd, *Dividing Line,* 120. Lower-class English people could still claim to be lighter than their Spanish or Irish counterparts. Theodore W. Allen, *The Invention of the White Race,* vol. 1, *Racial Oppression and Social Control* (London: Verso, 1994); Bernard Sheehan, *Savagism and Civility: Indians and Englishmen in Colonial Virginia* (Cambridge: Cambridge University Press, 1980), 54–56; Nicholas P. Canny, *The Elizabethan Conquest of Ireland: A Pattern Established, 1565–76* (New York: Barnes and Noble, 1976). On lower-class women brought to Virginia, see David Ransome, "Wives for Virginia," *William and Mary Quarterly,* 3d ser., 48 (1991): 3–18; Brown, *Good Wives, Nasty Wenches,* 80–83; Lois Green Carr and Lorena S. Walsh, "The Planter's Wife: The Experience of White Women in Seventeenth-Century Maryland," *William and Mary Quarterly,* 3d ser., 34 (1977): 543–71. The promotion of intermarriage, even though supported by few, represented a very different stance than that taken in the previous century by elites in Virginia who feared that intermarriage with Indians—especially when it involved the lower ranks of colonists—would lead to cultural disintegration and savagery. See Sheehan, *Savagism and Civility,* 63, and David D. Smits, "'Abominable Mixture': Toward the Repudiation of Anglo-Indian Intermarriage in Seventeenth-Century Virginia," *Virginia Magazine of History and Biography* 95, no. 2 (April 1987): 157–92, especially 178–84. Vaughan makes a similar point about the seventeenth-century apprehension that Englishmen could become Indianized: there were no biological barriers in the way of complete cultural assimilation. Vaughan, "From White Man to Redskin," 953, n. 97.

32. Lawson, *A New Voyage,* 90–91.

33. Waselkov and Braund, *William Bartram,* 150–51. Lawson, *A New Voyage,* 35–36.

34. Barlowe, "A New Land," 111. James H. Merrell, "The Racial Education of the Catawba Indians," *Journal of Southern History* 50, no. 3 (August 1984): 363–84, quote from 369. Merrell adds that the "Catawba could be unaware of the racial foundation of American slavery because they saw Indians as well as blacks enslaved and met white servants whose life on the surface resembled that of those held in bondage." Ibid.

35. When cultural differences threatened a useful alliance, Indians pragmatically stressed the similarities between themselves and others. See James Axtell, *Beyond 1492: Encounters in Colonial North America* (New York: Oxford University Press, 1992), 31–32, 39, 45, 102. Merrell, *The Indians' New World,* 30–31.

36. Lawson explained that slaves, together with "Dogs, Cats, tame or domestick Beasts, and Birds, are call'd by the same Name: For the *Indian* Word for Slave includes them all." A slave may be "a young Eagle, a Dog, Otter, or any other thing of that Nature, which is obsequiously to depend on the Master for its Sustenance." Lawson, *A New Voyage,* 210 (Slaves), 208 (foot mutilations). Lawson's guide, Eno Will, had a slave, Ibid., 48, 64. On slavery, see Theda

Perdue, *Slavery and the Evolution of Cherokee Society, 1540–1866* (Knoxville: University of Tennessee, 1979), chap. 1, especially 12–16. Bartram explains that the children of slaves were free. Waselkov and Braund, *William Bartram,* 52. The Virginia law is mentioned in Merrell, *The Indians' New World,* 35. Lawson, *A New Voyage,* 204 (wampum), 209 (Machapunga). Cherokee Indian quoted in Verner W. Crane, *The Southern Frontier, 1670–1732* (New York: Norton, 1981), 182. On wars for slaves, see Almon W. Lauber, *Indian Slavery in Colonial Times within the Present Limits of the United States* (New York: privately printed, 1913), 119–22, 133, 169–71, 183–87, 198. On efforts by the Proprietors and the South Carolina assembly to regulate (but not necessarily stop) the Carolina trade in Indian slaves, see Lauber, *Indian Slavery,* 173–85. On more women enslaved than men, see Perdue, *Cherokee Women,* 67–68; Wright, *The Only Land They Knew,* 148–49. According to Nash, the number of enslaved Indians "reached into the tens of thousands in the half-century after Carolina was settled by Europeans." Gary B. Nash, *Red, White, and Black: The Peoples of Early North America,* 3d ed. (Englewood Cliffs, N.J.: Prentice Hall, 1992), 132–34. See also Charles M. Hudson, *The Southeastern Indians* (Knoxville: University of Tennessee Press, 1976), 437–38; Crane, *The Southern Frontier,* 18–19, 113–14; Perdue, *Slavery and the Evolution of Cherokee Society,* chap. 1; J. Leitch Wright Jr., *The Only Land They Knew: The Tragic Story of the American Indians in the Old South* (New York: The Free Press, 1981), chap. 6; Peter Wood, *Black Majority,* 38–39, 143–44.

37. Lawson, *A New Voyage,* 210–11. On inebriation as a spiritual and empowering experience, see Peter C. Mancall, *Deadly Medicine: Indians and Alcohol in Early America* (Ithaca, N.Y.: Cornell University Press, 1995), 68–70, 75–76.

38. Mancall, *Deadly Medicine,* 60, 67, 89. Lawson, *A New Voyage,* 212. Keowee example cited in Perdue, *Cherokee Women,* 78. William Byrd, *The Secret Diary of William Byrd of Westover, 1709–1712,* ed. Louis B. Wright and Marion Tinling (Richmond: The Dietz Press, 1941), 423, 425. Waselkov and Braund, *William Bartram,* 65. Bartram's comment about ears referred to the Creek custom of cropping the ears of adulterers. See Richard A. Sattler, "Women's Status Among the Muskogee and Cherokee," in *Women and Power in Native North America,* ed. Laura F. Klein and Lillian A. Ackerman (Norman: University of Oklahoma Press, 1995), 214–29.

39. Lawson, *A New Voyage,* 212 (threats), 43 (Veneration). On Hagler, see William L. Saunders, ed. *Colonial Records of North Carolina,* 10 vols. (Raleigh: State of North Carolina), vol. 5, 143, 581; vol. 6, 902 (1754) (hereafter cited as CRNC). Letter from Governor Arthur Dobbs, November 30, 1757, General Assembly Papers, North Carolina State Archives (hereafter cited as NCSA). On Indian efforts to prohibit alcohol, see Mancall, *Deadly Medicine,* chap. 5. Comment of Aucus al Kanigut (made in 1767 after most Tuscarora had left North Carolina and become the sixth Nation of the Iroquois confederacy) cited ibid, 120.

40. On the deerskin trade, see Hudson, *Southeastern Indians,* 436, and Richard White, *The Roots of Dependency: Subsistence, Environment, and Social Change among the Choctaws, Pawnees, and Navajos* (Lincoln: University of Nebraska Press, 1983), chap. 4. Scholars debate how Indian women's status changed with colonial expansion. On the deterioration of Indian women's status, see Rebecca Brooks Edwards, "'Not Suspecting Such Usage': Siouan Indian Women in the Colonial Piedmont, 1600–1729," (M.A. thesis, University of Virginia, 1990); Karen Anderson, *Chain Her by One Foot: The Subjugation of Women in Seventeenth-Century New France* (London: Routledge, 1991); Carol Devens, *Countering Colonization: Native American Women and Great Lakes Missions, 1630–1900* (Berkeley: University of California Press, 1992). For the argument that the changes in women's status were more complicated, see Nancy Shoemaker, "The Rise and Fall of Iroquois Women," *Journal of Women's History* 2 (1991): 39–57, and the essays in Nancy Shoemaker, ed., *Negotiators of Change,* especially her historiographical introduction, 1–25. Theda Perdue argues that the new commercial economy and the centralizing of political authority in the hands of men reinforced Cherokee gender roles in ways that benefited women locally: men's extended absence from the villages enhanced women's responsibility for growing food and for raising children. By the late eighteenth century, however, increased warfare and the gradual weakening of traditional kinship systems had a deleterious impact on women. Perdue, *Cherokee Women,* 80–85, 90–94, 107. See also Theda Perdue, "Nancy Ward," in *Portraits of American Women: From Settlement to the Present,* ed. G. J.

Barker-Benfield and Catherine Clinton (New York: St. Martin's Press, 1991), 83–100; Thomas Hatley, "Cherokee Women Farmers Hold Their Ground," in *Appalachian Frontiers: Settlement, Society, and Development in the Preindustrial Era,* ed. Robert D. Mitchell (Lexington: University Press of Kentucky, 1991), 37–51. For rising tensions between Creek women and men, see Claudio Saunt, *A New Order of Things: Property, Power, and the Transformation of the Creek Indians, 1733–1816* (Cambridge: Cambridge University Press, 1999), 139–63. On the complexities of status, see Ramona Ford, "Native American Women: Changing Statuses, Changing Interpretations," in *Writing the Range: Race, Class, and Culture in the Women's West,* ed. Elizabeth Jameson and Susan Armitage (Norman: University of Oklahoma Press, 1997), 42–68. For the related argument over whether Indian women resisted or eagerly adopted the changes that came with European colonialism, see Kathryn E. Holland Braund, "Guardians of Tradition and Handmaidens to Change: Women's Roles in Creek Economic and Social Life during the Eighteenth Century," *American Indian Quarterly* 14, no. 3 (summer 1990): 239–58; Perdue, "The Traditional Status of Cherokee Women"; Perdue, "Southeastern Indians and the Cult of True Southern Womenhood"; Carol Devens, "Separate Confrontations: Gender as a Factor in Indian Adaptation to European Colonization in New France," *American Quarterly* 38, no. 3 (1986): 461–80.

41. John Archdale, *A New Description of That Fertile and Pleasant Province of Carolina* (London, 1707), 3. Lawson, *A New Voyage,* 17 (many thousands), 34, 232 (not a sixth), 243–44 (better to us). Merrell, *Indians' New World,* 18–27. Epidemics continued. According to Adair, in the 1730s the Cherokee "were a very numerous and potent nation" with "64 towns and villages" and at least 6,000 "fighting men." But a smallpox epidemic in 1738 "reduced them almost one half, in about a year's time." Adair, *History,* 238, 244. Decades later, Adair still shared Lawson's critique. He deplored the Indians' "evil habit of using spiritous liquors intemperately, which they have been taught by the Europeans," and he described how "lewd, idle white savages" engaged in unfair trade: "for by inebriating the Indians with their nominally prohibited, and poisoning spirits, they purchase the necessaries of life, at four or five hundred per cent cheaper, then the orderly traders." Adair called these opportunistic traders "the dreags and off-scourings of our colonies." Adair, *History,* 122–23, 444–45.

42. Lawson, *A New Voyage,* introduction by Lefler. On the enslavement of North Carolina Indians, see Merrell, *The Indians' New World,* 36–37; Hugh Talmage Lefler and Albert Ray Newsome, *North Carolina: The History of a Southern State* (Chapel Hill: University of North Carolina Press, 1954), 57; Nash, *Red, White, and Black,* 130–32.

43. This account by Von Graffenreid of the trial and death of Lawson is excerpted in Lawson, *A New Voyage,* xxxi–xxxvi. See also "De Graffenried's Manuscript," CRNC, vol. 1, 925–33. Lawson, *A New Voyage,* 207 (Torments).

44. CRNC, vol. 1, 875, 900 (Indian slaves); vol. 2, iv (Moore's description of casualties). On the Tuscarora War, see Chapman J. Milling, *Red Carolinians* (Chapel Hill: University of North Carolina Press, 1940), chap. 8; Thomas C. Parramore, "The Tuscarora Ascendency," *North Carolina Historical Review* 59 (Autumn 1982), 307–26; Nash, *Red, White, and Black,* 135–37; Lee, *Indian Wars,* 21–38; Crane, *The Southern Frontier,* 158–61; Lauber, *Indian Slavery,* 121–22; Hugh T. Lefler and William S. Powell, *Colonial North Carolina: A History* (New York: Scribner's, 1973), 65–80. On Cherokee involvement, see Perdue, *Cherokee Women,* 66–70. Pollock's "Letter Book," CRNC, vol. 1.

45. Walter Clark, ed., *Laws of North Carolina,* vol. 23, *The State Records of North Carolina,* ed. Walter Clark, 16 vols. numbered 11–26 (Winston and Goldsboro: State of North Carolina, 1895–1906), 65 (1715), 106 (1723), 160 (1741, emphasis added) hereafter cited as LNC. On the Virginia statute of 1691, see Brown, *Good Wives, Nasty Wenches,* 197–98. Robert Beverley, who advocated intermarriage in 1705, issued a revised edition of his *History* in 1722 that omitted the marriage promotion. Robert Beverley, *The History and Present State of Virginia* (Chapel Hill: University of North Carolina Press, 1947), 38–39, 170–71. See also Randolph, *British Travelers Among the Southern Indians,* 54. Jack D. Forbes argues that because Indians were often counted as mulattoes, historians fail to recognize the actual numbers of Indians in the colonial population. See Forbes, *Africans and Native Americans,* 219, 267.

46. For excellent discussions of how laws hardened racial boundaries in Virginia, see A. Leon Higginbotham and Barbara K. Kopytoff, "Racial Purity and Interracial Sex in the Law of Colonial and Antebellum Virginia," *The Georgetown Law Journal* 77, no. 6 (August 1989): 1967–2029, and Brown, *Good Wives, Nasty Wenches,* chap. 6. See also Peggy Pascoe, "Race, Gender, and Intercultural Relations: The Case of Interracial Marriage," *Frontiers* 12, no. 1 (1991): 5–18, and "Miscegenation Law, Court Cases, and Ideologies of 'Race' in Twentieth-Century America," *Journal of American History* 83, no. 1 (June 1996): 44–69.

47. In Linnaeus's categories one can see the influence of Galenic humor theory according to which the particular balance of four humors made up the human constitution. On naturalists' increasing tendency to emphasize degeneracy of Native Americans, see Vaughan, "From White Man to Redskin," especially 944–47. See also Arthur O. Lovejoy, *The Great Chain of Being: A Study of the History of an Idea* (Cambridge, Mass.: Harvard University Press, 1936).

48. Rev. James Fontaine, *Memoirs of a Huguenot Family,* trans. and ed. Ann Maury (Bungay: Morrow, 1986) 349–50.

49. Adair, *History,* 452. Vaughan, "From White Man to Redskin," 932–34, 948–49. Karen Ordahl Kupperman points out that only when Indians refused to assimilate with the English did the latter begin to see race as inherent and immutable. Kupperman, "Presentment of Civility," 227–28.

50. Adair, *History,* 1, 34. Waselkov and Braund, *William Bartram,* 156. Merrell, "The Racial Education of the Catawba Indians."

51. Nancy Shoemaker, "How Indians Got to be Red," *American Historical Review* 102, no. 3 (June 1997): 625–44. William G. McLoughlin and Walter H. Conser Jr., argue in "'The First Man Was Red'" that Native Americans took on a racial identity only after the American Revolution and in response to European ideas about race. James Merrell argues that the growth of racial slavery in the Piedmont after 1800 led the Catawba to perceive African Americans, especially enslaved men who did "women's work" in the fields, as different and degraded. In addition, the "Indians' own tenuous position in antebellum society hastened the drift toward racism." Merrell, "The Racial Education of the Catawba Indians," 365, 382.

52. Adair, *History,* 132. Adair did not give the year of Buck's death. See also Hatley, *The Dividing Paths,* 60–62.

53. Perdue, *Cherokee Women,* 82–83, 100–101. Hatley, *Dividing Paths,* 61–62. On the strains of occupying a liminal position between two cultures, see the essays in *The New Peoples: Being and Becoming Métis in North America,* ed. Jacqueline Peterson and Jennifer S. H. Brown (Lincoln: University of Nebraska Press, 1985); Nancy L. Hagedorn, "'Faithful, Knowing, and Prudent': Andrew Montour as Interpreter and Cultural Broker, 1740–1772," in *Between Indian and White Worlds: The Cultural Broker,* ed. Margaret Connell Szasz (Norman: University of Oklahoma Press, 1994), 44–60; Frances Karttunen, *Between Worlds: Interpreters, Guides, and Survivors* (New Brunswick, N.J.: Rutgers University Press, 1994); James Merrell, "'The Cast of His Countenance': Reading Andrew Montour," in *Through a Glass Darkly: Reflections on Personal Identity in Early America,* ed. Ronald Hoffman, Mechal Sobel, and Fredrika Teute (Chapel Hill: University of North Carolina Press, 1997), 13–39; Michele Gillespie, "The Sexual Politics of Race and Gender: Mary Musgrove and the Georgia Trustees," in *The Devil's Lane: Sex and Race in the Early South,* ed. Catherine Clinton and Michele Gillespie (New York: Oxford University Press, 1997), 187–201. See also Eric Hinderaker, "Translation and Cultural Brokerage," in *The Blackwell Companion to Native American History,* ed. Neal Salisbury and Phil Deloria (Oxford: Blackwell, forthcoming). On suspicions toward mixed-race people and cultural go-betweens, see James H. Merrell, *Into the American Woods: Negotiators on the Pennsylvania Frontier* (New York: Norton, 1999). For a more positive view of the flexible identities of mixed-race peoples and their crucial role in creating a Southern middle ground, see Andrew Frank, "A Peculiar Breed of Whites: Race, Culture, and Identity in the Creek Confederacy," (Ph.D. diss., University of Florida, 1998).

54. "Journal of Antoine Bonnefoy, 1741–1742," in *Travels in the American Colonies,* ed. Newton D. Mereness (New York: Macmillan, 1916), 248 (fled arrest). *South Carolina Gazette* ads quoted in Verner W. Crane, "A Lost Utopia of the First American Frontier," *Sewanee Re-*

view 27, no. 1 (January 1919), 54; Adair, *History,* 254 (painted himself). Information on Priber's background and thesis is in Knox Mellon Jr., "Christian Priber and the Jesuit Myth," *The South Carolina Historical Magazine* 59 (1960): 75–81.

55. Adair, *History,* 254–56; Ludovick Grant, "Historical Relations of Facts Delivered by Ludovick Grant, Indian Trader, to his Excellency the Governor of South Carolina," in *The South Carolina Historical and Genealogical Magazine* 10, no. 1 (January 1909): 59.

56. Anonymous writer, *South Carolina Gazette,* August 15, 1743 (Paradice; extreamly wicked); Grant, "Historical Relations," 59 (great scholar); "Journal of Antoine Bonnefoy," 248 (wrote German); Americus, "Characters," in *Annual Register . . . of the Year 1760* (London: J. Didsley, 1790), as quoted in Rennard Strickland, "Christian Gotelieb Priber: Utopian Precursor of the Cherokee Government," *The Chronicles of Oklahoma* 48, no. 3 (autumn 1970), 268 (hypothesis); Adair, *History,* 257. Grant, "Historical Relations," 59 (all Colours); Oglethorpe, "Account of Christian Pryber's Proceedings," April 22, 1743, in Candler, *The Colonial Records of Georgia,* vol. 36, 129; "Journal of Antoine Bonnefoy," 249 (no superiority). Anonymous writer, *South Carolina Gazette,* August 15, 1743 (whimsical Privileges; talks prophanely).

57. "Journal of Antoine Bonnefoy," 249 (no marriage contract; their genius); Grant, "Historical Relations," 59 (Children). *South Carolina Gazette,* August 15, 1743 (natural rights). On the influence of Thomas More's *Utopia,* see Crane "A Lost Utopia," and Rennard Strickland, "Christian Gotelieb Priber."

58. Grant, "Historical Relations," 60; Adair, *History,* 255–56.

59. Adair, *History,* 252, 256–57. Americus, in Strickland, "Christian Gotelieb Priber," 269.

60. Waselkov and Braund, *William Bartram,* 75. Lawson, *A New Voyage,* 61. On the Cherokee involvement in the Seven Years' War and its aftermath, see Hatley, *Dividing Paths,* chaps. 10–13. Perdue points out that towns may have become too vulnerable as targets for Indian war parties and eighteenth-century colonial armies. Perdue, *Cherokee Women,* 106. Waselkov and Braund, *William Bartram,* 75–77 (Keowee). Adair, *History,* 187. On the "demise" of Indian towns and the isolating effects on women, see Perdue, *Cherokee Women,* 107–108. For a complex view of the changing status of métis women, see Van Kirk, *Many Tender Ties,* passim, esp. 75–94. On métis women who learned dairying and other gender-specific Euroamerican tasks, see Lucy Eldersveld Murphy, "To Live among Us: Accomodation, Gender, and Conflict in the Western Great Lakes Region, 1760–1832," in *Contact Points: American Frontiers from the Mohawk Valley to the Mississippi, 1750–1830,* ed. Andrew Cayton and Fredrika Teute (Chapel Hill: University of North Carolina Press, 1998), 270–303. Murphy argues that native and métis women's negotiation of gender roles was crucial to the formation of culturally integrated communities.

61. Adair, *History,* 134–35.

62. On Indian women's selective appropriation of Christian symbols and rituals that allowed them to side-step patriarchal injunctions, see Nancy Shoemaker, "Kateri Tekakwitha's Tortuous Path to Sainthood," in *Negotiators of Change,* ed. Shoemaker, 49–71. For the example of a Creek woman who refused to let her child attend an English school, see Waselkov and Braund, *William Bartram,* 102. On the persistence of Indian gender roles that benefited women well into the nineteenth century (even as women's claims to property were curtailed by U.S. laws), see Theda Perdue, "Women, Men, and American Indian Policy: The Cherokee Response to 'Civilization,'" in *Negotiators of Change,* ed. Shoemaker, 90–114 and Clara Sue Kidwell, "Choctaw Women and Cultural Persistence in Mississippi," in ibid., 115–134. On cultural traditions that endured in the Piedmont, see Merrell, *The Indians' New World,* 125–33, 229–36. On methods of community-farming in the 1770s, see Waselkov and Braund, *William Bartram,* 127; Adair, *History,* 436–37.

63. On the shifting balance of power, see Merrell, *The Indians' New World,* chap. 5. On resistance to English values despite accommodation to new means of subsistence, see Hatley, *Dividing Paths,* 55, 161–63. On the continuation of women-dominated village economies that expanded to include larger markets, see Lucy Eldersveld Murphy, "Autonomy and the Economic Roles of Indian Women of the Fox-Wisconsin River Region, 1763-1832," in *Negotiators of Change,* ed. Shoemaker, 72–89.

Chapter 3

1. *Crown v. Mary Gorman.* Mary Gorman's confession, July 15, 1726; depositions of John West, John Ives, Thomas Collings, and Christopher Dawson, August 1, 1726, in Jury's indictment, [July 1726]; jury's presentment, October 1726, all in General Court Criminal Papers, 1726, Colonial Court Papers—Civil and Criminal, North Carolina State Archives, Division of Archives and History (hereafter NCSA). See also *North Carolina Higher-Court Minutes, 1724–1730*, ed. Robert J. Cain, vol. 6 of *The Colonial Records of North Carolina* [Second Series], ed. Mattie Erma Edwards Parker et al. (Raleigh: Division of Archives and History, 1963–), 324 (hereafter cited as Cain, NCHCR).

2. Tolerance for cross-dressing women was not a given: in colonial New York a woman was tarred for masquerading as a sailor. See Alfred F. Young, "English Plebian Culture and Eighteenth-Century American Radicalism," in *The Origins of Anglo-American Radicalism*, ed. Margaret Jacob and James Jacob (London: Allen and Unwin, 1984), 193. See also Alfred F. Young, *Masquerade: The Life and Times of Deborah Sampson Gannett, Continental Soldier* (New York: Knopf, forthcoming). An indispensable essay on the coexistence of multiple and sometimes clashing sets of mores is E. P. Thompson, "The Moral Economy of the English Crowd in the Eighteenth Century," in *Customs in Common* (London: Merlin, 1991), 185–258.

3. My understanding of resistance is greatly influenced by James C. Scott, *Domination and the Arts of Resistance: Hidden Transcripts* (New Haven, Conn.: Yale University Press, 1990) and *Weapons of the Weak: Everyday Forms of Peasant Resistance* (New Haven, Conn.: Yale University Press, 1985); Robin D. G. Kelley, *Race Rebels: Culture, Politics, and the Black Working Class* (New York: Free Press, 1994), esp. 35–75; Darlene Clark Hine, "Rape and the Inner Lives of Black Women in the Middle West: Preliminary Thoughts on the Culture of Dissemblance," *Signs* 14, no. 4 (summer 1989): 912–20; Michael Adas, "From Avoidance to Confrontation: Peasant Protest in Precolonial and Colonial Southeast Asia," in *Colonialism and Culture,* ed. Nicholas B. Dirks (Ann Arbor: University of Michigan Press, 1992), 89–126; Nicholas B. Dirks, "Ritual and Resistance: Subversion as Social Fact," in *Culture/Power/History: A Reader in Contemporary Social History,* ed. Dirks, Geoff Eley, and Sherry B. Ortner (Princeton, N.J.: Princeton University Press, 1994), 483–503.

4. *Laws of North Carolina,* ed. Walter Clark, vol. 23 of *The State Records of North Carolina,* ed. Clark, 16 vols. numbered 11–26 (Winston: State of North Carolina, 1895–1906), 3 (hereafter cited as LNC).

5. One historian estimated that between one half and two thirds of all white immigrants to the British colonies were indentured. Abbot Emerson Smith, *Colonists in Bondage: White Servitude and Convict Labor in America, 1607–1776* (New York: Norton, 1971), 3–4, 335–36. For a more recent confirmation that about half of the whites who came to the colonies from Britain and Europe (about 350,000 between 1580 and 1775) were servants, see Richard S. Dunn, "Servants and Slaves: The Recruitment and Employment of Labor," in *Colonial British America: Essays in the New History of the Early Modern Era,* ed. Jack P. Greene and J. R. Pole (Baltimore, Md.: Johns Hopkins University Press, 1984), 157–94. Convicted felons constituted as much as a quarter of all British emigrants to colonial America during the eighteenth century. Between 1718 and 1775 at least fifty thousand convicts were transported from Britain to the colonies. See A. Roger Ekirch, *Bound for America: The Transportation of British Convicts to the Colonies, 1718–1775* (Oxford: Clarendon Press, 1987), 27. On the everyday lives of women servants in the southern colonies, see Julia Cherry Spruill, *Women's Life and Work in the Southern Colonies* (reprint ed., New York: Norton, 1972).

6. Chowan County Miscellaneous Papers, 1695 (Microfilm C.024.99002), NCSA (Tarkentine). LNC, 62–66. *Chowan County North Carolina County Court Minutes (Court of Pleas and Quarter Sessions), 1730 thru 1745, Book I,* transcribed by Weynette P. Haun (Durham, N.C.: for the author, 1983), 101 (Mayer). Each of them served thirty-two extra days for their absence and three months more to reimburse their master for his expense in recapturing them. Chowan County Minute Docket of County Court, 1744. In 1741, any minister or justice of the peace who married servants without written permission from the master was fined five pounds. LNC,

159. Prior to this law, the North Carolina assembly presumably adopted the long-standing prohibition of servants' marriages without the consent of their master or mistress. British legal precedents (the Poor Laws) had for centuries prohibited servants from marrying. On the social control of servants in England, see Ann Kussmaul, *Servants in Husbandry in Early Modern England* (Cambridge: Cambridge University Press, 1981), esp. 83, and Martin Ingram, *Church Courts, Sex, and Marriage in England, 1570–1640* (Cambridge: Cambridge University Press, 1987). I use the term "free" to mark the legal status of someone who was not enslaved, even though "freedom" as an absolute condition did not exist for servants. The term "free black," for example, indicates a legally recognized condition as not enslaved, even if the person in question was subject to all the restrictions of servitude.

7. LNC, 64. The numbers of cases of fornication and bastardy are based on my research in the lower court records. They likely underestimate the incidence of illegitimate childbirth, in part because some records are missing. Given the lack of a census and irregular parish tallies, it is virtually impossible to establish the percentage of women in a county who gave birth to illegitimate children and how those numbers changed over time. In New Haven, Connecticut, between 1710 and 1730, men were charged with fornication in only half of the bastardy cases; after 1730, the father of an illegitimate child was not identified in nine out of ten cases. Fornication charges against men virtually ceased, while the prosecution of single mothers held fairly constant. Cornelia Hughes Dayton, *Women before the Bar: Gender, Law, and Society in Connecticut, 1639–1789* (Chapel Hill: University of North Carolina Press, 1995), chap. 4. For rituals of public penance in Virginia before 1662, see Kathleen M. Brown, *Good Wives, Nasty Wenches, and Anxious Patriarchs: Gender, Race, and Power in Colonial Virginia* (Chapel Hill: University of North Carolina Press, 1996), 189–92. Such penance rituals for fornication no longer occurred in North Carolina courts. During the seventeenth and eighteenth centuries "a significant change undoubtedly took place in the colonists' treatment of illegitimacy and bridal pregnancy: from treating both as serious sins the former was dealt with as a civil problem and the latter as a matter of moderate concern to religious groups, but not to the state." Robert V. Wells, "Illegitimacy and Bridal Pregnancy in Colonial America," in *Bastardy and Its Comparative History: Studies in the History of Illegitimacy and Marital Nonconformism in Britain, France, Germany, Sweden, North America, Jamaica, and Japan*, ed. Peter Laslett, Karla Oosterveen, and Richard M. Smith (Cambridge, Mass.: Harvard University Press, 1980), 357. On secularization and its accompanying sexual double standard, see Carol F. Karlsen, *The Devil in the Shape of a Woman: Witchcraft in Colonial New England* (New York: Vintage, 1989), 194–202; David H. Flaherty, "Law and the Enforcement of Morals in Early America," *Perspectives in American History*, vol. 5 (Cambridge, Mass.: Harvard University Press, 1971), 203–53.

8. LNC, 5, 174 (emphasis added). The preamble states the law's intent to keep the parish from paying child support. See *A Collection of the Statutes of the Parliament of England in Force in the State of North Carolina*, compiled by Francois-Xavier Martin (New Bern, 1792), 403. These financial concerns were not new: English laws passed in 1576 and 1610 sought to ensure the maintenance of poor children and the punishment of their parents. See Ingram, *Church Courts*, 152. In Virginia the majority of unwed mothers to appear in court were servant women. See Flaherty, *Law and the Enforcement of Morals in Early America*, 239; Brown, *Good Wives, Nasty Wenches*, 194. This was most likely the case in North Carolina as well, even though court clerks identified most of them simply as "single" or "spinsters." In South Carolina the accusation of paternity stuck despite a man's denials as long as a woman's accusation was taken under oath by magistrates and her charges remained constant during childbirth. See Spruill, *Women's Life and Work*, 319.

9. Laurel Thatcher Ulrich argues that the ritual questioning of a woman in labor to identify the child's father was not a form of harassment, it was "a formality allowing the woman . . . to claim child support." Thus, "confessing to fornication was simply a preliminary step to suing for the maintenance of one's child." Ulrich, *A Midwife's Tale: The Life of Martha Ballard, Based on Her Diary, 1785–1812* (New York: Vintage, 1991), 149, 151. For a discussion of women's "semi-professional sexual extortion" of men in sixteenth- and seventeenth-century England, see Barnard Capp, "The Double Standard Revisited: Plebian Women and Male Sexual Repu-

tation in Early Modern England," *Past and Present* 162 (February 1999): 70–100. Women's ability to find redress in the courts may be more true for New England than for the southern colonies, since "New England courts treated men and women more equally in sex crime prosecutions than did courts in the Chesapeake." See Mary Beth Norton, *Founding Mothers and Fathers: Gendered Power and the Forming of American Society* (New York: Knopf, 1996), 346. Faced with a court ruling, some men still fled their financial responsibilities. In May 1758 carpenter Richard Hickman "prevailed with" unwed Mary Johnston; when her child was born, Hickman "absconded," leaving Mary to rely on three other men to post bond for child support. Examination of Mary Johnston, October 23, 1758, Chowan County Bastardy Papers, NCSA.

10. On whippings for women and fines for men, see Donna J. Spindel, *Crime and Society in North Carolina, 1663–1776* (Baton Rouge: Louisiana State University Press, 1989), 131. On men's ability to substitute community service for a whipping, see Spruill, *Women's Life and Work,* 320. On the language of active men and acted-upon women, see Dayton, *Women before the Bar,* 176–79, and Lyndal Roper, *Oedipus and the Devil: Witchcraft, Sexuality, and Religion in Early Modern Europe* (London: Routledge, 1994), 60–62. On whippings as humiliating, especially for women who were stripped to the waist, see Norton, *Founding Mothers and Fathers,* 338–39.

11. *Crown v. Bordine,* Recognizance, Orders of [September?] Court, 1750, Hyde County Civil and Criminal Action Papers, NCSA. The complaint was found a true bill in March 1751, but the case was discontinued in June 1751. See Hyde County Appearance, Reference, Crown and Execution Docket, Court of Pleas and Quarter Sessions, 1744–61. More obscure is the slander suit brought by Ebenezer Gilbert against Abigail Gedings in 1759 for saying that "the Child which his wife had miscarred" had a head "as Big as his fist." Gedings's reference to the head size may have suggested Mrs. Gilbert had not miscarried inadvertently or legally. Gilbert won the case. Hyde County Civil and Criminal Papers, 1759, NCSA. Abortion before quickening—defined as the first moment the mother could feel the fetus move—was not considered criminal by English or colonial courts. See Cornelia Hughes Dayton, "Taking the Trade: Abortion and Gender Relations in an Eighteenth-Century New England Village," *William and Mary Quarterly,* 3d series, 48, no. 1 (January 1991): 19–49, esp. 20. For abortion cases in other colonies, see Susan E. Klepp, "Lost, Hidden, Obstructed, and Repressed: Contraceptive and Abortive Technology in the Early Delaware Valley," in *Early American Technology: Making and Doing Things from the Colonial Era to 1850,* ed. Judith A. McGaw (Chapel Hill: University of North Carolina Press, 1994), 68–113; Spruill, *Women's Life and Work,* 325–26; Roger Thompson, *Sex in Middlesex: Popular Mores in a Massachusetts County, 1649–1699* (Amherst: University of Massachusetts Press, 1986), 11, 24–26, 107–8, 182–83; Lyle Koehler, *A Search for Power: The "Weaker Sex" in Seventeenth-Century New England* (Urbana: University of Illinois Press, 1980), 205–6. On the age-old availability of different abortion techniques, see John M. Riddle, *Contraception and Abortion from the Ancient World to the Renaissance* (Cambridge, Mass.: Harvard University Press, 1992); Robert V. Schnucker, "Elizabethan Birth Control and Puritan Attitudes," *Journal of Interdisciplinary History* 4 (spring 1975): 655–67; Angus McLaren, *Reproductive Rituals: The Perception of Fertility in England from the Sixteenth Century to the Nineteenth Century* (London: Methuen, 1984), chap. 4; Linda Gordon, *Woman's Body, Woman's Right,* rev. ed. (New York: Penguin, 1990), chaps. 1–2. Due to very limited knowledge of women's reproductive anatomy, surgical abortion was performed infrequently in the colonial era. Cornelia Dayton has discovered the only known documented case (1742) of an abortion by instrument in colonial America, which she discusses in "Taking the Trade."

12. All of the depositions of this case are dated January 10, 1745, in Colonial Court Papers, Criminal Papers, General and Assize Courts, 1745–49, NCSA. I thank Marjoleine Kars for alerting me to this case and providing me with a photocopy of the document. Elizabeth Lang made her comments to Mary Sanders, who in turn reported them to the court. In the "Examination of Elizabeth King" I have inserted "wants" because it fits both the meaning in the sentence and the torn space in the document. For Sumner's indictment and acquittal, see Colonial Court Papers, Criminal Papers, General and Assize Courts, March 1745, NCSA. Cited in Spindel, *Crime and Society in North Carolina,* 49.

13. See, for example, the secret abortion of Sarah Grosvenor in Connecticut just two years earlier. Dayton, "Taking the Trade."

14. Catherine M. Scholten, *Childbearing in American Society: 1650–1850* (New York: New York University Press, 1985), 15 (natural condition). Spruill, *Women's Life and Work*, 52 (divine plan). D'Emilio and Freedman argue that in "early America, a unitary system of sexual regulation that involved family, church, and state rested upon a consensus about the primacy of familial, reproductive sexuality." Cases of abortion, however, attest to rifts in that consensus and suggest that not all sexual acts in early America had reproduction as their goal. John D'Emilio and Estelle B. Freedman, *Intimate Matters: A History of Sexuality in America* (New York: Harper and Row, 1988), xvii. Wealthy women could also find bearing and raising children burdensome. Elizabeth Drinker, a Philadelphia Quaker, "often thought that women who live to get over the time of Child-bareing, if other things are favourable to them, experience more comfort and satisfaction than at any other period of their lives." The cost and care involved in raising children was also a factor. One minister found that it was "folly tho common" for women with large families "to wish and resolve to have no more [children], and to be cast down with grief and anxious care if they find themselves with child again." Both quotes (without dates) in Scholten, *Childbearing in American Society*, 13. Laurel Thatcher Ulrich assumes that in early New England "reproduction was uncontrollable." Ulrich, *Good Wives: Image and Reality in the Lives of Women in Northern New England, 1650–1750* (New York: Oxford University Press, 1983), 159. For an argument to the contrary, see McLaren, *Reproductive Rituals*.

15. On infanticide, see Peter C. Hoffer and N. E. H. Hull, *Murdering Mothers: Infanticide in England and New England, 1558–1803* (New York: New York University Press, 1981); Rosalind Mitchison and Leah Leneman, *Sexuality and Social Control: Scotland, 1660–1780* (Oxford: Blackwell, 1989), 209–16; Ulrich, *Good Wives*, 195–201; Koehler, *A Search for Power*, 199–205; Sharon Ann Burnston, "Babies in the Well: An Underground Insight Into Deviant Behavior in Eighteenth-Century Philadelphia," *Pennsylvania Magazine of History and Biography* 106, no. 2 (April 1982): 151–86; R. W. Malcolmson, "Infanticide in the Eighteenth Century," in *Crime in England, 1550–1800*, ed. J. S. Cockburn (Princeton, N.J.: Princeton University Press, 1977), 187–209; Merril D. Smith, "'Unnatural Mothers': Infanticide, Motherhood, and Class in the Mid-Atlantic, 1730–1830," in *Over the Threshold: Intimate Violence in Early America*, ed. Christine Daniels and Michael V. Kennedy (New York: Routledge, 1999), 173–84.

16. LNC, 324. This was an adoption of the English statute made under James I in 1624 that a woman who concealed the birth of an illegitimate child could be hanged for murder. In medieval England infanticide was not homicide, but rather a lesser crime not distinguished from induced abortion. By the seventeenth century, however, infanticide was a capital crime in England and its colonies. See Lawrence Stone, *The Family, Sex, and Marriage in England, 1500–1800*, abridged ed. (New York: Harper Torchbooks, 1979), 326–27.

17. A bill of indictment was the written accusation of a crime based on the examination of the accused by a justice of the peace; a presentment was a written accusation based on information brought to a magistrate from someone other than the accused. See Paul M. McCain, *The County Court in North Carolina before 1750* (Durham, N.C.: Duke University Press, 1954), 37–38, 45–46. Criminal cases were prosecuted by the attorney general who represented the crown and the proprietors, and who was appointed by the deputy governor and his council. On Colliar: General Court of Oyer and Terminer, March 1720, in *North Carolina Higher-Court Minutes, 1709–1723*, ed. William S. Price Jr., vol. 5 of *The Colonial Records of North Carolina* [Second Series], ed. Mattie Erma Edwards Parker et al. (Raleigh: Division of Archives and History, 1963–), 212–13 (hereafter cited as Price, NCHCR, vol. 5). On Musick: General Criminal Court Records, 1720, NCSA; Cain, NCHCR, 327. On Pritlove: General Court Criminal Papers, January 1722/3, NCSA. On Bryan: General Court Criminal Papers, July 1729, NCSA; General Court Minutes, Oyer and Terminer, July 29, 1729, NCSA. On Morris: General Court Criminal Papers, October, 1735, NCSA. On Lynn: *Crown v. Lynn*, Salisbury District Supreme Court, Miscellaneous Papers, 1761. On women of color prosecuted for infanticide in New England, see Dayton, *Women before the Bar*, 211; Ulrich, *Good Wives*, 196. In England too, most of the women involved in infanticide cases were unmarried servant women. Middle-class and

aristocratic women seldom appeared in court on charges of infanticide, perhaps because they could afford to farm out illegitimate children to families in the countryside or pay others to dispose of their unwanted infants. See Malcolmson, "Infanticide in the Eighteenth Century," 192. In December 1711, "Betty J-r-d-n" of Virginia stood condemned to die for burglarizing the governor's house. She "plead her belly," a jury of matrons confirmed her pregnancy, and the sentence was stayed. William Byrd, *The Secret Diary of William Byrd of Westover, 1709–1712*, ed. Louis B. Wright and Marion Tinling (Richmond, Va.: Dietz, 1941), 452–53. See also Spruill, *Women's Life and Work*, 326–27. On the decline of convictions for infanticide, see Hoffer and Hull, *Murdering Mothers*, chap. 3; Dayton, *Women before the Bar*, 207–15. Donna J. Spindel and Stuart W. Thomas Jr. surmise that "the high rate of acquittal for infanticide combined with the high rate of conviction for bastardy suggests that the mother of an illegitimate child had a better chance of escaping punishment by killing the child than by allowing it to live." See their "Crime and Society in North Carolina, 1663–1740," *Journal of Southern History* 49, no. 2 (May 1983): 223–44, quote on 240.

18. LNC, 5. Chowan County Court Minutes, October 1715, NCSA. Chowan County Miscellaneous Papers, 1749, NCSA. Ingram notes economic motives behind such accusations in England: "Quite often the woman accused of incontinence was a widow holding lands by manorial customs which specified that her rights lasted only so long as she remained 'chaste and sole'; the accuser was usually someone who stood to benefit if the widow forfeited her holding." Ingram, *Church Courts*, 244–45.

19. LNC, 64. Information made by David Jones Sr., July Court, 1759, Hyde County Bastardy Papers, NCSA. Petition of Mrs. Rowden, April 20, 1732, Chowan County Court Minutes, NCSA. On Hamon: Chowan County Court Minutes, July 1737; 1739/40. In February 1740, Ann Hamon, now an indentured servant to John Pratt, acknowledged in court that she had two children during her time of service, and she was ordered to serve extra time according to the law. Bertie County Court Minutes, February 1739/40, NCSA. On Hamon's status as the free black granddaughter of a white woman, see Paul Heinegg, *Free African Americans of North Carolina and Virginia*, 3d ed. (Baltimore, Md.: Clearfield, 1997), vol. 1, 361.

20. Arrest warrant for William Swann and magistrates' judgment, August 3, 1709, Chowan County Miscellaneous Papers (Microfilm C.024.99002), NCSA. Sharon Block provides evidence of masters' sexual exploitation of servant women and explains how economic control could become sexual control as well, both shoring up patriarchal relations in the household. See Sharon Block, "Coerced Sex in British North America, 1700–1820" (Ph.D. diss., Princeton University, 1995), 70–73. For the constriction of servants' capacity to resist sexual coercion and for masters' ability to "manipulate forced sexual encounters into a mimicry of consensual ones," see Sharon Block, "Lines of Color, Sex, and Service: Comparative Sexual Coercion in Early America," in *Sex, Love, Race: Crossing Boundaries in North American History*, ed. Martha Hodes (New York: New York University Press, 1999), 141–63, esp. 143. On the sexual abuse of servant women, see also Norton, *Founding Mothers and Fathers*, 120–23.

21. On Jones: November 3, 1729, "Hue & Cry for a Runaway," General Court Miscellaneous Papers, Box 192. On Lambert: *North Carolina Gazette*, April 15, 1757, Microfilm copy in Williams R. Perkins Library, Duke University. In England, as in the colonies, court clerks generally used euphemisms such as "barbarous treatment" or "ill use" in place of "rape." Given this custom, we may never know how many suits against unspecified physical abuse involved sexual violence. See Anna Clark, *Women's Silence, Men's Violence: Sexual Assault in England, 1770–1845* (London: Pandora, 1987), 29–30; Margaret Hunt, "Wife Beating, Domesticity, and Women's Independence in Eighteenth-Century London," *Gender and History* 4, no. 1 (spring 1992): 10–33. Rape charges and their adjudication are discussed in greater detail in chapter 5.

22. LNC, 65. This law had its precedent in a Virginia statute of 1662. See Norton, *Founding Mothers and Fathers*, 103. Bertie County Court Minutes, November 10, 1731, NCSA. Musick paid a fine of fifty shillings for fornication and Ryall paid five pounds for adultery. The latter fine is remarkable because Musick was single and the law defined adultery as sex with a married woman. The courts apparently did not always abide by the legal double standard.

23. LNC, 5 (quote), 174 (1741). Chowan County Bastardy Bonds, 1752, NCSA (Ashley); Chowan County Bastardy Bonds, 1755 (Slaughter and Ford); 1759 (Halsey), NCSA. Mary Halsey, probably Rachael Halsey's sister, had an illegitimate child the year before in Chowan. On the role of midwives in cases of illegitimate births, see Ulrich, *A Midwife's Tale*, 147–61. For this tradition in England, see Ingram, *Church Courts*, 263. On the belief of honesty during labor, see Spruill, *Women's Life and Work*, 273.

24. Arrest warrant for Jacob Tice, July 24, 1739, Chowan County Miscellaneous Papers, NCSA. Bertie County Criminal Action Papers, 1758, NCSA. *Holland v. Ward*, July Court, 1747, Chowan County Civil Action Papers, NCSA. The outcome of this case is unknown. The Odums may also have brought a false charge against Ward to obtain the money. Either way, they were willing to pursue the case in a public suit. Christine Stansell explores diverging middle-class and working-class moralities in *City of Women: Sex and Class in New York, 1789–1860* (Urbana: University of Illinois Press, 1987).

25. "Hue and Cry for Bartholomew and Susanah MacGowan," January 15, 1725, General Court Criminal Papers, NCSA. *Allen vs. Davis alias McGreen* and *Metcalf v. Macgreen*, March 1725, in Cain, NCHCR, 88. The stolen goods are listed in the jury's presentment, January 11, 1725, General Court Criminal Papers, NCSA. The jury's uncertainty regarding Hanah's marital status appears in their reference to her as "Susanna McGowan wife of the said Bartho[lomew] Spinster." Her racial status is also ambiguous. Bartholomew McGowan had to serve 160 days for his eighty-day absence and two years extra to reimburse Mrs. Metcalf for her expense in capturing him. Bertie County Court Minutes, n.d., book 1, 1724–39, NCSA. Hanah Davis had run away from John Jones, another master, in 1717. See Margaret M. Hofmann, *Chowan Precinct, North Carolina, 1696 to 1723: Genealogical Abstracts of Deed Books* (Weldon, N.C.: Roanoke News, 1972), 231. George Allen's abuse of another servant woman is discussed in chapter 5.

26. On coverture, see Marylynn Salmon, *Women and the Law of Property in Early America* (Chapel Hill, N.C.: University of North Carolina Press, 1986), chaps. 3, 6.

27. LNC, 5. On the frequency of bigamy and the difficulty of detecting it, especially when a colonist left a spouse behind in England, see Edmund S. Morgan, "The Puritans and Sex," *New England Quarterly* 15, no. 4 (December 1942): 591–607. Cain, NCHCR, 420 (Brown). Pasquotank County Court Minutes, October 1748, NCSA (Diall). Diall's second marriage was apparently annulled, because two years later an unmarried West told the court that John Pendleton was the father of her illegitimate child. Pasquotank County Court Minutes, 1750; references to January and April Court, 1751, NCSA. Dayton found men more often prosecuted for bigamy than women because they had abandoned their roles as patriarchal providers of families. See Dayton, *Women before the Bar*, 172.

28. Dayton, *Women before the Bar*, 160. Brown, *Good Wives, Nasty Wenches*, chap. 6. Flaherty, "Law and the Enforcement of Morals in Early America," 203–53, especially 226. Norton, *Founding Mothers and Fathers*, 336, and Arthur P. Scott, *Criminal Law in Colonial Virginia* (Chicago: University of Chicago Press, 1930), 281, 291. Approximately 11.63 percent of the prosecutions in early North Carolina were for adultery, fornication, bastardy, and "keeping a disorderly house," and about half of the accused were convicted. See Spindel and Thomas, "Crime and Society in North Carolina," 223–44.

29. *Crown v. [William] Sikes*, jury's presentment, February Court, 1758, Edgecombe County Criminal Action Papers, NCSA. *Crown v. [Joseph] Sikes*, jury's presentment, February Court, 1758, Edgecombe County Criminal Action Papers, NCSA. *Crown v. Benjamin Sikes*, arrest warrant for Sikes, October 24, 1764, Edgecombe County Criminal Action Papers, NCSA. *Crown v. Alexander Jack*, jury's presentment, April Court, 1751, Pasquotank County Civil Action Papers, NCSA. Arrest warrant for Roads, June 28, 1743, Pasquotank County Civil Action Papers, NCSA. Ten years later, Mary Roads had another illegitimate child with shipwright John Smith. *Crown v. John Smith*, arrest warrant for Smith, August 15, 1753, Hyde County Civil and Criminal Action Papers, NCSA. Arrest warrant for Daniel Roads, December 3, 1746, Pasquotank County Bastardy Bonds, NCSA. Arrest warrant for John Burnham, November 4, 1746, Pasquotank County Bastardy Bonds, NCSA. Summons for Joseph Sawyer, July 25, 1748,

Pasquotank County Bastardy Bonds, NCSA. *Crown v. Lett and Butler,* jury's presentment, May Court, 1747, Bertie County Criminal Action Papers, NCSA. *Crown v. Williams,* jury's presentment, November Court, 1754, Bertie County Criminal Action Papers, NCSA. *Crown v. Butler and Mitchell,* jury's presentment, April Court, 1755, Bertie County Bastardy Bonds and Papers, NCSA; *Crown v. Butler and Mitchell,* arrest warrant for Butler and Mitchell, April 28, 1758, Bertie County Criminal Action Papers, NCSA. Martha Butler had a child out of wedlock in 1754: Bertie Criminal Actions Papers, NCSA. *Crown v. G[abriel] Manley,* arrest warrant for Manley, April 28, 1758, April Court, 1758, Bertie County Criminal Action Papers, NCSA. *Crown v. [Solomon] Manley,* jury's presentment, April Court, 1758, Bertie County Criminal Action Papers, NCSA. See also Heinegg, *Free African Americans of North Carolina and Virginia,* vol. 1, 145–48 (Butler family); vol. 2, 473–75 (Manley family). On the "subculture of mostly poor people who did not abide by the rules of polite society" and who created extended illegitimate families in nineteenth-century North Carolina, see Victoria E. Bynum, *Unruly Women: The Politics of Social and Sexual Control in the Old South* (Chapel Hill: University of North Carolina Press, 1992), 90–93.

30. Chowan County Miscellaneous Papers, 1739, NCSA (Hudson). Chowan County Miscellaneous Papers, July Court, 1745 (Microfilm C.024.99003), NCSA (Hudson as executrix). *Crown v. Barker and Braizer,* arrest warrant for Barker and Braizer, October 17, 1739; jury's presentment, [October] Court, 1739, Perquimans County Civil Action Papers, NCSA; *Perquimans County North Carolina County Court Minutes (Court of Pleas and Quarter Sessions), 1738–1754, Book II,* transcribed by Weynette Parks Haun (Durham, N.C.: for the author, 1988), 63–65, 72. Both Godwin and Hollamon were single at the time of the indictment, but Godwin's previous status as a married woman resulted in a charge of "adultery" rather than fornication. *Crown v. Hollamon and Godwin,* arrest warrant for Hollamon and Godwin, April 28, 1757; jury's presentment, April Court, 1757, Bertie County Criminal Action Papers, NCSA. Secretary of State Papers, will of William Godwin, May 4, 1752, NCSA. For Hollamon's assault on Isaac Middleton, see *Crown v. Hollamon,* jury's presentment, August Court, 1753, Bertie County Criminal Action Papers, NCSA. On common-law marriages in England, see John R. Gillis, "Married but Not Churched: Plebeian Sexual Relations and Marital Nonconformity in Eighteenth-Century Britain," in *'Tis Nature's Fault: Unauthorized Sexuality during the Enlightenment,* ed. Robert Purks Maccubbin (Cambridge: Cambridge University Press, 1987), 31–42. On discrepancies between what colonists considered legitimate marriages and the legal definitions, see Norton, *Founding Mothers and Fathers,* 66–69. On the acceptance of illegitimacy in certain societies, see Daniel Scott Smith and Michael S. Hindus, "Premarital Pregnancy in America, 1640–1971: An Overview and Interpretation," *Journal of Interdisciplinary History* 5 (spring 1975): 537–70; Peter Laslett, *Family Life and Illicit Love in Earlier Generations: Essays in Historical Sociology* (Cambridge: Cambridge University Press, 1977); Laslett, Oosterveen, and Smith, eds., *Bastardy and Its Comparative History.* For the argument that the sexual mores of plebeian women in England were often more lenient than those of middle-class women, see Anna Clark, "Whores and Gossips: Sexual Reputation in London, 1770–1825," in *Current Issues in Women's History,* ed. Arina Angerman et al. (London: Routledge, 1989), 231–48.

31. All of the quotes in this case are dated March 17, 1724, in Chowan County Miscellaneous Records, Miscellaneous Court Material, 1687–1745 (Microfilm C.024.40032), NCSA. In addition to the other penalties, Cotton also had to pay twenty-four shillings and two pence (for court attendance and traveling costs) to Martha Morris and Eleanor Clerk, who had saved their own skins by standing as a witness against Cotton. In July 1726 Kenyon sued Martha for the thirty-eight pounds she still owed him. The case was continued until October 1728 when the jury dismissed it. Cain, NCHCR, 27–28.

32. Upper House Journals, December 18, 1754, *Colonial Records of North Carolina,* ed. William L. Saunders, 10 vols. (Raleigh: State of North Carolina, 1886–1890), vol. 5, 224 (hereafter cited as CRNC). "Journal of a French Traveller in the Colonies, 1765," *American Historical Review* 26 (July 1921): 743, 738. Cotton may not actually have said any of these words, as they come from Morris's defensive deposition. Nonetheless, they could have been spoken, and at the very least Morris was capable of inventing them as plausible speech. This kind of

talk likely occurred more often than court records reveal. Anthropologist James C. Scott describes how people with less power often choose to express their anger against superiors in safe conversations with like-minded peers. In these "hidden transcripts" people air their grievances in insulting or reproachful speeches they *wish* they could give directly to those in power. To avoid punishment, such "backstage discourse" generally remains concealed, but it can also serve as a rehearsal for verbal assaults that eventually spill out into the public domain. See Scott, *Domination and the Arts of Resistance*, esp. xii. On deference as a cover for other feelings of disrespect, see E. P. Thompson, "Moral Economy of the English Crowd."

33. *Robert Parks v. Mary Collins* in Chowan County Minute Docket of County Court. Petition of Mary Collins, April 1744. Chowan Court. Chowan Miscellaneous Papers, 1744. Chowan Court, 1745.

34. Arrest warrant for Katherine Jolley, August 31, 1749, Hyde County Bastardy Papers, NCSA. We cannot know if Harvey was a "Rogue" or his daughter a "Strumpit," but Harvey did know how to write, and his script and signature appear on arrest warrants in the Hyde County Civil Action Papers, NCSA.

35. On the powers of a justice of the peace, see Paul M. McCain, "The County Court in North Carolina before 1750" (Ph.D. diss., Duke University, 1950), chap. 2. On plural office holding, see William S. Price Jr., "'Men of Good Estates': Wealth among North Carolina's Royal Councillors," *North Carolina Historical Review* 49 (January 1972): 72–82.

36. James Reed quoted in A. Roger Ekirch, *"Poor Carolina": Politics and Society in Colonial North Carolina, 1729–1776* (Chapel Hill: University of North Carolina Press, 1981), 30. On religion in North Carolina that was indeed passionate (if not Anglican), see Jon F. Sensbach, *A Separate Canaan: The Making of an Afro-Moravian World in North Carolina, 1763–1840* (Chapel Hill: University of North Carolina Press, 1998); Marjoleine Kars, *Breaking Loose Together: The Regulator Rebellion in Pre-Revolutionary North Carolina* (2002) (Chapel Hill: University of North Carolina Press).

37. *Chowan County North Carolina County Court Minutes (Court of Pleas and Quarter Sessions), 1735–1738; 1746–1748, Book II*, transcribed by Weynette Parks Haun (Durham, N.C.: for the author, 1983), 45.

38. LNC, 4, 80. This punishment was for the first offence. Repeat offenders received thirty-nine lashes and a month in prison without bail. LNC, 182–85. See also Alan D. Watson, "Ordinaries in Colonial Eastern North Carolina," *North Carolina Historical Review* 45, no. 1 (January 1968): 67–83. Widowed women were more likely to receive licenses than spinsters or married women, because men did not want their female relatives engaged in work notoriously connected with unseemly behavior. Judith Bennett explains the threat that English alewives posed to the patriarchal order: "in flirting with customers they undermined the authority of husbands; in handling money, goods and debts they challenged the economic power of men; in bargaining with male customers they achieved a seemingly unnatural power over men; in avoiding effective regulation of their trade they insulted the power of male officers and magistrates and, perhaps most importantly, in simply pursuing their trade they often worked independently of men." Judith M. Bennett, "Misogyny, Popular Culture, and Women's Work," *History Workshop Journal* 31 (1991): 168–88.

39. *Crown v. Young*, General Court Criminal Actions papers, July Court 1731, NCSA (unnamed woman). Robert Kingham was charged with giving George Kennard "a mortal wound in the head" with an ax but was acquitted in April 1724. CRNC, vol. 2, 553–55. On aid to prisoners, see *Crown v. Robert Kingham*, Jury's Presentment, March Court, 1733, General Court Criminal Papers, NCSA. For the May 1733 complaint that Robert Kingham attempted to rape Elizabeth Montgomery, a child, see General Court Criminal Action Papers, NCSA (and chapter 5). For theft, see *Crown v. Kingham*, Jury's Presentment, July Court, 1736, General Court Criminal Papers, NCSA. *Crown v. Walthams*, Jury's Presentment, March Court, 1736, General Court Criminal Papers, NCSA. In January 1738 William Waltham (also Wattham) was fined for "Keeping a Disorderly house and for profain Swearing." He had to give "bond no longer to keep a publick house." Mary Waltham was ordered put into the stocks for three hours and "Ducket in the publick Ducking pool" for

her "profane Swearing 163 Oaths." Haun, *Chowan County Court Minutes, Book II,* 53–54. Mary Waltham was also charged with stealing black silk stockings: *Crown v. Mary Waltham,* Jury's Presentment, October Court, 1738, General Court—Criminal and Assize, NCSA.

40. William Byrd met with varying degrees of success when he tried to obtain sexual favors in Williamsburg and its surroundings. Byrd, *The Secret Diary,* 90, 425. See also William Byrd, *Another Secret Diary of William Byrd of Westover, 1739–1741,* ed. Louis B. Wright and Marion Tinling (Richmond, Va.: Dietz, 1942), 31, 93, 70, 137, 155, 157, 166, 168, 174 for comments that he "committed folly with" and "played the fool" with various women, including a Sally in Williamsburg who was probably a servant. There is no extensive study on prostitution in the colonies, but on the availability of prostitutes in colonial Boston and New York, see D'Emilio and Freedman, *Intimate Matters,* 50–52. On women convicts, see Ekirch, *Bound for America,* 172–73; Smith, *Colonists in Bondage,* 141.

41. [No author], *An Essay on Conjugal Infidelity, Shewing the Great Mischief that Attend Those that Defile the Marriage Bed* (London: T. Warner, 1727), 12–13, quoted in Donna Andrew, *Philanthropy and Police: London Charity in the Eighteenth Century* (Princeton, N.J.: Princeton University Press, 1989), 57. See also Vern L. Bullough, "Prostitution and Reform in Eighteenth-Century England," in *'Tis Nature's Fault,* ed. Maccubbin, 61–74.

42. *Marston v. Trotter,* deposition of Elizabeth Marston, March Court, 1729, in Cain, NCHCR, 554–55. In 1725, Marston sued William and Mary Havett for Mary's claim that Marston "keeps a Common Bawdy house and that her two daughters are the young whores by which she carrys on her trade of whoring with her customers that use her house," and furthermore "that Six men hath been taken in bed with her daughters in one night in her house." *Marston v. Havett,* July 1725, General Court Records, Cain, NCHCR, 128, 153. In nineteenth-century North Carolina, indictments for prostitution "particularly targeted women who engaged in interracial social activity or who operated taverns at which blacks and whites were suspected of gambling, drinking, and exchanging illegal goods." Bynum, *Unruly Women,* 93. While the evidence is much more sparse for the eighteenth-century, it seems likely that establishments charged with prostitution also countenanced interracial socializing. In March 1777, for example, a free black woman named Sarah Moore was charged with keeping "a disorderly House, by harbouring Lewd Women, entertaining sailors & negroes and selling them spiritous Liquors without Licence." New Bern District Superior Court Records, Criminal, Oyer and Terminer, NCSA.

43. Haun, *Chowan County Court Minutes, Book II,* 46–47. On Abell's children, see Heinegg, *Free African Americans of North Carolina and Virginia,* vol. 1, 27. For a related discussion of torture as a public spectacle imposed and regulated by the eighteenth century French state, see Michel Foucault, *Discipline and Punish: The Birth of the Prison,* trans. Alan Sheridan (New York: Vintage, 1979), chaps. 1–2.

44. I first argued that the prohibition of interracial sex and the lengthy indentures of mixed-race children had a dramatic impact on generations of free blacks in "The Institution of Illegitimacy: Race, Class, and the Sexual Regulation of Servant Women in Colonial North Carolina," a paper delivered at the American Historical Association's Annual Meeting in San Francisco, California, January 6–9, 1994 and again in "Dangerous Acts: The Politics of Illicit Sex in Colonial North Carolina, 1660–1760" (Ph.D. diss., Duke University, 1994), 119–30. My argument was partly in rejoinder to Kathleen M. Brown, "Gender and the Genesis of a Race and Class System in Virginia, 1630–1750" (Ph.D. diss., University of Wisconsin–Madison, 1990), chap. 5, which maintained that laws about sex targeted white women and did not discuss the long-term impact on black families. Although I did not know it at the time, Reginald Butler also argued that "enforcement of miscegenation laws appears to have been directed towards the status of juvenile offspring rather than towards the sexual activity of the white mother." See Reginald Butler, "Evolution of a Rural Free Black Community: Goochland County, Virginia, 1728–1832" (Ph.D. diss., Johns Hopkins University, 1989), 33. Butler and I also explored black women's strategies of resistance. For a similar discussion, see Brown, *Good Wives, Nasty Wenches,* 205–206, 227–41.

45. LNC, 65 (1715), 106 (1723), 160 (1741). Price, NCHCR, vol. 5, 114 (Sarah Williamson). Her son was probably Joseph Williamson, a "mulatto fellow" who came before the Pasquotank County court in 1747 to petition for his freedom. Petition of Amy Dempsey, no date, Colonial Court Records, Miscellaneous Papers, 1677–1775, Folder: "Freedom of Slaves," NCSA. On Elizabeth Puckett, see Cain, NCHCR, 425. *Crown v. John Cotton,* July Court, 1725, General Court Criminal Papers, NCSA. Information made by John Blacknall, March 2, 1725, General Court Miscellaneous Papers, NCSA. Eastern Quarter Symons Creek Monthly Meeting (in Pasquotank), reel 1: Women's Minutes, 1715–1768, Friends Historical Collection, Guilford College, Greensboro, North Carolina. Damaris Symons indentured her mulatto daughter, Rachael, to Peter Symons for thirty-one years. Pasquotank County Court Minutes, July 1748, NCSA. Indenture of Patience Griffin, March 30, 1759, Pasquotank County Apprentice Bonds, Folder: "Name Unknown," NCSA. More examples of white mothers who had mulatto children can be found in the Apprentice bonds and court records, NCSA. Because the Albemarle settlement was more an extension of Virginia than part of South Carolina, North Carolina's laws were based on Virginia precedents. The first laws in South Carolina to address interracial children were enacted in 1717. See Peter H. Wood, *Black Majority: Negroes in Colonial South Carolina from 1670 through the Stono Rebellion* (New York: Norton, 1974), 99; A. Leon Higginbotham Jr., *In the Matter of Color: The Colonial Period,* vol. 1 of *Race and the American Legal Process* (Oxford: Oxford University Press, 1978), 158–59.

46. LNC, 65. On the tacit allowance of interracial sex for white men, see Higginbotham, *In the Matter of Color,* 43–46; Michael L. Nicholls, "Passing through This Troublesome World: Free Blacks in the Early Southside," *Virginia Magazine of History and Biography* 92 (January 1984): 50–70; Flaherty, "Law and the Enforcement of Morals in Early America," 240. On the courtroom appearances of white but not black women for illicit sex, especially with slaves, see Brown, *Good Wives, Nasty Wenches,* 239. Although there are no exact population numbers for free blacks before 1790, out of an estimated 5000 persons living in Bertie county in 1763, 96 were free people of color. By the mid eighteenth century, of the 100,000 blacks and whites in North Carolina, about 4000 were both black and free. Free blacks made up between 4 and 5 percent of the total colonial population (that is, not including Native Americans). See Marvin L. Michael Kay and Lorin Lee Cary, "A Demographic Analysis of Colonial North Carolina with Special Emphasis upon the Slave and Black Populations" in *Black Americans in North Carolina and the South,* ed. Jeffrey J. Crow and Flora J. Hatley (Chapel Hill: University of North Carolina Press, 1984), tables 3-9 and 3-10 on 106–9. Because the very existence of free blacks disrupted any facile conflation of race with status, the free African American community attained a symbolic significance that extended well beyond its actual numbers.

47. LNC, 65, 160. For a discussion of the white ancestry of most free blacks in early America, see Nicholls, "Passing through This Troublesome World," 50–70; Douglas Deal, "A Constricted World: Free Blacks on Virginia's Eastern Shore, 1680–1750," in *Colonial Chesapeake Society,* ed. Lois Green Carr, Philip D. Morgan, and Jean B. Russo (Chapel Hill: University of North Carolina Press, 1988), 275–305; Ira Berlin, *Slaves without Masters: The Free Negro in the Antebellum South* (New York: Pantheon, 1974), 6–7. Thirty-one years was most of a person's life in an era when well-nourished white males could expect to live only about fifty years. James M. Gallman, "Mortality among White Males, Colonial North Carolina," *Social Science History* 4, no. 3 (August 1980): 295–316.

48. Pasquotank County Apprentice Bonds, March 13, 1759; March 30, 1759, Folder: "Name Unknown," NCSA. This was not simply a matter of routine sexism since apprentice bonds for white girls included the clause that they be taught to read, write, and cipher.

49. Pasquotank Apprentice Bonds, July 10, 1746, Folder: "B," NCSA (Bright; emphasis added). Pasquotank Pleas & Quarter Sessions, 1738, NCSA (Doll). On Williamson: Pasquotank County Court Minutes, 1747, NCSA. On Olson: Pasquotank County Apprentice Bonds, September Court, 1756, Folder: "No Name," NCSA. In 1733, "divers Inhabitants" complained that justices of the peace had ordered "divers free People, Negroes & Mulattoes" bound out against their will until the age of thirty-one, and that these unlawful practices were "well known" and might lead such persons to leave the colony. The free people in question were most cer-

tainly the children of black mothers (and not of white women). The governor's Council agreed that such illegal practices should be "exploded," but as I discuss below, the courts continued to bind out inconsistently the children of free black mothers, sometimes for thirty-one years, like the "mulatto" children of white mothers, and sometimes until age twenty-one or eighteen (like white boys and girls). See CRNC, vol. 3, 556–57.

50. Jesse, George, and Squire Demsey were apprenticed to learn reading, writing, and husbandry until age twenty-one. Bertie County Apprentice Bonds, 1756, NCSA. Amy Demsey, born the mulatto daughter of a white women in 1723, was apprenticed until the age of thirty-one to Nathaniel Duckenfield. When he died in January 1756, Amy's mother and the managers of the Duckenfield estate paid ten pounds and twenty pounds respectively to hinder Amy from being sold. Amy Demsey petitioned that her indenture be annulled because her freedom had been purchased. The outcome of her petition is unknown, but even if Dempsey gained her freedom, she may have chosen to remain a servant to widow Duckenfield as a way of supporting herself and staying near her children. Petition of Amy Dempsey, no date, Colonial Court Records, Miscellaneous Papers, 1677–1775, Folder: "Freedom of Slaves," NCSA. Bertie County Apprentice Bonds, 1756, NCSA (Isaac and Pen Pugh). I have not found evidence of an indenture for Sarah Pugh, but it is possible that she also worked on the Duckenfield plantation. Bertie County Apprentice Bonds, 1759, NCSA (Jones). David and Mary Pugh would learn to read and write, David would become a cooper like Jones, and Mary would learn household business.

51. Petition of Peter Van Trump, February 3, 1726, General Court Criminal Papers, NCSA. Petition of Ruth Tillett, no date, Pasquotank County Slave Records, NCSA. The petition was granted in March court, 1783. Freedom Petition of William Derry, no date, Colonial Court Records—Miscellaneous, Box 192, NCSA. The outcome of Derry's petition is unknown. The first law against kidnapping free blacks in North Carolina and selling them as slaves elsewhere was passed only in 1779. LNC, 890. On enslavement of free blacks, see also John Hope Franklin, *The Free Negro in North Carolina, 1790–1860* (New York: Norton, 1971), 48–57; Wood, *Black Majority*, 101; Higginbotham, *In the Matter of Color*, 205; Kay and Cary, "A Demographic Analysis of Colonial North Carolina," 112–17; Nicholls, "Passing through This Troublesome World," 275–305.

52. General Assembly—Upper and Lower Houses, July 1733, NCSA.

53. All three petitions for Sarah's children were granted Chancey on April 17, 1742. Pasquotank County Apprentice Bonds, no date, Folder: "B"; Pasquotank Civil Action Papers, no date, NCSA. Sarah also had two daughters: Frank Boe who, with her two children, was bound out to Chancey, and Rachel Overton (perhaps the Rachel Boe in Chancey's will), a mulatto woman (indentured to Aron Jackson) who herself had three children by a "Negro Husband." These children, Daniel, Samuel, and Perthinia, were bound out to Aron Jackson until age twenty-one, with the stipulation that they be taught to read, write, and cipher crossed out on the indentures. Pasquotank County Court Minutes, 1745, 1746, NCSA.

54. See also Pasquotank County Court Minutes, July, 1738, Pleas & Quarters Sessions, NCSA. In the 1720s a Virginia law sought to end the confusion by stating that mulatto children were to be bound as their mothers were, i.e. for thirty-one years, but North Carolina law did not make this point. This stipulation remained on the Virginia books until 1765 when this particular form of discrimination was replaced with the usual terms of apprenticeship: twenty-one years for boys, sixteen (or eighteen) for girls. See Flaherty, "Law and the Enforcement of Morals in Early America," 52–53. In North Carolina by the 1740s, most mixed-race children of free mulatto mothers were apprenticed the same length of time as whites (twenty-one and eighteen years for boys and girls), but there were still some inconsistencies. Elizabeth Price, a free black servant, had a child who was indentured until age thirty-one to Price's mistress, Martha Reding. Pasquotank County Court Minutes, 1743, NCSA.

55. Sarah Overton's petition is in the Pasquotank County Apprentice Bonds, Folder "O," NCSA. The court's response in the Pasquotank County Court Minutes, October 1745, 179–86, is quoted in Heinegg, *Free African Americans of North Carolina and Virginia*, vol. 1, 117. Sue Boe's indenture is in the Pasquotank County Court Minutes, July 1748, NCSA. Will of

232 Notes to Pages *129–134*

Edmund Chancey, March 15, 1753, Secretary of State Papers, NCSA. To "mulato Jack," perhaps the father of Sarah's children, Chancey gave "Ten Shillings Cash."

56. Fischer, "Dangerous Acts," 119–31. On thirty-one-year indentures, see LNC, 65 (1715).

57. Pasquotank County Apprentice Bonds, no date, Folder: "B," NCSA. Heinegg, *Free African Americans of North Carolina and Virginia*, vol. 1, 118 (1790).

58. Letter from North Carolina merchants to the Commissioners of Trade, July 18, 1715, CRNC, vol. 2, 197. LNC, 62–66 (1715), 106–7 (1723), 191–204 (1741). On the Stono Rebellion and white fears of slave insurrections, see Wood, *Black Majority*, chaps. 8, 10, 12.

Chapter 4

1. Arrest warrant for Jolley, June 15, 1747, Hyde County Civil and Criminal Papers, Colonial Court Papers—Civil and Criminal, North Carolina State Archives: Division of Archives and History (hereafter cited as NCSA). I have found little information on Thomas Partree, except that he made his mark as a witness for the will of William Martin, Esquire, in 1744 and later sold 150 acres to Peter Harris (Hyde County Court Minutes, June 1755). A large and growing literature analyzes the performative aspects of "whiteness," those acts that reasserted the social meanings of whiteness as well as the actor's own racial status and identity as white. I have been most influenced by David Roediger, *The Wages of Whiteness: Race and the Making of the American Working Class*, rev. ed. (New York: Verso, 1999); Eric Lott, *Love and Theft, Black Face Minstrelsy and the American Working Class* (New York: Oxford University Press, 1995); Ariela J. Gross, "Litigating Whiteness: Trials of Racial Determination in the Nineteenth-Century South," *Yale Law Journal* 108, no. 1 (October 1998): 109–188; Walter Johnson, *Soul by Soul: Life inside the Antebellum Slave Market* (Cambridge, Mass.: Harvard University Press, 1999).

2. Slanderers underscore the boundaries of acceptable behavior with accounts of transgressive acts, as do the slanderer's targets who deny the misconduct and profess their allegiance to social norms. On insults as the reverse definition of respectability, see Peter N. Moogk, "'Thieving Buggers' and 'Stupid Sluts': Insults and Popular Culture in New France," *William and Mary Quarterly*, 3d ser., 36, no. 4 (October 1979): 524–47, esp. 526. For an anthropological discussion of slander, see F. G. Bailey, *Gifts and Poison: The Politics of Reputation* (New York: Schocken Books, 1971). On courts as sites of performance, see A. G. Roeber, "Authority, Law, and Custom: The Rituals of Court Day in Tidewater, Virginia, 1720 to 1750," *William and Mary Quarterly*, 3d ser., 37 (January 1980): 29–52; Rhys Isaac, *The Transformation of Virginia, 1740–1790* (Chapel Hill: University of North Carolina Press, 1982), esp. 88–94; and, more generally, Mindie Lazarus-Black and Susan F. Hirsch, eds., *Contested States: Law, Hegemony, and Resistance* (New York: Routledge, 1994). Slander suits do not allow insight into racial self-images of Africans Americans, but on the creation of an African American identity out of multiple African ethnicities, see Michael A. Gomez, *Exchanging Our Country Marks: The Transformation of African Identities in the Colonial and Antebellum South* (Chapel Hill: University of North Carolina Press, 1998); Ira Berlin, *Many Thousands Gone: The First Two Centuries of Slavery in North America* (Cambridge: Harvard University Press, 1998); Philip D. Morgan, *Slave Counterpoint: Black Culture in the Eighteenth-Century Chesapeake and Lowcountry* (Chapel Hill: University of North Carolina Press, 1998).

3. Laura Gowing explains how early modern defamation suits combined formulaic, repetitious legal language with distinctive, colorful quotes that appear to be verbatim records of the insult. Court clerks understood the importance of capturing the precise words, since the outcome of the suit hinged on the nuances of the slur and on whether or not it was said in malice. Laura Gowing, *Domestic Dangers: Women, Words, and Sex in Early Modern London* (New York: Oxford University Press, 1996), chap. 2.

4. For a discussion of competing explanations of racial difference in the nineteenth century (one of science and the other of performance), see Ariela Gross, "Litigating Whiteness." This chapter, which relies heavily on other scholars' accounts of the gendered nature of honor and speech, adds an analysis of racial slurs and their gender-specific impact. My discussion of gendered insults is particularly indebted to Clara Ann Bowler, "Carted Whores and White

Shrouded Apologies: Slander in the County Courts of Seventeenth-Century Virginia," *Virginia Magazine of History and Biography* 85 (October 1977): 411–26; Robert St. George, "'Heated' Speech and Literacy in Seventeenth-Century New England," in *Seventeenth-Century New En gland: A Conference Held by the Colonial Society of Massachusetts, June 18 and 19, 1982*, ed. David D. Hall and David Grayson Allen (Boston: Colonial Society of Massachusetts, 1984), 275–317; Mary Beth Norton, "Gender and Defamation in Seventeenth-Century Maryland," *William and Mary Quarterly*, 3d ser., 44, no. 1 (January 1987): 3–39; Helena M. Wall, *Fierce Communion: Family and Community in Early America* (Cambridge, Mass.: Harvard University Press, 1990), 30–48; Susan Juster, "'Surely the Tongue is an Unruly Member': Women and Words in the Evangelical Church," paper delivered at the Ninth Berkshire Conference on the History of Women, June 11–13, 1993; Cornelia Hughes Dayton, *Women before the Bar: Gender, Law, and Society in Connecticut, 1639–1789* (Chapel Hill: University of North Carolina Press, 1995), chap. 6; Mary Beth Norton, *Founding Mothers and Fathers: Gendered Power and the Forming of American Society* (New York: Knopf, 1996), chap. 4 and 253–77; Jane Kamensky, *Governing the Tongue: The Politics of Speech in Early New England* (New York: Oxford University Press, 1997). For a now classic discussion of the performativity of gender, see Judith Butler, *Gender Trouble: Feminism and the Subversion of Identity* (New York: Routledge, 1990).

5. Fundamental Constitutions of Carolina, drawn up by John Locke, March 1, 1669, William L. Saunders, ed., *Colonial Records of North Carolina*, 10 vols. (Raleigh: State of North Carolina, 1886–1890), vol. 1, 203 (hereafter cited as CRNC). Walter Clark, ed. *Laws of North Carolina*, vol. 23 of *The State Records of North Carolina*, ed. Walter Clark, 16 vols. numbered 11–26 (Winston and Goldsboro: State of North Carolina, 1895–1906), 38–39 (hereafter cited as LNC). On rare occasions the North Carolina courts also prosecuted perjury and lying, which I do not discuss here, but see Donna J. Spindel, "The Law of Words: Verbal Abuse in North Carolina to 1730," *American Journal of Legal History* 39, no. 1 (January 1995): 25–42. On the difference between contempt and sedition, see Larry D. Eldridge, *A Distant Heritage: The Growth of Free Speech in Early America* (New York: New York University Press, 1994), 8–13. Colonial historians argue about when rights of free speech began, but they generally agree that as the political structures in the colonies became more stable in the early eighteenth century, the number of prosecutions for seditious speech declined.

6. *Crown v. Elinor Moline* in Mattie Erma Edwards Parker, ed., *North Carolina Higher-Court Records, 1670–1696*, vol. 2 of *The Colonial Records of North Carolina* [Second Series], ed. Mattie Erma Edwards Parker et al. (Raleigh: Division of Archives and History, 1963–), 208, 220, 236 (hereafter cited as Parker, NCHCR, vol. 2). No record of Moline's offending words survived. Thomas Harvey, deputy governor from 1694 until his death five years later, was a member of one of the first English families to settle in North Carolina. The status of Elinor and Robert Moline is harder to measure as no will exists for either of them. Robert Moline was apparently able to give bond for Elinor's good behavior, and the suits for debt brought against him over the years indicate his participation in local commerce.

7. Kamensky, *Governing the Tongue*, 114. In seventeenth-century New England, women accounted for under 15 percent of the presentments for speech against authority. Ibid., 245, n. 68. See also Dayton, *Women before the Bar*, 297, 322–23. For the handful of women who defamed government officials or court magistrates in colonial Virginia, see Kathleen M. Brown, *Good Wives, Nasty Wenches, and Anxious Patriarchs: Gender, Race, and Power in Colonial Virginia* (Chapel Hill: University of North Carolina Press, 1996), 95, 148–49. The 160 contempt charges are noted in Donna J. Spindel, *Crime and Society in North Carolina, 1663–1776* (Baton Rouge: Louisiana State University Press, 1989), 92, table 12. Spindel found only 10 cases of women accused of riot, affray, or other offenses against the public order, 5 cases of contempt of authority, and 1 case of sedition (unfortunately, Spindel does not name the defendants), ibid., 89. However, Spindel's focus on the higher courts leads to an underestimation of the incidences of contemptuous speech by women. In the Civil and Criminal Action Papers of seven county courts before 1760 I found more examples of women's contemptuous speech than Spindel found in the Higher Courts for all of the counties during the entire colonial period, presumably because such cases were punished or dismissed before they reached the

higher courts. Elizabeth Joceline, *The Mother's Legacy* (1625), quoted in Anthony Fletcher, *Gender, Sex, and Subordination in England, 1500–1800* (New Haven, Conn.: Yale University Press, 1995), 380. Piney Woods Monthly Meeting Minutes (Perquimans), August 2, September 5, November 1, 1710, Friends Historical Collection ("bad languig"). For a careful analysis of the role of status in determining which insults came to court in early Maryland, see Norton, "Gender and Defamation in Seventeenth-Century Maryland," and Norton, *Founding Mothers and Fathers,* chap. 4. See also Moogk, "'Thieving Buggers' and 'Stupid Sluts'" on class-specific insults and court responses.

8. Chowan County Court Minutes, January, 1737, NCSA (Dalton). CRNC, vol. 1, 453 (Clapper). In 1699 Clapper became a constable, ibid., 524. This discussion of the restoration of men's respectability through public apology is based on Kamensky's explanation of the same in *Governing the Tongue,* chap. 5. See also Jane Kamensky, "Talk Like a Man: Speech, Power, and Masculinity in Early New England," *Gender and History* 8, no. 1 (April 1996): 22–47.

9. *Crown v. Castleton,* March 1724, Robert J. Cain, ed., *North Carolina Higher-Court Minutes, 1724–1730,* vol. 6 of *The Colonial Records of North Carolina* [Second Series], ed. Mattie Erma Edwards Parker et al. (Raleigh: Division of Archives and History, 1963-), 26–27 (hereafter cited as Cain, NCHCR). *Crown v. Robert Atkins,* March 1724, ibid., 24–26. In seventeenth-century New England, a public apology was seldom possible unless the offending male speaker was of the same status as the person he had offended. Kamensky, *Governing the Tongue,* 132–33.

10. *Crown v. Keeton,* October-November Court, 1697. Parker, ed., *North Carolina Higher-Court Records, 1697–1701,* vol. 3 of *The Colonial Records of North Carolina* [Second Series], ed. Mattie Erma Edwards Parker et al. (Raleigh: Division of Archives and History, 1963-). 89, 108 (hereafter Parker, NCHCR, vol. 3). *Crown v. Jolley.* Arrest warrant for Katherine Jolley, August 31, 1749, Hyde County Bastardy Papers, NCSA. (On this case, see also chapter 3.) *Crown v. Lackey,* Cain, NCHCR, 505–506.

11. William Sheppard, *A Grand Abridgment of the Common and Statute Law of England* (London, 1675), s.v. "scold." *Chowan County North Carolina County Court Minutes (Court of Pleas & Quarter Sessions), 1735–1738; 1746–1748, Book II* transcribed by Weynette Parks Haun (Durham: the author, 1983), 54 (Waltham).

12. *Crown v. Sylva,* March 1765, Salisbury District Court trial and Minute Docket, 1761–90, cited in Spindel, *Crime and Society,* 129. See also Bowler, "Carted Whores and White Shrouded Apologies." For Hassell's various misdeeds, see William S. Price Jr., ed., *North Carolina Higher-Court Records, 1709–1723,* vol. 5 of *The Colonial Records of North Carolina* [Second Series], ed. Mattie Erma Edwards Parker et al. (Raleigh: Division of Archives and History, 1963-) (hereafter cited as Price, NCHCR, vol. 5), 125, 202, 214–15, 225. In North Carolina in 1715 and again in 1741, fines for "Prophane Swearing & Cursing" were set at two shillings and six pence for every curse if the speaker was a private person, and five shillings per curse if the swearer was a "person of Office." Cursing in court (a perversion of solemn oath-taking) brought a five shilling fine and three hours in the stocks. LNC, 3, 4, 173. In 1662 the Virginia legislature allowed that "brabling women" whose slander involved their husbands in "vexatious suites" could be ducked in lieu of paying fines. See Brown, *Good Wives,* 147–48. I have found no North Carolina examples of ducking as a punishment for slander. As in many English examples, Waltham stood accused of multiple offenses, including petty larceny and keeping a tavern without a license (see chapter 3). On the many physical forms a ducking (or "cucking") stool could take, see John Webster Spargo, *Judicial Folklore in England, Illustrated by the Cucking Stool* (Durham: Duke University Press, 1944). Sixteenth-century duckings were increasingly reserved for scolding women (less for women accused of "whoredom") and as an alternative to a fine. Ibid., 39, 45.

13. The North Carolina assembly did not enact a defamation statute and generally adhered to English practice. On actionable words, see Kamensky, *Governing the Tongue,* 27–28 and Dayton, *Women before the Bar,* 301. For slander litigation in England, see J. A. Sharpe, *Defamation and Sexual Slander in Early Modern England: The Church Courts at York* (York: University of York, Borthwick Papers, No. 58, 1980); Martin Ingram, *Church Courts, Sex, and Marriage in England, 1570–1640* (Cambridge: Cambridge University Press, 1987), chap. 10; Gowing, *Domestic Dangers.*

14. Spindel has found only 16 slander cases out of a total of 1,501 civil cases in North Carolina's higher court records between 1702 and 1723. Spindel, "The Law of Words," 31, n. 32. For an extended discussion of the way expanding commerce and the growth of the colonial population after 1700 led to a decline in defamation suits regarding sexual mores and a focus instead on men's creditworthiness, see Dayton, *Women before the Bar*, chap. 6.

15. *Hunt and wife v. Moline*, General Court, November 1694, Parker, NCHCR, vol. 2, 210–11, 219, 223–24. Arguments over property often led to heated words that drew on the standard insults of "Rogues" for men and "Whores" for women. See, for example, *Richard and Mary Rookes v. Samual and Mary West*, October 1698. The Rookes were "whoores and Theives [sic] and had sold Cattle that were none of their own." Parker, NCHCR, vol. 3, 242, 255–56. In 1702 James Fewox declared that John Porter cheated in his business dealings and called "Mrs. Porter (who gave him not one word neither first nor last) all the Damned whores and biches his foule mouth Could Expresse." *Mr. John Porter v. James Fewox*, March/April 1702. Parker, NCHCR, *1702–1708*, 22–23.

16. Female plaintiffs (sometimes together with their husbands) brought twenty-five of the sexual slander suits; the other seven were brought by men alone on behalf of their wives or daughters. Of these thirty-two cases, seven involved accusations of interracial sex. As discussed below, male plaintiffs prosecuted allegations of sex with other men (1), sex with animals (4), sex with black or mulatto women (5). (I have counted twice Spence Hall's assertion that Mary Fisher was a "damned Mulatto Whore," once as a slur against Mary ("Whore"), and once as a slur against her husband, John (interracial sex), who brought the suit by himself. Hence the thirty-two female and ten male targets in forty-one cases of sexual slander.) Only four cases brought by female plaintiffs involved slander of a nonsexual nature: one sued for being labeled a thief, three for being called a witch. In the seventeenth century, men and women participated in sexual slander suits as plaintiffs and as defendants in more equal measure than they did in the eighteenth. See Dayton, *Women before the Bar*, 286–89, 293, 304–305; Brown, *Good Wives, Nasty Wenches*, 146–48. The split in insults that targeted women and men was already apparent by the seventeenth century. See Norton, "Gender and Defamation"; Susan Amussen, "Gender, Family, and Social Order, 1560–1725," in *Order and Disorder in Early Modern England*, 196–217; Gowing, *Domestic Dangers*, chap. 3. North Carolina's oldest extant court records (beginning in the 1680s) do not show white men refuting charges of "whoredom" with a white female partner. Standard slander cases brought by male plaintiffs involve being called a "Pick Pockett" or a "Thief." See, for example, *Ogilby v. Sale*, Declaration of Patrick Ogilby, March 1718, General Court Papers, NCSA. Morris v. Hill, Declaration of Thomas Morris, October Court 1744, Chowan Civil Action Papers, NCSA.

17. *Bartholomew and Ann Hewitt v. William Reed*. Parker, NCHCR, vol. 3, 406, 411–12. The Hewitts demanded twenty pounds sterling in damages, but when they did not appear in court the case was dismissed. Reed likely knew that adultery was defined as extramarital sex on the part of a *wife*, only. *Hosey v. Stafford*, Arrest warrant for Stafford, July 21, 1735; Examination of Thomas Stafford, July 22, 1735, Perquimans County Civil Action Papers, NCSA. (Stafford left a will which has not survived. Perquimans Precinct Court Minutes, July 1736, 077.301.3, NCSA.) *Hepsebeth Minshew v. Robert Hill*, Declaration of Hepsebeth Minshew, [July?] Court 1750, Chowan County Civil Action Papers, NCSA. Hill was found guilty in October 1750. Mary Garrett, a single woman under the age of twenty-one, sued Demsey Trottman for saying he had "been seen fucking [her] two Times." Garrett's case was discontinued in the same court session. *Garrett v. Trottman*, Declaration of Mary Garrett, Edenton District Superior Court, November 1763, NCSA. On the decline in slander suits, see Kamensky, *Governing the Tongue*, 186; Dayton, *Women before the Bar*, 304–307. On male bragging, see Dayton, ibid., 321. On public apologies, see Bowler, "Carted Whores and White Shrouded Apologies"; Kamensky, *Governing the Tongue*, chap. 5; Brown, *Good Wives, Nasty Wenches*, 189.

18. Advertisement of Thomas Perry, February 18, 1758, General Court Criminal Action Papers, NCSA. *Crown v. Perry*, Complaint of William Rice, March 20, 1758, and Recognizance of Thomas Perry, April 5, 1758 (both on one document), General Court Criminal Action

Papers, 1758, NCSA. Jury's presentment, October Session of the Supreme Court held at Edenton, 1758, NCSA. Perry was indicted for slander but the trial verdict is unknown.

19. *Hacket v. Nichols*, Arrest warrant for John Nichols, August 23, 1744; Declaration of Sarah Hacket, October Court, 1744, Chowan County Civil Action Papers, NCSA. *Sarah White v. Samuel Commander*, Declaration of Sarah White, June Court, 1755, Pasquotank County Civil Action Papers, NCSA. Declaration of Tamer Jones, October Court, 1754; Arrest warrant for Jones, June 27, 1755; *Tamer Jones v. Joseph Ferrill*, October Court, 1754, Pasquotank County Civil Action Papers, NCSA. Pasquotank Reference (Trial) and Appearance Docket, Court of Pleas and Quarter Sessions, References to June Court 1755, NCSA. Pasquotank County Execution Docket, Court of Pleas and Quarter Sessions, Executions issued at June Court, 1755, NCSA. *Lowry v. Cook*, Pasquotank County Civil Action Papers, January, 1749, NCSA.

20. *William and Elizabeth Ward v. Edward Whorton*, July Court, 1744, Pasquotank County Civil Action Papers, NCSA. In 1751, Thomas and Priscilla Gray sued planter John Sawyer for declaring Priscilla "a Common Strumpett." *Thomas Gray and his wife v. John Sawyer*, Declaration of Thomas and Priscilla Gray, April Court, 1751, Pasquotank County Civil Action Papers, NCSA. The following April a jury found the defendant not guilty. Haun, *Pasquotank County Court Minutes, 1747 thru 1753, Book 2*, 92. North Carolina women did not seem to enjoy the "phenomenal success rate of women represented by husbands" in slander suits in seventeenth-century Maryland. See Norton, "Gender and Defamation," 33. Elizabeth Riding, a widow who hoped to remarry, sued William Collins for slandering her as unchaste. The suit was abated in May 1764 after William Collins died. *[Elizabeth] Riding v. William Collins*, Declaration of Elizabeth Riding, Edenton District Superior Court, November 1763, NCSA. Sometimes fathers defended the reputation of their daughters. John Swindal, for example, sued William Beaker in 1746 for saying that he "did Lye with" John's daughter, Mary Swindal. *Swindal v. Beaker*, Arrest warrant for William Beaker, December 3, 1746, Hyde County Civil & Criminal Action Papers, NCSA.

21. Declaration of David and Mary Aires, Edenton Superior Court, November Term 1762, Edenton District Superior Court Records, 1763; Edenton District Superior Court Minute Docket, May 29, 1764, NCSA. See also Norton, "Gender and Defamation in Seventeenth-Century Maryland."

22. The Bible's Leviticus 20:13 mandated death for men who lay with each other as they lay with women. See also St. Paul's Epistle to the Romans 1:26–27. For agricultural metaphors of procreation, see Jonathan Ned Katz, ed., *Gay/Lesbian Almanac: A New Documentary* (New York: Harper and Row, 1983), 33. Katz discusses sodomy as a sin against marriage, private property, and the state on 31–35. Sir Edward Coke, the prominent English legal theorist who systematized English law in 1644, described sodomy as "mankind with mankind, or with brute beast, or by womankind with brute beast," but he did not include sex between women. Reverend John Cotton of Massachusetts wrote a legal code in 1636 that advocated the death penalty for "sodomy, which is carnal fellowship of man with man, or woman with woman, or buggery, which is carnal fellowship of man or woman with beasts or fowls." Cotton's code was adopted in New Haven in 1656, but no legal prosecution was instituted under that law and no other colonial statute referred to sex between women. Katz, *Gay/Lesbian Almanac*, 74 (Cotton), 88 (Coke). See also 58–60, 85–86, 92.

23. "Sodom Fair" quotes from Alan Bray, *Homosexuality in Renaissance England* (London: Gay Men's Press, 1982), 19. "Italian" quote in Ed Cohen, "Legislating the Norm: From Sodomy to Gross Indecency," *South Atlantic Quarterly* 88, no. 1 (winter 1989): 181–217, esp. 46, 56. Prior to 1533, sodomy in England was treated as a sin and punished by ecclesiastical authorities, but that year Henry VIII transformed the sin of sodomy into the more secular "sin-crime" of buggery and made it punishable by secular courts with loss of property and death. See Cohen, "Legislating the Norm," 185–86. See also Laurence Senelick, "Mollies or Men of Mode? Sodomy and the Eighteenth-Century London Stage," *Journal of the History of Sexuality* 1, no. 1 (1990): 33–67; Ann Rosalind Jones and Peter Stallybrass, "Fetishizing Gender: Constructing the Hermaphrodite in Renaissance Europe" in *Body Guards: The Cultural Politics of Gender Ambiguity*, ed. Julia Epstein and Kristina Straub (New York: Routledge, 1991), 80–111; Trumbach, "London's Sapphists," 112–41; Bray, *Homosexuality in Renaissance England*, chap. 4.

24. For sodomy in colonial New England, see John D'Emilio and Estelle B. Freedman, *Intimate Matters: A History of Sexuality in America* (New York: Harper and Row, 1988), chap. 2; Robert F. Oaks, "'Things Fearful to Name': Sodomy and Buggery in Seventeenth-Century New England," *Journal of Social History* 12, no. 2 (winter 1978); Jonathan Greenberg, "Bradford's 'Ancient Members' and 'A Case of Buggery . . . amongst Them,'" in *Nationalisms and Sexualities*, ed. Andrew Parker et al. (New York: Routledge, 1992), 60–76; Louis Crompton, "Homosexuals and the Death Penalty in Colonial America," *Journal of Homosexuality* 1 (1976): 277–93; Richard Godbeer, "'The Cry of Sodom': Discourse, Intercourse, and Desire in Colonial New England," *William and Mary Quarterly*, 3d ser., 52, no. 2 (April 1995): 259–86. For a comparison of the legal treatment of sodomy in New England and the Chesapeake, see Norton, *Founding Mothers and Fathers*, 347–57. Of the five southern colonies, only South Carolina incorporated the statute on "buggery" into its laws; the others assumed it to be in force without explicit mention. The first legal reference in North Carolina was a law of 1792 requiring the death penalty. Katz, *Gay/Lesbian Almanac*, 35–37, 104. Crompton, "Homosexuals and the Death Penalty," 278. Pennsylvania's revised criminal code in 1700 abolished the death penalty for whites convicted of sodomy or bestiality but allowed it for blacks convicted of buggery, burglary, murder, or the rape of a white woman. The most lenient statute for white sodomy offenders was thus also the first to provide a legal double-standard based on race. See Katz, *Gay/Lesbian Almanac*, 61. Henry Abelove argues that by the eighteenth century an array of nonreproductive sexual expressions (such as mutual masturbation, oral sex, anal sex, and same-sex activity) had come under negative pressure and been reformulated as foreplay, while heterosexual reproductive intercourse was newly privileged as "real" sex. Abelove, "Some Speculations on the History of Sexual Intercourse during the Long Eighteenth Century in England," *Genders* 6 (fall 1989): 125–30.

25. Price, NCHCR, vol. 5, 164–67. Since the law viewed as equally guilty any participants in the crime, the claim of the Winn brothers that they had been "buggered" by John Clark appeared as a local rumor rather than as (self-incriminating) depositions in court.

26. *Clark v. Wynn* and *Clark v. Wynn*, General Court Minutes, July 1718, in Price, ed., NCHCR, vol. 5, 173.

27. Mary Elizabeth Perry argues that "the real crime of sodomy" lay in "requiring a male to play the passive 'female' role and in violating the physical integrity of a male recipient's body." Perry, *Gender and Disorder in Early Modern Seville* (Princeton, N.J.: Princeton University Press, 1990), 125.

28. Bestiality may have been more common than sodomy, leading to more convictions. On the death penalty, see Oaks, "'Things Fearful to Name,'" 274–78; Roger Thompson, *Sex in Middlesex: Popular Mores in a Massachusetts County, 1649–1699* (Amherst: University of Massachusetts Press, 1986), 74. The last execution in Massachusetts for that crime was in 1673. No one was executed for sodomy in North Carolina. Sir Edward Coke described in 1644 how "a great Lady committed buggery with a Baboon, and conceived by it." Katz, *Gay/Lesbian Almanac*, 89. See also Jonas Liliequist, "Peasants against Nature: Crossing the Boundaries between Man and Animal in Seventeenth- and Eighteenth-Century Sweden," *Journal of the History of Sexuality* 1, no. 3 (1991): 393–423. Polly Morris, "Sodomy and Male Honor: The Case of Somerset, 1740–1850," *Journal of Homosexuality* 16 (1988): 383–406.

29. *Handcock v. Hughes*, deposition of Thomas Handcock, July 1724; *Handcock v. Hughes*, Retraxit, March 1725, in Cain, NCHCR, 48–49, 92. *Augustin Wright v. Robert Barnett*, declaration of Augustin Wright, October Court 1734, Pasquotank County Civil Action Papers, NCSA.

30. *Joshua Everet v. Thomas Garrett*, declaration of Joshua Everet, November Term 1762, Edenton District Superior Court, 1763, NCSA. Edenton District Superior Court Minute Docket, May 29, 1764, NCSA. *Crown v. Everitt*, jury's presentment, May 21, 1764, Edenton District Court Records, May 1764, NCSA. *Crown v. Robert Johnston*, jury's presentment, September 23, 1765, Salisbury District Superior Court Criminal Action Papers, NCSA. James Patrick was accused of "a venereal Affair with a Certain Red Cow." The grand jury dismissed the case as "no Bill," perhaps because at one point Carrol changed the alleged encounter to July 30th. *Crown v. James Patrick*, depositions of John Carrol, September 17, 1765 and October 19, 1765 (one docu-

ment); jury's verdict, n.d., Salisbury District Superior Court Criminal Action Papers, NCSA. *Taylor v. Davis*, declaration of Shadrick Taylor, November Supreme Court, 1764, Edenton District Superior Court Records, 1764, NCSA. Taylor sued for one hundred pounds in damages, but the outcome is unknown.

31. On the long-standing European assumption of an affinity between Africans and apes, see Winthrop D. Jordan, *White over Black: American Attitudes toward the Negro, 1550–1812* (Chapel Hill: University of North Carolina Press, 1968), 28–32. On Jamaican slaveholders who viewed and treated their human chattel as animals, see Philip D. Morgan, "Slaves and Livestock in Eighteenth-Century Jamaica: Vineyard Pen, 1750–1751," *William and Mary Quarterly*, 3d ser., 52, no. 1 (January 1995): 47–77.

32. Marvin L. Michael Kay and Lorin Lee Cary, "A Demographic Analysis of Colonial North Carolina with Special Emphasis upon the Slave and Black Populations" in *Black Americans in North Carolina and the South*, ed. Jeffrey J. Crow and Flora J. Hatley (Chapel Hill: University of North Carolina Press, 1984), 71–121, esp. 73. Winthrop Jordan points out that interracial sex "rivaled the slave revolt as a source of tension," and that rumors and fears of black male virility increased during times of interracial crisis, as whites projected a sexual element onto their opponents' political aggression. Jordan, *White over Black*, 136, 152–53. Peter Wood observes that whites increasingly feared and fantasized about the rape of white women by black men. Peter H. Wood, *Black Majority: Negroes in Colonial South Carolina from 1670 through the Stono Rebellion* (New York: Norton, 1974), 233–38. The North Carolina petition from 1755 is mentioned in Jordan, *White over Black*, 139–40.

33. *Hart v. Leaden*, declaration of Josiah Hart, October Court, 1745, Perquimans County Civil Action Papers, NCSA. The outcome of the case is unknown.

34. Other historians have noted this as well. See, for example, Peter W. Bardaglio, "Rape and the Law in the Old South: 'Calculated to excite indignation in every heart,'" *Journal of Southern History* 60, no. 4 (November 1994): 756–57.

35. For a path-breaking analysis of the dynamic by which slaveholders "represented themselves to one another by reference to their slaves," see Johnson, *Soul by Soul*, passim (quote on 13). Ariela J. Gross explores whites' self-representations in *Double Character: Slavery and Mastery in the Antebellum Southern Courtroom* (Princeton, N.J.: Princeton University Press, 2000). For contests over a "master's character," see esp. 98–121. For the "symbiosis of definitions of black and of white character," i.e., the ways in which white honor was defined in conjunction with the dishonoring of blacks, see ibid., 47–71, 120 (quote).

36. *Overman v. Towers*, Declaration of Samuel Overman, April Court, 1751, Pasquotank County Civil Action Papers, NCSA. Weynette Parks Haun, *Pasquotank County North Carolina County Court Minutes (Court of Pleas & Quarter Sessions), 1747–1753, Book II* (Durham: the author, 1990), 63, 73, 78, 80, 87, 92. The case resulted in a "Demurrer," meaning that even if Towers made the statement, he did not have to answer for it. *Black's Law Dictionary*, 3d. ed. (St. Paul, Minn.: West, 1933), 553–54. The indenture for Richard Towers is in the Pasquotank County Apprentice Bonds and Records, Folder: "T," NCSA.

37. *Horah v. Bower*, Declaration of Henry Horah, Salisbury District Superior Court Civil Action Papers, March Term, 1763, NCSA. The suit against Bower ended when he died in 1764. I thank Marjoleine Kars for bringing this case to my attention.

38. Hugh Davis case quoted in A. Leon Higginbotham Jr., *In the Matter of Color: Race and the American Legal Process: The Colonial Period* (Oxford: Oxford University Press, 1978), 23. Higginbotham states that the lack of a racial identification of Davis, combined with the claim that his sexual partner was a "negro," make it likely that Davis was "white." For the argument that this language did not necessarily refer to race, see Edmund S. Morgan, *American Slavery, American Freedom: The Ordeal of Colonial Virginia* (New York: Norton, 1975), 333. Quote from Jordan, *White over Black*, 141. Douglas Deal found evidence of whites' "growing hostility" toward blacks in three eighteenth-century slander suits involving tales of interracial sex (two brought by male plaintiffs). See Douglas Deal, "A Constricted World: Free Blacks on Virginia's Eastern Shore, 1680–1750," in *Colonial Chesapeake Society*, ed. Lois Green Carr, Philip D. Morgan, and Jean B. Russo (Chapel Hill: University of North Carolina Press, 1988), esp.

279–80. Brown argues that in Virginia, just after Bacon's Rebellion, "a new lexicon for colonial masculinity emerged, one in which differences of birth meant less than the privileges of whiteness." One rebel was smeared with the claim that he enjoyed the "dark imbraces" of his slave. See Brown, *Good Wives, Nasty Wenches,* 174–75. See also 210–11 for two cases of slander (1694, 1705) alleging interracial sex.

39. Arrest warrant for William Brounin, August 10, 1747, Hyde County Civil Action Papers, NCSA. Spence Hall was found guilty and fined forty shillings and six pence in damages plus court costs. Hall appealed to the Superior Court and the further outcome of the case is unknown. Complaint by John Adams Fisher, November Superior Court, 1767, misfiled in Edenton District Superior Court Records, 1765, 2.022.12, NCSA. *Spence Hall v. John Adams Fisher,* appeal by Spence Hall and jury's indictment, 1767, misfiled in Edenton District Superior Court Records, 1765, 2.022.12, NCSA. Written fragment regarding George Fisher, n.d., in Edenton District Superior Court Records, 1765, 2.022.12, NCSA. The "double levys" refer to the taxes levied on African American wives. See Brown, *Good Wives, Nasty Wenches,* 116–28.

40. Arrest warrant for Thomas Gidings, May 15, 1755, Hyde County Civil and Criminal Action Papers, NCSA. Bertie Criminal Papers, 1750, NCSA (Ratliffe). On mid-eighteenth century immigration, see Harry Roy Merrens, *Colonial North Carolina in the Eighteenth Century: A Study in Historical Geography* (Chapel Hill: University of North Carolina Press, 1964), 53–81. Historians have shown how the Irish became "white" in the nineteenth century—a process that had its roots in the colonial era. See Theodore W. Allen, *The Invention of the White Race,* vol. 1, *Racial Oppression and Social Control* (London: Verso, 1994); Roediger, *Wages of Whiteness;* Noel Ignatiev, *How the Irish Became White* (New York: Routledge, 1995); Dale T. Knobel, *Paddy and the Republic: Ethnicity and Nationality in Antebellum America* (Middletown, Conn.: Wesleyan University Press, 1986).

41. Deposition of Joseph McKeel, August 4, 1743, General Court, Criminal and Assize Court, NCSA. In a Georgia court case from 1853 involving the racial identity of one Jim Nuncz, whites commented that Nunez was more likely part Indian than black because he danced "as genteel as any man" with "no clumsiness" and was "very graceful." See Ariela Gross, "Litigating Whiteness," 159. On balls and dancing as performances of gentility, see Richard L. Bushman, *The Refinement of America: Persons, Houses, Cities* (New York: Knopf, 1992), 47–58, 68. On distinctive movements in African American dance and whites' efforts to interpret them, see Peter H. Wood, "'Gimme de Kneebone Bent': African Body Language and the Evolution of American Dance Forms," in *The Black Tradition in American Dance,* ed. Gerald E. Myers (Durham, N.C., 1988); Shane White and Graham White, *Stylin': African American Expressive Culture from Its Beginnings to the Zoot Suit* (Ithaca, N.Y.: Cornell University Press, 1998), 72–84.

42. On scientists' views, see Emmanuel Chukwudi Eze, ed., *Race and the Enlightenment: A Reader* (Cambridge, Mass.: Blackwell, 1997), and Jordan, *White over Black.* Jordan emphasizes that close proximity with blacks led whites to know of their shared humanity. Jordan, *White over Black,* chap. 6.

43. *Mary Low v. William Symons,* Declaration of Mary Low, July Court, 1732, Pasquotank County Civil Action Papers, NCSA. Given Quakers' penchant for resolving tensions within the Quaker meeting and their reluctance to prosecute each other in court, the fact that Low brought a suit against Symons underscores the egregious nature of his insult. The outcome of the suit—like the source of the conflict—remains unknown. Similarly, in April 1736 Moses and Mary Speight sued Sollomon Hendrickson for saying that Mary "is a Whore for that her own Negroe man lay with her." They requested fifty pounds. Hendrickson pleaded not guilty and was acquitted, and the Speights paid court costs. Weynette Parks Haun, *Old Albemarle County, North Carolina: Perquimans Precinct Court Minutes, 1688 through 1738, Book I* (Durham: the author, 1980), 113–14. To be called an animal (such as a pig or a dog) was to be labeled a degraded creature without a soul and without hope for salvation. See St. George, "'Heated' Speech and Literacy," 293–95.

44. *Mary Willabe v. William Clerk,* declaration of Mary Willabe, October Court, 1755, Bertie County Civil Action Papers, NCSA. By contrast, rumors of interracial sex that targeted white

men were not rhetorically linked to allegations of bestiality. In other words, sex with a black person debased white women more than white men.

45. *Crown v. Davis's Ned*, Arrest warrant for Ned, May 22, 1756, Hyde County Civil and Criminal Action Papers, NCSA (my emphasis). The warrant (the only document for this case) does not name the informant. Typically, it would have been Flimm herself. This case is different from other slander suits in that it was brought as a criminal case, suggesting that Ned's claim represented a breach of the peace.

46. Chapter 5 discusses rape charges brought against slaves. Historians have argued that the myth of the black rapist was invented only during and after the Civil War. See Angela Davis, "Rape, Racism, and the Myth of the Black Rapist," in *Women, Race, and Class* (New York: Vintage Books, 1983), 183–89; Diane Miller Sommerville, "The Rape Myth in the Old South Reconsidered," *Journal of Southern History* 61, no. 3 (August 1995): 481–518; Martha Hodes, *White Women, Black Men: Illicit Sex in the Nineteenth-Century South* (New Haven, Conn.: Yale University Press, 1997). Victoria Bynum points out that the nineteenth-century elite sometimes tolerated interracial adultery between white women and black men in preference to the larger social threat inherent in divorce, and she shows that whites in North Carolina were unwilling to prosecute black men for alleged rapes of white women even during the Civil War. Victoria E. Bynum, *Unruly Women: The Politics of Social and Sexual Control in the Old South* (Chapel Hill: University of North Carolina Press, 1992), 68–70, 109–10, 117–18. See also Laura F. Edwards, "Sexual Violence, Gender, Reconstruction, and the Extension of Patriarchy in Granville County, North Carolina," *The North Carolina Historical Review* 68:3 (July 1991): 237–60.

47. *Robert Gibbs and wife v. James Hall and wife*, Declaration of Robert and Judith Gibbs, September Court 1760, Hyde County Civil and Criminal Papers, NCSA. Hyde County Court Docket, 053.303.1.

48. Slander exemplifies how race, in the words of Barbara Fields, is "constantly created and verified in social life." See Barbara Jeanne Fields, "Slavery, Race, and Ideology in the United States of America," *New Left Review* 181 (May/June 1990): 95–118.

Chapter 5

1. Petition of Judith Spellman, October 3, 1729, Pasquotank County Civil Action Papers, Colonial Court Papers—Civil and Criminal, North Carolina State Archives, Division of Archives and History (hereafter cited as NCSA). General Court Papers, 1717–1754, NCSA; will of Joseph Stoakley, December 12, 1729, SS/AR, NCSA; Pasquotank County Civil Action Papers, October 1729; January 1729/30, NCSA. Spellman does not appear again in the Civil Action Papers or Criminal Action Papers of Pasquotank, nor in the General Court Papers. Unfortunately, the Pasquotank County Court Minutes are missing prior to 1737.

2. "An Act Concerning Servants and Slaves," 1715, *Laws of North Carolina*, ed. Walter Clark, vol. 23 of *The State Records of North Carolina*, ed. Clark, 16 vols. numbered 11–26 (Winston: State of North Carolina, 1895–1906), 63 (hereafter cited as LNC). Mary Sawyer's certificate, no date, Pasquotank County Slave Records, NCSA (freedom paper for Milly).

3. Foucault describes sexuality as "an especially dense transfer point for relations of power." Michel Foucault, *An Introduction*, vol. 1 of *The History of Sexuality*, trans. Robert Hurley (New York: Vintage, 1990), 103. I use the word *sexuality* with caution since it evokes sexual agency and desire. When women's bodies were used sexually, their own sexuality may not have been involved.

4. Walter Johnson explains how public inspections of slaves reproduced racial "knowledge": by projecting their hopes onto the bodies of slaves, "buyers read slaves' bodies as if they were coded versions of their own imagined needs . . . a dark complexion became a sign of an innate capacity for cutting cane, for example. Daily in the slave market, buyers 'discovered' associations they had themselves projected, treating the effects of their own examinations as if they were the essence of the bodies they examined." Johnson, *Soul by Soul: Life inside the Antebellum Slave Market* (Cambridge, Mass.: Harvard University Press, 1999), chap. 5, quote on 149. For Johnson's discussion of how slave owners built their reputations of "mastery" on their professed ability to read slaves' bodies for their profitability, see chaps. 3, 7.

5. *North-Carolina Gazette,* June 24, 1768, in Lathan A. Windley, ed., *Runaway Slave Advertisements: A Documentary History from the 1730s to 1790,* 4 vols. (Westport, Conn.: Greenwood, 1983), vol. 1, 434. On elaborate dress codes as markers of class, see Richard Bushman, *The Refinement of America: Persons, Houses, Cities* (New York: Knopf, 1992), 70–74; Jonathan Prude, "To Look upon the 'Lower Sort': Runaway Ads and the Appearance of Unfree Laborers in America, 1750–1800," *Journal of American History* 78 (June 1991): 124–59. A South Carolina law from 1735 specified suitable material for slave clothing and prohibited slaves from wearing fabrics "above" their station. See A. Leon Higginbotham Jr., *In the Matter of Color: The Colonial Period,* vol. 1 of *Race and the American Legal Process* (Oxford: Oxford University Press, 1978), 173–74. Clothing combined visual and physical experience. One former slave said wearing a flax shirt was like having "a hundred small pinpoints, in contact with his flesh," and that his older brother was most generous when he wore the new shirt until it was "broken in." Booker T. Washington, *Up from Slavery* (1901), quoted in Shane White and Graham White, *Stylin': African American Expressive Culture from Its Beginnings to the Zoot Suit* (Ithaca, N.Y.: Cornell University Press, 1998), 26–27.

6. LNC, 63. Petition of Ann James, n.d. [1758], Bertie County Civil Action Papers, NCSA. The court's response to her petition is unknown. John Brickell, *The Natural History of North Carolina* (Dublin, 1737), 276. William Attmore, "Journal of a Tour to North Carolina" (1787), ed. Linda Tunstall Rodman, *James Sprunt Historical Publications* 17, no. 2 (1922): 25, 44. Free black servants (like Judith Spellman) could and did petition the courts for redress when masters mistreated them or kept them poorly clad. In response to the complaint of a free black servant named Joseph Wakefield, the Chowan court ordered in 1730 that Major Thomas Holladay provide "good & sufficient cloathing" to Wakefield and no longer punish Wakefield himself but apply to a magistrate for the servant's "Correction." *Chowan County North Carolina County Court Minutes (Court of Pleas and Quarter Sessions), 1730 thru 1745, Book I,* trans. Weynette Parks Haun (Durham, N.C.: for the author, 1983), 3.

7. The Quaker abolitionist, John Woolman, analyzed this dynamic: "Placing on Men the ignominious Title, SLAVE, dressing them in uncomely Garments, keeping them to servile Labour, in which they are often dirty, tends gradually to fix a Notion in the Mind, that they are a Sort of People below us in Nature, and leads us to consider them as such in all our Conclusions about them." Quoted in Winthrop Jordan, *The Negro versus Equality, 1762–1826* (Chicago: Rand McNally, 1969), 4–5. But on slaves' ability to regain some control over their appearance by creatively altering the combination and fit of clothes, hats, and hairstyles (in ways that could parody white fashion), see White and White, *Stylin',* 5–62.

8. Marquis de Francois Jean Chastellux, *Travels in North America in the Years, 1780, 1781, and 1782,* vol. 1 (Chapel Hill: University of North Carolina Press, 1963), 585, n. 19. Entry of June 22, 1781, military journal of Lt. William Feltman, May 26, 1781 to April 25, 1782. Historical Society of Pennsylvania, quoted in Winthrop D. Jordan, *White over Black: American Attitudes toward the Negro, 1550–1812* (New York: Norton, 1977), 159. Deborah Gray White argues that the exposure of semiclad and naked women's bodies on the auction block, in the fields, in the Big House, and during whippings contributed to whites' belief in black promiscuity. Deborah Gray White, *Ar'n't I a Woman?: Female Slaves in the Plantation South* (New York: Norton, 1985), 32–33. Walter Johnson notes the erotic nature of examinations of black women in the slave market: they took place in separate screened off rooms, as if to protect the modesty of white men. Johnson, *Soul by Soul,* 137–39, see also 113–15, 147–49.

9. Entry of June 22, 1781, military journal of Lt. William Feltman, in Jordan, *White over Black,* 159.

10. William Byrd, *The Secret Diary of William Byrd of Westover, 1709–1712,* ed. Louis B. Wright and Marion Tinling (Richmond, Va.: Dietz, 1941), 90 (wench), 425 (Negro girl). William Byrd, *The London Diary (1717–1721), and Other Writings* (New York: Oxford University Press, 1958), 484 (felt the breasts). For comments that Byrd "committed folly with" and "played the fool" with various women, including a Sally in Williamsburg who was probably a servant, see William Byrd, *Another Secret Diary of William Byrd of Westover, 1739–1741,* ed. Louis B. Wright and Marion Tinling (Richmond, Va.: Dietz, 1942), 31, 93, 70, 137, 155, 157, 166, 168, 174.

On Byrd's sexual exploits, see Brown, *Good Wives, Nasty Wenches*, 328–34; Richard Godbeer, "William Byrd's 'Flourish': The Sexual Cosmos of a Southern Planter," in *Sex and Sexuality in Early America*, ed. Merril D. Smith (New York: New York University Press, 1998), 135–62. Explicit evidence of Anglo-American men's rape of enslaved women in the colonial period is sparse, but see Douglas Hall, ed., *In Miserable Slavery: Thomas Thistlewood in Jamaica, 1750–86* (London: Macmillan, 1989) for the overseer's diary entries on sex with numerous enslaved women. The sexual demands that black men made on black women seldom left a trace in the colonial records. I have not come across any colonial references to the rape of African American women by African American men, but Jordan found one Virginia lawsuit in 1778 that prosecuted one slave for raping another. Jordan, *White over Black*, 157. Sharon Block explains that the rape of servants and slaves did not always require violent assault, as masters could use indirect forms of coercion to make capitulation seem like the "best option"—and like consent. See Sharon Block, "Lines of Color, Sex, and Service: Comparative Sexual Coercion in Early America," in *Sex, Love, Race: Crossing Boundaries in North American History*, ed. Martha Hodes (New York: New York University Press, 1999), 141–63.

11. Brickell, *Natural History*, 274–75. Will of William Houghton, November 17, 1749, Chowan County Miscellaneous Papers (Microfilm C.024.99004), NCSA. Hester Gerbo's petition, Perquimans County Apprentice Bonds, no date, folder G, NCSA. Harriet A. Jacobs, *Incidents in the Life of a Slave Girl: Written by Herself*, ed. Jean Fagan Yellin (Cambridge, Mass.: Harvard University Press, 1987), 77. For a different argument about the effects of brutalization, namely that violence "ungendered" slaves, see Hortense J. Spillers, "Mama's Baby, Papa's Maybe: An American Grammar Book," in *Diacritics* 17 (summer 1987): 65–81. Elizabeth Fox-Genovese argues that for white women "gender constituted the invisible, seamless wrapping of the self," but that enslaved women's gender was neither as intrinsic nor as inalienable: "As a slave woman and her master confronted each other, the trappings of gender slipped away. The woman faced him alone. She looked on naked power." Elizabeth Fox-Genovese, *Within the Plantation Household: Black and White Women of the Old South* (Chapel Hill: University of North Carolina Press, 1988), 372–74. The assumption behind these writings is that brutality destroyed the social construct of gender; violence reduced (or returned) human bodies to a state of gender-neutrality that existed without (or prior to) socially imposed understandings of gender difference. For my purposes Fox-Genovese's term *naked power* is a fortuitous one, because it evokes the very gendered enactments of power that I want to discuss; it is hard to imagine a nakedness that is neither male nor female. For an excellent discussion of racialized sex and sexualized race, see Abdul R. JanMohamed, "Sexuality on/of the Racial Border: Foucault, Wright and the Articulation of 'Racialized Sexuality,'" in *Discourses of Sexuality: From Aristotle to AIDS*, ed. Domna C. Stanton (Ann Arbor: University of Michigan Press, 1992), 94–115. On the purposeful "breeding" of slave women, see Thelma Jennings, "'Us Colored Women Had To Go through A Plenty': Sexual Exploitation of African-American Slave Women," *Journal of Women's History* 1, no. 3 (winter 1990): 45–74. On the sexual exploitation of enslaved women in the antebellum South, see Darlene Hine and Kate Wittenstein, "Female Slave Resistance: The Economics of Sex," in *The Black Woman Cross-Culturally*, ed. Filomine Chioma Steady (Cambridge, Mass.: Schenkman, 1981), 288–99; White, *Ar'n't I a Woman?;* Michael Mullin, "Women and the Comparative Study of American Negro Slavery," *Slavery and Abolition* 6, no. 1 (May 1985): 25–40; Jacqueline Jones, *Labor of Love, Labor of Sorrow: Black Women, Work, and the Family from Slavery to the Present* (New York: Basic, 1985); Karen A. Getman, "Sexual Control in the Slaveholding South: The Implementation and Maintenance of a Racial Caste System," *Harvard Women's Law Journal* 7 (spring 1984): 115–52; Catherine Clinton, "'Southern Dishonor': Flesh, Blood, Race, and Bondage," in *In Joy and Sorrow: Women, Family, and Marriage in the Victorian South, 1830–1900*, ed. Carol Bleser (New York: Oxford University Press, 1991), 52–68; Hélène Lecaudey, "Behind the Mask: Ex-slave Women and Interracial Sexual Relations," in *Discovering the Women in Slavery: Emancipating Perspectives on the American Past*, ed. Patricia Morton (Athens: University of Georgia Press, 1996), 260–77. There is much less scholarship on the sexual abuse of enslaved women in the colonial period, but see Joan Gunderson, "The Double Bonds of Race and Sex: Black and White Women in a Colonial Virginia Parish," *Jour-*

nal of Southern History 52 (August 1986): 351–72; Jennifer Lyle Morgan, "Laboring Women: Enslaved Women, Reproduction, and Slavery in Barbados and South Carolina, 1650–1750" (Ph.D. diss., Duke University, 1995); Sharon Block, "Coerced Sex in British North America, 1700–1820" (Ph.D. diss., Princeton University, 1995), 73–78.

12. On rape as a means of negating another man's "role as a patriarch," see Block, "Coerced Sex in British North America," 46–58 (quote on p. 53), 77–78. For the argument that the rape of black women targeted the entire slave community and was meant, in part, to demoralize enslaved men, see Angela Davis, "Reflections on the Black Woman's Role in the Community of Slaves," *Black Scholar* 3, no. 4 (December 1971): 12–14. See also Nell Irvin Painter, "Soul Murder and Slavery: Toward A Fully Loaded Cost Accounting," in *U.S. History as Women's History: New Feminist Essays,* ed. Linda K. Kerber, Alice Kessler-Harris, and Kathryn Kish Sklar (Chapel Hill: University of North Carolina Press, 1995), 125–46. The enslaved African sailor, Olaudah Equiano, witnessed white sailors' "constant practice" of committing "violent depredations on the chastity of the female slaves; and these I was, though with reluctance, obliged to submit to at all times, being unable to help them." Equiano, *The Interesting Narrative of the Life of Olaudah Equiano, Written By Himself,* ed. Robert J. Allison (Boston: Bedford/St. Martin's, 1995), 93. There is a large literature on rape as a weapon of war; certainly slave societies were in a chronic state of violent repression and psychological warfare.

13. Byrd, *Secret Diary,* 205, 462, 494. On mistresses' abuse of slaves, especially enslaved women, see Jacobs, *Incidents in the Life of a Slave Girl;* Minrose C. Gwin, "Green-Eyed Monsters of the Slavocracy: Jealous Mistresses in Two Slave Narratives," in *Conjuring: Black Women, Fiction, and Literary Tradition,* ed. Marjorie Pryse and Hortense Spillers (Bloomington: Indiana University Press, 1985), 39–52; and Painter, "Soul Murder," esp. 135–37.

14. *Crown v. Hardy,* October, 1743, General Court Criminal Papers. Coroner's report, Northampton County, September 5, 1743, General Court, Criminal and Assize, NCSA. This became a legal case against Hardy for breach of the peace, possibly because other whites considered Hardy's violence an incitement to slave retaliation. Either way, Hardy was discharged, since it was not a felony to kill a slave. Equiano, *The Interesting Narrative,* 113 (shameful beating). On sadism as an effect of white men's dependence on slaves for their own self-image as powerful, see Robert Reid-Pharr, "Violent Ambiguity: Martin Delany, Bourgeois Sadomasochism, and the Production of a Black National Masculinity," in *Representing Black Men,* ed. Marcellus Blount and George P. Cunningham (New York: Routledge, 1996), 73–94; and Johnson, *Soul by Soul,* 105–7, 205–6.

15. For "sexually suggestive" whippings of slave women in the nineteenth century, see White, *Ar'n't I a Woman?,* 33. For whippings motivated by lust and thwarted sexual desire, see Frederick Douglass, *My Bondage and My Freedom* [1855] (New York: Dover, 1969), 85–88. On the growing popularity of sexualized flagellation in Europe, see Peter Wagner, *Eros Revived: Erotica of the Enlightenment in England and America* (London: Secker and Warburg, 1988), 21–24. Karen Halttunen explains that not until the eighteenth century did pornography include the infliction of pain "on any significant scale." See Karen Halttunen, "Humanitarianism and the Pornography of Pain in Anglo-American Culture," *American Historical Review* 100, no. 2 (April 1995): 303–34, esp. 315. Enslaved men and boys could experience sexualized violence as well. In nineteenth-century Edenton, North Carolina, Harriet Jacobs felt sorry for Luke, whose bedridden master, "a mere degraded wreck of manhood, . . . took into his head the strangest freaks of despotism" which Jacobs found "of a nature too filthy to be repeated. When I fled from the house of bondage, I left poor Luke still chained to the bedside of this cruel and disgusting wretch." Jacobs, *Incidents,* 192. On sadomasochism in slave/master relationships, see Reid-Pharr, "Violent Ambiguity." On the power-play behind one planter's homoerotic behavior, see Drew Gilpin Faust, *James Henry Hammond and the Old South: A Design for Mastery* (Baton Rouge: Louisiana State University Press, 1982), 18–19. Other acts of sadism involved the perversion of bodily functions. William Byrd of Virginia, for example, whipped his young slave Eugene "for pissing in bed" and twice in December 1709 "made him drink a pint of piss." Byrd, *The Secret Diary,* 112–13, 117. Thomas Thistlewood of Jamaica made slaves defecate in each other's mouths. See Hall, ed., *In Miserable Slavery,* 71–73.

16. Chowan County Court Records, January 20–21, July 21, 1732, NCSA. This was the same Dr. George Allen from whom Hanah Davis ran away in 1725 (see chapter 3). Another servant ran away from Allen in 1729. "Hue and Cry for Mary Jones," November 3, 1729, General Court Miscellaneous Papers, NCSA. Allen was prone to violence, see the General Court Criminal Action Papers, late 1720s and early 1730s, NCSA. For servants' suits against abusive masters, see Richard B. Morris, *Government and Labor in Early America* (New York: Columbia University Press, 1946), 470–500.

17. Only three depositions and the jury's presentment exist for this case (in a single document). Depositions of Jane McWilliams, Ann Collier, Richard Rigby, July 7, 1738, Chowan County Civil Action Papers, NCSA. Judith's last name is nowhere mentioned. Garzia was a minister for the Society for the Propagation of the Gospel in Foreign Parts (SPG), and on October 4, 1735, he took out a 1,280-acre land grant in St. Thomas's Parish in Beaufort County. *Colonial Records of North Carolina*, ed. William L. Saunders, 10 vols. (Raleigh: State of North Carolina, 1886–90), vol. 4, 64–65.

18. *Crown v. Garzia*, jury's presentment, General Court, July 1738, NCSA. The minister remained unpopular in his Beaufort County parish, and in August 1739 moved to Chowan County. Until he was thrown from a horse and killed in October 1744, Garzia criticized the "Immorality" of North Carolinians and complained that his salary was not paid. See the Letterbooks of the Society for the Propagation of the Gospel, Series A, 1735–1736, reel no. Z.5.262, vol. 26, 363; Series B, reel Z.5.287, vol. 7, Part 1, 203, 211; Part 2, 295–96; Series B, reel no. Z.5.288, vol. 9, 149, vol. 10, 131–132b; Series B, reel no. Z.5.225, vol. 12, 120–21, originals in the Archives of the United Society for the Propagation of the Gospel, London, England; copies on microfilm in NCSA.

19. Deposition of Mary Reed, July 11, 1734, General Court Criminal Papers, NCSA. The outcome of the case is unknown. I assume Reed is white because the records give a racial identification for Winslow, but not for her, and black women, whose immorality whites assumed, were not targeted for such public chastisement. E. P. Thompson suggests that "rough music"—the extralegal regulation of misconduct through crowd rituals of humiliation such as burning someone in effigy or making them ride a donkey backwards to loud music and insults—may have grown in eighteenth-century England as church courts policed sexual and social transgressions less effectively. The tarring of Mary Reed may have been prompted by a frustration with inefficient courts. Thompson also notes that "racism added a vicious tone to the ritual." E. P. Thompson, *Customs in Common* (London: Merlin, 1991), 482, 487 (racism). On the history of tar-and-feathering and its reappearance in the American colonies as a form of political protest in the 1760s (especially in seaports where tar was readily available), see Alfred F. Young, "English Plebian Culture and Eighteenth-Century American Radicalism," in *The Origins of Anglo-American Radicalism*, ed. Margaret Jacob and James Jacob (London: Allen and Unwin, 1984), 185–212 (see 193 for two colonial tarrings of women). On the 1722 example, see Bertram Wyatt-Brown, *Southern Honor: Ethics and Behavior in the Old South* (New York: Oxford University Press, 1982), 443. On the unwritten social rule that African Americans *not* meet whites' gazes, and on the way slaves could flaunt disregard for this custom or turn it into a protective mask, see White and White, *Stylin'*, 66–72.

20. Chowan County Criminal Action Papers, February 1747, NCSA. Depositions of Sarah Ricket, Jane Champion, Sarah Howcott, Deborah Thompson. Ricket's deposition did not mention the tarring. Perhaps she did not want to discuss the humiliating incident in court. I surmise that Ricket was a servant for the Champions because as a single women she was likely to work as a servant and Hannah Luton knew that Ricket could be found at the Champion household. Hannah Luton was the mistress of a household with at least ten servants and slaves. Thomas Luton did not leave a will, but the Chowan tax lists show that in 1740 he had two white and eight black tithables. By 1753 he had thirteen tithables in total. Colonial Court Records, Taxes and Accounts, 1679–1754, Folder: "Tax Lists, Chowan," NCSA. (On October 22, 1750, Hannah Luton was summoned to court to answer a complaint. It is unclear if this was the Ricket case.)

21. LNC, 192 (emphasis added), 194. The language in this law shows the transition from religion to race as a primary marker of difference: the statute still assumed that "Christian servants" were largely of European descent. Other laws written at the same time already used a language of race: "white," "African," "Indian," "mustee," etc. Similar rulings occurred in all of the colonies. See Abbot Emerson Smith, *Colonists in Bondage: White Servitude and Convict Labor in America, 1607–1776* (Chapel Hill: University of North Carolina Press, 1947), 276. On the Virginia law, see Higginbotham, *In the Matter of Color*, 36. Whipping continued to be the primary physical punishment for indentured servants and sailors. On the flogging of sailors, see Greg Dening, *Mr. Bligh's Bad Language: Passion, Power, and Theatre on the Bounty* (Cambridge: Cambridge University Press, 1992). On efforts to reform corporal punishment, including flogging, see Myra C. Glenn, *Campaigns against Corporal Punishment: Prisoners, Sailors, Women and Children in Antebellum America* (Albany, N.Y.: State University of New York Press, 1984).

22. LNC, 63–64 (1715), 201–203 (1741). For an explication of the 1715 and 1741 laws, see Marvin L. Michael Kay and Lorin Lee Cary, *Slavery in North Carolina, 1748–1775* (Chapel Hill: University of North Carolina Press, 1995), 61–69. The literature on slave resistance is huge, but for early works that have stood the test of time, see Herbert Aptheker, *American Negro Slave Revolts* (New York: Columbia University Press, 1943); Peter H. Wood, *Black Majority: Negroes in Colonial South Carolina from 1670 through the Stono Rebellion* (New York: Norton, 1974), Gerald W. Mullin, *Flight and Rebellion: Slave Resistance in Eighteenth-Century Virginia* (New York: Oxford University Press, 1972). See also Marvin L. Michael Kay and Lorin Lee Cary, "Slave Runaways in Colonial North Carolina, 1748–1775," *North Carolina Historical Review* 63, no. 1 (January 1986): 1–39. On runaways near the Virginia–North Carolina border, see Herbert Aptheker, "Maroons within the Present Limits of the United States," in *Maroon Societies: Rebel Slave Communities in the Americas*, ed. Richard Price (Garden City, N.Y.: Anchor, 1973), 157–59; Jeffrey J. Crow, *The Black Experience in Revolutionary North Carolina* (Raleigh: North Carolina Department of Cultural Resources, Division of Archives and History, 1977), 41–42.

23. Equiano, *The Interesting Narrative*, 122. Equiano's comments that sailors sexually exploited enslaved women "most shamefully" and that two white men once "beat and mangled me in a shameful manner" also show his disgust with white conduct (93, 113). On slave buyers whose fingers read whipping scars like a Braille that could disclose a slave's character, see Johnson, *Soul By Soul*, 145–46. On the gradual development of an African American racial identity out of a multiplicity of African ethnicities, see Michael A. Gomez, *Exchanging Our Country Marks: The Transformation of African Identities in the Colonial and Antebellum South* (Chapel Hill: University of North Carolina Press, 1998).

24. *North Carolina Gazette*, March 6, 1752; *William Brothers v. Samuel Cook*, search warrant for Ruth, Pasquotank County Civil Action Papers, November 7, 1753, NCSA. On the SPG brandings, see David Brion Davis, *The Problem of Slavery in Western Culture* (Ithaca, N.Y.: Cornell University Press, 1966), 220. William Bosman, "A New and Accurate Description of the Coast of Guinea . . . " [1705], in Elizabeth Donnan, ed., *Documents Illustrative of the History of the Slave Trade to America*, 4 vols. (Washington, D.C.: Carnegie Institution, 1930), vol. 1, 442 (tender women). One Edward Dyer in Maryland advertised for his runaway in 1767 by describing two "Certificates" of ownership: "Stripes, by Whipping scars" and "the letter D branded on his A-se." Quoted in Windley, *Runaway Slave Advertisements*, vol. 2, 70. As with whippings, the brandings of breasts and buttocks may have given some slaveholders a sexual charge. Spillers, "Mama's Baby, Papa's Maybe," 67 (hieroglyphics). Karen Sánchez-Eppler, *Touching Liberty: Abolition, Feminism, and the Politics of the Body* (Berkeley: University of California Press, 1993), 18 (slaves bodies acquired the "status of a text"). See also Collette Guillaumin, "Race and Nature: The System of Marks. The Idea of a Natural Group and Social Relationships," reprinted in Colette Guillaumin, *Racism, Sexism, Power, and Ideology* (London: Routledge, 1995), esp. 32. For a related discussion of the body as an object of torture and the site and symbol of oppression, see Michel Foucault, *Discipline and Punish: The Birth of the Prison*, trans. Alan Sheridan (New York: Vintage, 1979).

25. *North-Carolina Gazette,* November 16, 1769; May 5, 1775, in Windley, ed., *Runaway Slave Advertisements,* vol. 1, 434, 441. On the African-born population, see Kay and Cary, *Slavery in North Carolina,* 58. American-born slaves apparently did not often have "country marks," perhaps because African initiation rites to manhood seemed inappropriate in the context of slavery, and perhaps because slaves knew that such marks made it easier to identify runaways. See White and White, *Stylin',* 52. On Equiano's description of the forehead "weal," see Equiano, *The Interesting Narrative,* 34. While a young captive in Africa, Equiano traveled among people who "ornamented themselves with scars, and likewise filed their teeth very sharp" (52–53). He found such adornment disfiguring. For the idea that whippings and brandings covered up country marks, I am indebted to Caitlin Crowell, whose "Whipped into the Skin: Slave Mutilation and Racial Discourse in Colonial America" (Seminar paper, April 2000, in the author's possession) asks: "Did the lash, then, purport to take away scarring as a means of communication and self-naming? Or to write English meaning over African body languages?"

26. See Marvin L. Michael Kay and Lorin Lee Cary, "'The Planters Suffer Little or Nothing': North Carolina Compensations for Executed Slaves, 1748–1772," *Science and Society* 40 (1976): 288–306; Alan D. Watson, "North Carolina Slave Courts, 1715–1785," *North Carolina Historical Review* 60, no. 1 (January 1983): 24–36. Watson notes that special slave courts operated in New York, New Jersey, Pennsylvania, Delaware, and in the southern colonies from Maryland to Georgia (25). For the workings of the slave courts, see Kay and Cary, *Slavery in North Carolina,* chap. 3, and Andrew Fede, "Legitimized Violent Slave Abuse in the American South, 1619–1865: A Case Study of Law and Social Change in Six Southern States," *American Journal of Legal History* 28, no. 1 (January 1985): 145, n. 310.

27. Pasquotank County Court Minutes, 1745, NCSA (Chance); Perquimans County Civil Action Papers, Special Court, March 1754, NCSA (Judith); Craven County Court Minutes, 1764 (Bob and Simon), cited in Kay and Cary, *Slavery in North Carolina,* 80. New Bern Slave Records, 1766, NCSA (Sesor). Watson, "North Carolina Slave Courts," 33 (for punishment of 54 slaves).

28. Virginia law cited in Morris, *Government and Labor in Early America,* 462. Higginbotham, *In the Matter of Color,* 188 (South Carolina). The only amputation I found in North Carolina involved John Burnet, a "notorious felon" whose hand was amputated in 1767. See the Reports of the Committee of Public Claims, New Bern, December 11, 1767, in Walter Clark, ed., *The State Records of North Carolina,* 16 vols. numbered 11–26 (Winston and Goldsboro: State of North Carolina, 1895–1906; repr. Wilmington, N.C.: Broadfoot, 1994), vol. 22, 850. For Pricklove, see Mattie Erma Edwards Parker, ed., *North Carolina Higher-Court Records, 1670–1696,* vol. 2 of *The Colonial Records of North Carolina* [Second Series], ed. Mattie Erma Edwards Parker et al. (Raleigh: Division of Archives and History, 1963–), 9 (hereafter cited as Parker, NCHCR, vol. 2); for Manwaring, see Mattie Erma Edwards Parker, ed., *North Carolina Higher-Court Records, 1697-1701,* vol. 3 of *The Colonial Records of North Carolina* [Second Series], ed. Mattie Erma Edwards Parker et al. (Raleigh: Division of Archives and History, 1963-), 226, 236 (hereafter cited as Parker, NCHCR, vol. 3). In November 1693, Robert White and his son Vincent were branded in the hand with a "T" for larceny. Parker, NCHCR, vol. 2, 397, 325. In 1696, Peter Middleton was to be "stigmatized [and] branded with the letter T on [the] braun of his left thumb" but he was granted a suspension of the execution, and whether he was ever branded is unknown. Ibid., 291, 301, 309. Thomas Young and Roger Snell were to be branded on the "brawn of the Left Thum with a hott Iron with the Letter T" in 1698. Snell petitioned that he was "a very aged and poor man" whose family would suffer ruin if he was disabled by the branding; his sentence was suspended for twenty years. Parker, NCHCR, vol. 3, 192–93, 195. Thomas Dereham, described as a gentleman, was to have the letter "M" burned into his hand in 1702 for killing William Hudson. He petitioned for clemency and the outcome is unknown. Parker, NCHCR, vol. 3, 33–34. In 1722 Patrick Callihan was convicted for manslaughter and had the letter "M" burned into his hand "in open court." William S. Price Jr., *North Carolina Higher-Court Minutes, 1709–1723,* vol. 5 of *The Colonial Records of North Carolina,* Second Series (Raleigh: Division of Archives and History, North Carolina Department of Cultural Resources, 1977), 283–84 (hereafter cited as Price, NCHCR, vol. 5). In 1727 both Elijah Stanton, a planter, and

William Hughes, a labourer, were separately convicted of theft and branded in the hand with the letter "T." Robert J. Cain, ed., *North Carolina Higher-Court Minutes, 1724–1730,* vol. 6 of *The Colonial Records of North Carolina,* Second Series (Raleigh: Division of Archives and History, North Carolina Department of Cultural Resources, 1981), 423–34, 456–57 (hereafter cited as Cain, NCHCR). Bryan Conner had his hand branded for stealing eight shillings worth of goods in 1741, but sixty lashes ordered for a second act of petty larceny were remitted because Connor was in "a very sick and Low Condition," Robert J. Cain, ed., *Records of the Executive Council, 1735–1754,* vol. 8 of *The Colonial Records of North Carolina,* Second Series (Raleigh: Division of Archives and History, North Carolina Department of Cultural Resources, 1988), 123 (hereafter cited as Cain, REC). Charles Dent, convicted of manslaughter in the death of his daughter, was branded on the hand in 1743. *Crown v. Dent,* July 1743, General Court Criminal Papers, cited in Spindel, *Crime and Society,* 48. Moses Cornelius received an unspecified brandmark in 1766. Reports of the Committee of Public Claims, New Bern, November 6, 1766, in Clark, ed., *The State Records of North Carolina,* vol. 22, 845. The amelioration of penalties for whites was due partly to the decreasing numbers of European servants imported to the colonies in the late seventeenth century. See Richard S. Dunn, "Servants and Slaves: The Recruitment and Employment of Labor," in *Colonial British America: Essays in the New History of the Early Modern Era,* ed. Jack P. Greene and J. R. Pole (Baltimore, Md.: Johns Hopkins University Press, 1984), 157–94. Brandings were in place of execution and due to "Benefit of Clergy," a centuries-old privilege that initially protected English clergymen accused of a felony by entitling them to an ecclesiastical trial that could not impose the death penalty and ordered branding instead. Over time, this benefit applied to more and more people (including women in the seventeenth century), and by 1707 it was perfunctory for accused white felons in England and British America to "claim the Book." This benefit no longer required literacy and meant a de facto pardon for white felons found guilty of a first-time "clergyable" offense (most prominently manslaughter and theft, but not sexual offenses such as sodomy and rape that were capital crimes). See George Walton Dalzell, *Benefit of Clergy in America and Related Matters* (Winston-Salem, N.C.: J. F. Blair, 1955). Branding was abolished in England in 1779 after reformers argued that it "served no better purpose than to mark with indelible infamy those who suffer it and to give offence to every decent inhabitant." See Michael Ignatieff, *A Just Measure of Pain: The Penitentiary in the Industrial Revolution, 1750–1850* (New York: Columbia University Press, 1978), 90.

29. *Spires v. Daniel,* Cain, NCHCR, 251–53, 336. Certificate for John Stuart, March 18, 1735/6, Cain, REC, vol. 7, 329. On fighting and white men's honor, see Wyatt-Brown, *Southern Honor;* Elliott J. Gorn, "'Gouge and Bite, Pull Hair and Scratch': The Social Significance of Fighting in the Southern Backcountry," *American Historical Review* 90 (February 1985): 18–43.

30. Quote from Douglas Hay, "Property, Authority, and the Criminal Law," in *Albion's Fatal Tree: Crime and Society in Eighteenth-Century England,* ed. Douglas Hay et al. (New York: Pantheon Books, 1975), 23. LNC, 420. Discussions of the "new" bourgeois abhorrence of pain are in Halttunen, "Humanitarianism and the Pornography of Pain," and G. J. Barker-Benfield, *The Culture of Sensibility: Sex and Society in Eighteenth-Century Britain* (Chicago: University of Chicago Press, 1992). On the privatization of pain as part of the newer and more sophisticated forms of social control that replaced traditional displays of brute force, see Foucault's *Discipline and Punish.* On penal reform in America, see Glenn, *Campaigns against Corporal Punishment;* Louis P. Masur, *Rites of Execution: Capital Punishment and the Transformation of American Culture, 1776–1865* (New York, 1989); Michael Meranze, *Laboratories of Virtue: Punishment, Revolution, and the Transformation of Authority in Philadelphia, 1760–1835* (Chapel Hill: University of North Carolina Press, 1996).

31. "An additional Act to an Act, Intituled, An Act Concerning Servants and Slaves," 1758, LNC, 489. Brickell, *The Natural History of North Carolina,* 272–76. For Tom: Special Court, New Hanover County, February 10, 1755, Secretary of State Court Records, Magistrates and Freeholders Courts, NCSA. Isaac Faries, a physician, attested to the fact that Tom died of his wounds. Deposition of September 15, 1755, Secretary of State Court Records, Magistrates and

Freeholders Courts, NCSA. Kay and Cary, *Slavery in North Carolina*, 84 (Isaac). There was no mention of an alternative punishment for convicted slave women. A South Carolina statute from 1712 ordered castration for a man's third runaway attempt, and ear cropping (along with whipping and branding) for women on their fourth try. See Higginbotham, *In the Matter of Color*, 177. At different times castration was also lawful punishment in Pennsylvania (1700), New Jersey (1704), Virginia (1705), Antigua (1702), and Bermuda (1704). This was an American innovation, as there were no precedents for castration in English law (although Henry I had ordered emasculations in the twelfth century). See Jordan, *White over Black*, 154–56. In 1769 Virginia law called for the castration of slaves who even *attempted* to rape a white woman. Phillip J. Schwartz, *Twice Condemned: Slaves and the Criminal Laws of Virginia, 1705–1865* (Baton Rouge: Louisiana State University Press, 1988), 20. This figure of sixteen castrated slaves compares to none between 1748 and 1754 and one between 1755 and 1759. Kay and Cary, "'The Planters Suffer Little or Nothing,'" 298. The Reports of the Committee of Public Claims note reimbursements to physicians and slave owners for fourteen slaves castrated between 1755 and 1767. Clark, ed., *The State Records of North Carolina*, vol. 22, 819, 825, 830–31, 834, 837, 839, 843, 850. For evidence of fifty-nine slave executions in fifteen years, see Alan Watson, "Impulse toward Independence: Resistance and Rebellion among North Carolina Slaves, 1750–1775," *Journal of Negro History* 63 (1978), 319–20. For evidence of 115 executions between 1748–1772, see Marvin L. Michael Kay and Lorin Lee Cary, "'They Are Indeed the Constant Plague of Their Tyrants': Slave Defense of a Moral Economy in Colonial North Carolina, 1748–1772," *Slavery and Abolition* 6, no. 3 (December 1985): 37–56.

32. Jordan argues that white men treated slaves like "bulls and stallions whose 'spirit' could be subdued by emasculation." Jordan, *White over Black*, 156. Jordan claims that castrations were motivated by white men's sexual anxieties regarding black men's assumed sexual prowess, and that castrations served as a kind of "sexual retaliation." Ibid., 156–62. For a different view of castration as a rational aspect of the property-relationship of slavery, see Diane Miller Sommerville, "Rape, Race, and Castration in Slave Law in the Colonial and Early South," in *The Devil's Lane: Sex and Race in the Early South*, ed. Catherine Clinton and Michele Gillespie (New York: Oxford University Press, 1997), 74–89. My argument is not about whether white men's sexual anxiety was behind the choice of castration as a punishment for slaves, but rather that the castration of slaves interacted with whites' racial ideology, reinforcing their perceptions of racial difference.

33. On whites' perception that blacks were "both alike and different from themselves," see Jordan, *White over Black*, 137. On the way sadism made obvious the very humanity it sought to deny, see Reid-Pharr, "Violent Ambiguity," 82. See also Elaine Scarry, *The Body in Pain: The Making and Unmaking of the World* (New York: Oxford University Press, 1985).

34. *Crown v. Buttler*, July 27, 1721. Price, NCHCR, *vol. 5*, 250. *Crown v. David Oliver*. Recognizance of David Oliver, March 28, 1728, General Court Records, Criminal Action Papers, NCSA; jury's presentment against David Oliver, General Court, July 1728, General Court Records, Criminal Action Papers, NCSA. The plaintiffs in the seven criminal cases against white men included one widow, two married women (one of whom claimed attempted rape), three girls (ages fifteen, eleven, and a "child"), and one woman (who also complained of attempted rape) who was likely single. I have not included in this tally the 1697 case of *Crown v. Lee and Spelman*, because although the two men each received thirty-nine lashes for "Ravishing the wife and goods of Wm. Steele" (see chapter 1), Dorothy did not claim rape and was herself punished for adultery. For a detailed discussion of the evidence required for a successful prosecution of rape, see Block, "Coerced Sex in British North America," chaps. 1, 3, 5. On rape in colonial America, see also Dayton, *Women before the Bar: Gender, Law, and Society in Connecticut, 1639–1789* (Chapel Hill: University of North Carolina Press, 1995), chap. 5; Norton, *Founding Mothers and Fathers*, 347–57; Barbara Lindemann, "'To Ravish and Carnally Know': Rape in Eighteenth-Century Massachusetts," *Signs* 10, no. 1 (autumn 1984): 63–82. Wives did not charge their husbands with rape, but white wives could prosecute their husbands for assault, and some of the unspecified violence may have been sexual in nature. See Merril D. Smith, *Breaking the Bonds: Marital Discord in Pennsylvania, 1730–1830* (New York: New York University Press, 1991), chap. 4.

35. *Crown v. Joseph Pye*, jury's presentment, July General Court, 1736, General Court Records, Criminal Papers, NCSA. Chowan County Miscellaneous Papers, November 1757 (Microfilm C.024.99006), NCSA (Davis). Dayton charts the steep decline in the capital punishment of rape in New Haven after 1700 and notes that two thirds of that colony's eighteenth-century indictments for rape and all six death sentences involved "blacks, Indians, foreigners, or transients." See Dayton, *Women before the Bar* 243–74, 233 (quote). For the secularization of sex crimes in the eighteenth century, see Dayton, *Women before the Bar*; Brown, *Good Wives, Nasty Wenches*, 187–92. On the growing disinclination to order the death penalty for white felons, see Masur, *Rites of Execution*. For examples of capital punishment for whites convicted of nonsexual crimes, see Price, NCHCR, vol. 5, 78 (theft); Cain, NCHCR, vol. 6, 568–71 (murder). Spindel found sixty-seven whites sentenced to death in North Carolina between 1663 and 1776 (or 2.2 percent of all whites convicted in county and higher courts) but twenty-one received benefit of the clergy, two were pardoned, and one was deported. Spindel believes most of the remaining forty-three felons were also spared, as she can verify only two executions. Donna J. Spindel, *Crime and Society in Colonial North Carolina, 1663–1776* (Baton Rouge: Louisiana State University Press, 1989), 125. Kay and Cary assume instead that the forty-three convicts were likely executed (and that missing court records under-represent the numbers) but that whites were still executed in much smaller proportion than blacks. Kay and Cary, *Slavery in North Carolina*, 76–78.

36. Deposition of Elizabeth Montgomery (Jr.), and deposition of Mrs. Elizabeth Montgomery, May 7, 1733, General Court Records, Criminal Papers, NCSA. *Crown v. James Pritchard and James Ruffin*, jury's presentment, March 1746, General Court Records, Criminal Papers, NCSA. *Crown v. Samuel McCleneham*, jury's presentment, March 14, 1775, Pasquotank Criminal Action Papers, NCSA. On attempted rape as actionable, see Thomas D. Morris, *Southern Slavery and the Law, 1619–1860* (Chapel Hill: University of North Carolina Press, 1996), 308–12.

37. *Campbell v. Lenox*. Nov. 20, 1760, at a Superior Court held at Edenton, Cain, REC, vol. 8, 94–95, 398–404. In May 1764 Abraham Perry sued Robert Butterton for raping Perry's wife to the damage of two hundred pounds. The outcome is unknown. *Abraham Perry v. Robert Butterton*, May 1764. Edenton District Court Records, 1764. An earlier case was *George White v. James Fleming*, March 27, 1711, "for a Rape and for Burning his House etc." Both men gave twenty pounds recognizance to appear at next General Court. In July the case was continued, but it disappears from the record after that. (In 1713, Fleming served on a grand jury.) Price, NCHCR, vol. 5, 4–5, 55, 132.

38. Deposition of John Walles, Pasquotank County Civil Action Papers, May 17, 1739, NCSA. The deposition is all that remains of the incident.

39. *Turner v. Miller*, November Supreme Court, 1757, Salisbury District Supreme Court. *Leary v. Hall*. John Hall's bond, Perquimans County, May 2, 1763, Edenton District Court Records, May 1763, NCSA. Unless otherwise noted, the outcome of these cases is unknown. Single women who sued men for failing to fulfill promises of marriage seldom used a language of ravishment and admitted that on promises of marriage they had willingly had sex with their suitor. See, for example, *Elizabeth Stalling v. Abraham Riddick*, Edenton District Court Records, 1761, NCSA. Rachel Ming sued Jeremiah Halsey for a thousand pounds, not only because he married another woman but also for his claim that he had a "knocking bout" with Rachel and that he was drunk when he proposed marriage. *Rachel Ming v. Jeremiah Halsey* (1762, 1763), Edenton District Court Records, NCSA.

40. For a detailed analysis of the adjudication of rape cases involving black and white defendants, see Block, "Coerced Sex in British North America," chap. 4. On the less stringent requirements of evidence in rape charges against slaves, see ibid., 145–55. Block found an "extreme divergence in southern black and white conviction rates for rape," with the death sentences for white men ordered less often and then commuted at a much higher rate, ibid., 164–173. Brown found the same in Virginia, with at least twelve of nineteen accused black men executed for rape. See Brown, *Good Wives, Nasty Wenches*, 209. On different evidentiary standards and punishments for African Americans and other "outsiders" in colonial Connecticut, see Dayton, *Women before the Bar*, 233, 254–74.

41. The court records are incomplete, but of the twelve charges of rape brought against slaves in North Carolina before 1777, only two of them (Harry and Phill) dated prior to 1763. John Turner received 240 pounds as compensation for Harry. Special Court, Edgecombe County, July 15, 1740, Secretary of State, Magistrates and Freeholders Courts, NCSA. Special Court, Craven County, November 18, 1743, Secretary of State Court Records, Magistrates and Freeholders Courts, NCSA.

42. Special Court, Chowan County, November 14, 1766, Secretary of State Court Records, Magistrates and Freeholders Courts, NCSA (Cato). Special Court, Duplin County, May 1, 1770, Secretary of State Court Records, Magistrates and Freeholders Courts, NCSA (George). Special Court, Dobbs County, April 27, 1775, New Bern District Court, Miscellaneous Records, NCSA (Jem). Special Court, Craven County, September 13, 1775, Treasurer and Comptroller, Miscellaneous Records, NCSA (Ben). In August 1777, Titus was burned and hanged for the rape of Julin Rogers. Special Court, Onslow County, August 20, 1777, Secretary of State Court Records, Magistrates and Freeholders Courts, NCSA (Titus). Sheriff Ormond received fees for "Hanging etc" when Luke was executed in 1765 for the rape of Sarah Manning. Claim of Roger Ormond and Wyrnot Ormond, September 3, 1765, Treasurer's and Comptroller's Papers, Miscellaneous Records, NCSA. Other executions of slaves that do not mention but may have included mutilation are the following: Peter was hanged for the rape of Mary Woodward. Judgment against Peter, September 24, 1765, Edenton District Superior Court Records, NCSA. Boston was executed for raping Margaret Simmons. Claim of William Cray, September 10, 1767, Treasurer's and Comptroller's Papers, Miscellaneous Records, NCSA. Bacchus, the property of Martha Hill, was executed for rape in 1767. Reports of the Committee of Public Claims, New Bern, December 11, 1767, in Clark, ed., *State Records of North Carolina*, vol. 22, 850. Scipio was executed for the rape of an unnamed woman in 1773. Certificate of Payment for Francis Daniel, January/February Assembly 1773, Treasurer's and Comptroller's Papers, Miscellaneous Records, NCSA. These cases refer to rape convictions. The heads of executed slaves were stuck on pikes for other crimes as well, for example, Pompey's attempt in October 1765 to murder his owner, cited in Kay and Cary, *Slavery in North Carolina*, 79–80.

43. On the numbers of slaves executed and the diverging punishments of white and black convicts, see Kay and Cary, *Slavery in North Carolina*, 76–78, 90; Spindel, *Crime and Society*, 133–37. For the exhibit of slaves' corpses as "monuments to [whites'] fears," see Jordan, *White over Black*, 112. On the English custom of sticking heads on pikes, see Peter Linebaugh and Marcus Rediker, *The Many-Headed Hydra: Sailors, Slaves, Commoners, and the Hidden History of the Revolutionary Atlantic* (Boston: Beacon Press, 2000), 49–51. Indians were also singled out for lethal mutilation: in 1764 the assembly offered a thirty-pound bounty for every Indian scalp. See LNC, 601. On the Regulation, see Marjoleine Kars, *Breaking Loose Together: The Regulator Rebellion in Pre-Revolutionary North Carolina* (2002) (Chapel Hill: University of North Carolina Press). Elite men found public, punitive displays an egregious offense to their genteel status. William Cummings, for example, complained when three men assaulted him and "committed him to the *Publick and common* Stocks" for "a long time," namely half an hour. Edenton District Court Records, November Term, 1762, NCSA (emphasis added).

44. For a detailed investigation of sex between black men and white women in North Carolina, and for the argument that a white woman's class was crucial in determining the outcome of court cases involving rape allegations, see Martha Hodes, *White Women, Black Men: Illicit Sex in the Nineteenth-Century South* (New Haven: Yale University Press, 1997). See also Laura F. Edwards, "Sexual Violence, Gender, Reconstruction, and the Extension of Patriarchy in Granville County, North Carolina," *North Carolina Historical Review* 68 (July 1991): 237–60; Victoria E. Bynum, *Unruly Women: The Politics of Social and Sexual Control in the Old South* (Chapel Hill: University of North Carolina Press, 1992), esp. 109–10, 118.

45. Davis, *The Problem of Slavery in Western Culture*, 382, 408, 416, 443. On Martin Howard, see Don Higginbotham and William S. Price Jr., "Was it Murder for a White Man to Kill a Slave? Chief Justice Martin Howard Condemns the Peculiar Institution in North Carolina," *William and Mary Quarterly*, 3d ser., 36, no. 4 (October 1979): 598–600. On the way humanitarian

sentiments could be compatible with slavery, see Joyce E. Chaplin, "Slavery and the Principle of Humanity: A Modern Idea in the Early Lower South," *Journal of Social History* 24, no. 2 (winter 1990): 299–315.

46. Thomas Jefferson, *Notes on the State of Virginia* ed. William Peden (Chapel Hill: University of North Carolina Press, 1954). Elaine Forman Crane, "I Have Suffer'd Much Today": The Defining Force of Pain in Early America," in *Through a Glass Darkly: Reflections on Personal Identity in Early America,* ed. Ronald Hoffman, Mechal Sobel, and Fredrika Teute (Chapel Hill: University of North Carolina Press, 1997), 370–403. In her discussion of (whites') endurance of pain, Crane notes that "to be paralyzed by pain was to be rendered powerless. And to be powerless was to be impotent, unmanned, castrated, or emasculated." Ibid., 400. In what seems an ironic juxtaposition to the purposeful castration and execution of black men, Crane notes that whites' culture of sensitivity could extend to animals as well: Elizabeth Drinker, a Pennsylvania Quaker, complained that the "marks of cruelty that have been exercised on . . . horses, Hogs, Dogs etc . . . in what is called a civelized [sic] land, is intolerable." Ibid., 399.

47. Evangeline W. Andrews and Charles M. Andrews, eds., *Journal of a Lady of Quality; Being a Narrative of a Journey from Scotland to the West Indies, North Carolina, and Portugal, in the Years 1774 to 1776* (New Haven, Conn.: Yale University Press, 1934), 127. By the time Schaw visited Wilmington, North Carolina, she found a "most disgusting equality," a comment which indicates how inured she had become to the sight of people in bondage. Ibid., 153. For the assumption that "primitive" people tolerated pain more easily, see Crane, "I Have Suffer'd Much Today," 379.

48. Brickell, *The Natural History of North Carolina,* 168.

Epilogue

1. Benjamin Rush, "Observations intended to favor a supposition that the Black Color (as it is called) of the Negroes is derived from the LEPROSY," *Transactions of the American Philosophical Society* 4 (1799): 289–97. Quotes on 292–94.

2. Ibid., 295–97. Rush (1769) is cited in David Brion Davis, *The Problem of Slavery in Western Culture* (Ithaca, N.Y.: Cornell University Press, 1966), 443.

3. On the Bunch family, see Paul Heinegg, *Free African Americans of North Carolina and Virginia,* 3d ed. (Baltimore, Md.: Clearfield, 1997), vol. 1, 10, 134–39.

4. For a discussion of Thomas Jefferson's assimilationist fantasies regarding Indians (even as he saw them as doomed to extinction), see Peter S. Onuf, *Jefferson's Empire: The Language of American Nationhood* (Charlottesville: University Press of Virginia, 2000), chap. 1.

Index

An f indicates a page with a figure.

Abell, Elizabeth, 121–22
Abortion, 104, 112; and abortifacients, 104. *See also* Infanticide
Adair, James, 62, 73; and distinctions between Indians and Africans, 88; *History of the American Indians*, 59; on Native Americans and riches, 37; on Native American cooking and cooperative farming, 35; on skin color of Native Americans, 76; and Priber, 91
Adams, Anne, 108
Adams, Reverend James, 46
Adultery, 15, 112–13, 122; as a capital offense, 146; prosecutions for, 103
Africa, 177
African American men: castration of, 181, 187; and interracial sex, 123; seek their freedom in the courts, 125–26; and trial for rape, 181–82
African American women: assumed immoral, 151; could not sue for rape, 108; and interracial marriage, 113, 123–24; as sexual and savage, 28; and sexual exploitation, 161; and theft, 27. *See also* Free black women; Slaves
African Americans: and African-style dance, 155; and creole culture, 193; and English chauvinism, 28; and explanations of skin color, 191; and idea of inferiority, 132–33, 158, 188; and long indentures, 124–28; and natural right to freedom, 188; population of, 149; saw whites as sadistic, 167; and understanding of racial difference, 176. *See also* African American men; African American women; Free people of color; Slaves
Aires, David, 145
Aires, Mary, 145
Albemarle, 7, 24–25, 30, 39; promotion and settlement of, 20–21; Quaker monthly meetings in, 45
Albertson, Esau, 27
Alcohol, 58, 79, 80–82
Alexander (Indian), 48
Algonquian Indians: and disease, 30; linguistic group, 30, 31f. *See also* Native Americans
Allen, Doctor George, 109, 111–12, 169
Ambros, Susanah, 107
Ambrose (servant), 183
Ambrose, Alice, 44
American Revolution, 94, 96
"Americus" (writer), 93
Amputation, 10, 160, 179; display of severed heads, 185–88; of ears, 178–79
Andover, Tom, 14–15

Muskogee Indians. *See* Creek Indians
Mutilation: of feet, 79; and white and
black audiences, 166–67. *See also* Amputation; Branding; Castration

Nairne, Thomas, 72
Nakedness, 161–64, 189
Native American men: control of behavior
of, 41; and courtship rituals, 66–67; depiction of, 57, 67–68; and gender roles,
15, 34–35, 38; and role as hunters,
81–82; and supposed lack of sexual
prowess, 67–68, 70
Native Americans: and alcohol, 58, 79,
80–82; and child raising, 33–34; contrasts with English customs, 30; as depicted by English writers, 58–59, 60; and
disease, 30, 79, 82; effects of colonization on, 97; and English chauvinism, 28;
ethnocentrism of, 88; and European
manufactures, 58, 81, 96; and expanding colonial settlements, 58; and family
structure, 41; and gender norms, 8, 15,
30, 33–36, 41–42, 56; and an "Indian"
identity, 193; and inheritance of leadership positions, 37; and insiders and outsiders, 89–90; and intermarriage, 57,
78; and land use, 38–41; as the lost
tribes of Israel, 59, 75; and market of
prisoners of war to English, 79–80; and
marriage, 37–38; and matrilineage, 15,
30, 33–34; and notions of race, 78, 89;
and perceptions of white people, 88–89;
personal possessions of, 34, 36–40, 58;
population of, 30; and sexual behavior,
9, 56–57, 67; and skin color, 75–78; as
slaves, 79–80, 85; three linquistic groupings of, 30, 31f; and use of the term
"red," 89; and warfare, 79, 81–82. *See
also* Native American men; Native American women; *individual tribes*
Native American women: and alcohol and
sexual abuse, 80; bashfulness of, 62,
66f; and continued control over children, 73, 95; and control over fertility,
64, 66; and courtship rituals, 66–67; decline in status of, 97; depiction of,
56–57, 63f, 64f, 65f, 66f; English images of, 36, 61–70, 77; and extramarital
affairs, 37; and gender roles, 15, 34, 36,
38, 96; and influence over male activities, 82; and long-term marriages, 70,
71–72; and marriage rituals, 72–73, 96;
and matrilineal kinship, 95; and powers

of blood, 35; and property holding and
land use, 34–37, 41–42; and sexual self-determination, 41; and short-term liaisons, 70–71
Ned (slave), 157
Neuse River, 22f
Neusioc Indians, 83. *See also* Native Americans
"New and Correct Map of the Province of
North Carolina, A" (Moseley), 99f
New Bern, 83
New England: and colonies as religious settlements, 20
New Jersey: and religious dissenters, 44
New Voyage to Carolina (Lawson), 59
Newbold-White house, Perquimans
County, 46f
Newby, Gabriel, 45, 48, 51
Newby, Mary, 48
Newby, Nathan, 47
Newport, R.I.: slave trade in, 48
Nichols, John, 143–44
Nicholson household: and Quaker
monthly meeting, 45
Nonwhiteness, 86–87
Nopkehe, Catawba chief (also known as
King Hagler), 81
North Carolina: and the Anglican Church,
26, 44; and debt repayment, 24; government of, 7–8, 23f, 25; immigrants to,
ethnic makeup of, 21, 24–25; and importance of family, 18–19; and lack of
piety, 118; landholding in, 25; maps of,
60f, 99f; Native Indian linguistic
groups, 31f; and patriarchy and private
property, 15; population of, 7, 27, 149;
as a refuge, 24, 116; and religious dissenters, 44; settlement of, 7–8, 25–26;
settlers, disrespect of, 15
North Carolina Gazette, 176
North Carolina Yearly Meeting, 48–49
Nottaway Indians, 69. *See also* Native
Americans
Nowell, Margaret, 107
Nugent, Hannah, 119
Nussbaum, Felicity, 62, 64

"Observations intended to favor a supposition . . . " (Rush), 191
Odanell, William, 184
Odum, Elizabeth, 111
Oglethorpe, Governor James, 92
Olson, Mr., 125
"One sex" model, 4